W9-DAB-777

Bibliography of

New Religious Movements

in Primal Societies

Volume 3

Oceania

Bibliography of

New Religious Movements

in Primal Societies

Volume 3

Oceania

HAROLD W. TURNER

G.K. Hall & Co.

70 Lincoln Street • Boston, Mass.

MIDDLEBURY COLLEGE LIBRARY

All rights reserved.
Copyright 1990 by Harold W. Turner.

First published 1990
by G.K. Hall & Co.
70 Lincoln Street
Boston, Massachusetts 02111

10 9 8 7 6 5 4 3 2 1

Library of Congress Cataloging-in-Publication Data

(Revised for vol. 3)
Turner, Harold W.
    Bibliography of new religious movements in primal societies.

    (Bibliographies and guides in African studies)
    Includes bibliographies and indexes.
    Contents: v. 1. Black Africa. v. 2. North America. v. 3. Oceania.
    1. Religion – Bibliography. 2. Religion. Primitive – Bibliography.
I. Title. II. Series.
Z7833.T87BL80   016.291'046   77-4732
ISBN 0-8161-8984-6 (v. 3)   CIP

The paper used in this publication meets the minimum requirements of
American National Standard for Information Sciences – Permanence of
Paper for Printed Library Materials, ANSI Z39.48-1984.   ∞™

MANUFACTURED IN THE UNITED STATES OF AMERICA

For our daughter Helen.
In support of her concerns for the
Island peoples of the Pacific.

Contents

Introduction

This is the third in the series of bibliographic volumes on new religious movements in primal societies. When the two earlier volumes, on Black Africa and on North America, were published in 1977 and 1978 it was planned to complete the series with two further volumes covering the areas of Asia with Oceania and Latin America with the Caribbean. In the interval the available material has so increased that it is now proposed to devote a separate volume to each of these four areas. This third volume is therefore confined to Oceania as defined below, and three succeeding volumes will deal with Asia (to which Europe will be added, as well as smaller sections on theory and on general, or world-wide, discussions), with Latin America, and finally with the Caribbean area.

All these volumes draw on the extensive bibliographic and documentary resources of what was at first the Project for the Study of New Religious Movements in Primal Societies established in the Department of Religious Studies in the University of Aberdeen, which moved to Birmingham in 1981 to become the Centre for New Religious Movements within the Federation of the Selly Oak Colleges.

This removal and the consequent further developments of the Centre provide one of the reasons for the long interval before the series could be resumed. A second reason lies in the Centre's major activity in the years 1981-88, the microfilming of most of its documentation. While this task delayed the further volumes, it has both contributed to the bibliographical work itself and made available a set of nearly twelve hundred microfiches on the same subject. This represents approximately 120,000 pages of documentation, of which some 18,500 pages on Oceania are drawn from the items included in this volume. The bibliographic series and the microfiche set may therefore be seen as complementary resources.

The term Oceania is here taken to embrace the general area of the south-west Pacific: the three cultural areas of Melanesia, Micronesia, and Polynesia (including therefore Hawaii to the north and Easter Island to the east, as well as New Zealand to the south), together with Australia. It is generally understood that all these peoples originally came from the area now known as Indonesia. We trust that the Republic of Indonesia will understand why one of its political components, Irian Jaya, is included here and not with the rest of Indonesia in one of the future volumes; the reason of course is that the indigenous inhabitants of Irian Jaya have belonged culturally to Melanesia, as their new religious movements demonstrate. The same difference between political affiliation and cultural background applies also in our inclusion of Hawaii here rather than in the North American volume.

It may be a matter of surprise that the indigenous populations of Oceania, amounting to no more than a few million people, have produced such a large number of movements and so much literature about them, as is evidenced in the length of both the movements and the author indexes. A special wealth of material occurs in two regions, Melanesia (notably in Papua New Guinea) and New Zealand among the Maori people. In the former, the widespread reaction known as "cargoism" has led to hundreds of movements, many undocumented, and most of very limited expanse and of short duration. The dramatic and sometimes tragic nature of these movements led Europeans to dub them "cargo cults" (a name that is now inescapable), to record them in reports and then in more academic studies. From an early stage this area also had what was called the "largest Protestant mission in the world," that of the Lutherans, many of whom were of German origin or background and who engaged in systematic and detailed studies that were less common in other missionary circles.

A different set of factors operated in New Zealand, where the extent of the literature seems in inverse relation to the size of the population – there were at most no more than two or three hundred thousand Maoris, and this population had sadly declined to some forty thousand by the end of the last century. A dramatic recovery, however, to perhaps more than its original number has since occurred. Over sixty movements have been recorded (see B. M. Elsmore's study, entry 1656), although again many have been entirely local and of short life. Of the many factors at work we may note that the Maoris were a virile and intelligent people, who made an early and remarkably extensive response to Christian missions, and who attempted to preserve this response in their own ways when the problems of white settlers, new diseases, and eventually the Anglo-Maori wars arose.

A further factor derives from the intimate contact between the races from very early in the nineteenth century, together with the extent of the later white settlement, a situation not found elsewhere in Oceania. Europeans of all kinds documented the new religious movements in many different ways: missionaries and traders, travelers and settlers, the military men in the wars, government officers, politicians, journalists, and, more recently, academics, especially historians and anthropologists. In addition Maoris early achieved literacy (the King movement had its own newspaper well over a century ago – see entries 1749 and 1897; also 1734) and Maori writers and scholars have increasingly written on this subject.

Because this volume, like Volume 2, is the first systematic attempt on this scale, it is more comprehensive than selective. The criteria employed have been generous, to allow inclusion of almost all discovered items or references of any substance or of significance because of the context or the author. Annotations have not been provided where the titles are sufficiently indicative of contents, or where, as is sometimes the case, it has not been possible to examine the item itself. Evaluations have usually been avoided except in some instances that would seem fairly clear and where this may be helpful to the user.

The location of a few items, such as some in typescript, unpublished, or otherwise difficult of access has been indicated, and reference is sometimes made to the presence of these items in the documentary collection of the Centre for New Religious Movements, Selly Oak Colleges (Birmingham, B29 6LQ, United Kingdom), and in its slightly more limited microfiche version of the collection. The documentation there probably includes approximately seventy percent of the items in this volume.

In the bibliographic style used here, citations of periodicals that have two sets of enumeration show the alternative set in brackets without differentiating between old and new series of volume or issue numbers. Where this distinction can be made, the new series is indicated by "n.s." There remain, however, some periodicals with enumerations that defeat any system or logic. A certain measure of anglicization has been adopted for places of publication and also in references to the months of the year. Authors who use variant names when writing in different cultures are indexed under both forms, with cross-references; pseudonyms are cross-referenced to real names (where known), with entries indexed under the real name.

Omissions and errors of detail are inevitable in a work of this kind, and it is thought better to include the information contained in even obviously incomplete references, rather than to delay publication still further or to withhold these in the interest of an unachievable perfection. We trust that most errors will prove of little consequence for the reader, and we recognize that their later discovery also serves to keep the bibliographer humble.

Special acknowledgement is made for the assistance freely received from several libraries. The staff of the Turnbull Library in Wellington produced literature on movements unknown to me, and the Turnbull, together with the Hocken Library in Dunedin, was a major source of the older materials. The University of Papua New Guinea Library made its own unique contribution through its Special Collection of local materials. The inter-library loan office of the University of Aberdeen continued to be very helpful until 1981; since then the same office in the University of Birmingham has served an exceptionally large number of enquiries and neither this nor the succeeding volumes would have been possible without the privilege of this professional assistance. Other libraries used during two extended visits to the Pacific, Australia, and New Zealand (the compiler's homeland) have also been helpful, together with a host of individuals who have sent materials or information, often unsolicited.

In different ways the various staff of the Centre for New Religious Movements in Birmingham have all been involved in this project, especially the then-director, Dr. Jack Thompson, with his keen bibliographic sense. In the closing stages, considerable assistance in library checking and in formatting the computer-stored materials was received from three full-time volunteer staff members: Douglas Beck on a one-term internship from Hope College in Holland, Michigan, and Harold and Ruth Lehman during their two-year contribution after retirement from James Madison University in Harrisonburg, Virginia. Their cheerful participation in the chores was a great support to the compiler at the point where the task still seemed endless. And as for Maude there is no way of saying thanks to a wife who has managed to live with a bibliographer for some twenty-three years since this task first began, and who has to share in facing three further volumes.

Theory

The first group of items in the Oceania series consists of more theoretical materials oriented toward this area and should be used in conjunction with the more specialized Theory collection in the section on Melanesia, and with the theoretical sections of other volumes. There is sometimes no sharp distinction between these theory groups but the selection included here has some more explicit reference to movements in this area or some important focus that is relevant.

1 Boutilier, James A.; Hughes, Daniel T.; and Tiffany, Sharon W., eds. *Mission, church, and sect in Oceania.* Association for Social Anthropology in Oceania, Monograph Series no. 6. Ann Arbor: University of Michigan Press, 1978, 500 pp. Reprint. University of America Press, 1984.

   See essays on Australia by J. Beckett (entry 37), on the Bismarck Archipelago by D. E. Counts (entry 546), on Solomon Islands by F. Harwood (entry 1313) and by H. M. Ross (entry 1359), on Samoa by S. W. Tiffany (entry 2034), and on the Tonga Islands by S. R. D. Korn (entry 2069).

2 Burridge, Kenelm O[swald] L[ancelot]. *Encountering Aborigines: A case study. Anthropology and the Australian Aboriginal.* Pergamon Frontiers of Anthropology. Oxford: Pergamon Press, 1973, 260 pp.

   Pp. 221-32, "the contact situation": crises, and especially p. 227, adjustment movements.

3 Burridge, Kenelm [Oswald Lancelot]. *New heaven, new earth: A Study of millenarian activities.* Pavillion Series: Social Anthropology. Oxford: Blackwell, 1969, 191 pp.

Pp. 97-116, 165-69, problems of classification.

4 Firth, Raymond W[illiam]. *Tikopia ritual and belief.* London: Allen & Unwin; Boston: Beacon Press, 1967, 374 pp. Reprinted from *Man*, no. 142 (1955).

Pp. 157-61, a note on theory of cargo cults.

5 Guiart, Jean [Charles Robert]. "The millenarian aspect of conversion to Christianity in the South Pacific." In *Millennial dreams in action*, edited by S. L. Thrupp. The Hague: Mouton & Co., 1962, pp. 122-38. Reprint. New York: Shocken Books, 1970. Also in *Cultures of the Pacific: Selected readings*, edited by T. G. Harding and B. J. Wallace. London: Collier-Macmillan; New York: Free Press, 1970, pp. 397-411.

Importance of study of early Pacific missions with their eschatological emphasis, as one cause of new cults.

6 Keesing, Felix M[axwell]. "The changing life of native peoples in the Pacific area: A sketch in cultural dynamics." *American Journal of Sociology* 39, no. 4 (1934): 443-58.

Especially pp. 451-53, resistance to Western penetration beyond the "trader" level by "bizarre religious and mystical societies," with brief survey of the Philippines, the Pacific Islands and New Zealand.

7 Kilani, Mondher. "Cultes du cargo et changement social en Mélanesie: Problèmes d'interprétation." *Journal de la Société des Océanistes*, no. 68 [32, no. 1] (1980): 173-79, English and French summaries.

8 Leeson, Ida. "Bibliography of cargo cults and other nativistic movements in the South Pacific." Technical Paper no. 50. Sydney: South Pacific Commission, 1952, 16 pp. Mimeo.

An early scholarly instrument.

9 Pitt-Rivers, G. H. L. "The effect on native races of contact with European civilization." *Man* 27, no. 2 (1927): 2-10.

10 Prince, Raymond. "Delusions, dogma, and mental health." *Newsletter-Review* (Montreal, R. M. Bucke Memorial Society) 4, nos. 1-2 (1971): 54-59.

A follow-up to another paper in this issue on "religions of the oppressed" in general.

11 Tillett, G. J. "Prophetic movements as a form of social protest in the collective search for identity." B.A. (Hons.) thesis (anthropology), University of Western Australia, 1971.

12 Valentine, Charles A. "Social status, political power, and native responses to European influence in Oceania." *Anthropological Forum* (Perth) 1, no. 1 (1963): 3-55, bib. Reprinted in *Cultures of the Pacific: Selected readings*, edited by T. G. Harding and B. J. Wallace. London: Collier-Macmillan; New York: Free Press, 1970, pp. 337-84.

Pp. 35-39, various Polynesian movements; pp. 39-47, "Rejection, millenarianism and proto-nationalist movements in Melanesia"; pp. 52-52, typologies. A useful article.

13 Wilson, John. "Assimilation to what? Comments on the white society." In *Aborigines now*, edited by M. Reay. Sydney: Angus & Robertson, 1964, pp. 151-66.

14 Wilson, John. "Making inferences about religious movements." *Religion: Journal of Religion and Religions* 7, no. 2 (1977): 149-66.

Stresses the symbolic dimension, especially symbols of power and hierarchic order; follows Burridge and Cochrane in interpreting cargo cults and Maori Hau Hau, and rejecting explanations in terms of irrational deviations compensating those who are deprived.

General

This is a comprehensive section containing items in which the movements are discussed in a general way, Oceania is considered as a whole, or more than one of the individual countries and regions are covered. Important materials on any one movement or on any particular country or region may therefore be found in this general section as well as under the countries concerned. An exception has been made for major works that have only a minor reference to movements outside the countries or regions with which they primarily deal; it would be unfortunate if such important items were absent from their own sections merely on account of such brief references elsewhere.

15 Belshaw, Cyril Shirley. "The changing cultures of Oceanic peoples during the nineteenth century." *Cahiers d'histoire mondiale/Journal of World History* (Neuchatel) 3, no. 3 (1957): 647-64, bib.
   Pp. 652-60 cover religion, missions, and "religious resistance movements"; good survey of interactions with Western culture.

16 Burridge, K[enelm] O[swald] L[ancelot]. "Mouvements nés de l'acculturation en Océanie." In *Histoire des religions*, edited by H.-C. Puech. Encyclopédie de la Pléiades, vol. 3. Paris: Gallimard, 1976, pp. 1142-1219, bib.
   A systematic coverage of the main Polynesian and Melanesian movements, and of classification and explanatory problems.

17 Forman, Charles W. *The Island churches of the South Pacific.* American Society of Missiology Series, 5. Maryknoll, N.Y.: Orbis Books, 1982, 285 pp.
   Chap. 9 (pp. 154-63), "meeting the challenge of adjustment movements" in Melanesia and Micronesia (Modekgnei).

18 Garrett, John. *To live among the stars: Christian origins in Oceania.* Geneva and Suva: World Council of Churches and Institute of Pacific Studies, University of the South Pacific, 1982, 412 pp., illus., maps.

    Brief accounts of Papahurihia (pp. 69-70), Siovili (p. 85), Mamaia (p. 254), Tuka (p. 284), Christian Fellowship Church (pp. 300-301).

19 Guariglia, Guglielmo. *Prophetismus und Heilserwartungs-bewegungen als völkerkundliches und religionsgeschichtliches Problem.* Vienna: F. Berger, 1959, 332 pp.

    Pp. 63-82, introduction and background; pp. 72-73, Hapu; p. 76, Kaoni; pp. 83-123, the various regions of Oceania.

20 Guiart, Jean [Charles Robert]. *Les religions de l'Océanie.* Paris: Gallimard, 1963, 462 pp.

21 Harding, Thomas G[rayson], and Wallace, Ben J[oe], eds. *Cultures of the Pacific: Selected readings.* London: Collier-Macmillan; New York: Free Press, 1970, 496 pp.

    Essays by P. Lawrence (see entry 181), C. A. Valentine (entry 12), J. Guiart (entry 5), M. Mead (entry 427).

22 Keesing, Felix M[axwell]. "Cultural dynamics and administration." In *Proceedings of the 7th Pacific Science Congress, 1949.* Auckland: Board of Maori Ethnological Research, 1950, pp. 102-17.

    Useful discussion of acculturation, offering his own analytic system; pp. 114-15, brief account of nativistic movements.

23 LaBarre, Weston. *The Ghost Dance.* Garden City, N.Y.: Doubleday & Co., 1970, 677 pp.

    Pp. 236-52, Tuka, Water babies, Baigona, Vailala Madness, and other movements – a wide survey, with bibliography.

24 Latourette, Kenneth Scott. *Christianity in a revolutionary age.* Vol. 5, *The twentieth century outside Europe.* London: Eyre & Spottiswoode, 1963, 568 pp. Reprint. Grand Rapids: Zondervan Publishing House, 1970.

    Brief accounts of Ratana and other Maori movements (pp. 254-55), cargo cults (pp. 446-47), and Philippine Independent Church (pp. 361-62).

25 Lehmann, F[riedrich] R[udolf]. "Prophetentum in der Südsee." *Zeitschrift für Ethnologie* 66 (1934): 261-65, illus.

    Polynesian prophetism in general and as in Maori movements.

26 Mamak, Alexander F[rancis]; Alt, Ahmed; et al. *Race, class, and rebellion in the South Pacific.* Studies in Society, 4. Sydney and London: George Allen, 1979, 144 pp., map.

P. 72, Hahalis Welfare Society, briefly; pp. 98-107, Marching Rule (by H. Laracy); pp. 107-14, Parihaka revolt (by D. Lyons); p. 129, Apolosi's Viti Company; p. 134, Marching Rule and Parihaka likened to cargo cults.

27 Nevermann, Hans. "Die Südsee und der Kontinent Australien." In *Die heutigen Naturvölker im Ausgleich mit der neuen Zeit,* edited by D. H. Westermann. Stuttgart: F. Enke Verlag, 1940, pp. 198-269.

Pp. 260-62, new cults (mentions several) as religious, with misunderstood Christian doctrines and political aspirations.

28 Oliver, Douglas L. *The Pacific islands.* Cambridge, Mass.: Harvard University Press, 1958, 313 pp.

Pp. 132-33, Baker and the Tonga Free Church; pp. 129, 277, 288, 293, rather superficial remarks on cargo cults.

29 Orr J[ames] Edwin. *Evangelical awakenings in the South Seas.* Minneapolis: Bethany Fellowship, 1976, 245 pp.

Covers Indonesia and the Philippines. Many rather critical passing references to "strange delusions" or "syncretist sects." Revivals within churches due to local leaders rather than to missionaries.

30 "Survey of the year 1948: The South Pacific." *International Review of Missions,* no. 149 [38] (1949): 56-60.

P. 59, "disquieting symptoms . . . messianic cargo cults."

31 Taufa, Lopeti. "Change and continuity in Oceania." M.A. thesis, School of World Mission, Fuller Theological Seminary, 1968, 248 pp.

Pp. 102-4, Temudad's Modekne cult in Micronesia (based on H. G. Barnett, entries 1463-1464); pp. 189-91, nativistic movements and causes (using A. R. Tippett, entry 1365 , and D. L. Oliver, entry 28).

32 Thompson, Virginia, and Adloff, Richard. *The French Pacific islands: French Polynesia and New Caledonia.* Berkeley: University of California Press, 1971, 539 pp.

Pp. 264-65, a new cult, Toki, introduced to New Caledonia from Vanuatu and the Loyalty Islands after 1878.

33 Thrupp, Sylvia L[ettice], ed. *Millennial dreams in action: Essays in comparative study.* Comparative Studies in Society and History,

Supplement 2. The Hague: Mouton & Co., 1962, 229 pp. Reprint. New York: Schocken Books, 1970.

Conference papers, Chicago 1960 – case studies drawn from different societies and historical periods, relating these to a more general perspective.

34 Trompf, G[arry] W[inston], ed. *The Gospel is not Western: Black theologies from the Southwest Pacific.* Maryknoll, N.Y.: Orbis Books, 1987, 213 pp., maps.

Much useful background material. Pp. 49-66, essay by W. J. Opeba on Papua (see entry 444); pp. 67-89, E. Tuza on the Christian Fellowship church (entry 2087); and pp. 119-27, M. Maeliau (entry 415).

35 United States Government. Department of the Army. *Area Handbook for Oceania.* (Prepared by American University Foreign Area Studies Division) (PAM 550-94). Washington, D.C.: U.S. Government Printing Office, 1971, 555 pp.

Pp. 164-65, Cargo cults; p. 166, Gilbert Islands 1930 movement.

36 Watkins, June Elizabeth. "Messianic Movements: A comparative study of some religious cults among the Melanesians, Maoris, and North American Indians." M.A. thesis (anthropology), University of Sydney, 1951, 39 + 33 + 36 + 16 pp.

Maoris: Hau Hau and Pai Marire; U.S.: Ghost Dances of 1870 and 1890; Melanesia: cults from Tokerua to Bagasin; Bougainville cults; New Hebrides: Espirito Santo and Naked cults.

Australia

The category of Oceania is interpreted to include the Aboriginal peoples of Australia who differ from their Melanesian neighbors in the comparatively small number of distinct new religious movements they have produced, in the greater difficulty in identifying them, and in distinguishing these from older traditional forms. The most explicit examples are perhaps the older "adjustment movement" of Elcho Island described by R. M. Berndt and the more recent and more Christian revival movement originating in the same area and described in a number of articles by R. Bos. Closer study will probably reveal many more movements than have been publicly recorded.

37 Beckett, Jeremy. "Mission, church, and sect: Three types of religious commitment in the Torres Strait islands." In *Mission, church, and sect in Oceania*, edited by J. A. Boutilier, et al. Association for Social Anthropology in Oceania, Monograph Series no. 6. Ann Arbor: University of Michigan Press, 1978, pp. 222-29.

Pp. 222-29, appeal of whites' pentecostalism and its semi-independent development; p. 228, appeal in 1960s of new movement, the "World Church," although with a white leader.

38 Berndt, R[onald] M[urray]. *An adjustment movement in Arnhem Land, Northern Territory of Australia.* Cahiers de l'Homme, n.s. 2. The Hague: Mouton, 1962, 112 pp., illus.

The Elcho Island syncretistic movement. The fullest study of any one movement.

39 Berndt, Ronald M[urray]. "Influence of European culture on Australian Aborigines." *Oceania* 21, no. 3 (1951): 229-40.

Critique of A. Lommel (entry 66).

9

40 Berndt, Ronald M[urray]. "Looking back into the present: A changing panorama in eastern Arnhem Land." *Anthropological Forum* 4, no. 3 (1978-79): 281-95.

Pp. 288-93 passim, the Elcho Island movement.

41 Berndt, Ronald M[urray]. *A profile of good and bad in Australian Aboriginal religion.* Charles Strong Memorial Lecture, Sydney, August 1979. Melbourne: Charles Strong (Australian Church) Memorial Trust, 1979, pp. 17-32. Reprinted in *Colloquium* (Adelaide) 12 [1979]: 17-32.

Pp. 28-31, change and adaptation, but few attempts at combination with Christian elements, apart from on Elcho Island.

42 Berndt, R[onald] M[urray], and Berndt C[atherine] H[elen]. *The barbarians: An anthropological view.* New Thinkers Library, 38. London: C. A. Watts & Co., 1971, 192 pp., illus.

Pp. 77-79, and between pp. 80-88, plates 10(a) and 10(b) and notes: Elcho Island "memorial" of the movement.

43 Bos, Robert. "Australian Aboriginal Christian movements." In *Christianity: A world faith*, edited by R. Keely, et al. Tring, Hertfordshire: Lion Publishing, 1985, pp. 192-93.

The Arnhem Land revival and further developments.

44 Bos, Robert. "Christian ritual and the 'yolngu' domain." Nungalinya Occasional Bulletin 13. Darwin: Nungalinya Publications, 1981, 10 pp. Mimeo.

Report on the Elcho Island revival from 1979; rejects the "increasing stress" explanation of Wallace's revitalization theory.

45 Bos, Robert. "The Congress: A new movement in Aboriginal Christianity." In *The cultured pearl: Australian readings in cross-cultural theology and mission*, edited by J. Houston. Melbourne: Victorian Council of Churches, 1986, pp. 166-75.

The Uniting Aboriginal and Islander Christian Congress formed in 1982-83, with roots in the Arnhem Land revival.

46 Bos, Robert. "The Dreaming and social change in Arnhem Land." In *Aboriginal Australians and Christian Missions: Ethnographic and historical studies*, edited by T. Swain and D. B. Rose. Adelaide: Australian Association for the Study of Religion, 1988, pp. 422-37.

47 Bos, Robert. "Fusing Aboriginal and Christian traditions." In *The shape of belief: Christianity in Australia today*, edited by D. Harris, et al.

Homebush West (Sydney): Lancer Books, 1982, pp. 132-39. Revised from earlier version, *Digeridoo theology*, Nungalinya Occasional Bulletin 8.

Aboriginal rites and symbols as used in the Arnhem Land revival.

48 Bos, Robert. "Jesus and the Dreaming Religion and social change in Arnhem Land." Ph.D. dissertation (anthropology), University of Queensland, 1988, 416 pp.

49 Calley, Malcolm John Chalmers. "Aboriginal Pentecostalism: A study of changes in religion, North Coast, New South Wales." M.A. thesis, University of Sydney, 1955, xxii + 146 pp., illus., map.

Pentecostalism enabling conservation of important traditional elements under a Christian form.

50 Calley, Malcolm John Chalmers. "Bandjalang social organization." Ph.D. thesis (anthropology), University of Sydney, 1959, xxxi + 254 pp., maps, tables.

On the northern N.S.W. coast. Chap. 7 (pp. 193-240), the Pentecostal cult; Dick Piety led a secession from the United Aborigines Mission; this movement united the tribe, helps resist assimilation, and includes some non-Bandjalang.

51 Calley, Malcolm John Chalmers. "Pentecostalism among the Bandjalang." In *Aborigines now*, edited by M. Reay. Sydney: Angus & Robertson, 1964, pp. 48-58.

52 Eliade, Mircea. "Australian religions (Part V): Death, eschatology, and some conclusions." *History of religions* 7, no. 3 (1968): 244-68. Reprinted in *Australian religions*. Symbol, Myth, and Ritual Series. Ithaca and London: Cornell University Press, 1973, pp. 165-200.

An interpretative survey of published materials, including Kurangara, Elcho Island and "wandering cults, and millenaristic movements."

53 Elkin, A[dolphus] P[eter]. "Reaction and interaction: A food-gathering people and European settlement in Australia." *American Anthropologist* 53, no. 2 (April-June 1951): 164-86.

P. 177, a 1936 revival in northern N.S.W. of customs, language, and religion, the latter as equal to Christianity.

54 Elkin, A[dolphus] P[eter]. "The reaction of primitive races to the white man's culture: A study in culture contact." *Hibbert Journal* 35 (1936-37): 537-45.

With special attention to Aborigines in eastern Australia, reviving traditional religion after disillusion with whites' Christianity.

55 Glowczewski, Barbara. "Manifestations symboliques d'une transition économique: Le 'Juluru' culte intertribal du 'cargo.' (Australie occidentale et centrale)." *L'homme* 23, no. 2 (April-June 1983): 7-35, French and English summaries.

An intertribal cargo cult in western and central Australia.

56 Guariglia, Guglielmo. *Prophetismus und Heilserwartungs-bewegungen als völkerkundliches und religionsgeschichtliches Problem.* Vienna: F. Berger, 1959, 332 pp.

Pp. 124-25, summaries of movements, based on Lommel and Petri.

57 Hoeltker, Georg. "Zum 'prophetismus in Australien.'" *Neue Zeitschrift für Missionswissenschaft* 21, no. 4 (1965): 305-6.

58 Koepping, Klaus-Peter. "Religion in aboriginal Australia." *Religion: Journal of Religion and Religions* 11 (October 1981): 367-91.

A survey article.

59 Kolig, Erich. "*Bi:n* and *Gadeja*: An Australian aboriginal model of the European society as a guide in social change." *Oceania* 63, no. 1 (September 1972): 1-18.

Pp. 16-17, cargoism.

60 Kolig, Erich. "Djuluru: Ein synkretischer Kult Nordwest-Australiens." *Baessler-Archiv*, n.s. 27, no. 2 (1979): 419-48.

61 Kolig, Erich. "Quo Vadis, Australian aboriginal religion?" *Bulletin of the International Committee on Urgent Anthropological and Ethnological Research* 13 (1971): 99-113.

62 Kolig, Erich. "Tradition and emancipation: An Australian Aboriginal version of nativism." Supplement, *"Newsletter," Aboriginal Affairs Planning Authority* (Derby, W. Australia) 1, no. 6 (June 1973): 42 pp.

Pp. 5-8, 40-41, important critique of current views on "nativism"; passim, case study of nativism among groups at Fitzroy Crossing, both political and religious in form, with the latter (including the Worgaia cult) moving toward cargo ideas.

63 Kolig, Erich. "Woagaia: Weltanschaulicher Wandel und neue Formen der Religiosität in Nordwest-Australien." *Baessler-Archiv*, n.s. 29 (1981): 387-422.

64 Lanternari, Vittorio. *Occidente et terzo mundo: Incontri di civilta e religioni differenti*. Bari: Dedalo, 1967, 539 pp. Spanish translation. *Occidente y tercero mundo*. Buenos Aires: Argentina Editores, 1974.
     Chap. 1, Australian movements – Kurangara, Elcho Island, and Ungarinyin – as forms of "passive adjustment," when compared with Indian movements of Ram Mohan Roy, Ghandi, Vinoba Bhave, and Ambedkar as forms of "creative adjustment."

65 Lanternari, Vittorio. *The religions of the oppressed: A study of modern messianic cults*. English translation. London: MacGibbon & Kee, 1963, xx + 343 + xiii pp.; New York: A. A. Knopf, 1963, xvi + 286 pp. Reprint. New York: Mentor Books, 1965, xvi + 286 pp.
     Pp. 180-84 (Knopf edition), Aborigines, especially Kurangara cult – based on Lommel and Petri.

66 Lommel, Andreas. "Modern culture influences on the aborigines." *Oceania* 21, no. 1 (1950): 14-24.
     Especially on the Unambal. See also entry 39 for R. M. Berndt's critique.

67 Lommel, Andreas. *Die Unambal: Ein Stamm in Nordwest-Australien*. Monographie zur Völkenkunde ... Hamburgischen Museum für Völkenkunde, 2. Hamburg: The Museum, 1952, xii + 90 pp., illus., map, + 12 pp. of plates.
     Pp. 77-90, and plates 8-12, Kurangara movement, using a history-of-religions approach.

68 Long, Jeremy. "Papunya: Westernization in an Aboriginal community." In *Aborigines now*, edited by M. Reay. Sydney: Angus & Robertson, 1964, pp. 72-82.
     Papunya and Haast Bluff in Central Australia – forms of assimilation and of resistance – nothing on religion but useful background.

69 Maddock, Kenneth. *The Australian Aborigines: A portrait of their society.* London: Allen Lane, 1973, 210 pp., map. Reprint. Harmondsworth: Penguin Books, 1974.

Pp. 1-3, 4-6, Elcho Island movement; pp. 3-4, Pentecostalism developed as a syncretist cult by ex-United Aboriginal Mission Bandjalang in N.S.W.; p. 3, Molonga cult.

70 Massenzio, Marcello. *Kurangara: Una apocalisse australiana.* Chi Siamo, 4. Rome: Bulzoni Editore, 1976, 124 pp.

Pp. 9-25, editorial introduction; pp. 113-24, note on the ethnology of Australian religions, by D. Sabbatucci.

71 Meggitt, Mervyn J. *Desert people: A study of the Walbiri Aborigines of Central Australia.* Sydney: Angus & Robertson, 1962, 348 pp., illus.

Chap. 18 (pp. 331-40), "Reaction and interaction" – most changes are economic and organizational.

72 Meggitt, Mervyn J. "Djanba among the Walbiri, Central Australia." *Anthropos* (Freiburg) 50 (1955): 375-403.

Pp. 401-2, Kurangara as not significant among the Walbiri, or as much transformed.

73 Micha, Franz Josef. "Trade and change in Australian Aboriginal cultures: ... Australian Aboriginal trade as an expression of close culture contact and as a mediator of culture change." In *Diprodoton to Detribalization*, edited by A. R. Pilling and R. A. Waterman. East Lansing: Michigan State University Press, 1970, pp. 285-313.

Pp. 293-302, migration of cults (including new ones) along trade routes, but no details.

74 Mountford, Charles P[earcy]. *Brown men and red sand: Journeyings in wild Australia.* London: Phoenix House, 1950, 184 pp., illus. German translation. *Braune Menschen, roter Sand.* Zurich: Orell Fussli, 1951, 212 pp.

Pp. 133-34, Red Ochre ceremonies as transtribal and probably mainly social in function.

75 Nevermann, Hans; Worms, E. A.; and Petri, H., eds. *Die Religionen der Südsee und Australiens.* Die Religionen der Menschheit 5:2. Stuttgart: W. Kohlhammer, 1968, vii + 329 pp., illus. French translation. *Les religions du Pacifique et d'Australie.* Bibliothèque scientifique: Collection "Les religions de l'humanité." Paris: Payot, 1972.

See Petri (entry 79).

76 Nichols, Anthony H. "Psalms and hymns and didgeridoos." *On Being*, September 1984, pp. 22, 24, 26.
The Elcho Island movement from 1979, its spread and indigenizing features. By a C.M.S. missionary in Darwin.

77 Petri, Helmut. "Dynamik im Stammesleben Nordwest-Australiens." *Paideuma: Mitteilungen zur Kulturkunde* (Bamburg, West Germany) 6, no. 3 (1956): 152-68.
P. 156 *et seq.*, Kurangara.

78 Petri, Helmut. "Kuràngara: Neue magische Kulte in Nordwest-Australien." *Zeitschrift für Ethnologie* (Brunswick) 75 (1950): 43-51.

79 Petri, Helmut. "Nachwort." In *Die Religionene der Südsee und Australiens*, edited by H. Nevermann, E. A. Worms, and H. Petri. Die Religionen der Menschheit 5:2. Stuttgart: W. Kohlhammer, 1968, pp. 298-311. French translation. "Postface," pp. 359-73. (French, pp. 368-73; also p. 300, note.)
Pp. 303-11 (French, 368-73), and p. 300, note, on syncretisms including Kurangara.

80 Petri, Helmut. *Sterbende Welt in Nordwest-Australien*. Kulturgeschichte Forschungen, vol. 5. Brunswick: A. Limbach, 1954, 352 pp., illus.
Pp. 256-68, Kurangara; p. 264, Mulonga cult; pp. 265-67, Red Ochre cult.

81 Petri, Helmut. "'Wandji-Kuran-gara,' ein mythischer Traditionskomplex aus der westlichen Wüste Australiens." *Baessler-Archiv* (Berlin), n.s. 15 (1967): 1-32, diagrams.

82 Petri, Helmut. "Wandlungen in der geistigen Kultur nordwestaustralischer Stämme." *Veröffentlichungen aus dem Museum für Natur-, Völker- und Handelskunde in Bremen*, series B, vol. 1 (1950): 33-121.
Pp. 44-45, Kurangara.

83 Petri, Helmut. "Das Weltende im Blauben australischer Eingeborenen." *Paideuma* 4 (1950): 349-62.
Ungarinyin and Worora tribes in the Kimberly Division, and their new pessimistic eschatology.

84 Petri, Helmut, and Petri-Odermann, Gisela. "Nativismus und Millenarismus im gegenwärtigen Australien." In *Festschrift für Ad. E.*

Jensen. Vol. 2, edited by E. Haberland, et al. Munich: Klaus Renner Verlag, 1964, pp. 461-66.

85 Petri, Helmut, and Petri-Odermann, Gisela. "Stabilität und Wandel (Historische Gegenworts-Situationen unter farbigen Völkern Australiens)." *Ethnologica* (Cologne) 4 (1968): 420-54, illus., map.
Pp. 427ff., new syncretist forms–Jiniman-Jesus, Worgaia, Kurangara, Ngaru-Ngaru, etc. For English version, see entry 86.

86 Petri, Helmut, and Petri-Odermann, Gisela. "Stability and change: Present day historic aspects among Australian Aborigines." In *Australian aboriginal anthropology*, edited by R. M. Berndt. Nedlands, West Australia: University of Western Australia Press for Australian Institute of Aboriginal Studies, 1970, pp. 248-76.

87 Reece, R. H. W. *Aborigines and colonists: Aborigines and colonial society in New South Wales in the 1830s and 1840s*. Sydney: Sydney University Press, 1974, 254 pp.
Chap. 2 (pp. 63-103), "Christianization and civilization."

88 Rose, Frederick G[eorge] G[odfrey]. *The wind of change in central Australia: The Aborigines at Angas Downs, 1962*. Berlin: Akademie Verlag, 1965, 363 pp.
Pp. 11, 90-91, 100-102, 120, 180, 181, cargo beliefs and their relative rarity.

89 Roth, Walter E[dmund]. *Ethnological studies among the northwest-central Queensland Aborigines*. London: Queensland Agent-General's Office; Brisbane: Edmund Gregory, Government Printer, 1897, 199 pp.
Pp. 118, 120-25, Molonga cult.

90 Siebert, O. "Sagen und Sitten der Dieiri und nachbar Stämme in Zentral-Australien." *Globus* 97, no. 4 (1910): 53-59.
Mulunga dance, spreading from Queensland at turn of this century.

91 Sierksma, Fokke. *Een nieuwe hemel en een nieuwe aarde: Messianistische en eschatologische beweging en voorstellingen bij primitieve volken*. The Hague: Mouton, 1961, 312 pp.
Pp. 186-210 on Australia.

92 Warner, W[illiam] Lloyd. *A black civilization: A social study of an Australian tribe*. London: Harper & Row, 1937. Rev. ed. New York: Harper & Row, 1958, 618 pp., illus., charts, map.

   On the Murngin in northeast Australia. Pp. 536-37, two myths explaining why Aborigines were poor and backward compared with whites.

93 Worsley, Peter M. *The trumpet shall sound: A study of "cargo" cults in Melanesia*. London: MacGibbon & Kee, 1957, 290 pp. 2d ed., enl., with supplementary bib. New York: Shocken Books, 1968, 300 pp.

   P. 244 (1968 ed.), brief outline of cargo ideas he had found in an unnamed Aboriginal tribe.

Melanesia

Theory

This section indicates the theoretical discussion aroused, especially by cargo cults. Other types of movement in Melanesia have been somewhat neglected, although in the later 1970s the more recent indigenous "revival" movements began to receive attention, and these have been included in the various Melanesian sections below as being often semi-independent both in origin and in the course they have pursued.

94 Aberle, David F[riend]. "A note on relative deprivation theory as applied to millenarian and other cult movements." In *Cultural and Social Anthropology*, edited by P. Hammond. New York: Macmillan, 1964, pp. 338-42. Reprinted in *Millennial dreams in action*, edited by S. L. Thrupp. The Hague: Mouton & Co., 1962, pp. 204-14. Also in *A reader in comparative religion*, edited by W. A. Lesser and E. Z. Vogt. New York: Harper & Row, 1958. 2d ed. 1965, pp. 537-41; 3d ed. 1972, pp. 527-31.

95 Ahrens, Theodor. "Concepts of power in a Melanesian and biblical perspective." *Christ in Melanesia. Point* (Goroka), 1977, pp. 61-86. Reprinted in *Missiology* (Pasadena) 5, no. 2, (1977): 141-73. German translation. "Melanesische und biblische Perspectiven in der Erfahrung von Macht," in *Theologische Beitrag aus Papua Neuguinea*, edited by H. Bürkle. Erlangen Taschbucher, 43. Erlangen: Verlag Evang.-Luth. Mission, 1978, pp. 13-60.

An important paper at the Melanesian Institute seminar on adjustment cults, Lae, 1976, with revised references. Includes "Vailala

Theory

Madness" and two movements in the Hube area; cargo movements ideas of knowledge and power; church reactions.

96 Ahrens, Theodor. "'The Flower Fair Has Thorns as Well': Nativistic millennialism as pastoral and missiological issue." *Missiology* (Pasadena) 13, no. 1 (1985): 61-80.
     For expanded German version, see entry 99.

97 Ahrens, Theodor. "How right–or wrong–were we? The church's response to nativistic millenarianism reconsidered." *Point* (Goroka), no. 1 (1974), pp. 187-95.

98 Ahrens, Theodor. "Missionarische Präsenz in einem synkretischen Feld." In *Heisses Land Niugini: Beiträge zu den Wandlungen in Papua Neuguinea*, edited by R. Italiaander. Erlangen: Verlag der Evang.-Luth. Mission, 1974, pp. 229-49.

99 Ahrens, Theodor. *Unterwegs nach der verlorenen Heimat: Studien zur Identitätsproblematik in Melanesien*. Erlangen: Verlag der Evang.-Luth. Mission, 1986, 280 pp.
     Pp. 71-173 "Nativistischer Chilismus und Thaumaturgische Heiliggeistigbewegungen." An expanded version of entry 96.

100 Andrew, (Brother). "A psychiatrist looks at religious movements." In *Point*. Series 4, *Religious movements in Melanesia today (3)*, edited by W. Flannery. Goroka: Melanesian Institute, 1984, pp. 80-91.

101 Arbuckle, Gerald. "Man's aspirations to be man: Some reflections on adjustment cults." *Point* (Goroka), no. 1 (1974), pp. 113-22.

102 Baal, Jan van. "Changing religious systems." In *Micronationalist movements in Papua New Guinea*, edited by R. J. May. Monograph no. 4. Canberra: Department of Political and Social Change, Australian National University, 1982, pp. 622-27.
     On cargo cults as essentially religious, with a focus on specific goals; the general problems of acculturation.

103 Baal, Jan van. "Erring acculturation." *American Anthropologist* 62 (1968): 108-21.
     A former governor of Irian Jaya, later an anthropologist, on how modernization may go astray; pp. 108-11, examples in two cargo cults.

104 Baal, Jan van. "The political impact of prophetic movements." In *International Yearbook for the Sociology of Religion*, edited by J. Matthes (Cologne and Opladen) 5 (1969): 68-88, German summary.
P. 71, Irian Jaya movement of 1958-59; pp. 70-75, cargo and similar movements; distinguishes between political and religious movements.

105 Baal, Jan van. *De verhouding tussen de levende godsdiensten.* Publication no. 35. Kampen, Utrecht, etc.: Nederlands Gesprek Centrum, 1968, 52 pp.
P. 8, prophetic movements derive from traditional mythology and not merely from reactions to contact.

106 Barkun, Michael. *Disaster and the millennium.* New Haven: Yale University Press, 1974, 246 pp., bib.
Pp. 12-14, 117-18, etc., cargo cults set in a theoretical context.

107 Barnett, H[omer] G. "Peace and progress in New Guinea." *American Anthropologist* 61, no. 6 (1959): 1013-19.
The factors behind radical change voluntarily adopted in a Vogelkopt district as an example of modernization without cargo ideas; p. 1019, conversion to Christianity.

108 Barr, John. "The age of the spirit." In *Point.* Series 4, *Religious movements in Melanesia today (3)*, edited by W. Flannery. Goroka: Melanesian Institute, 1984, pp. 158-85.
On the new revival forms of movement.

109 Bastide, Roger. *Le sacré sauvage et autre essais.* Bibliothèque scientifique. Paris: Payot, 1975, 237 pp.
Pp. 113-16, discusses Burridge's "myth-dreams" of Melanesia and later employs the same idea for Western dreams.

110 Belshaw, Cyril S[hirley]. "Cargo cults." *South Pacific* 5, no. 8 (1951): 167.
Letter of interpretation in reply to J. Guiart (entry 332).

111 Bergmann, Ulrich. "Old Testament concepts of blessing: Their relevance for a theological interpretation of cargo cults." *Point* (Goroka), no. 1 (1974), pp. 176-86.

Theory

112 Berndt, Ronald M[urray]. *Excess and restraint: Social control among a New Guinea mountain people*. Chicago: University of Chicago Press, 1962, 474 pp.

   Pp. viii, 4, 218, 382, "reaction movements."

113 Berndt, Ronald M[urray]. "Reaction to contact in the Eastern Highlands of New Guinea." *Oceania* 24, nos. 3-4 (1954): 190-228, 255-75.

   Further "Ghost Wind" movement, 1948, and 1952; discussion of theory and suggests "adjustment movements" as best term.

114 Bird, N. M. "The 'cargo cult.'" *Pacific Islands Monthly* (Sydney), 16, no. 12 (1946): 45.

   Comments on letter of R. Inselmann (entry 163).

115 Bird, N. M. "Is there a danger of post-war flare-up among New Guinea natives?" *Pacific Islands Monthly* (Sydney) 16, no. 4, (1945): 65-70.

   "An old Territories resident" fears new forms of the "Vailala Madness," partly due to missions' teaching. See entries 147 and 163 for replies.

116 Bodrogi, Tibor. "Colonization and religious movements in Melanesia." *Acta Ethnographica* (Budapest) 1 (1951): 259-92.

   A Marxist view.

117 Brookfield, Harold C[hillingworth]. *Colonialism, development, and independence: The case of the Melanesian islands in the South Pacific*. Cambridge: Cambridge University Press, 1972, xvi + 226 pp., bib.

   Chap. 13 (pp. 159-77), "Melanesian reaction"–cargo cults, the Mataungan Association of the Tolai; by a social geographer.

118 Brouwer, Leo. "Little less than God: Pastoral-theological reflections on millenarian movements." *Point* (Goroka), no. 1 (1974), pp. 141-56.

119 Brown, Paula. "Social change and social movements." In *New Guinea on the threshold: Aspects of social, political, and economic development*, edited by E. K. Fisk. London and Canberra: Longmans Green, 1966. Reprint. Pittsburgh: University of Pittsburgh Press, 1968, pp. 149-65. Also in *Peoples and Cultures in the Pacific*, edited by A. P. Vadya. Garden City, N.Y.: Natural History Press, 1968, pp. 465-85.

   Cargo cults and theories about them.

Theory

120 Brunton, Ron[ald Gregory]. "Cargo cults and systems of exchange in Melanesia." *Mankind* 8, no. 2 (1971): 115-28.

Cults in Eastern Highlands, Madang and Manus districts as basis for discussion of theoretical questions.

121 Brunton, Ron[ald Gregory]. *Social stratification, trade, and ceremonial exchange in Melanesia*. M.A. thesis, University of Sydney, 1973, 166 pp., maps.

Pp. 144-46 on ritual leadership as in cargo cults, in relation to leadership based on economic status.

122 Bühler, Alfred. "Kulturkontakt und Kulturzerfall: Eindrucke von einer Neuguineareise." *Acta Tropica* (Basel) 14, no. 10 (1957): 1-35, illus., map; pp. 30-32, French and English summaries.

An ethnologist on cults caused by decline in *tambaram* houses, and inferiority before the whites, especially among the young; pp. 11ff. on cults under the surface in the Sepik district.

123 Bühler, Alfred. "Die messianischen Bewegungen der Naturvölker und ihre Bedeutung für Probleme der Entwicklungsländer." *Acta Tropica* (Basel) 21, no. 4 (1964): 362-82.

124 Burridge, Kenelm [Oswald Lancelot]. *New heaven, new earth: A study of millenarian activities*. Pavilion Series: Social Anthropology. Oxford: Basil Blackwell, 1969, 191 pp., bib.

Critical survey of theories, with examples from Melanesia (chaps. 5-6) and other areas; pp. 153-64, the "prophet" figure. A good study of the whole subject.

125 Burridge, Kenelm O[swald] L[ancelot]. "Racial tension in Manam." *South Pacific* 7, no. 13 (1954): 932-38.

The situation producing cargo cults, including misunderstandings between local and white peoples; p. 936, a form of independent "Catholic" church.

126 B[urton]-Bradley, [Burton] G. "The psychiatry of Cargo cult." *Medical Journal of Australia*, no. 2 (25 August 1973), pp. 388-92.

The importance of medical and psychological factors in understanding cargo cults (e.g., status anxiety as recruiting mentally disordered or marginal individuals).

Theory

127 Butinova, M. S. [The cargo cult in Melanesia: Towards the problem of millenarian movements (Russian text).] *Sovetskaya etnografiya* 2 (1973): 81-92, illus., English summary.
Discusses causes and criticizes bourgeois research for neglecting colonial oppression, which is now being opposed by "more mature forms . . . economic and political."

128 Carley, K[eith] W. "Prophets old and new." In *Prophets of Melanesia*, edited by G. W. Trompf. Port Moresby: Institute of Papua New Guinea Studies, 1977, pp. 238-65. Reprint. 1988.
On the parallels with Biblical prophecy.

129 Chatterton, Percy. "The missionaries – working themselves out of a job?" *New Guinea and Australia, the Pacific and South-East Asia* 3, no. 1 (1968): 12-18.
P. 17, cargo thinking not inevitable; by a veteran L.M.S. missionary.

130 Chinweizu. "Decolonizing the economy: The spirits of the cargo cult linger on to haunt modern development structures." *South* (London), May 1983, pp. 45-48, illus.
Modern development ideology and practice regarded as similar in principle to those of cargo cults – and equally ineffective.

131 Chowning, [Martha] Ann. "*Big men and cargo cults.*" *New Guinea and Australia, the Pacific and South-East Asia* 6, no. 3 (1971): 57-58.
Very critical review of G. Cochrane, entry 132.

132 Cochrane, Glynn. *Big men and cargo cults*. Oxford: Clarendon Press, 1970, xxix + 187 pp., illus., maps, bib.
A former government officer in Solomon Islands, studying movements there and in Papua, and replacing inadequate theories by functionalist explanations.

133 Colpe, Carsten. "Krisenkulte und prophetische Bewegungen, und Messianismus und Millenarismus." In *Handbuch der Religionsgeschichte*, edited by J. P. Asmussen, et al. Vol. 3. Göttingen: Vandenhoeck & Ruprecht, 1975, pp. 453-503.
Pp. 497-99, movements discussed in a theoretical context.

134 Douglas, Mary. *Natural symbols*. London: Barrie & Rockliff, 1970, 177 pp.

Pp. 136-239, cargo cults as millennial; passim, a typology of social structures and their relation to millennialism.

135 Dye, T. Wayne. *The Bible translation strategy: An analysis of its spiritual impact*. Ukarumpa, E.H.D.: Summer Institute of Linguistics, 1979, 256 pp.

Pp. 150-53, critique of A. F. C. Wallace's revitalization model as applied to church growth and the spread of Christianity; uses data from Mexico, the Philippines, and Papua New Guinea.

136 Eliade, Mircea. "Cargo cults and cosmic regeneration." In *Millennial dreams in action*, edited by S. L. Thrupp. The Hague: Mouton & Co., 1962, pp. 139-43.

Cults arise from disillusionment with Christianity after initial acceptance; congruence between Christian millennialism and indigenous ideas of cosmic regeneration.

137 Eliade, Mircea. *Mephistopheles et l'androgyne*. Paris: Gallimard, 1962. English translation. *The two and the one*. London: Harvill Press; New York: Harper & Row, 1965, 223 pp.

Chap. 3 (pp. 125-59), millenarian movements, especially the Naked Cult of Vanuatu (based on G. Miller, entry 1428) interpreted as "cosmic renewal."

138 Elkin, A[dolphus] P[eter]. *Social anthropology in Melanesia: A review of research*. London: Oxford University Press, 1953, 166 pp.

Pp. 141-60, culture change, and where research is needed; pp. 72-73, 153-56, et passim, cargo cults.

139 Firth, Raymond W[illiam]. *Elements of social organization* . London: Watts & Co., 1951, 257 pp. Reprint. London: Tavistock Publications, 1971.

Pp. 110-13, theory of cargo cults; chap. 6, moral standards and social organization; chap. 8, religion in social reality.

140 Firth, Raymond [William]. "Rumour in a primitive society." *Journal of Abnormal and Social Psychology* 53 (1956): 122-32.

Based on experiences in Tikopia; no special reference to new religious movements, but relevant to the means by which they may spread.

141 Firth, R[aymond] W[illiam]. "Social changes in the western Pacific." *South Pacific Commission Quarterly Bulletin* (Noumea) 3, no. 4 (1953):

Theory

25-28. Reprinted in *Colonial Review*, June 1953; in *Journal of the Royal Society of Arts*, no. 4909 [101], (October 1953): 803-19.
Pp. 25, 27-28, cargo cults as symbolic attempts to move into a new order and not necessarily opposed to economic development.

142 Firth, Raymond [William]. "The theory of 'cargo' cults: A note on Tikopia." *Man*, article 142, 55 (September 1955): 130-32.

143 Flanagan, Thomas. "Social credit in Alberta. A Canadian 'cargo cult.'" *Archives de Sociologie des Religions* 34 [17], no. 2 (1972): 39-48.
For comparative use of the term.

144 Flannery, Wendy. "Mediation of the sacred." In *Point*. Series 4, *Religious movements in Melanesia today (3)*, edited by W. Flannery. Goroka: Melanesian Institute, 1984, pp. 117-57.
The authority of ecstatic experience and dreams in contemporary "spirit" movements.

145 Forge, A. "Learning to see in New Guinea." In *Socialization: The approach from social anthropology*, edited by P. Mayer. ASA Monogram no. 55. London: Tavistock Publications, 1970, 352 pp.
P. 271, reasons for the resistance to cargo cults, as exemplified in the Abelam of the Sepik area, who are more developed and yet have retained traditional religion.

146 Gerritson, Rolf; May, R. J.; and Walter, M. A. H. B., eds. *Road belong development: Cargo cults, community groups, and selfhelp movements in Papua New Guinea*. Working Paper 3. Canberra: Australian National University, Research School of Pacific Studies, Department of Political and Social Change, 1981.

147 Gill, S. R. M. "Effect of war upon Papuan natives: Valuable observations by veteran Anglican missionary." *Pacific Islands Monthly* 16, no. 6 (1946): 52.
Discusses the causes found by N. M. Bird (entry 115) on New Guinea and asserts that the Papuan contact situation is different.

148 Goodenough, Ward Hunt. *Co-operation in change: An anthropological approach to community development*. New York: Russell Sage Foundation, 1963, 543 pp.
Chap. 11, revitalization movements and community development, including background, causes, government and missionary reactions.

149 Grimshaw, Beatrice. *The new New Guinea*. London: Hutchinson & Co., 1910, 322 pp., illus., maps.
Pp. 204-5, effects of cargo ships; p. 252, effects of Western goods.

150 Guiard, Jean [Charles Robert]. "Conférence sur les millénarismes, Université de Chicago, 8-9 Apr. 1960." *Archives de Sociologie des Religions* 9 [5] (1960): 105-9.
Comments on the conference that led to volume edited by S. L. Thrupp (entry 33).

151 Hayward, Douglas James. "Melanesian millenarian movements (an overview)." *Evangelical Missions Quarterly* 17, no. 4 (1981): 205-10. Reprinted in *Point*. Series 2, *Religious movements in Melanesia today (1)*, edited by W. Flannery. Goroka: Melanesian Institute, 1983, pp. 7-24.
Paper, October 1980, at Pyramid Seminar, Irian Jaya.

152 Hempenstall, Peter John. *Protest or experiment? Theories of cargo cults*. Occasional Paper 2. Melbourne: Research Centre for S. W. Pacific Studies, LaTrobe University, 1981.
Discusses precontact means of change, and cargo cult theories, emphasizing positive and rational features, and a multifactor view of causes.

153 Hoeltker, Georg. "How cargo cult is born: The scientific angle on an old subject." *Pacific Islands Monthly* 17, no. 4 (1946): 16, 70. Translated and abbreviated from *Nouvelle revue de science missionnaire*.

154 Hoeltker, Georg. "Nativismus." In *Entwicklungspolitik: Handbuch und Lexikon*, edited by H. Besters and E. E. Boesch. Mainz: Matthias-Grunewald Verlag, 1966, pp. 1424-26.

155 Hogbin, H[erbert] I[an] P[rietley]. *Social change*. London: C. A. Watts; New York: Humanities Press, 1958, pp. 207-49.
Chap. 8, local efforts in Melanesia to achieve further changes; cargo cults and their interpretation; clear account with useful summaries of various movements.

156 Hollenweger, Walter J. "Kilibob und der Mythos der Weissen." In *Völkschristentum und Völksreligion im Pazifik: Wiederentdeckung des Mythos für den christlichen Glaube*, by Theodor Ahrens and Walter J. Hollenweger. Perspektiven der Weltmission. Schriftenreihe der

Theory

Missionsakademie an der Universität Hamburg ... 4. Frankfurt: Verlag Otto Lembeck, [1977], pp. 82-105.

Reflections on Ahrens's material on the Kilibob myth, on myths in Christianity, and the criterion of truth in myth.

157 Horsfield, Donald. "Cargo comes on earth." *Outlook* (Christchurch, N.Z., Presbyterian Church) 80, no. 3 (1973): 12-13, illus. Also in *Reform* (London, United Reformed Church), April 1973, pp. 10-11.

An English missionary on the pragmatic and material emphases in Papuan religion.

158 Hours, B. "Melanesia: The three miracles." *South Pacific Bulletin* (Haymarket, N.S.W.) 26, no. 1 (1976): 35-40, illus.

Myths developed around three cataclysmic experiences: arrival of Europeans, arrival of American forces, and socioeconomic development.

159 Inglis, Judy. "Cargo cults and the problem of explanation." *Oceania* 27, no. 4 (1957): 249-63.

Ignores historical interpretations and denies possibility of a general theory in view of negative instances.

160 Inglis, Judy. "Interpretation of Cargo cults: Comments." *Oceania* 30, no. 2 (1959): 155-58.

161 Inglis, Judy. Review of *Mambu: A Melanesian millennium*, by K. O. L. Burridge (entry 892). *Journal of the Polynesian Society* 70, no. 3 (1961): 381-84.

162 Inglis, Ken. "With their fuzzy-wuzzy hair ... Myth and reality, 1939-1945." *New Guinea and Australia, the Pacific and South-East Asia* 3, no. 3 (1968): 23-38.

Historical comments on local background for some cults.

163 Inselmann, Rudolf. "'Cargo cult' not caused by missions." *Pacific Islands Monthly* 16, no. 11 (1946): 44-45.

Lutheran missionary's reply to criticisms by N. M. Bird (entry 115).

164 Janssen, Hermann. "Anthropologische Analyse und theologische Interpretation der Cargo-Kultbewegung in Papua Neuguinea." *Ordensnachrichten* (Vienna) 20, no. 5 (1981): 339-47.

165 Janssen, H[ermann]. "The development of the Melanesian way to fuller life." Melanesian Institute Orientation Course, Vunapope, 1969-70. 1970, 3 pp. Mimeo.
Based on discussion among J. M. Noss, S. White, G. Fahey, B. Miller, G. Arbuckle, and H. Janssen.

166 Janssen, Hermann. *Pacific cultures – Christianity and development.* Espiscopal Conference of the Pacific, Conference Booklet no. 3. N.p.: [Catholic] Episcopal Conference and CORSO (N.Z.), [1972], 14 pp. Reprinted as "Religion and secularization: Pacific cultures, Christianity, and development." *Catalyst* (Goroka) 2, no. 2 (1972): 50-68. German translation. "Religion und Säkularisierung," in *Heisses Land Niugini: Beiträge zu den Wandlungen in Papua Neuguinea,* edited by R. Italiaander. Erlangen: Verlag der Evang.-Luth. Mission, 1974, pp. 183-96.
Originally paper for Episcopal conference of the Pacific (Suva, 1972). An important theoretical analysis of acculturation.

167 Janssen, Hermann. "Political involvement of Christian communities in Papua New Guinea." *Point* (Goroka), no. 1 (1972), pp. 123-29.
Pp. 126-27, cargo cults as syncretistic developments of disappointed second-generation Christian communities.

168 Jarvie, Ian C[harles]. "On the explanation of Cargo cults." *European Journal of Sociology* 7 (1966): 299-312.

169 Jarvie, I[an] C[harles]. *The revolution in anthropology.* London: Routledge & Kegan Paul, 1964, 248 pp. 2d ed. New York: Humanities Press, 1964. Pp. 131-43 reprinted in *Rationality,* edited by B. R. Wilson. Oxford: Blackwell, 1970, pp. 50-61.
Chap. 2 (pp. 55-73), survey of three cults; chap. 3 (pp. 74-105), surveys theories of cults as a philosopher; chap. 4 (pp. 106-30), on explaining cults; chap. 5 (pp. 131-69), methodological discussion of theories (especially Belshaw, Hogbin, and Burridge); appendix 2 (pp. 229-33), surveys S. L. Thrupp essays (entry 33). Second edition adds discussion of P. Lawrence, who is also treated in entry 170.

170 Jarvie, Ian C[harles]. "Theories of cargo cults: A critical analysis." *Oceania* 34, no. 2 (1963): 1-31; 34, no. 2 (1963): 108-36. Reprint. Oceania Reprints. Sydney: Oceania Publications, 60 pp.
Rejects historical interpretations; surveys some eighteen views including those of James Mooney on the Ghost Dance in the U.S., and a few others outside Melanesia.

Theory

171 Juillerat, Bernard. "Research on 'possession' states: A request for contributions." *Research in Melanesia* (University of Papua New Guinea) 1, no. 2 (1975): 14.

Comments on lack of study compared with Africa, and urgency of research in view of decline of traditional ritual life.

172 Kilani, Mondher. "Cultes du cargo et changement social en Mélanesie: Problèmes d'interprétation." *Journal de la Société des Océanistes*, no. 68 [36] (1980 [appeared 1981]): 173-79, bib., English summary.

Cults as traditional means of social change rather than as acculturation phenomena.

173 Knoebel, J. "A pattern in dreaming and hoping." *Point* (Goroka), no. 1 (1974), pp. 81-92.

"The cultural rationale of adjustment movements" – in terms of Melanesian world views.

174 Kroef, Justus Maria van der. "The messiah in Indonesia and Melanesia." *Scientific Monthly* 75 (September 1952): 162-65. Rev. and enl. as "Racial messiahs," in *Race, individual, and collective behaviour*, edited by E. T. Thompson and E. C. Hughes. Glencoe: Free Press, 1958, pp. 357-64.

Pp. 360-62, Melanesian movements in a theoretical context.

175 LaBarre, Weston. "Materials for a history of studies of crisis cults: A bibliographical essay." *Current Anthropology* 12, no. 1 (1971): 3-44.

A major resource, with critical comments by various scholars.

176 Lacey, Roderic. "Local consciousness and national identity: Aspects of the Enga case." In *Priorities in Melanesian development.... 6th Waigoni Seminar ... 1972*, edited by R. J. May. Port Moresby: University of Papua New Guinea; Canberra: Australian National University, 1973, pp. 89-102.

No mention of religious movements but useful on the interaction of one of the largest groups with Western culture.

177 Lacey, Roderic. "Revitalization movements and cultural integration." Research paper, University of Wisconsin, Ph.D. program (history), 1971, 37 pp. Mimeo.

178 Lanternari, Vittorio. "Millennio." In *Mente Operazione*. Enciclopedia vol. 9. Turin, 1980, pp. 312-31.

179 Lanternari, Vittorio. *Origini storiche dei culti profetici melanesiana.* Bologna: N. Zanichelli, 1956. Extracted from *Studi e Materiali di Storia delle Religioni* 27, no. 2 (1956): 31-86.

180 Lawrence, Peter. "Chess bilong devil." *New Guinea and Australia, the Pacific and South-East Asia* 9, no. 2 (1974): 40-46. Reprinted as "European cultism: The skeleton in the scientific cupboard," in *Education in Melanesia. . . . 8th Waigoni Seminar . . . 1974.* Canberra: Australian National University; Port Moresby: University of Papua New Guinea, 1975, pp. 339-45.

Traces similarities between older European and current Papua New Guinea thought, as seen in cargo cult beliefs and myths.

181 Lawrence, Peter. *Daughter of time.* Brisbane: University of Queensland Press, 1968, 28 pp. Reprinted in *Cultures of the Pacific,* edited by T. G. Harding and B. J. Wallace. New York: Free Press, 1970, pp. 267-84.

Inaugural lecture. Surveys social sciences' change from positivist, reductionist views to accepting religious systems in their own right, with special reference to theories of cargo cults and to P. Worsley's interpretation.

182 Lawrence, Peter. "The fugitive years: Cosmic space and time in Melanesian cargoism and mediaeval European chiliasm." In *Millennialism and charisma,* edited by R. Wallis. Belfast: Queen's University, 1982, pp. 285-315.

Cargoism in Madang province – its backward-looking view of time compared with European views of a future millennium.

183 Lawrence, Peter. "Religion: Help or hindrance to economic development in Papua and New Guinea?" *Mankind* 6, no. 1 (1963): 3-11.

Southern Madang religious world-view as obscuring the facts of economic development and providing easy explanations of failures.

184 Lawrence, Peter. "Statements about religion: The problem of reliability." In *Anthropology in Oceania: Essays presented to Ian Hogbin,* edited by L. R. Hiatt and C. Jayawardena. Sydney: Angus & Robertson, 1971, pp. 139-54.

How he came to study cargo cults and the analytical approach used; the conditions under which he could accept statements about religion – all in relation to New Guinea.

Theory

185 Leahy, G. "Millenarianism as madness: A discussion of the psychoanalytic explanation of millenarian movements." B.A. (Hons.) thesis (anthropology), University of Sydney, 1973.

186 Lewy, Guenther. *Religion and revolution*. New York: Oxford University Press, 1974, 694 pp.

Chap. 10 (pp. 221-36), "The cargo cults of Melanesia: Their origins, features, explanations, and future prospects."

187 Little, Earl T. "Millennial movements and social change in Melanesia." M.Phil. thesis (anthropology), University of London, 1970, 177 pp.

Among the Tangu: review of theories; movements as responses to stress; special attention to leadership and followers.

188 Locher, G. W. "Myth, ideology, and changing society." In *Explorations in the anthropology of religion*, edited by W. E. A. Beek and J. H. Scherer. Verhandelingen van het Koninklijk Instituut voor Taal-, Land-, en Volkenkunde, 74. The Hague: M. Nijhoff, 1975, pp. 234-36.

Myth and ideology interact and produce social change.

189 Locher, G. W. "Myth in a changing world." *Bijdragen tot de Taal-, Land-, en Volkenkunde van Nederlands* (The Hague) 112 (1956): 169-92.

Discusses three theories, based on his own work in West Timor, Pouwer's work on the Mimika, and Kamma's work on Manseren movements in Biak-Numfor area; pp. 183-89, Indonesian messianism.

190 Long, Charles H. "Cargo cults as cultural historical phenomena." *Journal of the American Academy of Religion* 42, no. 3 (1974): 403-14.

191 Lusk, Keith. "Classifying new religious movements in Melanesia." School of World Mission, Fuller Theological Seminary, research paper, 18 April 1986, 35 pp.

Collates typologies of H. W. Turner, D. B. Barrett, G. Trompf, and J. Barr.

192 McArthur, Gilbert J. *Applied Christian ethics for Melanesian Churches*. N.p.: Stanmore Missionary Press, [1968?], 65 pp.

Pp. 47-51, Melanesian view of possessions, and outline of cargo cult history from 1871.

193 McLaren, Peter. "Religion and life." *Point* (Goroka), no. 2 (1975), pp. 105-12.

"Adjustment movements" as one of the three religious options open when traditional religion meets new challenges.

194 Mair, Lucy P[hilip]. "Independent religious movements in three continents." *Comparative Studies in Society and History* 1, no. 2 (1959): 113-26. Reprinted in *Gods and rituals*, edited by J. Middleton. New York: American Museum of Natural History, 1967, pp. 307-35. Reprint. London: Athlone Press; New York: Humanities Press, 1969, pp. 144-72.

Compares American Indian and Melanesian movements.

195 Mair, Lucy P[hilip]. "The pursuit of the millennium in Melanesia." *British Journal of Sociology* 9, no. 2 (1958): 175-82.

Critical review of P. Worsley (entry 529, 1957 ed.) for unproven Marxian-type sociological explanations in terms of economics and politics.

196 "Many 'still believe' in cargo cult." *Pacific Islands Monthly*, 28, no. 7 (1958): 59.

Interview with Peter Lawrence.

197 May, John d'Arcy. "Kontextuelle Theologie in Melanesien." *Zeitschrift für Missionswissenschaft und Religionswissenschaft* 71, no. 4 (1987): 279-91.

Largely on the search for authentic Melanesian theology, with sections on cargo cults and Holy Spirit movements.

198 May, R[onald] J. Conclusion to *Micronationalist movements in Papua New Guinea*, edited by R. J. May. Monograph no. 4. Canberra: Department of Political and Social Change, Australian National University, 1982, pp. 421-48.

199 Mead, Margaret, and Schwartz, Theo. "The cult as a condensed social process." In *Group processes: Transactions of the Fifth Conference, 1958*, edited by Bertram Schaffner. New York: Josiah Macy, Jr., Foundation, 1960, pp. 85-187.

Based on Manus Island with its Paliau movement.

200 Merton, Thomas. "Cargo theology." Transcription from tape, 1968, 28 pp.

Copy at Holy Spirit Seminary library, Bomana, Papua.

Theory

201 Moritzen, Niels-Peter. "Der Stein der Weisen, oder Wohin fuhrt die Kargo-Kult-Forschung?" In *Theologische Beiträge aus Papua Neuguinea*, edited by H. Bürkle. Erlangen Taschenbücher 43. Erlangen: Verlag Ev.-Luth. Mission, 1978, pp. 136-41.

202 Namunu, Simeon. "Spirits in Melanesia and the Spirit in Christianity." In *Point*. Series 4, *Religious movements in Melanesia today (3)*, edited by W. Flannery. Goroka: Melanesian Institute, 1984, pp. 92-116.

203 Narokobi, Bernard M. "Who shall take up Peli's challenge? A philosophical contribution to the understanding of Cargo cults." *Point* (Goroka), no. 1 (1974) pp. 93-104.
By a Papua New Guinea lawyer.

204 Oosterwal, Gottfried. "Cargo cults as a missionary challenge." *International Review of Missions*, no. 224 [56] (1967): 469-77. Reprinted in *Insight and Opinion* (Cape Coast, Ghana) 4, no. 3 (1969): 107-13.
Nonreligious factors inadequate as explanations.

205 Pataki-Schweizer, K. J. "Meth-drinkers and lotus-eaters." *Australian and New Zealand Journal of Psychiatry* 10 (1976): 129-31.
A medical anthropologist suggests a theoretical connection between methylated spirits drinkers and cargo cultists in periods of cultural stress.

206 Queiroz, Maria Isaura Pereira de. "Les mouvements messianiques en Océanie." In *Réforme et révolution dans les sociétés traditionelles*. Paris: Éd. Anthropos, 1968, pp. 233-44.
By a Brazilian anthropologist, from another perspective.

207 Reed, Stephen W. *The making of modern New Guinea, with special reference to culture contact in the mandated territory*. Memoirs, American Philosophical Society, 18, 1942. Philadelphia: American Philosophical Society, 1943, 326 pp.
Pp. 234-43, agencies of change (missions, etc.); pp. 252-65, effects of contact.

208 Richardson, Paul. "New religious movements and the search for a Melanesian spirituality." *Melanesian Journal of Theology* 2 (1986): 66-75.

209 Saake, Wilhelm. "Probleme der Akkulturation bei primitiven Völkern." *Zeitschrift für praktische Psychologie* (Paderborn) 7, nos. 1-2 (1967): 8-24.

Pp. 21-23, cargo cults as an example; by the director of Anthropos Institute.

210 Sackett, Lee. "A note on 'measurable prediction' theory as applied to cargo cults." *Oceania*, 44, no. 4 (1974): 294-300.

211 Scheffler, Harold W. "The social consequences of peace on Choiseul Island." *Ethnology* 3 (1964): 398-403.

P. 402, brief reference to "breakaway churches" elsewhere in Solomon Islands as providing uniting or cohesive factors lacking on Choiseul.

212 Schmitz, Carl A. "Gesellschaftsordnung und Wandel in einer Bergbauern-Kultur in Nordost-Neuguinea." *Kölner Zeitschrift für Soziologie* 9 [1957?]: 258-82.

Pp. 273-82, acculturation processes in relation to the indigenous culture outlined in the first part.

213 Schwartz, Theodore. "Cultural totemism: Ethnic identity, primitive and modern." In *Ethnic identity: Cultural continuities and change*, edited by G. DeVos and L. Romanucci-Ross. Palo Alto: Mayfield Publishing Co., 1975, pp. 108-31.

The search for identity under changing social conditions in the Admiralty Islands; references to Paliau, and to apparent immunity of Seventh Day Adventists.

214 Schwarz, Brian H. "The symbolic significance of cargo in Melanesian cargo cults." M.Litt. dissertation (religion in primal societies), University of Aberdeen, 1976, 103 pp.

An important theoretical analysis, by a Lutheran missionary.

215 Seiler, Donald. "Aspects of movement and socio-economic development in the Maprik sub-district of Papua New Guinea." Bachelor of Economics (Hons.) thesis (geography), University of Queensland, 1972, 416 pp.

Pp. 54, Cargo cults as indicators of change.

216 Selem, Tioty Munepen. "Cargo cult." In *Tertiary students and the politics of New Guinea. Papers presented at the second seminar of Papua*

Theory

New Guinea tertiary students ... Lae ... August 1971. Lae: PNG Institute of Technology, 1971, [3 pp.].

Cargo cults, as "fruits of racialism and white power" can be turned to good account by better biblical teaching and direction of resources to development; example of the Tutukuval Isukul Association (Association of Planters) formed among Johnson cultists on New Hanover by a Catholic priest.

217 Sharp, Nonie. *Millenarian movements: Their meaning in Melanesia.* LaTrobe University, Department of Sociology Papers, 25. Bundoora, Victoria: LaTrobe University, 1976.

218 Smith, Jonathan Z. "The influence of symbols upon social change: A place on which to stand." *Worship* 44, no. 8 (1978): 469-74.

Pp. 469-70, a theory of social change, with cargo cults arising where a "locative culture" has its sense of place disrupted by "cargo" or money.

219 Smith, Jonathan Z. "A pearl of great price and a cargo of yams: A study of situational incongruity." *History of Religions* (Chicago) 16, no. 1 (1976): 1-19.

Application of concepts used in study of cargo cults and revitalization movements to the Babylonian New Year festival and the Ceramese myth of Hainuwele.

220 Stanner, W[illiam] E[dward] H[anley]. "On the interpretation of cargo cults." *Oceania* 29, no. 1 (1958): 1-25.

Recognizes their distinctively religious nature.

221 Stanner, W[illiam] E[dward] H[anley]. *The South Seas in transition.* Sydney, Wellington, and London: Australasian Publishing Co., 1953, 448 pp.

Pp. 57-73, problems of analysis and interpretation of cargo cults, with reference to prophetess Philo, Marafi and Vailala Madness, and outlines of other movements.

222 Steinbauer, Friedrich. "The Melanesian cargo cults–an example for religious adjustment movements." Paper, New ERA Advanced Seminar paper, "How does orthodoxy assimilate heterodoxy?" St. Croix, Virgin Islands: April 1987, 14 pp. Photocopy.

223 Steinbauer, Friedrich. "Der religiöse Bezug im Cargo-Kult-Komplex." *Evangelische Missions Zeitschrift* 26, no. 4 (1969): 211-29.

Theory

224 Stephen, Michele. *Cargo cult hysteria: Symptom of despair or technique of ecstasy?* Research Centre for Southwest Pacific Studies, Occasional Paper 1. Melbourne: LaTrobe University, 1977, 16 pp.

A positive form of breaking from the old and validating the new.

225 Stephen, Michele. "Dreams of change: The innovative role of altered states of consciousness in traditional Melanesian religion." *Oceania* 50, no. 1 (1979): 3-22. Reprinted as "Dream, trance, and spirit possession: Traditional religious experiences in Melanesia," in *Religious experience in world religions*, edited by V. Hayes. Adelaide: Australian Association for Study of Religions, 1979, pp. 25-49.

These experiences as means of communication with ancestors and divinities, and as innovative and validating change both in precontact and postcontact movements.

226 Strehlan (*sic*, for Strelan) John G[erhard]. "Christliche Eschatologie und Cargo-Kulte / Christian eschatology and cargo cults." *Evangelium: Gospel.* Bimonthly for Lutheran Theology and the Church (Berlin German Lutheran Hour) 3, no. 1 (1976): 4-11. [Parallel German and English texts.]

Analysis of the interaction of Melanesian eschatologies (as embodied in myths, with five themes identified) and Christian eschatology (as in various mission teachings, and supported by the place of whites in some local myths, and by their wealth).

227 Strelan, John G[erhard]. "Der Cargo-Kult Melanesiens im Lichte der Paulinischen Theologie." *Zeitschrift für Mission*, 12, no. 3 (1986): 152-60.

228 Strelan, John G[erhard]. "Eschatology, myth, and history." In *Christ in Melanesia. Point* (Goroka), 1977, pp. 197-207.

Paper, Melanesian Institute Seminar on Adjustment Cults, Lae, 1976. While myth and eschatology are familiar categories in Melanesia, case studies of Mambu and the Vailala Madness suggest that history is not a meaningful category.

229 Strelan, John G[erhard]. "Our common ancestor: Toward a theological interpretation of Cargo cults." *Catalyst*, 5, no. 2 (1975): 33-40.

"Cargo" as Melanesian symbolic equivalent of the biblical "salvation," equally corporate and cosmic in scope; differences in the means – through ritual and return of ancestors.

Theory

230 Strelan, John Gerhard. "The return-to-origins motif in Pauline theology and its significance for a theological interpretation of messianic and millenarian movements in Melanesia." Dissertation, Graduate School, Concordia Seminary (St. Louis, Mo.), 1973, 226 pp., bib.

Chap. 2, history and morphology of Melanesian movements; chap. 7, theological interpretation.

231 Tahu, Atabani. "The concept of 'God the holy mama' as the basis of a belief in a Christian God in Melanesia." Thesis, Rarongo Theological College, 1985.

232 Talmon, Yonina. "Pursuit of the millennium: The relation between religion and social change." *Archives Européennes de Sociologie* (Paris) 3, no. 1 (1962): 125-48. Reprinted in *Studies in social movements*, edited by B. McLaughlin. New York: Free Press; London: Collier-Macmillan, 1969, pp. 400-427. Abridged in *Protest, reform, and revolt*, edited by J. R. Gusfield. New York: John Wiley & Sons, 1970, pp. 436-52.

233 Taussig, Michael. "The genesis of capitalism amongst a South American peasantry: Devil's labour and the baptism of money." *Comparative Studies in Society and History* 19, no. 2 (1977): 130-55.

Barren money, through magical baptism, can become unnaturally fertile – rational theory in its own context, and useful for comparison with Melanesian cargo-thinking.

234 Toch, Hans. *The social psychology of social movements*. Indianapolis: Bobbs-Merrill Co., 1965, 257 pp.

Chap. 2, illusions as solutions; pp. 39-42, cargo cults.

235 Toit, Brian M[urray] du. "Misconstruction and problems in communication." *American Anthropologist* 71, no. 1 (1969): 46-53.

A "negative instance" in East Central Highlands, New Guinea, in 1962, where sun's eclipse produced no new cult.

236 Trompf, Garry W[inston]. "'Doesn't colonialism make you mad?' The so-called 'Mun Madness' as an index for the study of new religious movements in Papua New Guinea during the colonial period." In *Papua New Guinea: A Century of colonial impact, 1884 to 1984*, edited by S. Latukefu. Port Moresby: National Research Institute and University of Papua New Guinea Press, 1989, xv + 494 pp.

237 Trompf, Garry W[inston]. *Religion and money: Some aspects.* The Young Australian Scholar Lecture Series, 1. Bedford Park, S. Australia: Australian Association for the Study of Religions, for the Charles Strong Memorial Trust, 1980, 16 pp.

   Pp. 6-8, 14-15, cargo cults as test case on importance of money in religion.

238 Trompf, Garry W[instone], ed. *Cargo cults and millenarian movements: Transoceanic comparisons and connections in the study of new religions movements.* Religion and Society series. Berlin: de Gruyter, Mouton Publishers, 1990, xvii + 456 pp.

   See pp. 8-35, Introduction, and pp. 37-87, "The cargo and the millennium on both sides of the Pacific" (the Brotherhood of the Sun in California; equivalent movements and tendencies in eastern Australia; Melanesian cargo cults) – both by the editor. See also essays by P. Gesch (on New Guinea), L. Lindstrom (on Vanuatu), and G. Brookes (on Spirit movements in Timor).

239 Trompf, Garry W[inston], ed. *Prophets of Melanesia.* Port Moresby: Institute of Papua New Guinea Studies, 1977, pp. 20-107. Reprint. 1988.

   Especially pp. 1-19, introduction by the editor, and pp. 238-66, "Prophets old and new," by K. W. Carley (Melanesian prophets in the context of the history of religion). See area sections for five case studies – on Papua, by the editor, D. Fergie, and W. Jojoga; on New Guinea, by M. Tamoane; and on Solomon Islands, by E. Tuza.

240 Turner, Harold W[alter]. "New and ongoing religious movements in Melanesia: What to look for: a guide for the study of revivals within churches and missions and new religious movements in Melanesia." Paper presented at the Melanesian Institute seminar (Goroka) 1980, 4 pp. Typescript.

241 Turner, Harold W[alter]. "New religious movements in primal societies." In *Point.* Series 2, *Religious movements in Melanesia today (1),* edited by W. Flannery. Goroka: Melanesian Institute, 1983, pp. 1-6.

   General survey of such movements, with a four-fold classification applied to Melanesia.

242 Turner, Harold W[alter]. "Old and new religions in Melanesia." *Point* (Goroka), no. 2 (1978), pp. 5-29.

Theory

243 Waiko, John [D.]. "Cargo cults: The Papua New Guinea way." In *Nuigini Reader,* edited by H. Barnes. North Melbourne: Australian Union of Students, 1972, pp. 43-50.
An expansion of paper cited in entry 244.

244 Waiko, John D. "European-Melanesian contact in Melanesian tradition and literature." In *Priorities in Melanesian development. . . . 6th Waigoni Seminar . . . 1972,* edited by R. J. May. Port Moresby: University of Papua New Guinea; Canberra: Australian National University, 1973. Reprint. 1974, pp. 417-28.
Cults before 1942 were not solely due to contact with whites but represented a traditional response to dangers, of which the advent of the whites was but an extraordinary example. Baigona and Taro cults as case studies.

245 Walter, Michael A. H. B. "Cargo cults: Forerunners of progress." In *Point.* Series 2, *Religious movements in Melanesia today (1),* edited by W. Flannery. Goroka: Melanesian Institute, 1983, pp. 190-204.

246 Walter, Michael A. H. B. "Cult movements and community development associations: Revolution and evolution in the Papua New Guinea countryside." In *Road belong development: Cargo cults, community groups, and selfhelp movements in Papua New Guinea,* edited by R. Gerritson, R. J. May, and M. A. H. B. Walter. Working Paper 3. Canberra: Australian National University, Research School of Pacific Studies, Department of Political and Social Change, 1981, pp. 81-116 (bib., pp. 107-16).
Relation between cult movements and new "dynamic community groups," with discussion of significance of the former.

247 Watson, Avra Peter Ginieres. "Melanesian cargo movements: A developmental analysis." Ph.D. dissertation (cultural anthropology), University of Pittsburgh, 1976, pp. 247 pp., maps.
Historical process and diffusion in culture change, emphasizing economic factors. Uses an eighteen-feature scale for analysis of transition from initial religious to final secular forms.

248 Watters, R. F. "Cargo cults and social change in Melanesia." *Pacific Viewpoint* 1, no. 1 (1960): 104-7.

249 Weiss, Robert Frank. "Defection from social movements and subsequent recruitment to new movements." *Sociometry* (New York) 26, no. 2 (1963): 1-20. Reprinted in *Studies in Social Movements,* edited

by B. McLaughlin. New York: Free Press; Collier-Macmillan, 1969, pp. 328-48.
>Cargo cults discussed only on p. 5 (p. 332 in reprint), but are included as illustrating the overall theory.

250 Whisson, Michael G. "Gods in new guise." *Breakthrough* (U.K., Student Christian Movement), [ca. 1965], pp. 13-15.
>Explains movements in terms of indigenous myth and ritual, and as rational within a local world view.

251 Whiteman, Darrell L[averne]. "The Christian mission and culture change in New Guinea." *Missiology* 2, no. 1 (1974): 17-33, bib.

252 Whiteman, Darrell L[averne]. "The cultural dynamics of religious movements." In *Point*. Series 4, *Religious movements in Melanesia today (3)*, edited by W. Flannery. Goroka: Melanesian Institute, 1984, pp. 52-79.

253 Worsley, Peter M. "Cargo cults." In *Contemporary anthropology: An anthology*, edited by D. G. Bates and S. H. Lees. New York: A. A. Knopf, 1981, 266-72.

General

This section includes items on the Melanesian culture area as a whole or covering more than one of the Melanesian countries or regions. It therefore includes material on Papua New Guinea as a national unit, although most items on this country are more conveniently treated separately under its four geographic regions. Most of the literature on cargo cults as such will be found in the Melanesia: General section, although further discussions occur in many of the other sections. It should be remembered, however, that despite the pervasiveness of cargo ideology there are many other movements than "cargo cults."

254 Adams, R. "The Pitenamu society." In *Micronationalist movements in Papua New Guinea*, edited by R. J. May. Political and Social Change Monograph 1. Canberra: Department of Political and Social Change, Research School of Pacific Studies, Australian National University, 1982, pp. 63-110.

General

255 Aeerts, Theo[dore Joseph Arnold]. "The birth of a religious movement: A comparison of Melanesian cargo cults and early Christianity." *Verbum SVD* 20, no. 4 (1979): 323-44.
     The common pattern compared with Christianity, all illustrated with detailed references to the movements and to the Bible.

256 Ahrens, Theo[dor]. "Christian syncretism." *Catalyst* (Goroka) 4, no. 1 (1974): 8-10, 33. German translation in *Zeitschrift für Mission* 1, no. 3 (1975): 180-85.

257 Ahrens, Theo[dor]. "The Church's response to nativistic millenarianism reconsidered." Melanesian Institute Orientation Course, 1976, 5 pp. Mimeo.

258 Ahrens, Theo[dor], and Murphy, K., eds. "The Church and adjustment movements." *Point* (Goroka), no. 1 (1974), 216 pp.
     A theme issue, with thirteen essays (listed separately) and a bibliography.

259 Arbuckle, Gerald. "Man's aspirations to be man: Some reflections on adjustment cults." *Point* (Goroka), no. 1 (1974), pp. 113-22.

260 Arndt, G. "From whence the cargo? A look into the understanding of origins." In *Anthropological Study Conference Amapyaka, Western Highlands District, 1968*. N.p.: New Guinea Lutheran Mission (Lutheran Church Missouri Synod), 1968, 5 pp. Mimeo.

261 Australian Board of Missions. "Cults: Nationalism in the Pacific." Field survey no. 7. *Australian Board of Missions Review* (Sydney) 4, no. 7 (July 1952): 101-3.
     A general survey of cargo cults.

262 Avi, Dick. "Cargo cult: Seeking the Kingdom of God." *Mission Review* (Sydney–Uniting Church in Australia), no. 8 (July-September 1979), pp. 9-11; and letters in criticism (by R. F. Burns) and in support (by Rex Matthews) in no. 9 (October-December 1979), p. 11.
     An executive officer of Melanesian Council of Churches attempts a positive appreciation of the meaning of cults.

263 Baal, Jan van. "Algemene sociaal-culturele beschouwingen." In W. Klein (ed.), *Nieuw-Guinea* (The Hague) vol. 1, 1956, 243-46.
     Mentions Seventh Day Adventists and some "spiritualistic movements" in connection with cargo cults.

264 Baal, Jan van. *Mensen in verandering: Ontstaan en groei van een nieuwe cultuur in ont wikkelingslanden.* Amsterdam: De Arbeiderspers, 1967, 192 pp.
Pp. 69-80, cargo cults; pp. 81-90, prophetic movements across various continents; for an English summary, see F. C. Kamma (entry 761), pp. 260-62, 272-73.

265 Bader, Otto. "Im Dunkel des Heidentums." *Steyler Missionsbote* (St. Augustin-bei-Bonn) 63 (1935-36): 237-88.

266 Barr, John. "The age of the spirit." In *Point*. Series 4, *Religious movements in Melanesia today (3)*, edited by W. Flannery. Goroka: Melanesian Institute, 1984, pp. 158-85.

267 Barr, John. "Spiritistic tendencies in Melanesia." In *Point*. Series 3, *Religious movements in Melanesia today (2)*, edited by W. Flannery. Goroka: Melanesian Institute, 1983, pp. 1-34 (bib., pp. 22-34).

268 Barr, John. "A survey of ecstatic phenomena and 'Holy Spirit movements.'" *Oceania* 54, no. 2 (1983): 109-33.

269 Barr, J[ohn], and Trompf, G[arry] [Winston]. "Independent churches and recent ecstatic phenomena in Melanesia: A survey of materials." *Oceania* 54, no. 1 (September 1983): 48-50.

270 Beek, W. E. A. van, and Scherer, J. H., eds. *Explorations in the anthropology of religion: Essays in honour of Jan van Baal.* The Hague: Martinus Nijhoff, 1975, vi + 303 pp. + portrait.
See essays under Locher (entry 188), Ploeg (entry 451), Pouwer (entry 811), and Schoorl (entry 818).

271 Belshaw, Cyril S[hirley]. "Cargo cults." In *Encyclopaedia Britannica*, 1969. Vol. 4, pp. 901a-b.
A good brief survey.

272 Belshaw, Cyril S[hirley]. *Changing Melanesia: Social economics of culture contact.* Melbourne: Oxford University Press, 1950, 197 pp., maps.
Includes cargo cults; pp. 74-75, syncretism; p. 112, Jon Frum.

273 Belshaw, Cyril S[hirley]. "The significance of modern cults in Melanesian development." *Australian Outlook* 4, no. 2 (June 1950): 116-25. Reprinted in *A reader in comparative religion*, edited by W. A.

General

Lesser and E. Z. Vogt. New York: Harper & Row, 1958; 2d ed. 1965, pp. 517-22; 3d ed. 1972, pp. 523-27.

Surveys thirteen movements between 1900 and 1950, from Fiji to Papua; suggests a common cause in the search for a halfway position between the old life and the new.

274 Benz, Ernst. *Neue Religionen*. Stuttgart: Ernst Klett Verlag, 1971, 179 pp.

Chap. 8 (pp. 125-39), cargo cults, by an historian of religion.

275 Berndt, Ronald M[urray]. "Looking back into the present: A changing panorama in eastern Arnhem Land." *Anthropological Forum* 4, nos. 3-4 (1978-79) [issued 1980]: 281-96.

Pp. 289-90, brief comments on the Elcho Island movement; whole article is useful on interaction processes.

276 Bettison, David G.; Hughes, Colin A.; and Veur, Paul [W.] van der, eds. *The Papua-New Guinea elections, 1964*. Canberra: Australian National University, 1965, 545 pp.

Cargo cults, passim (e.g., pp. 196-211, 267-69, 276-77, 459-60); conclusions, p. 508. See also M. S. Dewdney (entry 905), and "The Rai Coast open electorate" (entry 957).

277 Blumanthal, Gary B. "Elcong Bena circuit." In *A study of the Lutheran Church in the Bena area*, by T. Ahrens, et al. Goroka: Melanesian Institute, [1975], separate pagination, pp. 1-55, map.

An American missionary on movements in 1966 and 1969 in the Bena area.

278 Bodrogi, T[ibor]. "Colonization and religious movements in Melanesia." *Acta Ethnographica Academiae Hungaricae Scientiarum* (Budapest, Magyar Tudomanyos Akademia) 2, nos. 1-4 (1951): 259-92, notes and bib. Russian summary (pp. 290-92).

A Marxist view, with colonialism as a major cause.

279 Brouwer, Leo. "Theological evaluation of millenarian movements." Melanesian Institute Orientation Course, Bomana, 1971-72, 6 pp. Mimeo. *Idem*, Alexishafen, 1974 and 1979, 10 pp. Mimeo.

280 Brown, Paula. "Social change and social movements." In *New Guinea on the threshold: Aspects of social political and economic development*, edited by E. K. Fisk. Canberra: Australian National University, 1966, 290 pp., illus.

Pp. 152-65, various forms of change with special reference to Tommy Kabu's Kompani, Kondom's more secular Chimbu movement, Yali, and Paliau.

281 Budruan, S. "Kago Kal I Pinis Olgeta Siwa Budruan i Raitim." *New Voices* 2 (1972): 5-6.

282 Bürkle, Horst, ed. *Theologische Beiträge aus Papua Neuguinea*. Erlangen Taschenbücher 43. Erlangen: Verlag Ev.-Luth. Mission, 1978, 345 pp.

See items by Ahrens (entry 95), Moritzen (entry 201), Steinbauer (entry 487), Strelan (entries 491 and 492).

283 Burridge, K[enelm] O[swald] L[ancelot]. "The cargo cult." *Discovery* (London) 23, no. 2 (February 1962): 22-27, illus.

A survey of the ideas behind cargo cults, interpreted as symbols of the "new man" aspired to.

284 Burridge, K[enelm] O[swald] L[ancelot]. "The Melanesian manager." In *Studies in Social Anthropology*, edited by J. H. M. Beattie and R. G. Lienhardt. Oxford: Clarendon Press, 1975, pp. 86-104.

Cargo influence on new form of leader.

285 Burton-Bradley, B[urton] G. "Cargo anxiety." Paper presented at World Congress of Psychiatry, November 1971, Mexico City, 6 pp. Mimeo.

286 Burton-Bradley, B[urton] G. "Cargo cult." In *Historical Dictionary of Oceania*, edited by R. D. Craig and F. P. King. Westport, Conn., and London: Greenwood Press, 1981, pp. 45-47.

287 Burton-Bradley, B[urton] G. "Guilty or not guilty. A review of fifteen years experience in the law courts." *Papua New Guinea Medical Journal* 18, no. 3 (1975). Reprinted in *Catalyst* 7, no. 1 (1977): 38-49.

Pp. 41-45, cargo cult activities as seen in individuals within the author's psychiatric practice.

288 Burton-Bradley, B[urton] G. "Human sacrifice for cargo." *Medical Journal of Australia* 2 (16 September 1972): 667-71.

289 Burton-Bradley, B[urton] G. "Longlong!" 1973. Mimeo.

Pp. 121-35, prophets, cargo cults and case studies relevant to these, from a psychiatric viewpoint.

General

290 Burton-Bradley, B[urton] G. *Stone age crisis: A psychiatric appraisal.* Abraham Flexner Lectures in Medicine, 1973. Nashville: Vanderbilt University Press, 1975, 128 pp.
Chap. 2 (pp. 10-31), cargo cults.

291 Butinov, N. A. Review of *The Melanesian cargo cult: Millenarianism as a factor in cultural change,* by P. Christiansen (entry 301). *Sovetskaja Etnografija* (Moscow), no. 4 (1971), pp. 179-81.
In Russian.

292 Butinova, M. S. "Cargo cultism and the election." *Inside New Guinea* (Boroko) 3, no. 14 (10 November 1971).
On alleged manipulation of cargo ideas by Pangu party before the elections of 1972. On microfiche, the Centre, Selly Oak Colleges.

293 Butler, J[ohn] F[rancis]. *Christianity in Asia and America after A.D. 1500.* Leiden: E. J. Brill, 1979, 47 pp. + 48 leaves of plates.

294 "Cargo: Government waging war on wishful thinking and the 'spirit' world." *Focus: New Guinea,* no. 5 (September 1971), pp. 11, 18. Reprinted from *Bisnis Newsletter,* August 1971.
Critique of cargoism by the Department of Business Development, prompted by the Mt. Turu movement.

295 Carley, Keith. "Prophets old and new." In *Prophets of Melanesia,* edited by G. W. Trompf. Port Moresby: Institute of Papua New Guinea Studies, 1977, pp. 238-66, index. Reprint. 1988.
An important theoretical article.

296 Chalk, Peter G. "Acculturation and change in Melanesia: Towards an understanding of the cargo movements." Thesis (social sciences), Gregorian University, Rome, 1973, 80 pp. Typescript.
Based on eighteen movements, drawn from P. Worsley (entry 529) and P. Lawrence (entry 1025). Copy at Melanesian Institute, Goroka.

297 Chatterton, Percy. "Headaches ahead for the lawyers?" *Pacific Islands Monthly* 43, no. 5 (May 1972): 43, 45, illus.
Cargo cults cannot be outlawed, but fund-raising might be controlled. By a veteran missionary.

298 Chatterton, Percy. "Magic." *Pacific Islands Monthly* 37, no. 12 (1966): 39, 41.

Increased reliance on magic in imported forms, especially in towns, as evidence of stress.

299 Chatterton, Percy. "The missionaries working themselves out of a job?" *New Guinea and Australia, the Pacific and South-East Asia* 3, no. 1 (1968): 12-18.
Pp. 16-17, cargo thinking.

300 Christiansen, Palle. "Cargo kult." *Jordens Folk* (Copenhagen) 1, no. 2 (1965): 52-56, illus.

301 Christiansen, Palle. *The Melanesian Cargo cult: Millenarianism as a factor in cultural change*. English translation. Copenhagen: Akademisk Forlag, for Institute of Ethnology and Anthropology, University of Copenhagen, 1969, 1248 pp.

302 Cochrane, Glynn. *Big men and cargo cults*. Oxford: Clarendon Press, 1970, xxxix + 187 pp., illus., maps., bib.
Pp. 1-66, Papuan background and "Vailala Madness"; pp. 67-96, Marching Rule; pp. 97-118, Doliasi 'Custom' movement; pp. 138-71, general and theoretical.

303 Cotlow, Lewis N. *In search of the primitive*. Toronto: Little, Brown & Co.; London: Robert Hale, 1966, 454 pp., illus., maps.
Pp. 367-70, cargo cults.

304 Dammann, Ernst. *Grundriss der Religionsgeschichte*. Theologische Wissenschaft: Sammelwerk für Studium und Beruf, 17. Stuttgart: Verlag W. Kohlhammer, 1972, 127 pp.
Pp. 109-14, cargo cults, by a historian of religions.

305 Davenport, William. Review of *Road belong cargo: A study of the cargo movement in the Southern Madang District, New Guinea*, by P. Lawrence (entry 1025). *American Anthropologist* 68, no. 1 (1966): 326-28.

306 Dawia, Alexander. "Indigenizing Christian worship." *Point* (Goroka), no. 1 (1980), pp. 49-60.
Learning from small revivalist churches and Pentecostal groups.

307 De'Ath, Colin. "Cargo cults, millennial thinking and salvation history." *Bikmans: A Journal of Papua New Guinea Affairs, Ideas, and Arts* (Boroko) 2, no. 1 (1981): 25-35.

General

308 Devereux, George. "An ethnopsychiatric note on property destruction in cargo cults." *Man*, article 221, 64 (November-December 1964): 184-85.

309 Downs, Ian. "Cargo cult: It's a way of protest." *Papua New Guinea Post-Courier* (Port Moresby), 11 May 1972, p. 5.

310 Eckert, Georg. "Prophetentum in Melanesien." *Zeitschrift für Ethnologie* 69 (1937): 135-40.

311 Eckert, Georg. "Prophetentum und Kulturwandel in Melanesien." *Baessler Archiv* 23, no. 1 (1940): 26-41.
    A wideranging scholarly survey with many useful extracts from German mission periodicals.

312 Elkin, A[dolphus] [Peter]. Review of *The trumpet shall sound: A study of 'cargo' cults in Melanesia,* by P. M. Worsley (entry 529). *Oceania* 28, no. 3 (March 1958): 242-44.
    Critical of "provocative, armchair, Marxian interpretation," rendering it unsuitable for introduction for nonspecialist.

313 Ellenberger, John D. "Schismatic movements in mission-founded churches." *Catalyst* (Goroka) 11, no. 4 (1981): 224-36.

314 Epstein, A. L.; Parker, R. S.; and Reay, Marie. *The politics of dependence: Papua New Guinea, 1968.* Canberra: Australian National University Press, 1971, 398 pp., maps.
    See essays by E. Ogan (entry 654), T. G. Harding and P. Lawrence (entry 958) on New Guinea, and by R. S. Parker (entry 449).

315 Essai, Brian. *Papua and New Guinea: A contemporary survey.* Melbourne: Oxford University Press, 1961, 255 pp.
    Pp. 52-56, Vailala Madness, Sanop movement (Buka Passage), and Paliau movement.

316 Farb, Peter. "Ghost dance and cargo cult." *Horizon* (New York) 11, no. 2 (1969): 58-65.
    A. F. C. Wallace's revitalization theory used to analyse "millenarian" movements.

317 Fenbury, David [M.]. "The white cassowary: 'I would like to see this cargo. . . .'" *New Guinea and Australia, the Pacific and South-East Asia* 1, no. 5 (March-April 1966): 48-65.

Fiction. Written in 1957 by senior administrator to show the United Nations Trusteeship Division that cargo cults were more than burgeoning nationalism.

318 Fine, Michael. "An analysis of adopted cults in central Australia: Social groups and ritual amongst the Walbiri and Aranda." B.A. (Hons.) thesis, University of Sydney, 1975, 60 pp., diag., map.

319 Finnane, Paul. "The prophet–a symbol of protest: A study of the leaders of cargo cults in Papua New Guinea." M.A. thesis (anthropology), Loyola University (Chicago), 1972, 88 pp.
      Note especially pp. 58-64, the "myth-dream" as the heart of cargoism, and pp. 74-77, conclusions; chap. 2 surveys the leaders of many movements.

320 Fischer, Hans. "Cargo-Kulte und die 'Amerikaner.'" *Sociologus* (Berlin) 14, no. 1 (1964): 17-30.
      The "Americans" as a category of people seen as more friendly than other whites (e.g., colonial administrators), and identified with ancestors bringing the millennial age.

321 Flannery, Wendy. "The authority of ecstatic religious experiences and drama in contemporary Melanesian 'spirit' movements." In *Point.* Series 4, *Religious movements in Melanesia today (3)*, edited by W. Flannery. Goroka: Melanesian Institute, 1984, pp. 117-57.

322 Flannery, Wendy, ed. *Religious movements in Melanesia: A selection of case studies and reports*. Goroka: Melanesian Institute, 1983, 213 pp., maps. Mimeo.
      Supplements to *Point* Series 2, 3, and 4. Sections 1 and 2, movements with affinity with cargo cults; section 3, renewal or revival movements. Irian Jaya movements are in section 2.

323 Flannery, Wendy, ed. "Searching for life in all its fulness." *One World* (Geneva), no. 85 (April 1983), pp. 15-17, map.
      Cargo cults and the more recent and more Christian revival movements.

324 Forster, Robert. "The cargo cults today." *New Society* (London), no. 432 (7 January 1971), pp. 10-12, illus. Also letter by Lucy Mair, no. 433 (14 January 1971), p. 75.
      A survey, with special reference to Yali's cult; cults regarded as rudimentary nationalism; nothing on religious dimensions.

General

325 Freund, A. P. H. "Papua New Guinea had cargo cults long before the white men came." *Papua New Guinea Post-Courier* (Port Moresby), 11 February 1976, p. 14.
A letter.

326 Gaiyer, Patrick P. "Cargo cult hysteria undermines our people's pride, productivity." *Papua New Guinea Post-Courier* (Port Moresby), 4 March 1976, p. 2.

327 Gesch, Patrick [Francis]. "Cargo cults: The village-Christian dialogue." In *Point*. Series 4, *Religious movements in Melanesia today (3)*, edited by W. Flannery. Goroka: Melanesian Institute, 1984, pp. 1-13.

328 Gesch, Patrick F[rancis]. Review of *Melanesian Cargo cults: New salvation methods in the South Pacific*, by Friedrich Steinbauer (entry 485). *Catalyst* (Goroka), 10, no. 2 (1980): 128-32.

329 Godschalk, Jan A. Foreword to *Point*. Series 2, *Religious movements in Melanesia today (1)*, edited by W. Flannery. Goroka: Melanesian Institute, 1983, pp. vii-x.
An introduction to seminars held in Irian Jaya in 1980 and 1981, and later at Goroka; by a missionary of Regions Beyond Missionary Union.

330 Goody, Jack. *Literacy in traditional societies*. Cambridge: Cambridge University Press, 1968, 349 pp.
Pp. 298-99, editorial preface to M. J. Meggitt's essay (entry 428).

331 Gott, K. D. "'Cargo cult' in New Guinea." *Eastern World* (London) 9, no. 10 (October 1955): 20-21.
Brief survey since 1870, suggesting occurrence where white contact has been limited, rather than nonexistent or extensive.

332 Guiart, Jean [Charles Robert]. "'Cargo cults' and political evolution in Melanesia." *Mankind* (Sydney) 8, no. 5 (May 1951): 227-29. Reprinted in *South Pacific* (Sydney) 5, no. 7 (1951): 128-29.
Criticism of C. Belshaw (entry 273) on movements outside Papua New Guinea.

333 Guiart, Jean [Charles Robert]. "Forerunners of Melanesian nationalism." *Oceania* 22, no. 2 (December 1951): 81-90.
Brief survey, with some fresh data on New Caledonian movements – on Lifu, and the Doki cult.

334 Guiart, Jean [Charles Robert]. "Les tendances modernes de l'evolution des sociétés Mélanésiennes." In *Men and Cultures*, edited by A. F. C. Wallace. Philadelphia: University of Pennsylvania Press, 1960, 810 pp.
Pp. 265-66, messianic and cargo movements in Melanesia.

335 Guiart, Jean [Charles Robert], and Worsley, Peter. "La répartition des mouvements millénaristes en Mélanésie." *Archives de Sociologie des Religions*, 3e année, 5 (January-June 1958): 38-46, maps.
Lists and locates 73 movements.

336 Haney, William Edward. "An analysis of the influence of environment and contact history on the form of two millenarian movements." M.A. thesis, Washington State University, 1965, 86 pp.
North American Ghost Dance and cargo movements.

337 Hannet, Leo. "Em rod bilong kago." *Kovave* (Milton, Queensland, Jacaranda Press), June 1969 (pilot issue), pp 47-51.
A one-act play in Pidgin.

338 Harris, Marvin. *Cows, pigs, wars, and witches: The riddles of culture.* New York: Random House, 1974, 276 pp. Reprint. London: Hutchinson, 1975, 276 pp. New York: Vintage, 1978.
Pp. 114-32, "Phanton cargo" – a survey, with special reference to Yali.

339 Harrison, Tom. *Savage civilization.* London: Victor Gollancz, 1937, 461 pp., illus., folding map, bib.
Pp. 271n, 381n, Vailala Madness as "an embryonic anti-white religion"; pp. 380-381, summaries of Runovoro movement and the Clapcott murder.

340 Hastings, Peter, ed. *Papua/New Guinea: Prospero's other island.* Sydney: Angus & Robertson, 1971, 226 pp.
Cargo cults, passim, and especially p. 153 (by E. P. Wolfers) and pp. 189-90, 196 (by Tokari); and P. Lawrence (entry 394).

341 Hayward, Douglas J. "An overview of Melanesian millenarian movements." *Evangelical Missions Quarterly* 17, no. 4 (1981): 205-10.
By a missionary in Irian Jaya.

342 Hertle, Rudolph. Review of *Melanesische Cargo-Kulte: neureligiöse Heilsbewegungen in der Südsee,* by F. Steinbauer (entry 485). *Practical Anthropology* 19, no. 5 (1972): 238-40.

General

343 Hilliard, David [Lockhart]. *God's gentleman: A history of the Melanesian Mission, 1849-1942*. St. Lucia: University of Queensland Press, 1978, 342 pp.
   See also under Solomon Islands.

344 Hinton, Peter D. "The Melanesian cargo cult and the development of secular organizations: A study in social process." B.A. thesis, University of Sydney, 1961.
   Not catalogued in the university library.

345 Hoeltker, Georg. "Neues zum Cargo-Kult in Melanesia." *Neue Zeitschrift für Missionswissenschaft* 28, no. 1 (1968): 56-57.
   Uses M. J. Meggitt (entry 428) and other sources.

346 Hogbin, H[erbert] I[an] P[riestley]. "Report on Vailala madness and other cargo cults." *Papua New Guinea Department of Native Affairs Circular 37*, 8 January 1947.

347 Horne, John R. "Vailala madness." *Pacific Islands Monthly* 48, no. 10 (1977): 33.
   Earlier cults were Tokeriu, Baigona, and Taro, and German Wislin.

348 Horsfield, Donald. [Letter.] *Reform* (London), April 1973, pp. 10-11, illus.
   A missionary on cargo thinking.

349 Hovey, Kev. "Understanding cargoism: Melanesia's challenge to the Church or the Church's challenge to Melanesia?" Fuller Theological Seminary, School of World Mission course paper, April 1979, 35 pp.

350 Hueter, Dick. "The battle for the abundant life: The problems of cults and the church." *Point* (Goroka), no. 1 (1974), pp. 123-40.

351 Hughes, C. A., and Veur, Paul W. van der. "The elections, an overview." In *The Papua-New Guinea elections, 1964*, edited by D. G. Bettison, C. A. Hughes, and P. van der Veur. Canberra: Australian National University, 1965, pp. 388-429.
   P. 403, ideas about Yali; pp. 403-4, beliefs about the Johnson cult, New Hanover.

352 Hughes, Jenny. "Cargo cults demythologized." Essay submitted for the 1970 Te Rangi Hiroa Essay Competition, Port Moresby, 1970, 8 pp.

A general account using "revitalization" concept and surveying different theories. Copy in Papua New Guinea Special Collection, University of Papua New Guinea.

353 Inder, Stuart, ed. *Pacific Islands Year Book*. 12th ed. Sydney: Pacific Publications, 1977, 431 pp., map.
   Pp. 233-35, John Frum, p. 235, Nagriamel, pp. 321-22, Marching Rule, Eto's Church and Moro movement – all brief outlines.

354 Italiaander, Rolf, ed. *Heisses Land Niugini: Beiträge zu den Wandlungen in Papua Neuguinea*. Erlangen: Verlag der Evang.-Luth. Mission, 1974, 368 pp., illus.
   See T. Ahrens (entry 256) and H. Wagner (entry 1157).

355 Janssen, H[ermann]. "A church self-study in Papua New Guinea." *Pro Mundi Vita Dossier* (Brussels), 1975.

356 Janssen, Hermann. "The development of the Melanesian way to fuller life." Melanesian Institute Orientation Course, Vunapope 1969-70, 3 pp. Mimeo.

357 Janssen, Hermann. "Missionary attitudes towards cargo cults." Melanesian Institute Orientation Course, Bomana, 1971-72, 8 pp., Mimeo. Also at Alexishafen, 1974 and 1979, 12 pp., Mimeo.

358 Janssen, H[ermann]. "Population movements and the role of socio-religious relationships in changing societies of South Pacific islands." *Teaching all nations* (Manila) 13, no. 1 (1976): 40-55, bib.

359 Janssen, Hermann. "Religion and secularisation: Pacific cultures, Christianity and development." *Catalyst* (Goroka) 2, no. 2 (1972): 50-68.

360 Janssen, Hermann. "What to do? Missionary attitudes to cargo cult movements." *Point* (Goroka), no. 1 (1974), pp. 157-75.

361 Janssen, H[ermann], ed. "Self-Study of the Catholic Church in Papua New Guinea: Seminar Handbook." Goroka: Self-Study Secretariate, [Melanesian Institute], 1972, [213 pp.]. Mimeo.
   Thirty-three short papers from a national workshop at Alexishafen; paper 4 by Janssen on Christian Churches and changing cultures in Papua New Guinea (pp. 2, 3-4, on cargo ideas and

General

syncretism); paper 12 by Leo Brouwer on Liturgy in Melanesia, old and new (pp. 2-3 on syncretism and misunderstandings of Christianity).

362 Jarvie, Ian C. "Cargo cults." In *Encyclopaedia of Papua and New Guinea*. Vol. 1. Melbourne: Melbourne University Press, 1972, pp. 133b-137a.

363 Jarvie, Ian C. "Cargo cults." *Man, myth, and magic* 1 [1970-72]: 2109-12.

364 Jawodimbari, Arthur. *"Cargo: A play.*" In *Five New Guinea Plays*, edited by U. Beier. Milton, Queensland: Jacaranda Press, 1971, pp. 11-19.

365 Johnston, George H. "Cargo cult natives await their Great White Ship." *Sun* (Sydney) 21 (June 1950): 21.

366 Jojoga [Opeba], Willington. "Prophets in traditional society." Draft paper, Department of History, University of Papua New Guinea, [ca. 1975], 20 pp. Mimeo.
    Same as his essay published in G. Trompf (entry 239), with introductory survey of prophets from Tokeriu. P. 11a, new information on a prophet in 1973.

367 Joyce, Peta. "Melanesian cargo cults: The European reaction." Essay submitted for the Te Rangi Hiroa Essay Competition, Port Moresby, 1975, 12 pp.
    Copy in P.N.G. Special Collection, University of Papua New Guinea.

368 Julius, Charles. "Cargo cults in Papua and New Guinea." *Australian Territories* (Canberra) 2, no. 4 (1962): 14-20, illus.
    By the government anthropologist.

369 Kaima, Sam Tua. "Politics as cargo in Papua New Guinea." *Catalyst* (Goroka) 17, no. 2 (1987): 149-62.
    Shows the ideological and historical connections between cargo cults and political parties, and the common leadership patterns; refers to Yaliwan, Yali, Paliau, Tommy Kabu, etc.

370 Kanadi, John. "Cargo cult comes to reality." In University of Papua New Guinea, P.N.G. Special Collection.
    A play.

371 Keesing, Felix M[axwell]. *Native peoples of the Pacific world*. New York: Macmillan Co., 1945, 144 pp.
Pp. 130ff., local "sects."

372 Kelty, Matthew. "What cargo cults reflect to me." *Catalyst* 13, no. 4 (1983): 289-300.
Cultural and spiritual dimensions.

373 Kerpi, Kama. "Cargo." *Kovave: A Journal of New Guinea Literature* (Milton, Queensland) 5, no. 1 (June 1975): 30-36, illus.
Fiction.

374 Kerr, Martin D. *New Guinea patrol*. London: Robert Hale, 1973, 192 pp. + 12 pp. illus. Reprint. London: Travel Book Club, 1974.
Pp. 33-34, a government officer on cargo cults including Johnson cult, and Hohalis (sic) Welfare Society "set up to entice Europeans to produce mixed race offspring at baby farms"!

375 Keysser, Christian. "Aus dem Bericht an den Völkerbund." *Neuendettelsauer Missionsblatt* 25, no. 1 [92, no. 11] (10 November 1935): 89.

376 Kiki, Albert Maori. *Kiki. Ten thousand years in a lifetime: A New Guinea autobiography* [recorded by Ulli Beier]. London: Pall Mall Press, 1968, 190 pp., map, illus. German translation. *Ich lebe seit 10,000 Jahren*. Frankfurt: Ullstein, 1969, 189 pp.
Pp. 48-52, current local interpretation of the Vailala Madness; pp. 52-53, two Orokolo prophets from 1945; pp. 104-25, the Buka affair (Hahalis Welfare Society); p. 170, Tommy Kabu as not a cult leader; by a distinguished politician.

377 Kilani, Mondher. *Les cultes du cargo mélanésiens: Mythe et rationalité en anthropologie*. Lausanne: Éditions d'en Bas, 1983, 108 pp., bib.

378 Knauft, Bruce M. "Cargo cults and relational separation." *Behavior Science Research* (New Haven) 13, no. 3 (1978): 185-240, bib. (pp. 229-40).
Empirical analysis of twenty-one cargo cults in support of the view that the disruption caused by a cult varies directly with the degree indigenes become separated from agents of Western culture directly prior to the cult outbreak.

General

379 Knoebel, J[oseph]. "The history and development of adjustment movements." Melanesian Institute Orientation Course, Mt. Hagen and Bomana, 1971, 8 pp. Mimeo.

380 Knoebel, J[oseph]. "A history of adjustment movements in Melanesia." Melanesian Institute Orientation Course, Alexishafen, 1974 and 1976, 16 pp. Mimeo.
See also entry 381.

381 Knoebel, Joseph. "In search of tomorrow's new world: A history of adjustment movements in Melanesia." *Point* (Goroka), no. 1 (1974), pp. 50-73.

382 Knoebel, Joseph. "A pattern in dreaming and hoping: The cultural rationale of adjustment movements." *Point* (Goroka), no. 1 (1974), pp. 81-92.

383 Knuf, Joachim. *Cargo-Kulte und situationale Logik: Zur situationslogischen Analyse millennarischer Bewegungen*. Weisbaden: Edition Ethnos, [reported in press 1980].

384 Krige, Willem Adolf. "Die problem van eiesoortige kerkvorming by Christian Keysser." Doctoral dissertation, Free University of Amsterdam, 1954.
Pp. 99-100, outline of cargo cults, in the context of missionary Keysser's theory of church planting.

385 Kroef, Justus M. van der. "Racial messiahs." In *Race, individual, and collective behavior*, edited by E. T. Thompson and E. C. Hughes. Glencoe: Free Press, 1958, pp. 357-74. Rev. and enl. version of "The Messiah in Indonesia and Melanesia," *Scientific Monthly* 75, no. 3 (September 1952): 161-65.
Pp. 360-62 especially on Melanesia.

386 Krug, Werner G. *Paradis mit kleinen Fehlern: Südsee zwischen Bali und Hawaii*. Hamburg: Hoffman und Campe Verlag, 1957, 339 pp., illus., map.
Pp. 134, 163-78, cargo cults.

387 Kuder, John. [The cargo cult and its relation to the task of the Church.] In *Lutheran Mission New Guinea 18th Annual Field Conference, Minutes, 1964*. Lae: The Mission, 1964, pp. 23-25. Mimeo.

Summary of his paper on 31 January 1964 at Wau, and of ensuing discussion. For full version in German translation, see entry 388.

388 Kuder, John. "Der Cargo-Kult und sein Verhältnis zur Aufgabe der Kirche." *Evangelische Missions-Zeitschrift*, n.s. 22, no. 2 (1965): 58-72.
A German translation of a paper given at Wau in 1964 along with J. F. Wagner's major study: see Kuder (entry 387) and Wagner (entry 513) for details.

389 "Kult mit Gutern." *Ruf in die Welt* (Neuendettelsau, Evangelische Jugendmissionsblatt) 20, no. 2 (1972): 1-11, illus.
A well-illustrated general article with special reference to Mt. Hurun and Johnson cults.

390 Laboi, Anton. "Cargo king." *Papua New Guinea Writing* (Literature Bureau, Konedobu), no. 6 (June 1972), pp. 3-5.
Fiction: a cargo cult in progress, involving a death. In English.

391 Lanternari, Vittorio. *The religions of the oppressed: A study of modern messianic cults.* English translation. London: MacGibbon & Kee, 1963, xx + 343 + xiii pp.; New York A. A. Knopf, 1963, xvi + 286 pp. Reprint. New York: Mentor Books, 1965, xvi + 286 pp.
Chap. 5, "Messianic movements in Melanesia," and paucity in Australia.

392 Laufer, Carl. "Religiöse Wahnideen unter Naturvölkern: Einige grundsätzliche Gedanken zu einem Aktuellen Missions-Problem." *Neue Zeitschrift für Missionswissenschaft* (Beckenried) 3 (1947): 216-21.

393 Laufer, Carl. "Schwärmgeisterei in der Südsee." *Hiltruper Monatshefte*, 1955, pp. 175-79.

394 Lawrence, Peter. "Cargo cult and politics: Seeking a way to the white man's goods." In *Papua/New Guinea: Prospero's other island*, edited by P. Hastings. Sydney: Angus & Robertson, 1971, pp. 106-22.

395 Lawrence, P[eter]. "Cargo cults." In *The encyclopedia of religion*, edited by M. Eliade. Vol. 3. New York: Macmillan, 1987, pp. 74-81.

396 Lawrence, Peter. "Cargo thinking as a future political force in Papua and New Guinea." *Journal of the Papua and New Guinea Society* 1, no. 1 (1966): 20-25.

General

Explanation of cults in terms of motivation, means and effects, each being defined in local religio-cultural terms; long-term effects of cargo-thinking on economics, education and politics.

397 Lawrence, Peter. "Politics and 'True Knowledge' . . . when God is managing director?" *New Guinea and Australia, the Pacific and South-East Asia* 2, no. 1 (1967): 34-49.
    Especially pp. 42-42, primal religion, with the Highlands more empirical than the coast; pp. 47-49, "cargoism" as major problem among coastal peoples.

398 Lawrence, P[eter], and Meggitt, Mervyn J[ohn], eds. *Gods, ghosts, and men in Melanesia: Some religions of Australian New Guinea and the New Hebrides*. Melbourne and New York: Oxford University Press, 1965, 198 pp.
    See index, "cargo beliefs" for passing references; p. 278, South Pentecost as a "negative instance"; pp. 184-90, C. A. Valentine on the Sumua cult in Bismarck Archipelago (see entry 620).

399 Lea, David A. M., and Irwin, P. G. *New Guinea, the territory, and its people*. Melbourne: Oxford University Press, 1967, 116 pp. Reprint. 1971.
    P. 96, briefly on Vailala Madness and similar cults "falling back on old beliefs."

400 L[ehmacher], G. "'Christliche' Schwärmgeister in Melanesien (Solomon Islands)." *Die Katholischen Missionen* 62, no. 11 (1934): 309-10.
    Buka Island movements, also in the Admiralty Islands, Rabaul, etc.

401 Lepani, Charles. "New Guinea's cargo cults." *Sunday Review*, 6 June 1971, p. 983.
    Long letter from a Trobriand Island student in New South Wales, defending cargo cults as restoring the cultural dignity undermined by Christian churches.

402 Lidz, Ruth W.; Lidz, Theodore; and Burton-Bradley, Burton G. "Cargo cultism: A psychosocial study of Melanesian millenarianism." *Journal of Nervous and Mental Disease* 157, no. 5 (1973): 370-88.
    By psychiatrists, using psychoanalytical terms and Piaget's concepts of cognitive development to explain progress of cult beliefs from "mass hysteria to mass paranoia" as disillusionment increased and

self-esteem declined; the political evaluation of such movements, with Hahalis, Yaliwan, Vailala, Letub, Tagarab, and Yali cults as examples.

403 Lindall, Edward. *A time too soon: A novel.* London and New York: William Morrow & Co., 1967, 221 pp.

Built around the common image of a cargo cult with political aspects.

404 Lindstrom, Lamont C. [Monty Lindstrom, pseud.]. "Cargo cults, sexual distance, and Melanesian social integration." *Canberra Anthropology* (Canberra, A.C.T.) 1, no. 2 (1977): 42-58.

405 Linklater, Eric [Robert Russell]. *The faithful ally.* London: Jonathan Cape, 1954, 257 pp. Reprint. London: Reprint Society, 1956, 254 pp.

A novel about the contrasting methods of the hereditary ruler (the "faithful ally") and the colonial service in a cargoist uprising under a charismatic leader using unexplained magic in an imaginary British protectorate on the north side of New Guinea.

406 Loeliger, Carl [Ernest]. "New myths: The cargo cults." In *The world's religions: A Lion handbook.* Tring, Herts.: Lion Publishing, 1982, p. 146.

A compact summary.

407 Loeliger, Carl [Ernest], and Trompf, Garry [Winston], eds. *New Religious movements in Melanesia.* Suva: Institute of Pacific Studies, University of the South Pacific; University of Papua New Guinea, 1985, xvii + 188 pp., maps, illus.

Fourteen items – student essays, missionary reports, papers and documentary studies of many kinds of new movements – cargo cults, independent churches, spirit movements, etc., with introduction (pp. xi-xvii) by the editors and good maps.

408 Luke, Harry [Charles]. *From a South Seas diary, 1938-42.* London: Nicholson & Watson, 1945, 255 pp., illus.

Pp. 123-24, a governor's negative view of Apolosi, Fiji; pp. 203-4, how he saw Jon Frum.

409 Lusk, Keith. "Revivals in Papua New Guinea and the Solomon Islands since 1970." Seminar paper (Dr. J. Edwin Orr), School of World Mission, Fuller Theological Seminary, 11 February 1986, 52 pp.

On how revival movements begin and spread, based on a survey of all reported movements.

General

410 Lynch, Mark. "Communication and cargo: Some roles performed by members of Papua New Guinea's House of Assembly, 1964-1972." M.A. thesis, University of Sussex, 1972, 113 pp.

By a former Australian *kiap*, in the 1960s, Wonenara area. References to cargo expectations and sundry movements, especially those with a political reference and expectations of "electoral cargo."

411 McCarthy, Jack [John Desmond McCarthy]. "Monster was the key figure in cargo cult." *Papua New Guinea Post-Courier* (Port Moresby), 24-29 April 1972.

By a journalist long resident in Papua New Guinea.

412 McCarthy, Jack [John Desmond McCarthy]. "Old government saying: Cargo cult is false." *Papua New Guinea Post-Courier* (Port Moresby), 24-29 April 1972.

413 McCarthy, J[ohn] K[eith]. *Patrol into yesterday: My New Guinea years.* Melbourne: F. W. Cheshire, 1963. Reprint. London: Angus & Robertson, 1964, 252 pp., illus., maps.

By experienced Australian administrator. Pp. 180-83, 188-89, 210, Batari's movement in New Britain; pp. 223-28, "Rise and fall of a prophet" – Yali in Madang; pp. 240-41, Lagit and the human sacrifice near Alexishafen; the first two accounts are primary sources, the author's reports.

414 McLaren, Peter. "Religion and life: A problem of adjustment." *Point* (Goroka), no. 1 (1974), pp. 105-12.

415 Maeliau, Michael. "Searching for a Melanesian way of worship." In *The Gospel is not Western: Black theologies from the Southwest Pacific*, edited by G. W. Trompf. Maryknoll: Orbis Books, 1987, pp. 119-27.

Especially pp. 119, 125-26 on recent revival movements as indigenous examples.

416 Mair, Lucy P[hilip]. *Australia in New Guinea.* London: Christophers, 1948, xvii + 238 pp., illus., map. 2d ed. Melbourne University Press, 1971, 254 pp.

P. 68, first use of term "cargo cult" in academic literature; pp. 64-68, 200-202, native reaction to white rule, including new cults.

417 Mair, Lucy P[hilip]. "Cargo cults today." *New Society* (London), no. 433 (14 January 1971), p. 75.

Comments on R. Forster (entry 324); suggests that both cargo cults and political parties lack a nationwide basis and uniting capacity.

418 Malefijt, Annemarie de Waal. *Religion and culture: An introduction to the anthropology of religion.* New York: Macmillan; London: Collier-Macmillan, 1968, 407 pp.

Pp. 329-32, theory of millennialism; pp. 332-42, Melanesian movements – Tokeriu, German Wislin, Vailala, Taro and Naked cults, and Chair-and-Rule and Marching Rule movements.

419 Malenwie, Peter Kopunye. "Cargo cult: The thinking of men." University of Papua New Guinea, New Guinea collection.

A play.

420 Margull, Hans-Jochen. *Aufbruch zur Zukunft.* Gutersloh: G. Mohn, 1962, 128 pp.

Includes cargo cults along with Kimbanguism and Bantu movements in South Africa.

421 Margull, Hans-Jochen. "Aufsatz über die 'Cargo'-Bewegungen." *Das Wort in der Welt* 1 (1962): 9-14.

422 Martin, P. H. "Modern cults in Melanesia." B.Litt. thesis, University of Oxford, 1956-57.

423 Martin Luther Seminary. "Cargo cults in Melanesia: Five study papers by students of Martin Luther Seminary, Lae." Lae: The Seminary, 1972, unpaged typescript in library.

Final-year student essays supervised by F. Steinbauer: David P. Piso, Baigona cult, Papua, 19 pp. Michael Maie, Vailala Madness, Papua, 5 pp. Yerr B. Komndi, Mansren Movement, West Irian, 7 pp. Zage Rupenu, Yali Movement, Madang (1939-46), 13 pp. Peyandi Lepi, Yeliwan cult, Sepik, 8 pp.

424 Matthews, Rex. [Letter to the Editor.] *Mission Review* (Sydney, Uniting Church in Australia), no. 9 (December 1979), p. 11.

A reply to R. F. Burns's letter in same issue which criticized D. Avi's article in previous issue, and defending Avi's views.

425 May R[onald] J., ed. *Micronationalist movements in Papua New Guinea.* Political and Social Change Monograph 1. Canberra: Department of Political and Social Change, Research School of Pacific Studies, Australian National University, 1982, 486 pp., illus., maps.

General

Pp. 31-62, Peli Association; pp. 63-110, Pitenamu society, Bougainville (by R. Adams); pp. 6-12, useful summaries of Paliau, Hahalis, Pitenamu and Johnson cults; chap. 14 (pp. 421-48), theoretical survey, including place of cargoism.

426 May, Ron[ald J.]. "The micronationalists." *New Guinea and Australia, the Pacific and South East-Asia* (Sydney) 10, no. 1 (May-June 1975): 38-53.

Pp. 41-42, Hahalis Welfare Society; pp. 48-49, Peli Association and Yaliwan, in context of self-development economic and political movements.

427 Mead, Margaret. "The rights of primitive peoples, Papua New Guinea: A crucial instance." *Foreign Affairs* 45, no. 2 (January 1967): 304-18. Reprinted in *Cultures of the Pacific*, edited by T. G. Harding and B. J. Wallace. New York: Free Press, 1970, pp. 419-29.

Pp. 426-27, brief comment on leadership as seen in cargo cults, with Paliau as an unusual example.

428 Meggitt, M[ervyn] J. "The uses of literacy in New Guinea and Melanesia." *Bijdragen tot de Taal-, Land-, en Volkenkunde* 123 (1967): 71-82. Reprinted in *Literacy in Traditional Societies*, edited by J. Goody. Cambridge: Cambridge University Press, 1968, pp. 300-309.

Cargo cults' ritual attitude to writing; literacy may reinforce such movements.

429 Melanesian Institute (Goroka). Orientation Courses, various years and places, mimeo papers, usually bound in a volume for that course:

(1) Vunapope 1969-70: G. Fahey (S.M.), Cargo cult movements in Bougainville, 6 pp. (mainly on Hahalis); H. Janssen (M.S.C.), The development of the Melanesian way to fuller life (place of cargoism in local thought – similar to his paper on development in *Catalyst* 2, no. 2 (1972), 3 pp.; B. Miller (M.S.C.), Cargo cult movements – the birth of a cult (Johnson cult and United Farmers' Association which sought to replace it); J. M. Noss (S.V.D.), Cargo cult in Madang district (comprehensive survey) 30 pp.; S. White (M.S.C.), Cargo cult in New Britain, 1970, 7 pp.

(2) Mt. Hagen, 1971: H. Bammler (Lutheran), Cargo cult movements in the Highlands; H. Bammler, Attitudes of the Lutheran Church in New Guinea towards cargo cult; H. Janssen (M.S.C.), Missionary attitudes towards cargo cultism (repeated at Alexishafen, 1974); J. Knoebel (S.V.D.), The history and development of adjustment movements (cargo cult), 8 pp.

(3) Alexishafen, 1974 (404 pp.): T. Ahrens (Lutheran), the "Lo-Bos" congregation, 9 pp.; L. Brouwer, Pastoral-theological evaluation of millenarian movements, 10 pp.; H. Janssen, Missionary attitudes towards cargo cults (repeated from 1971), 13 pp.; M. Wagewa, Cargo cults in the Sepik District (in Pidgin and English versions), 7 pp.

(4) 1976: Theo Ahrens, The Church's response to millenarianism reconsidered, 5 pp.

(5) 1979: J. Strelan, Towards a theological interpretation of cargo cults, 5 pp.

430 Merton, Thomas. "Cargo cults of the South Pacific." *America*, no. 3500 [137, no. 5] (27 August-3 September 1977): 94-99.

431 Merton, Thomas. *The geography of Lograire*. New York: New Directions, 1968, 153 pp.

Pp. 91-95, "cargo songs"; pp. 100-104, similar material and "cargo catechism"; pp. 105-14, John Frum and "Dialog with Mr. Clapcott" – on Vanuatu; pp. 115-16, "A few more cargo songs"; pp. 147-51, an editor's notes on Merton's sources.

432 *Missio: Probleme des Umbruchs-Cargo-Kult, In Dokumentation Papua-Neuguinea an der Schwelle zur Unabhängigheit*. Aachen: Missio: Internationales Katholisches Missionswerke Verlag, 1974, 47 pp.

Pp. 34-35 on cargo cults, reprinted from *Weltmission* (1971): 14-15.

433 Moritzen, Niels-Peter. "Der Stein der Weisen, oder: Wohin führt die Kargo-Kult-Forschung?" In *Theologische Beiträge aus Papua Neuguinea*, edited by H. Bürkle. Erlangen Taschenbücher 43. Erlangen: Verlag der Evang.-Luth. Mission, 1978, pp. 136-41.

434 Mortimer, Rex. "A case of cricket cargo." *Pacific Islands Monthly* 51, no. 2 (1980): 51, 53.

Review of F. Steinbauer's "Melanesian cargo cults" (entry 222).

435 Moses, Robinson. "A theological assessment of revival movements." In *Point*. Series 4, *Religious movements in Melanesia today (3)*, edited by W. Flannery. Goroka: Melanesian Institute, 1984, pp. 186-94.

436 Moulik, T. K. "Creating productive tensions. ..." In *Priorities in Melanesian development. ... Sixth Waigoni Seminar ... 1972*, edited by R. J. May. Port Moresby: University of Papua New Guinea; Canberra: Australian National University, 1973. Reprint. 1974, pp. 207-321.

General

P. 317, cargo cults as examples of economically productive activity.

437 Moulik, T. K. "A review of village industries: The urban rural choice in entrepreneurial development." In *Change and development in rural Melanesia. ... 5th Waigoni Seminar ... 1971*, edited by M. Ward. Canberra: Australian National University; Port Moresby: University of Papua New Guinea, 1972, pp. 520-29.
Village industries that failed showed less cargo mentality than those that succeeded. Also p. 27, cargo motivations (by the editor).

438 Namunu, Simeon. "Spirits in Melanesia and the Spirit in Christianity." In *Point*. Series 4, *Religious movements in Melanesia today (3)*, edited by W. Flannery. Goroka: Melanesian Institute, 1984, pp. 92-116.

439 Nevermann, Hans. "Der 'Cargo-Kult.'" In *Die Religionen der Südsee und Australiens*. Die Religionen der Menschheit 5, 2, edited by H. Nevermann, et al. Stuttgart and Berlin: W. Kohlhammer Verlag, 1968, pp. 106-13. French translation. "Le 'culte-du-cargo,'" in *Les religions du Pacifique et d'Australie*. Paris: Payot, 1972, pp. 135-43, 149.

440 New Guinea, Territory of. *Annual report to the United Nations, 1950-51*. Canberra: Commonwealth of Australia, 1952.
Pp. 24-30, information on cargo cults as requested by the Trusteeship Council–general characteristics; pp. 16-30, Paliau movement.

441 Newman, Paul. "Cargo cults and other Melanesian revitalization movements." M.A. thesis (anthropology), University of Pennsylvania, 1961, 65 pp., illus., tables.
Pp. 25-56 survey 29 cargo cults from published sources, with data tables (pp. 57-59); classifies them into noncargo millenarian, traditional, socio-political-economic, communist, communist-cargo.

442 O'Donnell, T. "Attitudes of the administration on cargo cults." Melanesian Institute Orientation Course, Bomana, 1971-72. Mimeo.

443 Opeba, Jojoga Willington. "Taro or cargo?" Honours subthesis, University of Papua New Guinea, 1983.

444 Opeba, Willington Jojoga. "Melanesian cult movements as traditional religious and ritual responses to change." In *The Gospel is not Western:*

Black Theologies from the Southwest Pacific, edited by G. W. Trompf. Maryknoll, N.Y.: Orbis Books 1987, pp. 49-66.

Baigona and Taro cults in Northern Province, Papua, with criticism of colonial government and missionary interpretations, and reinterpretation as nonmillenarian "prosperity movements"; the trauma from interaction with the whites and Christianity as a subordinate factor.

445 O'Reilly, Patrick [Georges Farell]. "Le mouvement du Cargo: Son origine et sa recrudescence du fait de l'occupation japonaise: Les représailles japonaises." In *Jaunes noirs et blancs*, edited by P. O'Reilly and J. M. Sedes. Éditions du Monde Nouveau, 1949, pp. 191-200.

Cargo cults during the Japanese occupation, and reprisals against them.

446 O'Reilly, Patrick [Georges Farell]. "Mouvements messianiques en Océanie." *Vie Intellectuelle* 28 (December 1956): 22-30.

A survey of movements and their causes; pp. 28-30, John Frum.

447 Papua New Guinea Parliament. *House of Assembly Debates, 1964*. 1st meeting of the first session, 12 June 1964. Vol. 1, no. 1, 1964, pp. 65-72.

On Johnson cult, New Hanover, and general discussion of cults.

448 Papua New Guinea Tertiary Students. *Tertiary students and the politics of New Guinea. Papers presented at the second seminar of Papua New Guinea tertiary students ... Lae ... August 1971*. Lae: PNG Institute of Technology, 1971, [86 pp.].

See papers by William Hawarry (entry 961) and T. M. Selem (entry 216) referring to cults.

449 Parker, R. S. "From dependence to autonomy." In *The Politics of Dependence, Papua New Guinea 1968*, edited by A. L. Epstein, et al. Canberra: Australian National University, 1971, 398 pp.

Pp. 322-24, cargoist ideas.

450 Parsonson, Gordon S. "A new heaven and a new earth: Some post-Christian reactions in Melanesia." Seminar on Christianity and the Non-Western World, University of Aberdeen, 31 October 1974, 16 pp. Mimeo.

451 Ploeg, A[nton]. "Wok kago and wok bisnis." In *Explorations in the anthropology of religion*, edited by W. E. A. Van Beek and J. H.

General

Scherer. Verhandelingen van het Koninklijk Instituut voor Taal-, Land-, en Volkenkunde, 74. The Hague: M. Nijhoff, 1975, pp. 190-212.

Pp. 190-94, Melanesian culture before World War II; pp. 194-96, various interpretations of cults; pp. 198-207, indigenous efforts at development ("bisnis") and the relation to supernatural factors; pp. 207-8, Mataungan association among the Tolai.

452 Pokawin, Stephen Polonhou. "Cargo cults and development." *Point* (Goroka), no. 1 (1979), pp. 83-95. Reprinted in *Cargo cults and development in Papua New Guinea*, edited by W. Ferea. Port Moresby, 1985, chap. 27. Computer printout.

453 Posern-Zielinski, A[leksander]. "Melanezyjskie ruchy millenarystyczne jako. . . ." *Etnografia Polska* (Breslau) 11 (1967): 349-65; pp. 364-65, English summary.

Cargo cults interpreted as reactions to colonialism, as "undeveloped forms of the struggle for national liberation" that pass over into "sects limited in influence" or are replaced by political movements.

454 *Post-Courier* (Port Moresby). The main daily newspaper in Papua New Guinea carries frequent reports of alleged cargo cults and ideas, and similar phenomena, and letters and comments on these. The following are cited as samples of many in the 1970s:

19 May 1971, p. 5 (by B. Yembanda, on a money-creating cult); 10 June 1971, p. 5 (by A. Sapias, Pomio cultists, East New Britain); 3 July 1971, p. 5 (by G. Robinson, cult events on Mt. Turu).

10 March 1972, p. 1 (Red boxes money cult at Muglum, Mt. Hagen); 10 May 1972, p. 4 (Visiting Catholic missionary's comments); 11 May 1972, p. 5 (by Ian Downs, on cults); 22 May 1972, p. 4 (Pomio area, East New Britain); 6 July 1972, p. 1 ("Their plots . . . and helpers"); 18 July 1972, 1 ("They have a new chance"); 13 November 1972, p. 1 (Wulupu cult, East Sepik), also on 14, 15, 16 November and 5 December 1972.

2 April 1974, p. 3 (Homa village, Southern Highlands); 11 December 1974, p. 4 (Pondona village, Bougainville).

4 March 1975, p. 2 (H. Aufenanger on cults and the great Father); 23 April 1975 ("Money without faces on it has no power"); 28 April 1975, p. 1 ("The king lives").

25 March 1976 ("Gambling with cards is a cargo cult"); 8 September 1976 (Hahalis village, Bougainville).

18 August 1977, p. 19 ("Robbery–Highlander's version of cargo cult"); 25 August 1977, (Pomio area, East New Britain); *idem*, p. 18

(Buka Island, North Solomons); 7 September 1977, p. 15 (Pomio area); 22 September 1977, p. 16 (Pomio); 19 October 1977, p. 1 (Pomio); 21 October 1977, p. 3 (Pomio).

455 Price, Willard. *Odd way round the world.* New York: John Day Co., 1969, 310 pp., illus., maps.
Pp. 135-39, cargo cults, including Johnson cult on New Hanover; a traveler's popular account.

456 Prowse, Duncan. "The secret of heaven's treasure." *Walkabout* (Sydney), November 1972, pp. 40-43, illus.
A useful general survey, especially of recent cargo movements.

457 "Religious movements in Melanesia today." *Umben* (Goroka) 2, no. 2 (1984).
Four articles in Tok Pisin, or neo-Melanesian.

458 Review of "The New Guinea prophet: Is the cultist always normal?" by B. G. Burton-Bradley (entry 895). *R. M. Bucke Memorial Society Newsletter-Review* (Montreal) 4, nos. 1-2 (1971): 60-61.

459 Rich, H. "'Cargo': A Melanesian philosophy." B.A. thesis, University of Sydney, 1964.

460 Riesenfeld, Alphonse. "Baigona and Figona." *Man*, article 66, 46 (May-June 1946): 71-72.
On the similarity between Baigona of Orokaiva and the Figona cult, a traditional cult in Solomon Islands, where the snake is also central.

461 Rousseau, Madelaine. "L'Océanie devant l'Occident." In *L'art Océanien: Sa Présence.* Collection Le Musée Vivant, 38. Paris: APAM, 1951, 138 pp., illus.
Pp. 136-37, cargo cult has as its myth a new materialistic concept.

462 Rowley, Charles D[unford]. *The New Guinea villager.* Melbourne: F. W. Cheshire, 1965, 225 pp. Reprint. New York: Praeger; London: Pall Mall, 1966.
Pp. 160-88, cargo cults.

463 Ryan, D. "Millenarian movements as adaptive mechanisms." Paper, Symposium, 42d ANZAAS Congress, Port Moresby, August 1970.
Reported in *Man in New Guinea* 2, no. 2 (1970).

General

464 Ryan, John. *The Hot land: Focus on New Guinea.* Melbourne: Macmillan; New York: St. Martin's Press, 1969, 390 pp., illus., maps.

Chap. 23, cargo movements, including Vailala, Tommy Kabu, Paliau, Yali, Johnson cult, Koriam's "money cult" in 1969, and other recent developments; chaps. 24-25, Hahalis Welfare Society and the "baby garden" in Buka, especially the clash with the government; chap. 26, Kuraio cult, Bougainville, from about 1959.

465 Salisbury, R[ichard] F[rank] [Roswell]. *From stone to steel: Economic consequences of technological change in New Guinea.* London: Cambridge University Press; Victoria: Melbourne University Press, 1962, 237 pp.

Pp. 114-15, 121, 159, etc., brief references to cargo cults and effects of white contacts.

466 Sanders, J[ohn] Oswald. *Planting men in Melanesia: The first decade of development of the Christian Leaders' Training College of Papua New Guinea.* Mt. Hagen, Papua New Guinea: Christian Leaders' Training College, 1978, 180 pp., illus.

Pp. 22-24, a common earlier missionary interpretation of cults as confusing "religious aberrations" aiding "the powers of darkness," but not now representative of this College; pp. 113-210, an entirely positive account of the Enga revival from 1975, and of its roots in the 1970-71 revival in Solomon Islands.

467 Schlesier, Erhard. *Die melanesischen Geheimkulte.* Göttingen: Musterschmidt, 1958, 390 pp., map, bib. (pp. 373-90).

A Habilitationsschrift, Göttingen.

468 Schulz, Th. "Die Dämonie des Cargo-Kultes." *In Alle Welt* 6 (1954): 126-28.

469 Schwartz, Theodore. "Cargo cult: A Melanesian type response to culture contact." Paper written for DeVos Conference of Psychological Adjustment and Adaptation to Culture Change, Hakone, Japan, 1968. Also read in brief form at the 8th International Congress of Anthropological and Ethnological Sciences, Tokyo, 1968. 120 pp. Mimeo. Published in *Responses to change: Society, culture, and personality,* edited by G. A. DeVos. New York: Van Nostrand Reinhold Co., 1976, pp. 157-206.

470 Schwartz, Theodore. "Cargo cults and social movements in psycho-cultural adjustment to cultural change in Melanesia." 8th International

Congress of Anthropological and Ethnological Sciences, Tokyo and Kyoto, September 1968. *Symposia Abstracts* 8, no. 2 (1968): 5-14.
Brief form of entry 469.

471 Schwartz, Theodore. "Cult and context: The paranoid ethos in Melanesia." *Ethos* 1, no. 2 (Summer 1973): 153-74.
Shortened version of entry 469; cargo cults as a form of "psychocultural adjustment."

472 Schwarz, Brian. "African movements and Melanesian movements." In *Point*. Series 4, *Religious movements in Melanesia today (3)*, edited by W. Flannery. Goroka: Melanesian Institute, 1984, pp. 14-28.

473 Schwarz, Brian. "Seeking to understand cargo as a symbol." *Catalyst*, no. 10 [no. 1 of 1980], pp. 14-27.
An important interpretation, by a Lutheran missionary.

474 Seligman, Charles G. "Temperament, conflict, and psychosis in a stone-age population." *British Journal of Medical Psychology* 9, no. 3 (1929): 187-202.
Impulsiveness and suggestibility as common features; pp. 200-202, new cults and prophets.

475 Sharp, Nonie. *Millenarian movements: Their meaning in Melanesia.* LaTrobe University, Department of Sociology Papers, 26. Bundoora, Victoria: LaTrobe University, 1976, 50 pp.

476 Shevill, Ian. "'Cargo cults' in the Pacific." *World Dominion* 31, no. 1 (1953): 27-29.
A brief survey, with more detail on the Assisi cult in Anglican mission areas.

477 Siikala, Jukka. "The cargo proper in cargo cults." *Temenos* 15 (1979): 68-80.
Theoretical discussion of money and the economic aspects, with special reference to Philo's movement in 1941.

478 Smith, Robin (photos), and Willey, Keith (text). *New Guinea: A journey through 10,000 years.* Melbourne: Lansdowne Press, 1969, 168 pp., illus.
Pp. 84-88, cults, illustrated by Paliau, Baining "cargo egg" prophet, Johnson cult, and Hahalis Welfare Society, but nothing on religious dimensions.

General

479 Souter, Gavin. *New Guinea: The last unknown*. Sydney: Angus & Robertson, 1963, 296 pp., illus., maps. Reprint. New York: Taplinger Publishing Co., 1966.

P. 151, Vailala Madness and an aeroplane; pp. 238-42, various cults.

480 Stanner, W[illiam] E[dward] H[anley]. *The South Seas in transition: A study of post-war rehabilitation and reconstruction in three British Pacific dependencies*. Sydney, Wellington, and London: Australasian Publishing Co., 1953, 448 pp.

Chap. 5 (pp. 57-73), native social changes, including Vailala Madness and prophetess Philo.

481 Stanner, W[illiam] E[dward] H[anley]. "The 'Vailala Madness' or 'Cargo cult.'" In *Reconstruction in the South Pacific Islands: A preliminary report. Part I: Papua-New Guinea*. New York: International Secretariat, Institute of Pacific Relations, 1947, pp. 31-34. Mimeo.

Includes analyses of cargo cults and other modern movements.

482 Stayte, Terry. "'Work for good life' Cargo cultists are told." *Straits Times* (Singapore), 25 August 1976.

By a reporter in Port Moresby. General survey, with special reference to Albert Kiki Maori's youthful experience of cults and to the Kopani movement on Bougainville.

483 Steinbauer, Friedrich. "Cargo cults: Challenge to the churches?" *Lutheran World* 21, no. 2 (1974): 160-72. German version as "Die Cargo-Kulte in der gegenwärtigen kirchlichen Situation in Papua-Neuguinea," *Lutherische Rundschau* 24, no. 2 (1974): 179-94. Slightly altered and extended version as "Der Traum von Glück," in *Theologische Beiträge aus Papua Neuguinea*, edited by H. Bürkle. Erlangen Taschenbücher 43. Erlangen: Verlag Ev.-Luth. Mission, 1978, pp. 123-35.

A summary of his 1971 book (entry 485, together with a fuller account of the Yeliwan cult (1971-) and a summary of 12 others not included in the book.

484 Steinbauer, Friedrich. "Die Cargo-Kulte als religionsgeschichtliches und missionstheologisches Problem." Vol. 1, "Gesamt Darstellung der Melanesischen Heilserwartungsbewegungen 1957-1970. Vol. 2, "Erklarung und missionstheologische Uberlegungen zu den Melanesischen Heilserwartungbewegungen." Th.D. dissertation (theology), University of Erlangen-Nurnberg, 1970, 495 pp. (bib., pp.

467-95) + 200 pp. (bib., pp. 172-99) + folding table analyzing movements.
Many bibliographic items not directly on the subject.

485 Steinbauer, Friedrich. *Melanesische Cargo-Kulte: Neureligiöse Heilsbewegungen in der Südsee*. Munich: Delp'sche, 1971, 208 pp., 46 plates, folding map and chart. English translation. *Melanesian Cargo cults: New salvation movements in the South Pacific*. St. Lucia: University of Queensland Press; London: George Prior Publishers, 1979), 215 pp., illus., map, tables, glossary.
   German edition abridged from his doctoral dissertation – omits glossary and footnotes and selects from bibliography; English edition (a poor translation) abbreviates vol. 2 (analysis and theological material) but restores the glossary and enlarges and adapts the bibliography for English speakers, adds literary source notes and an index.

486 Steinbauer, Friedrich. "Der religiöse Bezug in Cargo-Kult-Complex." *Evangelische Missionszeitschrift*, n.s. 26, no. 4 (1969): 211-29.

487 Steinbauer, Friedrich, and Knoebel, Joseph. "Selected bibliography." *Point* (Goroka), no. 1 (1974), pp. 196-214.
   On "Cargo cults" or "adjustment movements."

488 Sterly, Joachim. "Helige Männer und Medizinmänner in Melanesian ... Aufweisung des Zauberpriestertums in Süwestlichen Pazifik." Doctoral dissertation, University of Cologne, 1965.
   Pp. 424ff., cargo cults.

489 Strelan, John G[erhard]. "A bibliography for the study of the history and morphology of cargo cults and related movements in Melanesia." Martin Luther Seminary, Lae, New Guinea, 1975, 25 pp. Mimeo.

490 Strelan, John G[erhard]. "Our common ancestor." *Catalyst* (Goroka) 5, no. 2 (2d quarter 1975): 33-40.

491 Strelan, John G[erhard]. Review of *Völkschristentum und Völksreligion im Pazifik. . . .*, by T. Ahrens and W. J. Hollenweger (entry 860). *Catalyst* 8, no. 4 (1978): 289-94.

492 Strelan, John G[erhard]. *Search for salvation: Studies in the history and theology of cargo cults*. Foreword by H. W. Turner. Adelaide: Lutheran Publishing House, 1977, 131 pp., maps. Chap. 5, "The response of the

General

church to cargo cults," translated into German as "Die Antwort der Kirche auf die Cargo-Kulte," in *Theologische Beiträge aus Papua Neuguinea*, edited by H. Bürkle. Erlangen Taschenbücher 43. Erlangen: Verlag Ev.-Luth. Mission, 1978, pp. 99-122.

A most useful and sympathetic survey and theological interpretation, by a Lutheran missionary scholar.

493 "A Survey of the Year 1948: The South Pacific." *International Review of Missions*, no. 149 [38], (January 1949), pp. 57-60.

P. 59, "Messianic cults" as "disquieting symptoms" of new hopes engendered by the war.

494 Swinger, J. W. "A review of material presented at the University of Papua New Guinea, Department of Extension Studies Seminar on Churches and Missions, on 4 January 1979: Religious cults and revivalist movements." Pp. 5-6.

495 "Theologische Stimmen: Christlicher Synkretismus. . . ." *Zeitschrift für Mission* 1, no. 3 (1975): 180-85.

Based on T. Ahrens in *Catalyst* 4, no. 1 (1974).

496 Thomas, Gordon. "A plea for better regulation of mission activities in New Guinea." *Pacific Islands Monthly* 6, no. 4 (1935): 25-26.

Asserts a connection between native denominational enthusiasm and recent cults at Aitape and Buka.

497 Tippett, Alan Richard. *Solomon Islands Christianity: A study in growth and obstruction*. London: Lutterworth; New York: Friendship Press, 1967, 407 pp., maps. Reprint. South Pasadena, Calif.: William Carey Library, [1974].

See Index for: S. Eto and Etoism (Christian Fellowship Church) especially chaps. 15-17; Marching Rule (and John Frum); Messianism; Millenarianism; Nativistic Movements (Buka cults, Chair and Rule Movement, Freedom Movement, Lontis cult) especially chap. 14 with comparative analysis of nativistic movements; Pokokogoro cult; Christo-paganism.

498 Tokolila, William. "The cargo cult." *Kingdom Overseas* (London, Methodist Missionary Society), November 1969, pp. 16-17, photo.

499 Trompf, G[arry] W[inston]. "A brief introduction to the so-called cargo cults." In *Religion in Melanesia*. University of Papua New Guinea teaching materials, Part B, 1980, pp. 17-21.

500 Trompf, G[arry] W[inston]. "The effects of religious change on society." Humanities Foundation Course, University of Papua New Guinea, 1976, pp. 3-6.

501 Trompf, G[arry] W[inston]. "Independent churches in Melanesia." *Oceania* 54, no. 1 (1983): 51-72, illus. Originally presented as a paper at the Melanesian Institute Seminar, Goroka, November 1980, 18 pp. Mimeo.

Surveys twelve movements, the first three in more detail – Christian Fellowship Church, Hehela "Church," Kwato Church, Paliau, Remnant "Church," Congregation of the Poor, Nagriamel, Peli Association, Yali, Moro, Sulphur Bay and Lenakel movements. An important account of forms overshadowed by cargo cults.

502 Trompf, G[arry] W[inston]. "Melanesian 'cargo cults' today." *Current Affairs Bulletin* 58, no. 1 (1981): 19-22.

The Nagriamel revolt and its religious aspects in relation to similar movements with political features.

503 Trompf, G[arry] W[inston]. Review of *Search for salvation: Studies in the history and theology of cargo cults*, by John G. Strelan (entry 492). *Catalyst* (Goroka) 7, no. 4 (1977): 308-10.

Supports Strelan's interpretation and his exposition of "Christ the ancestor" as point of contact with cults; suggests movements that might have been included.

504 Trompf, G[arry] W[inston]. "What has happened to Melanesian 'cargo cults'?" In *Point*. Series 4, *Religious movements in Melanesia today (3)*, edited by W. Flannery. Goroka: Melanesian Institute, 1984, pp. 21-59.

505 Trompf, G[arry] W[inston], and J. G. Strelan. *A story of Christianity in Papua New Guinea*, edited by Joan Walker. Goroka: Liturgical Catechetical Institute, 1979, 101 pp., illus., + 11 pp. summary.

Prepared for Religious Education in Grade 10 in Catholic high schools. Pp. 90-94, cargo cults, with case study of a Papuan movement in 1940 vividly told.

506 Tudor, Judy, ed. *Pacific Islands Yearbook*. 11th ed. Sydney: Pacific Publications, 1972, 542 pp.

P. 459, Jon Frum and Nagriamel; p. 435, Masinga, Moro, and Eto – outline histories. Similar references in earlier editions (e.g., 10th ed., 1968).

General

507 Turner, Harold Walter. "Cargo cult." In *Encyclopaedia Britannica*, 1974. Micropaedia, vol. 2, pp. 564b-c.

508 Turner, Harold Walter. "Old and new religions in Melanesia." *Point* (Goroka), no. 2 (1978) [issued 1979], pp. 5-29.
    The closing address at the Lae seminar of the Melanesian Institute on "adjustment cults," 1976. Pp. 5-13, varieties of movement and their future development; pp. 5-29, practical relationships with new movements.

509 United States Government. Department of the Army. *Area handbook for Oceania*. Prepared by American University, Foreign Area Studies Division. (PAM 550-94.)Washington, D.C.: U.S. Government Printing Office, 1971, 555 pp.
    Pp. 164-66, "cargo cults and other post-Christian developments."

510 Uplegger, Helga, and Mühlmann, W. E. "Die Cargo-Kulte in Neuguinea und Insel-Melanesien." In *Chiliasmus und Nativismus*, edited by W. E. Mühlmann, et al. Berlin: D. Reimer, 1961, pp. 165-90, maps. French translation. "Les cultes du Cargo en Nouvelle-Guinée et dans les îles de la Mélanésie," in Messianismes révolutionnaires du tiers monde, by W. E. Mühlmann. Paris: Éditions Gallimard, 1968, pp. 119-46.
    In German edition, pp. 167-71, Tuka; pp. 171-80, Mambu; pp. 180-85, Paliau.

511 Valckx, Wim. "Roep om mensenoffers." *Bijeen* (Hertogenbosch), October 1971, pp. 20, 45.

512 Valentine, C[harles] A. "Social and cultural change." In *Encyclopaedia of Papua and New Guinea*. 3 vols. Carlton, Victoria: Melbourne University Press, with the University of Papua New Guinea, 1972, pp. 1048-50, illus., maps. Extensively revised as "Changing indigenous societies and cultures," in *Anthropology in Papua New Guinea*, edited by I. Hogbin. Melbourne University Press, 1973, pp. 227-34.
    In revised version, pp. 228-34, innovative and cargo movements, and theories about them.

513 Wagner, J[ohann] F[riedrich]. "The outgrowth and development of the cargo cult." Paper presented at 18th Field Conference, Lutheran Mission New Guinea, Wau, 1964. Ulap: Luther Mission New Guinea, 1964, 203 pp., bib. Mimeo.

Pp. 7-14, Upikno movement since 1933; pp. 15-25, Yali since World War II; pp. 26-45, pseudopentecostal movement since 1958; then discusses explanations of movements, pp. 192-97, and lists some seventy examples of cargo ideas between 1952 and 1962, as reported, with sources. A valuable primary source.

514 Waiko, John D[ouglas]. "European-Melanesian contact in Melanesian tradition and literature." In *Priorities in Melanesian development. ... 6th Waigoni Seminar ... 1972*, edited by R. J. May. Port Moresby: University of Papua New Guinea; Canberra: Australian National University, 1973, pp. 427-28.

515 Waiko, John Douglas. "A religious response of the stateless society to colonial rule: A comparison of some East African and Melanesian examples." M.A. thesis (African history), S.O.A.S. University of London, 1973, 40 pp.
    Pp. 23-32, Baigona and Taro movements (the latter among the author's own people); pp. 33-35, conclusions, questioning explanations entirely as interaction movements and asking for research on indigenous explanations.

516 Walter, Michael A. H. B. "Cult movements and community associations: Revolution and evolution in the PNG countryside." IASER Discussion Paper 36. Boroko: Institute of Applied Social and Economic Research, 1981, 30 pp. Mimeo.
    Follows up R. Gerritsen's suggestion on relations between cargo cults and community groups, and hence on the dynamic of rural society today.

517 Warren, Max A. C. "The 'Messianic' movements of New Guinea." In *Revival – an enquiry*. London: S.C.M. Press, 1954, pp. 33-37.

518 Watson, Avra Peter Ginieres. "Melanesian cargo movements: A developmental analysis." Ph.D. dissertation (anthropology), University of Pittsburgh, 1976, 253 pp.
    Comparative analysis of more than sixty movements over the last century, with intensive study of the Admiralty Islands.

519 Watters, R[ay] F. "Cargo cults and social change in Melanesia." *Pacific Viewpoint* (Department of Geography, Victoria University, Wellington, N.Z.) 1, no. 1 (1960): 104-7.

General

520 Weymouth, Ross. "The Bible and revival movements." In *Point*. Series 4, *Religious movements in Melanesia today (3)*, edited by W. Flannery. Goroka: Melanesian Institute, 1984, pp. 195-208.

521 White, Osmar. *Parliament of a thousand tribes: A study of New Guinea.* London: William Heinemann, 1965, 256 pp., illus. Rev. ed., with subtitle *Papua New Guinea. The story of an emerging nation.* Melbourne: Wren, 1972, 273 pp., illus.
　　See index and especially pp. 113-20, Vailala; pp. 131-35, Mansren myth and causes; pp. 147-51, Rai coast; pp. 149-51, Yali; pp. 151-55, Paliau; p. 190, Johnson cult.

522 Whiteman, Darrell L[averne]. "The Christian mission and culture change in New Guinea. " *Missiology* 2, no. 2 (1974): 17-33, bib.
　　Pp. 19-20, uses J. K. McCarthy (entry 413) on Lagit; pp. 23-23, misunderstandings involved in cargo ideas; whole article relevant to development of cargo cults.

523 Whiteman, Darrell L[averne]. "The cultural dynamics of religious movements." In *Point*. Series 4, *Religious movements in Melanesia today (3)*, edited by W. Flannery. Goroka: Melanesian Institute, 1984, pp. 52-79.

524 Whiteman, Darrell L[averne]. *Melanesians and missionaries: An ethnological study of social and religious change in the Southwest Pacific.* Pasadena, Calif.: William Carey Library, 1983, 559 pp.

525 Willey, Keith. *Assignment in New Guinea.* Brisbane: Jacaranda Press, 1965. Reprint. Sydney: Angus & Robertson, 1966, 263 pp., illus., maps.
　　Pp. 25-26, cargo cults; pp. 48-56, Yali and cultists in the elections; pp. 62-64, 72-75, Johnson cult; pp. 95-97, Batari and recent cults; pp. 98-117, Hahalis Welfare Society. By an Australian journalist; popular and impressionistic.

526 Wilson, Bryan R[onald]. *Magic and the millennium: A sociological study of religious movements of protest among tribal and third-world peoples.* London: Heinemann Educational Books; New York: Harper & Row, 1973, 547 pp. Reprint. Frogmore, St. Albans: Granada Publishing, Paladin Books, 1975, 547 pp.
　　Pp. 73-75, Papua (Baigona, Kava Keva movements); pp. 199-206, Koreri and Mansren movements; pp. 216-18, New Guinea highlands; pp. 309-47, cargo cults (pp. 325-27, in the Mamberamo area); pp. 317-22, Vailala; pp. 322-26, Jonfrum; pp. 327-32, Madang; pp. 333-38, Yali;

pp. 468-74, Marching Rule; pp. 474-75, Malekula Cooperative; pp. 475-76, Tommy Kabu; pp. 476, 483, Paliau; all placed in the context of his theoretical system.

527 Worsley, Peter M[aurice]. "Cargo cults." *Scientific American* 200, no. 6 (1959): 117-22, 125-26, 128, maps.

528 Worsley, Peter M[aurice]. "Millenarian movements in Melanesia." *Rhodes-Livingstone Journal* 21 (1957): 18-31. Reprinted in *Gods and rituals*, edited by J. Middleton. Garden City, N.Y.: American Museum of Natural History, 1967, pp. 337-52. In Bobbs-Merrill Reprint Series in Social Sciences, no. A-248, Indianapolis: Bobbs-Merrill. French translation in *Anthropologie religieuse: Les Dieux et les Rites. Textes fondamentaux*. Paris: Larousse, 1974, pp. 167-80.

    Includes comparative reference to millennial movements in Africa.

529 Worsley, Peter [Maurice]. *The trumpet shall sound: A study of "cargo" cults in Melanesia.* London: MacGibbon & Kee, 1957, 290 pp. Pp. 153-59 reprinted in *From primitives to Zen*, edited by M. Eliade. New York: Harper & Row, 1967, pp. 413-17. 2d ed., enl., with supplementary bib. New York: Schocken Books, 1968, 300 pp. Italian translation. *La tromba suonerà.* Turin: Einaudi, 1961, 362 pp. German translation. *Die Posaune wird erschallen: Cargo-Kulte in Melanesien.* Frankfurt: Suhrkamp, 1973, 498 pp., map. French translation. *Elle sonnera la trompette: Le culte du cargo en Mélanésie.* Paris: Payot, 1977, 318 pp.

    The first comprehensive survey, by a sociologist, using colonialism and political factors rather than religious concerns as explanation of causes.

Bismarck Archipelago (within Papua New Guinea)

This geographical term includes much of the island world of the nation of Papua New Guinea, stretching from the Admiralty Islands in the north to New Britain in the south, but excluding Buka and Bougainville. The four political divisions included are Manus, West New Britain, East New Britain, and New Ireland, and the term Bismarck Archipelago is used as a convenient way of grouping these.

530 Adam, Keith. "Police move in on the New Hanover cargo cult." *Pacific Islands Monthly* 35, no. 8 (1964): 9-10.

Bismarck Archipelago

A very offhand journalistic account of dealing with refusal to pay taxes, under the influence of the Johnson cult.

531 Australia, Commonwealth of. "Cargo cults: Paliau movement." In *Territory of New Guinea Annual Report 1950-51.* Canberra: Commonwealth Government, 1951, 24-30, 33, 116ff.

General account of cargo cults and detailed account of Paliau movement, supplied at request of Trusteeship Council.

532 Australia, Commonwealth of. *Report to the Council of the League of Nations on the administration of the Territory of New Guinea . . . 1937 to . . . 1938.* Canberra: Commonwealth Government Printer, 1939, 148 pp.

P. 30, para. 64, cargo movement in Namatarai subdistrict of New Ireland.

533 Bailoenakia, Philip, and Koimanrea, Francis. "The Pomio Kivung movement." In *Point.* Series 2. *Religious movements in Melanesia today (1),* edited by W. Flannery. Goroka: Melanesian Institute, 1983, pp. 171-89.

534 Baluan Christian Church. *Sing Sing: Baluan United Kristian Chech, founded 1946, Paliau Maloat prepared by Madang branch.* Madang: Baluan Christian Church, n.d.

A booklet.

535 Beerman, Laurenz. "Ist Paliau noch der Herr?" *Hiltruper Monatsheft* 63 (1955): 78-79, 102-3.

536 Beyerhaus, Peter. *In der Inselwelt südostasiens erlebt: Zweiter Teil der Reiseberichts.* Weltweite Reihe 27-28. Stuttgart: Evangelische Missionsverlag, 1973, 160 pp.

Chap. 4: Die Liebenzeller Mission und die Paliaubewegung auf Manus.

537 Billings, Dorothy K. "The Johnson cult of New Hanover." *Oceania* 40, no. 1 (1969): 13-19.

"Johnson" refers to President Lyndon B. Johnson of the United States.

538 Biskup, Peter, ed. *The New Guinea memoirs of Jean Baptiste Octave Mouton.* Pacific History Series, 7. Canberra: Australian National University, 1974, 161 pp.

Bismarck Archipelago

A Belgian planter among the Tolai at Vunamanri, southeast of Rabaul. Pp. 112-15, bullet-proof ointment from a "wizard" (*Tavalai*); cf. Salisbury (entry 593) p. 80.

539 Brenninkmeyer, Leo. *15 Jahre beim Bergvolke der Baininger. Tagebuchblätter.* Hiltrup: Herz-Jesu-Missionshaus, 1928, 96 pp., illus.
Pp. 47-49, Bainings' beliefs concerning a Golden Age to come about 1930.

540 Brown, Rodger S. "Tribute to a New Guinea pastor." *Mission Review* (Sydney, Uniting Church in Australia), no. 6, January 1979, p. 14.
On Rev. Mikael To Bilak (1910-78), who worked as a Methodist minister among the Baining, 1933-48, and again in the 1950s, and dealt with Baining cargo cults.

541 Budruan, Siwa. "Kago kal i pinis olgeta." *New Voices* (Rabaul, Christian Writers' Association in Melanesia) 2 (1972): 5-6, illus.
In Pidgin.

542 Cadogan, William. "Kilenge prophets." *Annals of Our Lady of the Sacred Heart* (Cork) 66, nos. 10, 11, 12 (October, November, December 1949). Reprinted in *Annals of Our Lady of the Sacred Heart* (Geneva, Ill.) 5, nos. 5 and 6 (May and June 1949): 4-5, 24-27, and 4-5.
A first hand account of a "classic" cargo movement under Nakovai in the Kilenge Catholic mission area in far west of New Britain in 1942; second movement under Varan in 1945.

543 Chowning, Ann, and Goodale, J. C. "The Passismanua Census Division." In *The Papua-New Guinea elections, 1964*, edited by D. G. Bettison, C. A. Hughes, and P. van der Veur. Canberra: Australian National University, 1965, pp. 266-79.
P. 267, cargo beliefs; pp. 267-69, 272, Koriam movement existing for a generation and determining his winning the election; sundry cargo ideas.

544 Counts, David R., and Dorothy E. A[yers]. "Apprehension in the backwaters." *Oceania* 46, no. 4 (1976): 283-305.
On the opposition among the Kaliai of west New Britain between the "Law of the Story" (traditionalists) and the "Rule of Money" (progressives). Pp. 285-86, 291-303, the Story cargo movement; pp. 303-5, common features among cultists and noncultists.

Bismarck Archipelago

545 Counts, Dorothy E. [Ayers]. "Cargo or Council: Two approaches to development in north-west New Britain." *Oceania* 41, no. 4 (1971): 288-97, maps.
The Kaliai, and Aitele's movement, 1964.

546 Counts, Dorothy E. [Ayers]. "Christianity in Kaliai: Response to missionization in North west New Britain." In *Mission, church, and sect in Oceania*, edited by J. A. Boutilier, et al. Association for Social Anthropology in Oceania, Monograph Series no. 6. Ann Arbor: University of Michigan Press, 1978, pp. 355-94.
Pp. 378-94, the Story movement.

547 Counts, Dorothy E. [Ayers]. "The Kaliai and the Story: Development and frustration in New Britain." *Human Organization* 31, no. 4 (1972): 373-83.
Relations between cultists and progressives; frustrations as cause of the cult.

548 Counts, Dorothy E. A[yers], and Counts, David R. "Independence and the rule of money in Kaliau." *Oceania* 48, no. 1 (1977): 30-39.

549 Dahmen, J. "Schwärmgeisterei auf Neubritannien und Manus in den letzten Jahren." In *Christen und Antichristen*, edited by Kilger. Tagung zu Munster, 25-29 Mai 1953. Hiltruper: N.d., pp. 36-57.

550 Epstein, [T.] Scarlett. "The Mataungan affair: The first radical mass political movement." *New Guinea and Australia, the Pacific and South-East Asia* (Sydney) 4, no. 4 (1969-70): 8-14.
The secular alternative to cargoism among the Tolai in east New Britain.

551 Errington, Frederick [Karl]. "Indigenous ideas of order, time, and transition in a New Guinea cargo movement." *American Ethnologist* 1, no. 2 (1974): 255-67.
The Kaun, or Dog, movement on Duke of York Islands from late 1930s, but in decline in late 1960s, with some comment on P. Lawrence's ideas.

552 Flannery, Wendy. "Unea (Bali) Island cargo movement." In *Religious movements in Melanesia: A selection of case studies and reports,* edited by W. Flannery. Goroka: Melanesian Institute, 1983, pp. 17-26. Mimeo.

553 Goodenough, Ward Hunt. "Some observations on the Nakanai." In *Papua and New Guinea Scientific Society Annual Report and Proceedings, 1954*. Port Moresby: The Society, 1956, pp. 40-45.

Pp. 40, 45, Batari movement defunct by 1951; pp. 43-45, similar successor movement seeking "the road to salvation."

554 Gorohauve. "Enigmatic man from Manus." *Pacific Islands Monthly* 36, no. 12 (1965): 65, 67.

555 Guariglia, Guglielmo. *Prophetismus und Heilserwartungs-bewegungen als völkerkundliches und religionsgeschichtliches Problem*. Vienna: F. Berger, 1959, xvi + 332 pp., maps.

Pp. 107-10.

556 Hannet, Leo. "Disillusionment with the priesthood." In *Black writing from New Guinea*, edited by U. Beier. Asian and Pacific Writing, 3. St. Lucia: University of Queensland Press, 1973, pp. 39-51.

Pp. 45-46, his problem with and interpretation of the Hahalis Welfare Society.

557 "Hanover awaits Christ." *Post Courier* (Port Moresby) 17 August 1983.

558 Hogg, Donald M. (text), and Anderson, J. L. (photos). *New Guinea*. Sydney: A. H. & A. W. Reed, 1969, 216 pp., illus.

Pp. 42-45, Johnson cult, and more briefly on Baining movement in 1964; by a sympathetic New Zealand journalist.

559 Inder, Stuart. "Quick action wanted on New Hanover cargo cult." *Pacific Islands Monthly* 35, no. 7 (1964): 12-13.

560 Isaiah, R. N. "Constable Lapaniuva and the Johnson cult." *Oral History* 4, no. 3 (1976): 18-26.

Interview with a policeman; especially pp. 21-26 on the Johnson cult troubles from a law-and-order viewpoint, with suggestion that a cult contributed to development.

561 Janssen, Hermann. "Creative deities and the role of religion in New Britain: An evaluation of Carl Laufer's anthropological concern." In *Carl Laufer MSC: Missionar und Ethnologe auf Neu-Guinea*, edited by H. Janssen, et al. Basel, Freiburg, and Vienna: Herder, 1975, pp. 19-39.

Pp. 31-32, cargoism; pp. 34-36, syncretistic communities.

Bismarck Archipelago

562 Janssen, Hermann. "Götter geben kein Geld: Cargo-kult auf Neubritannien." *Hiltruper Monatshefte* (Munster) 77, no. 5 [1969]: 104-6, illus.

563 Janssen, Hermann. "Güterkult in Kaliai." *Hiltruper Monatshefte* (Munster) 77 (1969): 195-98, illus.

564 Janssen, Hermann. "Der Mythos der Kaliai: Phänomenologie einer Cargo-Kultbewegung in Papua Neuguinea." *Ordensnachrichten* (Vienna) 20, no. 5 (1981): 334-38.

565 Janssen, Hermann. "The story cult of Kaliai in New Britain." Melanesian Institute Orientation Course, Alexishafen, 1974, 14 pp. Mimeo.
     See also entry 566.

566 Janssen, Hermann. "The story of Kaliai. A cargo cult in West New Britain." *Point* (Goroka), no. 1 (1974), pp. 4-28.

567 Jhabvala, D. S. "The cargo cultists' bid for Johnson." *Herald Tribune* (New York), 13 June 1965.

568 Kohnke, Glenys. *Time belong Tumbuna: Legends and traditions of Papua New Guinea.* Port Moresby: Robert Brown & Associates; Milton, Queensland: Jacaranda Press, 1973, 111 pp., color paintings by the author.
     Pp. 14-15, text and painting, "The Egg Prophet" (i.e., Melki of the Baining from ca. 1955).

569 Landi, J. C. "A discussion of the importance of traditional religious beliefs for the emergence of cargo cult activity among the Bainings." Undergraduate seminar paper, University of Papua New Guinea, 1975. Cited and used by G. W. Trompf (entry 239) p. 103.

570 Laufer, Carl. "Psychologische Grundlagen religiöser Schwärmgeistbewegungen in der Südsee." *Kairos: Zeitschrift für Religionwissenschaft und Theologie* 1, no. 3 (1959): 149-61.

571 Longgar, W. "The Johnson cult of New Hanover." In *Melanesia and Judaeo-Christian religious traditions*, edited by G. W. Trompf. Port Moresby: University of Papua New Guinea Extension Studies, 1975, Book 4, op. 3, pp. 25ff.

Bismarck Archipelago

572 Maloat, Paliau. "Histori bilong mi taim mi bon na I kamap tede." In *The politics of Melanesia. ... 4th Waigoni Seminar ... 1970*, edited by M. W. Ward. Port Moresby: University of Papua and New Guinea, 1970, pp. 144-61. English and Pidgin versions on facing pages.

The distinguished founder, Paliau Maloat, O.B.E., M.P., of the Paliau movement and church, gives his own story of his life.

573 Maloat, Paliau. *Manus Kastam Kansol: Stori*. N.p.: [after 1980], 14 pp., illus., diagrams. English translation by J. D. May. *Point*. Series 8, *Living theology in Melanesia: A reader*, edited by J. D. May. Goroka: Melanesian Institute, 1986, pp. 31-43.

On what is now known as Makasol, its history, and the theology of "Wing, Wang, Wong."

574 Maurer, Henry [Sudsee, pseud.]. "Make ready! A story of that strange cargo madness." *Annals of Our Lady of the Sacred Heart* (Kensington, Australia) 63, no. 5 (1952): 119-210.

A Catholic missionary neutralizing a new cult on the Island of Tanga, off New Ireland.

575 Mead, Margaret. *Continuities in cultural evolution*. Terry Lectures Series. New Haven, Conn: Yale University Press, 1964, 471 pp., illus. Reprint. 1965.

Chap. 9 (pp. 192-234), the Paliau movement; photo of Paliau.

576 Mead, Margaret. *New lives for old: Cultural transformation, Manus, 1928-1953*. New York: William Morrow; London: Gollancz, 1956, 548 pp.

Much on Paliau and the religious aspects of his movement, "the Noise" of 1947, and the transition to Christianity. See especially pp. 192-97, 208-11, 120-241, 322-42.

577 Miller, B. "Cargo cult movements–The birth of a cult." Melanesian Institute Orientation Course, Vunapope, 1969-70, 5 pp. Mimeo.

The Johnson cult and the society that sought to replace it–Tutukuval Isukal (United Farmers) Association.

578 [Report.] *Monatshefte zur Ehren unserer Lieben Frau vom Heiligsten Herzen Jesu* (Hiltrup and Munster), 1894, pp. 137, 166.

Reports in the journal of the Sacred Heart Mission of the attack by Tolai in New Britain in 1983, supported by a magician's bullet-proof magic ointment.

Bismarck Archipelago

579 Moses, Robinson. "A theological assessment of revival movements." In *Point*. Series 4, *Religious movements in Melanesia today (3)*, edited by W. Flannery. Goroka: Melanesian Institute, 1984, pp. 186-94.

580 Murphy, Leslie. "No swift end to New Guinea's odd Johnson cult." *Pacific Islands Monthly* 37, no. 9 (1966): 45-47.

581 Namunu, Simeon. "The charismatic renewal in the United Church on Gazelle Peninsula." Paper presented at Melanesian Institute Seminar on New and Ongoing Religious Movements in Melanesia, Goroka, November 1980, 11 pp. Mimeo.
    Promoted by John Pastorkamp, a Dutch missionary with "Youth with a Mission" on Thursday Island, and later partly accepted as an evangelistic influence by and within the United Church. On microfiche, the Centre, Selly Oak Colleges.

582 *New York Times*. Various reports on the Lyndon B. Johnson cult on New Hanover:
    "Cult that tried to 'buy' Johnson and tax revolt in New Guinea," 28 June 1964, p. 7. "64 Johnson cultists arrested by Australians," 9 August 1964, p. 46. "Johnson cultists jeer American in U.N. group," 4 April 1965, p. 5.

583 Niskaram, Norlie. "Cargo cultism on New Hanover: A psychopathological phenomenon or an indication of unequal development?" In *New Religious movements in Melanesia*, edited by C. Loeliger and G. Trompf. Suva: Institute of Pacific Studies, University of the South Pacific; University of Papua New Guinea, 1985, pp. 75-89.
    Also known as the Johnson movement, from the 1960s; interpreted as representing a desire for real development, as against government neglect.

584 *Pacific Islands Monthly*. Items on cargo cults, 1935-77:
    "Scientists consider future of native races in Pacific," 5, no. 7 (1935): 62-63. See entry 1269.
    "'Fanaticism' reported," 7, no. 1 (1936): 68.
    "Another native messiah goes to gaol," 22, no. 5 (1951): 1-104 [Paliau, on Manus.]
    "Baining natives killed in New Britain patrol," 25, no. 12 (1955): 67.
    "Evidence on cargo cult outbreak in Bainings area," 26, no. 1 (1955): 163.
    "Manslaughter charge now dropped," 26, no. 2 (1955).

[Johnson cult], 35, no. 10 (1964): 9.
[Johnson cult], 36, no. 12 (1965): 11.
"Johnson NG president still," 37, no. 1 (1966): 14.
"Johnson cultist loses faith," 37, no. 2 (1966): 29.
"Cargo cultism on rise," 48, no. 2 (1977): 29-30. [Mentions Baining and Pomio areas.]

585 Panoff, Michel. "Les caves du Vatican: Aspects d'un cargo-cult mélanésien." *Les Temps Modernes*, no. 276 [24] (June 1969): 2222-44.
Cargo beliefs among the Maenge of east New Britain.

586 Peniel, Kakesek. "The cargo cult." *Tatuma* (Goroka Teachers' College), [pp. 50-51].
A student article relating his earlier experiences of the Johnson cult in New Hanover.

587 Pokawin, Polonhou. "Wing, Wang, Wong–developments in the Paliau movement." Paper presented at Melanesian Institute Seminar on New and Ongoing Religious Movements in Melanesia, Goroka, November 1980, 10 pp. Mimeo. Published in *Point*. Series 2, *Religious movements in Melanesia today (1)*, edited by W. Flannery. Goroka: Melanesian Institute, 1983, pp. 104-14.
History and theology of the Paliau movement; recent revivals of the church dimension by Paliau Lukas and Peter Kuwoh, and their political potentiality; by a lecturer in politics, son of a pastor on Manus.

588 Pongi, T. "Nabo of Bulutangalon." *Oral History* 4, no. 3 (1976): 41-47.
By an undergraduate at University of P.N.G. On a Nabo (b. 1914, near Manus) who met Paliau Maloat during police training in Rabaul, became a zealous modernizer who prepared the way for Paliau's movement from ca. 1947.

589 Porai, B. R. "Paliau Maloat." *Oral History* (Boroko) 1, no. 7 (1973): 41-45.
By a man from Manus, with first hand information.

590 Ramstad, Yngvar. *The TKA movement in New Ireland*. Canberra: Research School of Pacific Studies, Department of Anthropology and Sociology, [1970?], 20 pp.
TKA (the "communal planting association") from 1969, under Arao as cult leader.

Bismarck Archipelago

591 [Report.] *Nachrichten aus Kaiser Wilhelmsland und dem Bismarck Archipel.* [Deutsche Neu-Guinea Compagnie], 1893, p. 67; 1894, p. 18.
Reports on the bullet-proof ointment of the magician among the Tolai in 1893 in New Britain.

592 Rowley, Charles D[unford]. *The New Guinea villager: The impact of colonial rule on primitive society and economy.* London: Pall Mall; New York: F. A. Praeger, 1966, 225 pp. Reprint. Melbourne: F. W. Cheshire, 1968.
Pp. 157-58, Paliau; pp. 160-88, cargo cults.

593 Salisbury, Richard F. *Vunamami: Economic transformation in a traditional society.* Berkeley and Los Angeles: University of California Press, 1970, 398 pp., maps.
Pp. 79-80, magician with bullet-proof vest among the Tolai in 1893.

594 Samol, Melchior. "The Paliau movement–Manus Island." In *Socio-Economic change Papua New Guinea*, edited by R. Adams. Lae: University of Technology, 1977, pp. 140-58.

595 Sapias, Austin. "Pomio cultists were ready for their ship to come in . . . but the cargo just did not arrive." *Papua New Guinea Post-Courier* (Port Moresby), 10 June 1971, p. 5.

596 Scharmach, Leo. In *Manuale Missionariorum*. Kokopo: [Catholic Mission, Vunapope, New Britain], 1953, 65 pp.
P. 7, "cargo dreams" and Batari; pp. 58-65, "cargo madness," including Batari and "Manus, etc., Kings." By a Catholic bishop, Vicar-Apostolic, of Rabaul.

597 Scharmach, Leo. *This crowd beats us all.* Surrey Hills: Catholic Press Newspaper Co., 1960, 295 pp., illus., map.
Pp. 127-30, 235-39. Batari's movement among the Nakanai.

598 Schutte, Andries Gerhardus. "Die nativistischen Bewegungen als Handlungsabläufe. Eine Untersuchung nach den Ablaufsregeln." Doctoral dissertation (philosophy), University of Heidelberg, 1969, 235 + 21 pp., bib.
A comparative sociological study of Mau Mau and Kimbangu/Ngunza movements, and the Paliau movement in the Admiralty Islands.

599 Schwartz, Theodore. "The co-operatives–'Ol i-bagarapim mani. . . .'"
New Guinea Quarterly 1, no. 8 (1967): 36-47.

600 Schwartz, Theodore. "The Noise. Cargo cult frenzy in the South Seas."
Psychology Today (New York) 4, no. 10 (1971): 54-54, 102-3, col. illus.
Comparisons with youth culture cults in Western society; pp. 54,
102-3, theoretical considerations.

601 Schwartz, Theodore. "The Paliau Movement in the Admiralty Islands,
1946 to 1954." Ph.D. dissertation, University of Pennsylvania, 1957.
Published under the same title in *Anthropological Papers of the
American Museum of Natural History* (New York) 49, no. 2 (1962):
211-421, illus., map.
A major anthropological study of Paliau and his modernizing
movement in 1945, his reinterpretation of the mainly Catholic
Christianity of the area, his secular programs, and the two forms of
cargo cult interrelated to the movement–the "Noise" of 1949, and the
"Ghost" or "Cemetery" cult of about 1953.

602 Schwartz, Theodore. "Relations among generations in time-limited
cultures." In *Socialization as cultural communication,* edited by T.
Schwartz. Berkeley, etc.: University of California Press, 1976, pp. 216-
30. Reprinted from special issue of *Ethos* 3, no. 2 (Summer 1975).
Pp. 223-25, Paliau movement summarized and evaluated; some
further more recent information.

603 Schwartz, Theodore. "Systems of a real integration: Some
considerations based on the Admiralty Islands of Northern Melanesia."
Anthropological Forum 1, no. 2 (1963): 56-59.
P. 93, a useful summary of the Paliau movement.

604 Schwartz, Theodore, and Romanucci-Ross, Lola. "Drinking and
inebriate behaviour in the Admiralty Islands, Melanesia." *Ethos* 2, no. 3
(Fall 1974): 213-31.
Pp. 215-16, a Catholic village which resisted the Paliau
movement; p. 218, Paliau as anti-alcoholic.

605 Seelen, P. "Mission: Rabaul: 'Cargo Talk,' De Mythe der
Scheepsladingen." *Annalen Missiehuis Tilburg* 64, no. 5 (1950): 10ff.
By a missionary priest.

606 Smales, Gus. "Cultists' ship in but not with cargo." *Pacific Islands
Monthly* 47, no. 7 (1976): 17-18.

Bismarck Archipelago

The Bali-Witu Island (in the Bismarck Sea) cult since the mid-1940s, and its recent refusal to pay taxes.

607 Steinbauer, Friedrich. "Eine reise durch Melanesien." *Wort und Sending: Beilage zum Rothenburger Sonntagsblatt*, nos. 5 and 6 (1967), pp. 3 + 2.

Report by Lutheran missionary on the Hahalis Welfare Society.

608 Suziki, M. "Higashi New Guinea no Paliau Undo." *Kaigai Jijo* 12, no. 10 (1964): 33-41.

On the Paliau movement.

609 Threlfall, Neville. *One hundred years in the islands: The Methodist/United Church in the New Guinea Islands region, 1875-1975.* Rabaul: Toksave na Buk Dipatmen, United Church New Guinea Islands Region, 1975, 288 pp., illus., maps.

Brief references to cargo cults, passim, especially the 1955 clash with the Baining cult of Alagasam when a Baining Methodist was martyred; p. 226, modern pentecostal experiences.

610 Tirpaia, C. "The *Kivung Lavurua* movement among sections of the Tolai community in East New Britain Province." In *Melanesian religion: Collected essays*, edited by G. W. Trompf. Suva: Institute of Pacific Studies, forthcoming.

611 Tovalele, P. "The Pomio cult – East New Britain." In *Socio-economic change Papua New Guinea*, edited by R. Adams. Lae: University of Technology, 1977, pp. 124-39.

612 Trompf, G[arry] W[inston]. "Keeping the *Lo* under a Melanesian messiah: An analysis of the Pomio *Kivung*, East New Britain." *Christianity in Oceania: Ethnographic perspectives on emerging religions in Pacific Island societies*. Association for Social Anthropology in Oceania Monograph. New York: Association for Social Anthropology, forthcoming.

613 Trompf, G[arry] W[inston]. "The life work of Paliau Maloat: An introduction." In *Religion in Melanesia (University of Papua New Guinea) Part B, 1980*, pp. 35-37, 48-49.

614 United Nations Trusteeship Council. "The Paliau movement in Manus." *United Nations Trusteeship Council – Official records*. 8th

session, 334th meeting, 2 March 1951, pp. 156b-157a, 158; 337th meeting, 7 March 1951, pp. 180b-182b, 184b-185a.

615 United Nations Visiting Mission to Trust Territories in the Pacific. *Report on New Guinea.* 15 August 1950; section on "Paliau movement in Manus" reprinted in *South Pacific* 4, no. 11 (1950): 207-8.

616 University of Papua New Guinea. Notes by Jack Chawanin, Manus, 1974, in University of Papua New Guinea, Department of Literature, Archives. Ref. FA/03 and FA/05.
    On ancestors manufacturing the "cargo," but only Europeans having ships to get it.

617 Valentine, Charles A[bernathy]. "Cargo cults and social stratification in New Guinea." In *Abstracts of Symposium Papers: Tenth Pacific Science Congress 1961.* Honolulu: Pacific Science Association, 1961, pp. 117-18.
    Cargo movements as response to the new caste-like social stratification, to deal with the problems of those outside the new system.

618 Valentine, Charles A[bernathy]. "Documents in Pacific Manuscripts Bureau." In *Miscellaneous Reports 1952-1959.* Pacific Manuscripts Bureau, no. 608. Canberra: The Bureau, 1973. Microfilm.
    Includes C. A. Valentine III, "Cargo beliefs and cargo cults among the West Nakanai of New Britain," 15 January 1955, 74 + 3 pp.

619 Valentine, Charles A[bernathy]. "An introduction to the history of changing ways of life on the island of New Britain." Ph.D. dissertation (anthropology), University of Pennsylvania, 1958, 836 pp.
    Among the Lakalai in New Britain; on the sequence of different types of movement.

620 Valentine, Charles A[bernathy]. "The Lalakai of New Britain." In *Gods, ghosts, and men in Melanesia,* edited by P. Lawrence and M. J. Meggitt. Melbourne, etc.: Oxford University Press, 1965, pp. 184-90.
    Especially pp. 188-90, the Sumua cult and later developments as a small-scale revitalization movement.

621 Valentine, Charles A[bernathy]. "Men of anger and men of shame. Lalakai ethnopsychology. . . ." *Ethnology* 2, no. 4 (1963): 441-47.
    P. 455, cargo cults influence social change, eliminating warfare, evil magic, shame, etc.

Bismarck Archipelago

622 Valentine, Charles A[bernathy]. "Uses of ethnohistory in acculturation." *Ethnohistory* 7, no. 1 (1960): 1-15.
Illustrated from the Lakalai; pp. 11-14, history of Christianity, including a nativistic movement.

623 Veur, Paul van der. "The first two meetings of the House of Assembly." In *The Papua-New Guinea elections, 1964,* edited by D. G. Bettison, C. A. Hughes, and P. van der Veur. Canberra: Australian National University, 1965, pp. 445-504.
P. 460, a debate on the Johnson cult in New Hanover, introduced by Nicholas Brokam.

624 Walter, Friedrich. "Der Cargo Kult auf den Admiralitätsinseln." *Mitteilungen der Liebenzeller Mission*, nos. 3-4 (1951), pp. 17-21; no. 7 (1951), pp. 3-5.
A Lutheran missionary on Manus, on the Paliau movement.

625 Walter, Friedrich. *Das Kreuz unter Palmen, ein Bericht über die Missionsarbeit auf den Admiralitätsinseln in den Jahren 1939-1959.* Bad Liebenzell: Liebenzeller Mission, 1959.
Includes the Paliau movement on Manus.

626 Walter, Friedrich. "Vom Missionsfeld auf den Admiralitätsinseln Besuch im Kargokult-Dorf Bunai." *Mitteilungen der Liebenzeller Mission*, nos. 3-4 (1954), pp. 3-10.
A Lutheran missionary on Manus, on the Paliau movement.

627 "What price LBJ?" *Newsweek*, 22 June 1964, pp. 47.
News report of Bos Malik and his move to get President L. B. Johnson to New Hanover.

628 Whitaker, J. L., et al. *Documents and readings in New Guinea history: Prehistory to 1889.* Milton, Queensland: Jacaranda Press, 1975, 552 pp.
Pp. 23-26, Paliau Maloat reflecting on his childhood, and first experiences of the outside world; a reprint of T. Schwartz (entry 601, pp. 239-41), with introduction.

629 White, S[tephen]. "Cargo cult – New Britain 1970." Melanesian Institute Orientation Course, Vunapope, 1969-70, 7 pp. Mimeo.

630 Wilson, Bryan R[onald]. *The noble savages: The primitive origins of charisma and its contemporary survival.* Berkeley: University of California Press, 1975, 131 pp.

Pp. 89-92, the Johnson cult as case study.

631 Wilson, Thomas. "Cargo cult and economic development in transitional Melanesia." M.A. thesis, McMaster University, 1970, 67 pp.
    With special reference to the Admiralty Islands.

Bougainville (within Papua New Guinea)

Together with the small island of Buka, Bougainville Island forms the separate political unit of Bougainville. Culturally it has more in common with the adjacent Solomon Islands than with Papua New Guinea. History, however, has left it within the latter nation, and we consider it here as a distinct region within Papua New Guinea, both politically and in terms of new movements. The Hahalis Welfare Society has achieved notoriety, but there have been many other movements going back at least to 1913.

632 Australia, Commonwealth of. *Reports to the Council of the League of Nations on the administration of the Territory of New Guinea*. Canberra: Commonwealth Government.
    For 1933-34 (1935), pp. 22-23, Sanop's movement, Gogohei village, east side of Buka.
    For 1935-36 (1937), pp. 21-23, movements of Pako and Muling at Lontis, Buka Island, and of Sanop and his arrest in 1935.

633 Burton-Bradley, B[urton] G. "Human sacrifice for cargo." *Medical Journal of Australia* (Glebe, N.S.W.), no. 2 (16 September 1972), pp. 668-70.
    Lagit on Buka Island who sought to become God and initiate arrival of cargo by killing his grandnephew.

634 Fahey, G. "Cargo cult movements in Bougainville." Melanesian Institute Orientation Course, Vunapope 1969-70, 6 pp. Mimeo.
    Mainly on Hahalis Welfare Society.

635 Hagai, Francis. "Explaining Hahalis: 'We are not in Buka.'" *New Guinea and Australia, the Pacific and South-East Asia* (Sydney) 1, no. 6 (1966): 12-14, photo.
    By the secretary of the Hahalis Welfare Society on Buka Island. Lengthy extracts in A. M. Kiki (entry 376), pp. 117-19.

636 Hannet, Leo. "The case for Bougainville secession." *Meanjin Quarterly* 34, no. 3 (1975): 286-93.

Bougainville

P. 288, Koratsi as member of Hahalis protonationalist movement.

637 Hannet, Leo. "Disillusionment with the priesthood." In *Black writing from New Guinea 1973*, edited by U. Beier. Asian and Pacific Writing, 3. St. Lucia: University of Queensland Press, 1973, pp. 39-51.
Pp. 45-46, criticism of Church and administration attitudes to Hahalis, whose founder Hannet knew well.

638 Inder, Stuart. "On the trail of the cargo cultists." *Pacific Islands Monthly* 31, no. 2 (1960): 57, 59, 61, 63, illus.
Offhand journalistic account of a cargo movement at Kieta, and short biography of Kearei, a seminary dropout, in the administration.

639 Inder, Stuart. "Prosperity, changing ways are killing off Buka's weird cargo cult." *Pacific Islands Monthly* 37, no. 4 (1966): 40-41, 43-45, 47, illus.
Comments from Fr. Paul Demers, Catholic missionary with alternative Haku Development Society, on Hahalis, outlining the history and reprinting a long extract on new religions in Indonesia for perspective.

640 Latu, Francis. "The history and development of the Hahalis Welfare Society." *New New Guinea Writing III* (Port Moresby, Bureau of Literature), 1969, pp. 1-4.

641 Luana, Caspar [pseud.]. "Buka! a retrospect." *New Guinea and Australia, the Pacific and South-East Asia* 4, no. 1 (1969): 15-20.
Imaginative account of origins of Hahalis, after John's visit to Rabaul to discover the secret of cargo.

642 Mamak, Alexander [F.]. "The setting and history of inequality." In *Race, class, and rebellion in the South Pacific*, edited by A. Mamak and A. Ali. Sydney and Boston: G. Allen & Unwin, 1979, 144 pp.
Hahalis and its clash with government.

643 Mamak, Alexander [F.], and Bedford, Richard D. *Bougainvillean nationalism: Aspects of unity and discord*. Bougainville Special Publication 1. Christchurch, N.Z.: Bougainville Special Publications, Department of Geography, University of Canterbury, 1974, 88 pp.
Pp. 6-7, Hahalis in relation to politics; p. 9, Napidoe Navitu association and politics.

Bougainville

644 Middlemiss, B. J. A. "Napidakoe Navitu." In *The politics of Melanesia.*
... *4th Waigoni Seminar* ... *1970,* edited by M. W. Ward. Port
Moresby: University of Papua and New Guinea, 1970, pp. 100-104.
Reprint. 1973.
   An anagramic name for a self-help and independence
organization on Bougainville; not overtly religious but unites all
religions, including cultists.

645 Montauban, Paul. "Faux prophètes aux Salomon." *Annales de Marie*
(Lyon), July 1934.
   Buka Island prophets about 1932.

646 Montauban, Paul. "Le grand rêve Buka depuis la guerre: S'emparer du
cargo." *Missions Maristes d'Océanie (Missions des Îsles)* (Paris), no. 15
[2] (September-October 1948): 135-39.

647 Montauban, Paul. "Schwärmgeister auf den Salomonen." *Kreuz and
Karitas*, no. 42, May 1934, pp. 137-40.
   Buka Island cargo movements; see extracts in G. Eckert (entry
311), pp. 32-33.

648 Nash, Jill. "Matriliny and modernization: The Nagovisi of south
Bougainville." *New Guinea Research Bulletin* (Canberra and Port
Moresby), no. 55 (1974), pp. 108-15.
   Matriliny is able to survive and even strengthen under Christian
and modernizing influences; pp. 111-15, Bipo na Tede development
society with Christian religious dimensions.

649 New Guinea, Territory of. "Native religious outbreaks: Cargo cult in
Buka and Bougainville." In *Territory of New Guinea Annual Report,
1935-6.* Canberra: Government Printer, 1936.
   Recent cargo cult in Buka.

650 New Guinea, Territory of. "Outbreaks of a quasi religious nature ...
Buka passage." In *Territory of New Guinea Annual Report, 1933-4.*
Canberra: Government Printer, 1934, pp. 22-23.
   Aftermath of the movement under Pako in 1932; Sanop, on of its
leaders, recommenced a movement in 1934; reflections on such
movements.

651 Ogan, Eugene. *Business and cargo: Socio-economic change among the
Nasioi of Bougainville.* New Guinea Research Bulletin 44. Canberra

Bougainville

and Port Moresby: New Guinea Research Unit, Australian National University, 1972, 204 pp.

On the Kieta subdistrict, Bougainville; chap. 3, missions and social change; chap. 8, "bisnis" and "kago," material and spiritual riches undifferentiated and both obtained by supernatural means; incipient cults, but no leaders.

652 Ogan, Eugene. "Cargoism and politics in Bougainville, 1962-1972." *Journal of Pacific History* 9 (1974): 117-29.

653 Ogan, Eugene. *The changing life of the Nasioi people.* New Guinea Research Bulletin 4. Pidgin translation of summary version, "Ol senis i wok long Pkamap long sindaun bilong ol Nasioi pipal," by H. Pora-Schmidt, in *Luksave* 3 (1972): 11 pp., illus.

654 Ogan, Eugene. "Charisma and race." In *The politics of dependence: Papua New Guinea, 1968,* edited by A. L. Epstein, et al. Canberra: Australian National University Press, 1971, pp. 132-61.

Pp. 144-47, 152-59 on cargo cults.

655 Ogan, Eugene. "An election in Bougainville." *Ethnology* 4, no. 4 (October 1965): 397-407, map.

Pp. 400-406, cargo expectations, contributing to the success of the elected candidate.

656 Ogan, Eugene. "The Nasioi vote again." *Human Organization* 29, no. 3 (1970): 178-88, maps, bib.

References to cargoism on pp. 181 (general), 185, 187 (comparative table of "cargoist" areas voting) among the Nasioi of Bougainville.

657 Oliver, Douglas L. *Bougainville: A personal history.* Melbourne: Melbourne University Press, 1973, 231 pp., illus.

Pp. 121-23 et passim, cargo cults; pp. 150-57, Hahalis.

658 O'Reilly, Patrick [Georges Farell]. "Sorcellerie et civilisation européenne aux Îles Salomon." In *La sorcerie dans les pays de mission: Compte rendu de la 14e Semaine de Missiologie de Louvain, 1936.* Brussels: l'Édition Universelle; Paris: Brouwer, 1937, pp. 142-56.

Contains account of an abortive revolt in Buka.

659 Ouellette, Mary Leo. "The Hahalis Welfare Society and the baby garden." *Papua New Guinea Medical Journal* 14, no. 1 (1971): 3-6.

By a Catholic sister.

660 *Pacific Islands Monthly.* Sundry reports and comments as follows:
"Fanaticism: Outbreak of religious mania in New Guinea," 3, no. 5 (1932): 46 [two "rival prophets" on Buka];

"Buka 'fanaticism' waning: Twelve natives imprisoned; ringleader uncaptured," 6, no. 4 (1935): 10;

"Fanaticism in New Guinea: Buka natives wait for 'Ship of the Millennium,'" 6, no. 3 (1935): 32 [brief news item of a "fresh outbreak"];

"Buka 'fanaticism' leader imprisoned," 6, no. 6 (1936): 67 [arrest and imprisonment of Sanape];

"Complicated aftermath of the New Guinea Buka troubles," 32, no. 2 (1962): 27-19, illus.;

"3,500 Buka Islanders pose a cargo cult problem," 34, no. 3 (1963): 58-59;

"Cult leader is 'doing well,'" 37, no. 10 (October 1966): 18, illus. [on Francis Hagai];

"A human sacrifice, he says," 40, no. 12 (1969): 36 [report by a planter of a proposed sacrifice];

"Hahalis becomes respectable. . . ." 43, no. 11 (1972): 39;

"Resurrected cult on Bougainville," 46, no. 2 (1975): 8-9 [Damen Damien's cult of the mid-1960s at Pondoro village, Koromira census division, under Paul Mena];

"Graves pillages [*sic*]," 47, no. 10 (1976): 25 [brief news items on cargo cult activity in central Bougainville at Kopani village];

"Two die by ritual," 47, no. 11 (1976): 34-35 [at Hahalis village, Buka Island; Hahalis cult described, but these killings are not directly attributed to it].

661 Rimoldi, Max. "The Hahalis Welfare Society of Buka." Ph.D. dissertation (anthropology), Australian National University, 1972.

662 Roberts, Mark. "The Kiriaka 'cargo cult.'" In *New religious movements in Melanesia*, edited by C. Loeliger and G. Trompf. Suva: Institute of Pacific Studies, University of the South Pacific; University of Papua New Guinea, 1985, pp. 40-44.
A strong reaction in 1960 among the Kiriaka people in northwest Bougainville against the Catholic mission. Subsequent mission use of the cargo theme to secure extensive economic development.

663 Ross, A[nthony] Clunies, and Langmore, J[ohn]. *Alternative strategies for Papua New Guinea.* Melbourne: Oxford University Press, 1973, 263 pp.

Bougainville

Pp. 116-21, cults from Pako in 1932 to Hahalis.

664 Sharp, Nonie. "The Republic of the Northern Solomons." *Arena* (Greensborough, Victoria), no. 40 (1975), pp. 119-27.

Pp. 123-24, 127, the contribution of "millennial movements" in Northern Solomons' independence, proclaimed 1 September 1975.

665 Sipari, Herman. "Friday religion." In *New Religious movements in Melanesia*, edited by C. Loeliger and G. Trompf. Suva: Institute of Pacific Studies, University of the South Pacific; University of Papua New Guinea, 1985, pp. 26-33.

A "separatist Catholic church movement" in North Solomons Province from 1958, and spreading into central Bougainville.

666 Sipari, Herman. "The Kopani 'cargo religion.'" In *New religious movements in Melanesia*, edited by C. Loeliger and G. Trompf. Suva: Institute of Pacific Studies, University of the South Pacific; University of Papua New Guinea, 1985, pp. 34-39.

In central Bougainville from the 1960s, anti-Christian and antidevelopment, stimulated by the copper mine development.

667 Tohiana, R. "The Hahalis welfare society of Buka." Honours subthesis, University of Papua New Guinea, Port Moresby, 1982.

668 Willey, Keith. "Cargo cultists cast their shadow on independence." *Sunday Times* (Perth), 24 May 1964.

On Hahalis Welfare Society.

Fiji

Fiji became independent in 1970 after having been a British colony from 1874. It lies at the extreme eastern side of the Melanesian culture area and shares also in Polynesian cultural influences. It is here included in the former culture area, and some of its movements reveal characteristic cargo-cult features. Contemporary movements in Fiji are as yet inadequately reported.

669 Asmis, Rudolf. "Die Farbigenpolitik der Briten auf den Fidji-Inseln." *Koloniale Rundshau* 29 (1938): 79-96.

P. 84, a cargo movement.

670 Blanc, Joseph [-Felix]. *Histoire religieuse de l'Archipel Fidjien.* 2 vols. Toulon: Imprimerie Saint-Jeanne d'Arc, 1926, 1:269 pp.; 2:340 pp., bib.

Vol. 2, pp. 179-81, Apolosi. By a Catholic bishop.

671 Brewster, A[dolf] B[ruce]. *The hill tribes of Fiji*. Philadelphia:
Lippincott; London: Seeley Service & Co., 1922, 308 pp., illus. Reprint.
New York: Johnston Reprints, 1967, 323 pp., illus.

Firsthand account by a colonial officer who changed his name
during World War I. Pp. 222-31 (1922 ed.), Luveniwai; pp. 236-60, 268-
70, 278-80, Tuka cult and its prophet Navosakandua.

672 Cato, A. C[yril]. "Disintegration, syncretization and change in Fijian
religion." *Mankind* 5, no. 3 (1956): 101-6.

673 Cato, A. C[yril]. "A new [religious] cult in Fiji." *Oceania* 18, no. 2
(December 1947): 146-56.

Kelevi's cult, 1942-, including sections from his dictated
"catechism"–"The Good News Written by the Word," and from
interviews with Kelevi in 1947.

674 Chambers, W. J., and Suckling, J. B. "Bau Circuit"; "Nadgroga Circuit."
Missionary Review (Australian Methodist Church) 18, no. 10 (1919): 8-
9; 19, no. 7 (1919): 12-13.

On Sailosi or "No. 8" religion–by the Methodist missionaries
involved.

675 Couper, A[lastair] D[ougall]. "Protest movements and proto-
cooperatives in the Pacific islands." *Journal of the Polynesian Society* 77
(1968): 263-74.

Pp. 268-71, Apolosi's trading Viti Company, in the early more
secular periods.

676 Derrick, R[onald] A[bert]. *A history of Fiji*. Suva: Printing and
Stationery Department, vol. 1-, 1946, vii + 250 + xxviii pp. 2d ed. 1950,
illus., maps, bib. 3d rev. ed. Suva: Government Press, 1957, 334 pp.,
illus., maps, bib. (vol. 1, pp. iv-viii of last group).

Pp. 113-15 (1946 and 1950 eds.), history of Kaba-Daku area in
the 19th century; p. 115, Daku's "obduracy" and late acceptance of
Christianity; p. 84, map of Rewa delta–as background to the Daku
movement.

677 Destable, P. "Aux Îles Fidji: Intrigues criminelles." *Les missions
Catholiques* (Lyons), 1919, pp. 127-28.

On Apolosi in 1914, and successor "false prophet" Sailosi at the
end of World War II. By a Catholic priest.

Fiji

678 Fossen, Anthony B[elgrano] van. "Priests, aristocrats, and millennialism in Fiji." *Mankind* (Sydney) 16, no. 3 (1986): 158-66.

Millennial movements as hostile to, chiefly, European and Indian values, and representing the concerns of a decaying priesthood. Pp. 161-62, Tuka; p. 162, Kelevi; pp. 162-64, Apolosi; p. 164, three unrecorded current movements.

679 Garrett, John. "Motivation, values, and goals for economic development–the case of Daku." In *Tourism in Fiji*. Ray Parkinson Memorial Lectures. Suva: University of the South Pacific, 1973, pp. 57-61.

Historical background and development of the Daku community; history and personality of Ratu Emosi, its founder, and influence of the Tuka and Apolosi cults on him.

680 Gittins, John. "The co-operative movement in Fiji." *South Pacific* (Australian School of Pacific Administration) 4, no. 11 (1950): 193-98.

P. 195, failure of Apolosi and the Fijian Trading Co. from 1914.

681 Guariglia, Guglielmo. *Prophetismus und Heilserwartungs-bewegungen als völkerkundliches und religionsgeschichtliches Problem.* Vienna: F. Berger, 1959.

Pp. 77-78, Tuka; pp. 78-79, Luvenai; p. 121, Apolosi; pp. 121-22, Kelevi movement.

682 Guiart, Jean [Charles Robert]. "Institutions religieuses traditionelles et messianismes modernes à Fiji." *Archives de Sociologie des Religions*, no. 4 [2, no. 2] (1957): 3-30, footnote refs.

Pp. 24-25, Apolosi.

683 Hocart, A. M. "Myths in the making." *Folklore* (London) 33 (1922): 61-69.

Pp. 61-62, etymological myths developed by the Tuka movement, with some biblical influence.

684 Lester, R. H. "Magico-religious societies of Viti Levu, Fiji." *Transactions and Proceedings of the Fiji Society for Science and Industry* (Suva) 2, no. 2 (1953): 117-34.

A paper read in 1941, reporting contents of a manuscript by Robert Boyd (then chairman of Native Lands Commission). Translated from the Fijian original. Pp. 128-33, Luvenai; pp. 133-34, Kalourere (as Luvenai became known under different forms in inland areas) interpreted as based on the Tuka cult; both treated as traditional societies sporadically revived.

685 Luke, Harry [Charles]. *From a South Seas diary, 1938-42*. London: Nicholson & Watson, 1945, 255 pp., illus.

Pp. 123-24, 140, Apolosi as seen negatively by the governor.

686 Macnaught, Tim[othy A.]. "Apolosi R. Nawai: The man from Ra." In *More Pacific Islands portraits*, edited by Deryck Scarr. Canberra: Australian National University Press, 1979, pp. 173-92, 271-72.

A detailed biography using archival and oral resources.

687 Naivolasiga, Eparaman. "Evangelization." B.D. thesis, Pacific Theological College (Suva), 1970, 68 pp., bib.

Chap. 1 (pp. 1-21), Na Lami (The Lamb) Group founded by Emosi Nasove (former follower of Apolosi) and continued by his son Kitione (a local Methodist preacher) as a cooperative society with an ambiguous relation to the Methodist Church and hostility to some traditional Fijian customs; pp. 56-57, recommendations about Methodist approach to Na Lami.

688 [News item.] *Missionary Review* (Sydney, Methodist Church of Australia), 4 February 1919, pp. 8-9.

On Apolosi.

689 Parr, Arnold R. "Origins of cults in South Pacific societies: A study of the Messiah Organization in Fiji." Paper presented at Annual Meeting, New Zealand Association of Social Anthropology, Palmerston North, August 1977, 20 pp. Mimeo.

690 Rakato, Aporoso. "Cacaka ni Gauna: Lauwaki, Vuda." Paper presented at School of Social and Economic Development, University of the South Pacific, 1973, 12 pp. Mimeo.

On the Apolosi movement, Lauwaki branch at Vuda, from the 1960s, led by an old lady.

691 Rokotuiviwa, Paula S. *The congregation of the poor*. Suva: South Pacific Social Services Association, 1975, 58 pp., illus.

Loaniceva's healing church in Suva, etc., as a "reformist sect" from about 1963.

692 Rokotuiviwa, Paula S. "The Congregation of the Poor." In *New religious movements in Melanesia*, edited by C. Loeliger and G. Trompf. Suva:

Fiji

Institute of Pacific Studies, University of the South Pacific; University of Papua New Guinea, 1985, pp. 163-84.
Abridged version of entry 691.

693 Shaheem, F. "2000 wait on return: Police investigating." *Times of Fiji* (Suva), 15 March 1984, p. 3.
Current reemergence of the Tuka cult at Ndugumoi's home, with prophecies of his return.

694 Spate, Oskar H[ermann] K[ristian]. "Under two laws: The Fijian dilemma." *Meanjin* (Melbourne University) 19, no. 2 (1961): 166-81.
Pp. 174-80, Daku community of Ratu Emosi as "the New Testament among the mangroves," and a later substitute for cargo cults.

695 Spencer, Dorothy M[ary]. *Disease, religion, and society in the Fiji Islands*. American Ethnological Society Monographs, 2. New York: J. J. Augustin, 1941, ix + 82 pp. Reprint. Seattle: University of Washington Press, 1966.
Chap. 2 (pp. 9-18), religious beliefs and practices; pp. 16-18, Luvenai cult.

696 Sutherland, William. "The Tuka religion." *Transactions of the Fijian Society*, 1908-10, pp. 51-57.
One of the most reliable sources for the earliest known cargo movement in Fiji, in 1885.

697 Thompson, Laura [Maud]. *Fijian frontier: Secret cults*. Studies in the Pacific, 4. New York, etc.: American Council, Institute of Pacific Relations, 1940, xxiii + 150 pp.
Pp. 114-21, Water Babies, Tuka, Immortality cult, etc.; based on A. B. Brewster (entry 671).

698 Thompson, Laura [Maud]. *Southern Lau, Fiji: An ethnography*. Bernice P. Bishop Museum Bulletin 162. Honolulu: Bishop Museum, 1940, 228 pp., illus., maps, bib.
Pp. 116-19, secret societies.

699 Thomson, Basil H[ome]. *The Fijians: A study of the decay of custom*. London: William Heinemann, 1908, xviii + 396 pp., illus, map. Reprint. London: Dawsons of Pall Mall, 1968.
P. 134, Ndengai cult equated with Christianity; pp. 140-45, "Tuka heresy"; pp. 145-46, Seankanka revolt.

700 Thomson, Basil H[ome]. "The Kalou-Vu (ancestor gods) of the Fijians and a new religion (the Tuka cult)." *Journal of the Royal Anthropological Institute of Great Britain and Ireland* 24 (1895): 340-59. Pp. 356-59, Tuka cult.

701 Tippett, Alan R[ichard]. "A diachronic study of religious innovation in the Fiji Islands." Paper presented at International Association for Mission Studies, Third Biennial Meeting, Frankfurt, 1974, 65 pp. Mimeo.

Pp. 1-35, advent of Christianity and innovative responses; pp. 35-53, innovative nativism – Tuka, Apolosi, Matuku Island movement, John the Christ, Kelevi cult, Daku community, Livai's cult.

702 Verlingue, Charles-Edouard. Review of "Institutions religieuses traditionelles et messianismes modernes à Fiji," by J. [C. R.] Guiart (entry 682). *Journal de la Société des Océanistes*, no. 14 (1958), pp. 159-60.

Regards the treatment of messianism as thorough, but notes lesser examples not included, such as Daku.

703 Vollmer, A. "Der Tuka-Aberglaube der Fidschi-Insulaner." *Petermans Mitteilungen* 38 (1892): 148-50.

704 Worsley, Peter [Maurice]. *The trumpet shall sound: A study of "cargo" cults in Melanesia.* London: MacGibbon & Kee, 1957, 290 pp. 2d ed., enl., with supplementary bib. New York: Schocken Books, 1968, 300 pp.

Chap. 1 (pp. 17-31, 1968 ed.), Tuka movement.

Irian Jaya (Republic of Indonesia)

This is the western half of the large island called New Guinea by geographers. It has borne various names: Netherlands or Dutch New Guinea (1928-62), Irian Barat or West Irian, and finally Irian Jaya. Politically, it is part of the Republic of Indonesia and we trust that Indonesians will understand that it is only for reasons of convenience that this territory is considered here along with the rest of Melanesia, to which its indigenous peoples have belonged culturally. Its new religious movements resemble those of the eastern half of the island that lies within the nation of Papua New Guinea, and they go back to at least as far as the beginnings of Christian missions in the 1850s.

Irian Jaya

705 Arsdale, Peter W. van. "Reactive change and the redistribution of power: The 'Lord of the Earth' cult." In *Perspectives on development in Asmat.* Asmat Sketch Book no. 5, edited by F. A. Trenkenschuh. Jayapura, Irian Jaya: [Catholic] Diocese of Agats; Asmat: Asmat Museum of Culture and Progress; distributed by Crosier Missions, 3204 East 43d St., Minneapolis, 1975. 2d ed. 1978, pp. 146-72, 312.

706 Arsdale, Peter W. van, and Gallus, David E. "The 'Lord of the earth' cult among the Asmat: Prestige, Power and politics in a transitional society." *Irian* (Jayapura) 3, no. 2 (1974): 1-31 (with summary in Indonesian).

707 Baal, Jan van. *Mensen in verandering: Ontstaan en groei van een nieuwe cultuur in ontwikkelingslanden.* Amsterdam: De Arbeiderpers, 1967, 192 pp.
      Pp. 69-80, cargo cults; pp. 81-90, prophet movements in other continents; pp. 185-86, notes.

708 Baal, Jan van. *The Nimboran community development project.* Technical Paper 45. Sydney: South Pacific Commission, June 1953.
      Pp. 11-14, two Nimboran Kesjep movements, of the early 1950s, as cargo cults based on traditional dance-induced visions.

709 Baal, Jan van. "The Nimboran development project." *South Pacific* 6, no. 8 (December 1952): 492-98, 503.
      P. 494, cargo (kasiep) practices and movements.

710 Baas, P. R. "Heilsbeweging op Irian." *Tot Aan de Eiden der Aarde* 9, no. 9 (1985): 198-99.
      A salvation movement on Irian, a general explanation including belief in a secret Bible not shared.

711 Bijerk, Jac. "Pamai." In *Kruis en Korwar: Een honderdjarig waagstuk op Nieuw Guinea*, edited by F. C. Kamma. The Hague: J. N. Voorhoeve, 1953, pp. 137-50.
      The Pamai movement, 1928-29.

712 Bout, D. C. A. *Groeiende arbeid op Jappen.* Oegstgeest: [Netherlands Reformed Church], 1928.
      Pp. 9-13, prophet Saumira on Japen, 1925 – see extracts reprinted in F. C. Kamma (entry 761), p. 144.

713 Bout, D. C. A. "Een leugenprofeet." *Het Penningske. Maanblaadje, uitgaande van de samenwerkende Zendings-Vereenigingen* (Utrecht), no. 5 (May 1926), pp. 3-4.
> On prophet Saumira at Serewin on Japen in 1925. See extract reprinted in F. C. Kamma (entry 761), p. 143.

714 Bromley, H. Myron. "The year of the Balien." *Alliance Witness* 109, no. 12 (5 June 1974): 18-20, map.
> Pp. 19-20, brief account of a cargo cult led by an ex-teacher claiming to be Christ among the Grand Valley Dani; by a missionary of the Christian and Missionary Alliance.

715 Bruijn [Bruyn], J. V. de. *Het verdwenen volk*. Bussum, Netherlands: Van Holkema & Warendorf, 1978.
> Pp. 89, 153-54, 217, notes on the Situgumina myth. See also L. Rhys (entry 812).

716 Bruyn, J. V. de. "De Mansren-cultus der Biakkers." *Tijdschrift voor Indische Taal-, Land-, en Volkenkunde* 83, no. 4 (1949): 313-30. Shortened English translation in *South Pacific* (Sydney) 5, no. 1 (1951): 1-10.
> An important account, with emphasis on cultural nationalism rather than religion.

717 Bruyn, W. K. H. Feuilletau de. "De legende van Manseren Mangoendi." *Tijdschrift Nieuwe Guinea* 6, no. 4 (1941-42): 99-110.
> A slightly revised version of entry 718.

718 Bruyn, W. K. H. Feuilletau de. "De Schouten–en Padaidoeilanden." In *Mededeelingen Encyclopaedisch Bureau*. Vol. 21. Batavia: Javasche Boekhandel & Drukkerij, 1920.
> Pp. 72-74, "konoors" disturbances.

719 Bureau for Native Affairs, Hollandia. "Anthropological research in Netherlands New Guinea." *Oceania* 29, no. 2 (1958): 142-45. Reprint. Oceania Monographs, no. 10. 1959, pp. 12-15.

720 "Comoro Cargo cult." *Asmat Drums* (Hastings, Nebraska), no. 49 (Fall 1983), [p. 8].
> A cargo cult among the Sawi people of Comoro village on the Ayip river in 1981-82, led by Mare, in a Regions Beyond missionary Union area.

Irian Jaya

721 Drabbe, P. "Folk tales from Netherlands New Guinea." *Oceania* 18, no. 2 (1947): 157-75; no. 3, (1948): 248-170; 19, no. 1 (1948): 75-90.

The myth of the flood among the Mimika, related to their being a "negative instance" in relation to new movements.

722 Dubbeldam, L. F. B. "Some thoughts on nativistic movements." *Working Papers in Dani Ethnology* (United Nations Temporary Executive Authority in West New Guinea–West Irian, Bureau of Native Affairs), no. 1 (October 1962): Section D, p. 48.

See entry 838.

723 Eechoud, J[an] P. K. van. "Mau Mau bij de Papoea's. Bedreiging voor Nieuw-Guinea?" *Elseviers Weekblad* (Amsterdam), 20 December 1952, p. 19.

Effects of the Manseren myth and its *konoor* explained, and compared culturally to Mau Mau in Kenya.

724 Eechoud, J[an] P. K. van. *Woudloper gods*. Amsterdam: DeBoer, 1955, 304 pp.

Pp. 260-62, references to concept of *hai* but no mention of a *hai* movement; this was discovered by Father Kammerer, Catholic missionary at Kugapa.

725 Ellenberger, John D. "A century of 'Hai' movements among the Damal of Irian Jaya." In *Religious movements in Melanesia: A selection of case studies and reports*, edited by W. Flannery. Goroka: Melanesian Institute, 1983, pp. 104-10. Mimeo.

726 Ellenberger, John. "The planting of the church among the Damals of West Irian." In *The Gospel and frontier peoples*, edited by R. P. Beaver. South Pasadena: William Carey Library, 1973.

P. 161, lists ten small "messianic movements" that flowered and died; expanded in his "A century of 'Hai' movements . . ." (entry 725).

727 Ellenberger, John. *Schismatic movements in mission-founded churches.* Christian and Missionary Alliance Precouncil Missionary Conference, 1975. Reprint. *Catalyst* 11, no. 4 (1981): 224-36.

728 "Eine Erweckungsbewegung auf Hollandisch Neuguinea." *Barmer Missionsblatt*, May 1929, pp. 35-38.

The Pamai movement, 1928-29.

729 Finsch, Otto. *Neu-Guinea und seine Bewohner*. Bremen: C. E. Müller, 1865, 185 pp.
Pp. 45-46, 108, a prophet in Mansinam – see extract reprinted in F. C. Kamma (entry 761), p. 109.

730 Galis, K[laas] W[ilhelm]. *Papua's van de Humboldt-Baai: Bijdrage tot een ethnografie*. The Hague: J. N. Voorhoeve, 1955, 293 pp., illus., maps.
Pp. 139-40, 145-47, the mythological basis of Koreri and other movements on the northeast coast.

731 Gallus, David. "Report to the Provincial Chapter, 1981 – from the Asmat Mission." In *Asmat Sketch Book no. 8*. Agats, Irian Jaya: Asmat Museum of Culture and Progress; distributed by Crosier Missions, 3204 East 43d St., Minneapolis, 1982, pp. 139-49.
P. 145 summary of cult-based revolt in December 1980.

732 Gibbons, Alice. *The people time forgot*. Chicago: Moody Press, 1981, 347 pp., illus., maps.
On the Damal people in the highlands. Pp. 297-302, the great fetish-burning of 1957 as a group response early in the contact period; p. 326, brief mention of cargo ideas in the *hai* belief.

733 Gibbons, Don. "The cargo myth and the threat it poses for the Evangelical Church in Irian Jaya." 1978, 24 pp. Mimeo.
Unpublished paper presented to the Christian and Missionary Alliance annual conference, July 1978, by one of their missionaries of many years standing. Includes some new material on movements as encountered by the C. and M. A.

734 Godschalk, Jan A. "How are myth and movement related?" In *Point*. Series 2, *Religious movements in Melanesia today (1)*, edited by W. Flannery. Goroka: Melanesian Institute, 1983, pp. 62-77.
Definitions of myth; Irian Jaya examples of myth and movement (including Koreri, Jewme, Damal, and Dani movements); Koreri myth without movement; the Yali, no myth and no movement; Muyu, movement without myth.

735 Godschalk, Jan A. "A survey of salvation movements in Irian Jaya." In *Religious movements in Melanesia: A selection of case studies and reports*, edited by W. Flannery. Goroka: Melanesian Institute, 1983, pp. 52-101. Mimeo.

Irian Jaya

736 Godschalk, Jan A. "Where the twain shall meet: A study of the autochthonous character of some movements in New Guinea." Doctoraal scriptie [master's degree thesis], Rijksuniversiteit te Utrecht, Faculteit der Godgeleerdheid, 1977, 64 pp.

Pp. 5-16, Koreri movements; pp. 17-20, Jewme movement, Mamberamo area; pp. 21-25, *kasiep* movements, Nimboram area; pp. 26-29, two movements among the Muyu; pp. 30-34, Ain's cult among the Taro Enga; pp. 35-37, Taro cult among the Orokaiva – all based on the main writers on these movements; pp. 38-42, the mythical framework; pp. 43-48, role of ancestors; pp. 49-53, meaning of "cargo"; useful summaries and interpretations.

737 Goudswaard, A. *De Papoewa's van de Geelvinksbaai.* Schiedam: H. A. M. Roelants, 1863, 105 pp., map.

Pp. 83-94, appendix on Papuan culture; p. 93, the first known description of a movement in Biak-Numfor, based on Captain Fabritius – see extract in F. C. Kamma (entry 761); also on the Konor and Manseren myths, passim. By an early missionary.

738 Grootenhuis, G. W. "Nativistic movements." *Working Papers in Dani Ethnology* (United Nations Temporary Executive Authority in West New Guinea – West Irian, Bureau of Native Affairs), no. 1 (October 1962): Section D, pp. 49-53.

See entry 838.

739 Grootenhuis, G. W. *De "wege"-beweging in Paniai en Oost-Tigi.* Hollandia: Gouvernement van Nederlands Nieuw-Guinea, Bureau of Native Affairs, no. 150, 15 September 1960, 20 pp.

740 Guariglia, Guglielmo. *Prophetismus und Heilserwartungs-bewegungen als völkerkundliches und religionsgeschichtliches Problem.* Vienna: F. Berger, 1959, 332 pp.

Pp. 79-81, Koreri; p. 88, Pamai; pp. 104-5, Simson; p. 105, Nimboram, and Ninigo Island; pp. 105-7, Koreri movements.

741 Haes, F. I. M. de. "Nota over de Wege-beweging. 5 Jan 1960." 3 pp. Mimeo.

A report to the Government of Netherlands New Guinea, Wissel Lakes area administration, dated 22 December 1959, on Wege-Bage; attached to report of J. Massink, entry 787.

742 Hale Naua. "Memorie van Overgave van de Onderafdeling Hollandia, 1926-1930." 1930.

Memorandum as "handing-over notes" by government officer. Pp. 27-31, 59, Pamai movement, 1928, in the district of Hollandia.

743 Hartweg, F. W. Letter. *Het Penningske. Maandblaadje, uitgaande van de samenwerkende Zendings-Vereenigingen* (Utrecht), no. 7 (July 1928), pp. 2-3.

A missionary's brief report of a Biak movement in Kerem, 1927-28; see extract reprinted in F. C. Kamma (entry 761), p. 142.

744 Hartweg, F. W. "Das Lied von Manseren Mangundi (Biak-Sprache)." *Zeitschrift für Eingeborenen-Sprachen* 23 (1932): 46-58.

A song in Biak (Numfor dialect) on the culture hero redeemer, Manarmaker, with German translation, introduction and notes.

745 Hasselt, F[rans] J[ohannes] F[rederick]. "Iets over de roem seram en over Namggi." *Tijdschrift voor Indische Taal-, Land-, en Volkenkunde* (Batavia) 60 (1921): 108-14.

Remarks taking issue with W. K. H. Feuilletan de Bruyn entry 718.

746 Hasselt, F[rans] J[ohannes] F[rederick]. "I. Noemfor. Een geschiedenis van vijf jaren zendingsarbeid." *Lichtstralen op den akker de Wereld* (Rotterdam) 20, no. 1 (1914): 6-7, 13-14, 18, 27-29, 35.

Pp. 16, 28, etc., on *konoor* Mangginomi on Numfor in 1910 – see extracts reprinted in F. C. Kamma (entry 761), pp. 138-39.

747 Hasselt, F[rans] J[ohannes] F[rederick]. "De legende van Mansren Mangoendi." *Bijdagen tot de Taal- Land-, en Volkenkunde van Nederlandsch Indie. . . .* 69, no. 1 (1914): 90-100.

748 Hasselt, F[rans] J[ohannes] F[rederick]. *Petrus Kafiar.* Utrecht: De Utrechte Zendingsvereeniging, n.d., 62 pp.

P. 33, attempt to make local mission agent, Petrus, into a *konor* on Biak in 1898; p. 53, similar attempt in 1908. See F. C. Kamma (entry 761), p. 137.

749 Hasselt, J. L. van. "Eenige aanteekeningen aangaande de bewoners der Noord-Westkust van Nieuw-Guinea, meer bepaaldelijk den stam der Noefoorezen" (Parts 1-2). *Tijdschrift van het Bataviaasch Genootschap voor Kunsten en Wetenschappen* 31 (1886): 576-93; 32 (1889): 261-72.

Pp. 265-68, Manseren Mangoendi myth – cited by F. C. Kamma (entry 761), p. 308.

Irian Jaya

750 Hasselt, J. L. van. "De toovenar van Doreh." *Het Penningsken.*
Hulpvereeniging der Utrechte Zendingsvereeniging (Utrecht), no. 73
(1871), pp. 1-4.
Report by a missionary intimately involved with a pseudo-*konoor*
(or "magician") at Dore in 1868; extensive extracts in F. K. Kamma
(entry 761), pp. 116-18.

751 Hayward, Douglas J[ames]. *The Dani of Irian Jaya before and after
conversion.* Sentani, Irian Jaya: Regions Press, 1980, 223 pp. Originally
an M.A. project (missiology), School of World Mission, Fuller
Theological Seminary, 1977, 272 pp.
Pp. 125-53 (1977 version, pp. 156-76), a fetish-burning movement
from 1955 under Moses Kelangin (Catholic teacher) among the Damal
and Dani; with missionary reactions.

752 Hayward, Douglas J[ames]. "The millenarian features of the rebel
movements which swept through the western Dani area in 1976-1977."
Paper presented at Pyramid Seminar, October 1980, 10 pp. Mimeo.

753 Heider, Karl G. "Societal intensification and cultural stress as
determining factors in the innovation and conservation of two Dani
cultures." *Oceania* 46, no. 1 (1975): 53-67.
Compares the massive response of Western Dani to Western
contact and Christianity, with the lack of response by Grand Valley
Dani; suggests latter have a higher level of cultural satisfaction and a
lower level of cultural stress.

754 Held, G[errit] J[an]. *De Papoea: cultuurimprovisator.* Gravenhage: W.
Van Hoeve, 1951, 231 pp.
Pp. 40-42, 70-71, 192-93, salvation movements; pp. 192-93,
Orakaiva (Kladi) cult; pp. 188-90, myth of the two brothers; pp. 223-24,
some traditional assumptions relevant to cargo cults.

755 Held, G[errit] J[an]. *Papoea's van Waropen.* Leiden: E. J. Brill, 1947.
English translation. *The Papuas of Waropen.* Koninklijk Instituut voor
Taal-, Land-, en Volkenkunde. Translation Series, 2. The Hague:
Martinus Nijhof, 1957, 384 pp., illus., map.
English translation, pp. 317-21, culture heroes and a wonderful
future; revivals of Koreri and Manseren movements among the
Waropen of east Geelvink Bay in the 1930s.

756 Hitt, Russell T[rovillo]. *Cannibal valley*. New York: Harper & Row, 1962, 253 pp., illus. Reprint. London: Hodder & Stoughton, 1969. Reprint. Grand Rapids: Zondervan, 1970, 254 pp.

Pp. 163-81, the *hai* myth and movement among the Uhunduni; pp. 216-23, prophet Jabonep among the Dani. By a missionary.

757 Hogerwaard, T. "Herlevend heidendum." *Zendings-tijdschrift "De Opwekker*." (Surabaya and Bandung. Ned. Indischen Zendings Bond) 86 (1941): 487-98.

Simson's cargo cult of 1940 near Hollandia.

758 Horne, Shirley. *An hour to the stone age*. Chicago: Moody Press, 1973, 208 pp., illus., map.

Pp. 123-34, Western Dani fetish-burning movement, from 1955; pp. 146-49, Papinggawe's incipient cult and currency destruction. By the wife of a pioneer missionary of the Unevangelized Fields Mission.

759 Hughes, Earl J. "Kobakma Cargo cult." In *Religious movements in Melanesia: A selection of case studies and reports*, edited by W. Flannery. Goroka: Melanesian Institute, 1983, pp. 102-3. Mimeo.

760 Kabel, J. P. "De Kesjep-beweging in Nimboran, geschetst tegen de achtergrond van het oude heidendom en de overgang naar het Christendom." *De Heerbaan* (Amsterdam) 6, no. 3 (1953): 106-45; no. 4 (1953): 148-71.

A good study from inside the situation.

761 Kamma, F[reerk] C[hristiaans]. *Koreri: Messianic movements in the Biak-Numfor culture area*. Koninklijk Instituut voor Taal-, Land-, en Volkenkunde. Translation Series, 15. The Hague: M. Nijhoff, 1972, xii + 328 pp., illus., 2 folding maps, bib. (pp. 301-19, with 350 items).

See entry 764. Note the new chap. 10 discussing the literature since 1954, and the appendix updating the movements in other parts of Irian Jaya to 1962. The bibliography is especially valuable.

762 Kamma, F[reerk] C[hristiaans]. "Kringloop en burchten" (Parts 1-2). *Zendings-tijdschrift "De Opwekker"* (Surabaya and Bandung, Ned. Indischen Zendings Bond) 86 (1941): 524ff.; 88 (1943): 3ff.

On Manseren and Koreri movements.

763 Kamma, F[reerk] C[hristiaans]. "Levend heidendom" (Parts 1-2). *Tijdschrift voor Zendingswetenschap* (Rotterdam) 83 (1939): 187-207; 289-316; 387-422.

Irian Jaya

On the Manseren and Koreri movements, passim.

764 Kamma, F[reerk] C[hristiaans]. *De messiaanse Koreri-bewegingen in het Biaks-Noemfoorse cultuurgebied.* The Hague: J. N. Voorhoeve, 1954, 250 pp., map.
A doctoral dissertation, the standard work on Irian Jaya. English translation, revised and extended, see entry 761.

765 Kamma, F[reerk] C[hristiaans]. "Messianic movements in western New Guinea." *International Review of Missions*, no. 162 [41] (April 1952): 148-60.
Forms of the Mansren myth and cult.

766 Kamma, F[reerk] C[hristiaans]. "Oude verwachtingen in de Nieuwe tijd." In *Raaiboek van Nieuw Guinea*, edited by G. L. Tichelman. The Hague: Het Nationaal Nieuw Guinea Comite, and Hollandia: Het Nieuw Guinea Verbond, 1951, pp. 39-43.

767 Kamma, F[reerk] C[hristiaans]. "Papoesch Adventisme." *Zendings-tijdschrift "De Opwekker"* (Surabaya and Bandung, Ned. Indischen Zendings Bond) 85 (1940): 259ff.
"Papuan adventism."

768 Kamma, F[reerk] C[hristiaans]. "Religieuze voorstellingen." In *Kruis en Korwar: Een honderdjarig waagstuk op Nieuw Guinea*. The Hague: J. N. Voorhoeve, 1953, pp. 20-30.
Pp. 29-30, messianic movements.

769 Kamma, F[reerk] C[hristiaans]. "Toekomstverwachtingen bij Papoea's." *Schakels* (The Hague, Government Information Service), no. 62 (January 1953), p. 28.

770 Kamma, F[reerk] C[hristiaans]. *"Dit wonderlijke werk": Hetprobleem van de communicatie tussen oost en west gebaseerd op de ervaringen in het zendingswerk op Nieuw-Guinea (Irian Jaya) 1855-1972; een socio-missiologische benadering.* 2d rev. ed. 2 vols. Oegstgeest: Raad voor de Zending van de Nederlands Hervormde Kerk, 1977, pp. 1-416, 417-836 pp.

771 Kamma, F[reerk] C[hristiaans]. "Zending en messianisme in de Geelvinkbaai: Een roos die bloeit op een mesthoop of een honderjarig misverstand?" *Vox Theologica* (Groningen) 42 (1972): 254-75.

772 Koentjaraningrat, and Bachtiar, Harsja W. *Penduduk Irian Barat.* Djakarta: Penerbitan Universitas, 1963, 380 pp.
See chapter, "Reaksi penduduk terhadap perobahan Zaman"–the reaction to changing times, for Koreri movements.

773 Kooijmann, S. "Die Messianischen Koreri-Bewegungen auf Neuguinea." *Evangelisches Missions-Magazin* (Basel) 99 (November 1955): 180-88.

774 Kouwenhoven, W[illem] J[an] H[endrik]. "Nimboran: A study of social change and socio-economic development in a New Guinea society." The Hague: J. N. Voorhoeve, 1956, 240 pp., maps. Reprint. Ca. 1978.
A Leiden University dissertation. Pp. 75-81, Kasiep movements; pp. 141-47, Kasiep movement in Gressie, 1953, and its failure; p. 81, Pentacost (an individual).

775 Kroef, J[ustus] M[aria] van der. "Culture contact and culture conflict in Western New Guinea." *Anthropological Quarterly* 32, no. 3 (1959): 134-60.
Pp. 134-46, the Muju and their prophets.

776 Kroef, J[ustus] M[aria] van der. "Patterns of cultural change in three primitive societies." *Social Research* 24, (1957): 427-56.
Pp. 428-46, Koreri movements in Biak-Numfor society (north coast); pp. 439-46, in the Mimika people (south coast); pp. 446-52, Nimboram development project (north coast); pp. 453-56, conclusions.

777 Lagerberg, C. S. I. J. *Jaren van reconstructie: Nieuw-Guinea van 1948 tot 1961.* s'Hertogenbosch: Zuid-Nederlandsche Drukkerij N.V., 1962.
Pp. 41-47, Biak area cargo cults.

778 Land, C. op't. *Werk in uitvoering: Structuur en dynamiek van het ontwikkelingswerk.* Meppel: Boom, 1970.
Pp. 210-24, and pp. 468-76, notes: early Nimboram and Kasiep movements, 1910-52; pp. 517-19, English summary.

779 Larson, Gordon F. "The fetish burning among the Western Dani Papuans." *Working Papers in Dani Ethnology* (United Nations Temporary Executive Authority in West New Guinea–West Irian, Bureau of Native Affairs), no. 1 (October 1962): Section D, pp. 54-58.
See entry 838.

Irian Jaya

780 Leeden, A. C. van der. "Sarmi'ers in het contact met het Westen." *Bijdragen tot de Taal-, Land-, en Volkenkunde van Nederlandsch-Indie* (*Anthropologica* 2) 117 (1961): 51-63.

A pre-1931 cargo movement at Martewar, northwest of Samai.

781 Lekahema, S. "De 'Manseren'-beweging." *Tijdschrift "Nieuw-Guinea"* (The Hague) 8, no. 4 (1947): 97-102. English summary.

Based on F. C. Kamma (entry 767)).

782 Logchem, Jan Theo van. *De Argoeniers: Een Papoea-volk in West Nieuw-Guinea.* Utrecht: Schotanus & Jens, 1963, 207 pp.

The Arguians: a Papuan people in Western New Guinea. A Utrecht University doctoral dissertation, 1963. Pp. 186-202, *manggarega* messianic movements.

783 Mampioper, A. *Mitologi dan Pengharapan Masyarakat Biak-Numfor.* Jayapura: April 1976, 133 pp.

784 Marjen, Chris. "Cargo cult movement, Biak." *Journal of the Papua and New Guinea Society* (Port Moresby) 1, no. 2 (1967): 62-65.

By a West Irian medical student, on the Manseren Koreri movement of the 1940s and the myth behind it.

785 Massenzio, Marcello. "Progetto mitico e opera umana" (Parts 1-2). *Culture: Quadrimestrale di studi Storico-Culturali* 2 (1977): 71-89; 4 (1979): 3-31.

Analysis of the Manseren Manggundi movement in Biak, and critique of P. M. Worsley (entry 529) with respect to the myth-cult relation and the millenarian concept.

786 Massenzio, Marcello. *Progetto mitico e opera umana. Contributo all'analisi storico-religiosa dei millenarismi.* Collana Anthropos, 4. Naples: Liguori Editore, 1980, 182 pp.

Part 1, Koreri myths; part 2, Manseren myths; pp. 171-75, prospects for research; pp. 176-82, bibliography on cults.

787 Massink, J. "Onderwerp: Wege-beweging: An de Resident van Centraal Nieuw Guinea te Biak." 1959, 4 pp. Mimeo.

A government report, to which the report by F. I. M. de Haes (entry 741) was attached. On the Wege-Bage movement.

788 May, Kevin R. "Cargo thinking in Nimboran." In *Point*. Series 2, *Religious movements in Melanesia today (1)*, edited by W. Flannery. Goroka: Melanesian Institute, 1983, pp. 52-62.
The basis in Nimboram mythology for *kasiep* movements.

789 Merkelijn, P. J. "'Spreken in vele talen' Vreemde verschijnselen bij Papoea's op Nieuw-Guinea en hum oorzaak." *Sociaal Spectrum van de Archipel* 1, no. 8 (1948): 4-5.
Includes Simson movement, and Sarmi movement of 1947.

790 Metz, J. "Op Roon begint Victorie" (Parts 1-2). *Tijdschrift voor Zendingswetenschap* (Rotterdam) 84 (1940): 34-74, 296-325.
Pp. 311, 312, 319, 325, local missionary's reports of a *konoor*, Marisi, on island of Room, 1900-1908; see extracts in F. C. Kamma (entry 761), p. 135.

791 Moszkowski, Max. "Die Völkerstämme am Mamberamo in Holländisch-New Guinea, und auf den vorgelagerten Inseln." *Zeitschrift für Ethnologie* 43 (1911): 315-46.
Pp. 327-28, 344-45, Manseren myth culture hero, Manggundi, among the Mamberam in 1910, and discussion with Neuhaus in which the author supports a precontact view of the origins of the story.

792 Mote, Yacob. "Later Belakang Weege-Bage Menolak Kulit Kerang sebagai Mata Uang Adat Suku Ekagi di Daerah Paniai." Thesis, Sekobah Tinggi Teologi Katolik di Jayapura (Irian Jaya), November 1976, 73 pp. Typescript.
Pp. 15-36, Wege-Bage movement.

793 Müller, Ernst Wilhelm. "Die Koreri-Bewegung auf den Schouten-Inseln (West-Neuguinea)." In *Chiliasmus und Nativismus*, edited by W. E. Mühlmann. Berlin: D. Reimer (1961) 1964, pp. 141-64.

794 O'Brien, Denise. "Nativistic movements." *Working Papers in Dani Ethnology* (United Nations Temporary Executive Authority in West New Guinea – West Irian, Bureau of Native Affairs), no. 1 (October 1962): Section D, pp. 59-60.
See entry 838.

795 O'Brien, Denise, and Ploeg, Anton. "Acculturation movements among the western Dani." *American Anthropologist* 66, no. 4, pt. 2 (1964): 281-92.

Irian Jaya

Pp. 284-92, movements with cargo cult features, 1959, 1963, in Swart valley and among the Bokondini Dani.

796 Oosterwal, Gottfried. "A cargo cult in the Mamberamo area." *Anthropological Report* (Hollandia) 3 (1962): 12-22. Reprinted in *Ethnology* 2, no. 2 (1963): 1-14.

Simple explanation of the cargo ideology; first detailed report of a movement among the Kaowerabedj people.

797 Oosterwal, Gottfried. "Cargo cults and Seventh-Day Adventism." *Ministry* (Washington), October 1962, pp. 10-13.

By an Adventist missionary anthropologist.

798 Osborne, Robin. *Indonesia's secret war: The guerrilla struggle in Irian Jaya*. Sydney: Allen & Unwin, 1985, xvi + 212 + 12 pp., plates, maps.

A journalist's account of the rebel movement's relation to the Koreri movement, interpreted solely as nationalist opposition to Indonesian hegemony; cf. Frank Tucker's essay (entry 837).

799 Ottow, C. W. [Letters.] In *Die Biene auf dem Missionsfelde*. Berlin: 1861.

Pp. 83-84, Koreri in Numfor, 1860 – see extracts in F. C. Kamma (entry 761), p. 107.

800 Ottow, C. W., and Geissler, J. G. "Kort oversigt van het land en de bewoners der Kust van Noord-Oostelijk Guinea (van de Zendelingen Ottow en Geissler) Mansiman, 2.3.1857." *Bijblad bij de Christelijke Stemmen* (Amsterdam) 6 (1868): 154-59.

A published version of the report: a different Dutch version of the original text.

801 Ottow, C. W., and Ottow-Letz, A. [Letters.] *Licht en Schaduw in het Oosten* (Amsterdam, Amsterdamsche Vroumen-Vereeniging tot bevorderung der Zendingszaak), no. 22 (1860), pp. 176-79.

On Koreri in Numfor, 1860 – see extract in F. C. Kamma (entry 761), p. 108. By a missionary couple.

802 Peters, H. L. "De Amungwe in het centrale bergland van Nederlands-Nieuw Guinea." *Nederlands Nieuwe-Guinea* (The Hague) 9, no. 1 (1961): 11-13, illus.

Cargo expectations associated with the arrival of missionaries.

803 Pijnappel, J. "Eenige bijzonderheden betreffende de Papoea's van de Geelvinksbaai van Nieuw-Guinea (1854)." *Bijdragen tot de Taal-, Land-, en Volkenkunde van Nederlandsch-Indie* 2, no. 4 (1854): 371, 383 (with translation included).
Probably the earliest published reference to Koreri beliefs.

804 Ploeg, Anton. "Nativistic movements among the Bokondini Dani." *Working Papers in Dani Ethnology* (United Nations Temporary Executive Authority in West New Guinea – West Irian, Bureau of Native Affairs), no. 1 (October 1962): Section D, pp. 61-62.
See entry 838.

805 Pos, Hugo. "The revolt of 'Manseren.'" *American Anthropologist* 52, no. 4 (1950): 561-64.
The movement under Stephanus on the north coast during the Japanese occupation.

806 Pospisil, Leopold. *The Kapauku Papuans of West New Guinea.* 2d ed. New York: Holt, Rinehart & Winston, 1978, 129 pp., illus., map.
Pp. 99, 110-12, Wege-Bage, "the crazy people," among the Kapauka.

807 Pouwer, J[an]. "Cargo cults." *Oceania* 28, no. 3 (1958): 247-49.
Letter from the then government anthropologist in Dutch New Guinea, presenting Kamma's work, and an appendix (pp. 250-52) containing Kamma's English summary.

808 Pouwer, J[an]. *Enkele aspecten van de Mimika-cultuur. . . .* The Hague: Staatsdrukkerij-en Uitgeversbedrijf, 1955, 323 pp., maps, diagrams.
A University of Leiden doctoral dissertation, 1955. Pp. 254, 263, "messianism"; Mimika mythology, maintained by the older people, facilitated relations with whites, but younger people, influenced by outside ideas, reveal cargo ideas.

809 Pouwer, J[an]. *The flood: A Mimika myth (West New Guinea).* 10 pp. + table. Mimeo.
Course material used at Victoria University, Wellington, in the 1970s. Four versions of the myth, with a diagram of its structure and movements. This myth accounts for the existence and wealth of the whites, and is a factor in the absence of cargo cults among older Mimika. The first version is drawn from P. Drabbe (entry 721).

Irian Jaya

810 Pouwer, J[an]. "Memorandum over een cargo-cult onder de Muju in Merauke." Report to the Bureau for Native Affairs, Hollandia, Netherlands New Guinea, 1953. Typescript.
Brief notes on a cargo cult among the Muju in Merauke.

811 Pouwer, J[an]. "Structural history: A New Guinea case study." In *Explorations in the anthropology of religion*, edited by W. E. A. van Beek and J. H. Scherer. The Hague: M. Nijhoff, 1975, pp. 80-111.
A theoretical discussion of the relation between structures in myth, and history, with the Mimika, as in his other cited works, as case study. Pp. 102-11 give the text of one version of the flood myth.

812 Rhys, Lloyd. *Jungle Pimpernel: The story of a District Officer in Central Netherlands New Guinea*. London: Hodder & Stoughton, 1947, 293 pp., illus., map.
Pp. 183-84, 187-89, the myth of Sitoegoemina, the woman who went to the land of the whites, who are thus of the same ancestors as the Mingani people.

813 Saf, F. X. *Gerakan "cargo cult" di pulau Kolepom*. Jayapura: Catholic Theological College, 1981.
A thesis on some movements on Kolepom island.

814 Saulnier, T. *Les Papous, coupeurs de têtes*. Édition du Port Royal, 1961. Dutch translation. *Tussen hemel en moeras*. Lochem: De Tijdstroom, 1962. English translation. *Headhunters of Papua*. London: P. Hamlyn, 1963, 309 pp., illus.
P. 35 (English translation), a policeman's incipient cargo movement on the south coast in 1959 among the Asmat.

815 [Schneider, G. J.] "Eine Erweckungsbewegung auf Holländisch Neuguinea." *Missionsblatt Barmen* (Neuendettelsau) (May 1929): 535ff.
The Pamai movement, based largely on missionary Schneider's report.

816 Schneider, G. J. "Schwärmerei in Holländische-Neuguinea." *Neuendettelsauer Missionsblatt* 29, no. 11 [96, no. 8] (1939): 64.
The Pamai movement.

817 Schneider, G. J. "Sentani ontwaakt." *Nederlands Zendingsblad* 24 (1929): 108-9.
The Pamai movement, Lake Sentani, 1928; by a local missionary.

818 Schoorl, J. W. "Salvation movements among the Muyu-Papuas of West Irian." In *Explorations in the anthropology of religion*, edited by W. E. A. van Beek and J. H. Scherer. The Hague: M. Nijhoff, 1975, pp. 166-89, map. Reprinted in *Irian* (Jayapura) 7, no. 2 (1978): 3-35.

English translation of his 1957 dissertation on four Muyu movements, except for the fourth, which is included in entry 819. The 1950 (under Terenem) and 1951-52 (under Jeknon and Kawon) movements are regarded as arising outside Western influence; Koeram's movement of 1953; pp. 167-70, 185-88, interpretation as social movements merely using religious forms for material ends.

819 Schoorl, J. W. "Shell capitalism among the Muyu people." *Irian* (Jayapura) 5, no. 3 (October 1976): 3-78.

The essence of his 1957 dissertation, including the fourth movement, and with interpretation as in entry 818.

820 Souter, Gavin. *New Guinea – The last unknown*. Sydney, etc.: Angus & Robertson (1963) 1967, 296 pp., illus.

Pp. 129, 151, 238-42, Mansren and other cults from 1880s in Geelvink Bay; a brief popular outline.

821 Sowada, Alphonse A. "An appeal for justice: 'The Ayam revolt.' (August 1975-July 1977)." In *Asmat Sketch Book no. 7*. Asmat: Asmat Museum of Culture and Progress; distributed by Crosier Missions, 3204 East 43d St., Minneapolis, 1980, pp. 5-55, illus.

By a Catholic Missionary bishop.

822 Spreeuwenberg, H. "De Simson-beweging." In *Kruis en Korwar. Een honderd-jarig Waagstuk op Nieuw-Guinea*, edited by F. C. Kamma. The Hague: J. N. Voorhoeve, 1953, pp. 155-60.

823 Sunda, James. *Church-growth in the Central Highlands of West New Guinea*. Lucknow: Lucknow Publishing House, 1963, 51 pp., graphs.

Pp. 24-31, the 1955 fetish-burning movement in the Ilaga valley, culminating among the Dani in 1960; the missionaries' debate on the issue.

824 ten Haaft, D. A. "De betekenis van de 'Manseren'-beweging van 1904 voor het Zendgswerk op de Noordkust van Nieuw-Guinea." *De Heerbaan* (Amsterdam) 1, no. 3 (1948): 71-81.

Irian Jaya

825 ten Haaft, D. A. "De Manseren-beweging op Noord Nieuw-Guinea 1939-1943." *Tijdschrift Nieuw-Guinea* (The Hague) 8, no. 6 (1948): 161-65; 9, no. 1 (1948): 1-8. English summaries.

826 ten Haaft, D. A. "De Manseren-Mangoendi-beweging op Biak." *Tijdschrift Nieuw-Guinea* (The Hague) 7 (1946-47): 144.

827 Teutscher, H[endricus] J[acobus]. "Die Messianische Bewegung auf Japen (Niederlandisch-Neuguinea)." *Evangelische Missions-Zeitschrift* 12, no. 2 (1955): 33-39.

828 Teutscher, H[endricus] J[acobus]. "Some mission problems in post-war Indonesia: Experiences in Dutch New Guinea." *International Review of Missions*, no. 148 [37] (1948): 410-20.
    The Manseren myth and its revival during and after World War II.

829 Thimme, Hans-Martin. "Manarmakeri: Theological evaluation of an old Biak myth." *Christ in Melanesia. Point* (Goroka), 1977, pp. 21-49.
    By a theological teacher in the Reformed Church Seminary, Jayapura. Claims that the text of this influential myth has a literal meaning the reverse of millenarian.

830 Thimme, Hans-Martin. "Some notes on the myth of Koreri (with text in Biak)." *Irian: Bulletin of Irian Jaya Development* 6, no. 1 (1977): 3-45.

831 Tichelman, G. L. *Draaiboek van Nieuw Guinee*. The Hague: National Nieuw Guinee Comite, 1951, pp. 39-43.
    The Manseren Manggundi myth and its various manifestations in movements–in 1914, 1942-43 (suppressed by the Japanese), 1945-47.

832 Tichelman, G. L. "Messianisme op Nieuw-Guinea." *Salvo* 2, no. 12 (1948-49): 240.

833 Tichelman, G. L. "Papoese Heilsverwachtigen." *Studium Generale* (West Berlin and New York) [6?], no. 2 (1960?): 41-44.

834 Tijdeman, E. "De legende van Meok Woendi." In *Mededeelingen van het Bureau voor de Bestuurszaken der Buitenbezittingen, bewerkt door het Encyclopaedisch Bureau*. Vol. 2. The Hague: M. Nijhoff, 1912, pp. 253-56.

A later report on a *konoor* in the Biak area from 1884–extract in F. C. Kamma (entry 761) p. 131; p. 256, imprisonment of *konoor* Mangginomi of Numfor in 1914.

835 Trenkenschuh, F[rank A.]. "The Ayam revolt, April 1981: A report and analysis." In *Asmat Sketch Book no. 8.* Agats, Irian Jaya: Asmat Museum of Culture and Progress; distributed by Crosier Missions, 3204 East 43d St., Minneapolis, 1982, pp. 95-120.

836 Trenkenschuh, F[rank A.]. "Cargo cult in Asmat: Examples and prospects." In *Asmat Sketch Book no. 2.* Djajapura, Irian Jaya: [Catholic] Diocese of Agats; Asmat: Asmat Museum of Culture and Progress; distributed by Crosier Missions, 3204 East 43d St., Minneapolis, 1970, pp. 97-109.

Two examples of cargo cults; future prospects. By a Catholic missionary-anthropologist.

837 Tucker, Frank. "The relationship between cargo cult and rebel movement in Irian Jaya." *Catalyst* (Goroka) 18, no. 2 (1988):163-86.

An important survey by an Australian missionary, using several unpublished studies, of the relation of OPM (Operasi Papua Merdeka) to the Koreri movement (from which it developed historically) and to cargoism among the Ekagi and the Moni people, the western Dani, the Asmat, and in the Lakes Plains area; millennialism as the common basis; how to minister in these situations.

838 United Nations Temporary Executive Authority in West New Guinea–West Irian. Bureau of Native Affairs. *Working Papers in Dani Ethnology*, no. 1 (October 1962): Section D, pp. 47-62, 92-96.

P. 48, L. F. B. Dubbeldam, "Some thoughts on nativistic movements"; pp. 49-53, G. W. Grootenhuis, "Nativistic movements" (surveys types and theories of causes); pp. 54-58, Gordon F. Larson, "The fetish burning movement among the Western Dani Papuans" (by a missionary from Ilaga who followed Jabonep's fetish-burning, in 1960, to correct the effects); pp. 59-60, Denise A. O'Brien, "Nativistic movements" (on mass burnings of ritual and other objects among the Bokondini Dani in the Swart valley, 1960-1962 [see entry 795 for a revised and extended version]); pp. 61-62, Anton Ploeg, "Nativistic movements among the Bokondini Dani" (burning of ritual objects, 1960); pp. 92-96, discussion by the above authors. All on similar or connected movements after a short contact with missions.

Irian Jaya

839 Venema, H. "De weg naar het Koninkrijk" (Parts 1-3). *Tot Aan de Einden der Aarde* 11, no. 2 (1986): 26-28; no. 3 (1986): 50-51; no. 4 (1986): 74-75.
Report of a salvation movement in southern Irian Jaya, 1984-85, by a Reformed missionary in the area.

840 Vries, James A. de. "Cargo expectations among the Kwerba people." In *Point*. Series 2, *Religious movements in Melanesia today (1)*, edited by W. Flannery. Goroka: Melanesian Institute, 1983, pp. 25-30.

841 Vries, Jan B. K. de. "De hitte en de papierwinkel." *Tot Aan de Einden der Aarde* 9, no. 9 (1985): 246-47.

842 Vries, Jan B. K. de. "Salvation movement in the Mandobo area, Irian Jaya 1976/77." *Arsip Raad voor de Zending*. Mimeo. Reprinted in *Point*. Series 2, *Religious movements in Melanesia today (1)*, edited by W. Flannery. Goroka: Melanesian Institute, 1983, pp. 31-51.

843 "'Wege Bage' beweging." *Nederlands Nieuw-Guinea* (National New-Guinea Comite) 10, no. 4 (1962): 31.

844 "De wege-bage, een Messias-beweging aan Wisselmeren." *De Tifa*, no. 204 (26 March 1960), pp. 2-3.

845 Werkman, O. "Het daghet in het osten." *Het Penningske: Maandblaadje, uit-gaande van de samenwerkende Zendings-Vereenigingen* (Utrecht), no. 4 (April 1931), pp. 1-4.
P. 2, a Martawar movement about 1930.

846 Wilden, J. J. van der. "The road of the Kuasep." *Irian* 10, no. 2 (1982): 1-49.
A study about background and motivations behind the Kemtuik millennial movements.

847 Yost, James A. "A preliminary report on the Comoro 'Cargo cult' movement." In *Religious movements in Melanesia: A selection of case studies and reports*, edited by W. Flannery. Goroka: Melanesian Institute, 1983, pp. 111-15. Mimeo.

848 Yost, Jim, and Yost, Joan. "Cargo cult to church growth." *Regions Beyond* (Philadelphia, R.B.M.U.) 34, no. 2 (1983): 12-13.
Mare's movement among the Sawi in Comoro, and how missionaries dealt with it in the early 1980s.

849 Zevering, K. H. "Een heilsbeweging onder de Auwjoe. Schets van een acculturatieproces." Archief Ministrie Overzeese Gebiedsdelen. The Hague, [1961?], 79 pp. Typescript.

A cargo movement among the Auyu, 1953; a sketch of an acculturation process, its religious and revolutionary aspects and spread to the Yakai in 1960.

New Caledonia

In relation to its size, New Caledonia has fewer recorded movements than other parts of Melanesia; only two are documented here. One cannot be sure whether this is a characteristic it shares with some other French-controlled territories in the Pacific or whether it is due to lack of research and reporting. It was annexed to France in 1853 and has been an "overseas territory" since 1946, with a large French population.

850 Clifford, James. *Person and myth: Maurice Leenhardt in the Melanesian world*. Berkeley: University of California Press, 1982, xii + 270 pp., illus., bib.

Pp. 163-70, Pwagach's neoprimal movement from the 1920s and Leenhardt's "conversion" of him in 1939.

851 Dousset, Roselene. *Colonialisme et contradictions: Étude sur les causes socio-historiques de l'insurrection de 1878 en Nouvelle-Calèdonie*. Le Monde d'Outre-Mer Passé et Présent. 3d ser., Essais, 10. Paris and The Hague: Mouton, 1970, 208 pp., illus.

Useful as study of a "negative case" or reaction alternative to cargoism.

852 Guiart, Jean [Charles Robert]. "Forerunners of Melanesian nationalism." *Oceania* 22, no. 2 (December 1951): 81-90.

Pp. 83-84, the new "red god" or Doki cult of 1939; pp. 84, 88, the Communist-inspired cargo-type movement of Pwagac on Lifu, Loyalty Islands, 1945.

853 Guiart, Jean [Charles Robert]. "Naissance et avortement d'un messianisme: Colonisation et décolonisation en Nouvelle-Calédonie." *Archives de Sociologie des Religions*, no. 7 [4] (1959): 3-44.

On Pwagac from 1932, a healer-diviner converted by Leenhardt in 1938, exiled to the New Hebrides and died there in 1955.

New Caledonia

854 Kroef, J[ustus] M[aria] van der. "Racial messiahs." In *Race, individual, and collective behaviour*, edited by E. T. Thompson and E. C. Hughes. Glencoe: Free Press, 1958, 357-74.

> P. 361, brief account of the movement on Lifu described by J. Guiart entry 852 and based on this article.

New Guinea (within Papua New Guinea)

This term is sometimes found in a geographical sense for the whole island of New Guinea. Items here refer to the political unit that has been known as New Guinea, the northeastern area of the island. This was known as German New Guinea (1899-1914), then as New Guinea while a League of Nations mandate to Australia (1921-46) and while a United Nations Trust territory under Australia (1946-75). In 1975 it united with Papua, etc., as independent Papua New Guinea. In view of the historical and geographical distinctions, we retain this term in a political sense to include the seven provinces of West and East Sepik, Western and Eastern Highlands, Chimbu, Madang, and Morobe. Some new movements may be regarded as independent churches and most have expressed a cargo ideology, but in the 1970s some remained within or more connected with the churches as "revivals."

855 Adams, Robert. "The Pitenamu society." In *Micronationalist movements in Papua New Guinea*, edited by R. J. May. Department of Political and Social Change, Monograph 1. Canberra: The Department, Research School of Pacific Studies, Australian National University, 1982. Reprinted in *Point*. Series 2, *Religious movements in Melanesia today (1)*, edited by W. Flannery. Goroka: Melanesian Institute, 1983, pp. 310-170.

856 Aenyo, Amos. "Report on the Spirit movement: Mareanda area of Kandep–Enga Province." Paper presented at Melanesian Institute Seminar on New and Ongoing Religious Movements in Melanesia, Goroka, November 1980, 5 pp. Mimeo.

857 Ahrens, Theodor. "Christian syncretism: A study from the Southern Madang District." *Catalyst* (Goroka) 4, no. 1 (1974): 3-40.

> Uses the "Lo-bos" congregation in Astrolabe Bay as the case study.

858 Ahrens, Theodor. "Kirche, Volkschristentum und Volksreligion in Melanesien." In *Volkschristentum und Volksreligion im Pazifik: Wiederentdeckung des Mythos für den christlichen Glaube*, by Theodor

Ahrens and Walter J. Hollenweger. Perspektiven der Weltmission. Schriftenreihe der Missionsakademie an der Universität Hamburg . . . 4. Frankfurt: Verlag Otto Lembeck, [1977], pp. pp. 11-80.

Pp. 11-14, the "Lo-bos" movement of Astrolabe Bay as producing more valuable answers than the local Christian congregations; pp. 43-72, the dialogue between Christianity and primal religions, especially pp. 47-51 on withholding of revealed knowledge; pp. 75-80, local versions of the Kilibob and Manuba myth. An important study.

859 Ahrens, Theodor. "New buildings on old foundations? 'Lo-bos' and Christian congregations in Astrolabe Bay." *Point* (Goroka), no. 1 (1974), pp. 29-49.

By a German Lutheran missionary scholar. For fuller version see entry 860.

860 Ahrens, Theodor, and Hollenweger, Walter J. *Volkschristentum und Volksreligion im Pazifik. Wiederentdeckung des Mythos für den christlichen Glaube.* Perspektiven der Weltmission. Schriftenreihe der Missionsakademie an der Universität Hamburg . . . 4. Frankfurt: Verlag Otto Lembeck, [1977], 124 pp.

See T. Ahrens (entry 859).

861 Ahrens, Theodor, et al. "Cargo cult movements." In *A study of the Lutheran Church in the Bena area.* Goroka: Melanesian Institute, [1975], separate pagination, 1-40.

P. 15, outlines of Yali cult 1966, and Muliapo's cult 1969.

862 Allen, B[ryant] J[ames]. "Information flow and innovation diffusion in the East Sepik district, Papua New Guinea." Ph.D. thesis (geography), Australian National University, 1976, 452 pp., illus., maps, tables.

The relations of "bisnis" and "kago"—their motivations, tenets, and channels through which they spread, with the latter liable to displace the former when it fails to fulfil expectations; pp. 103-4, 257-65, Kirapkirap movement; pp. 265-67, Red Box movement 1963-64; pp. 140-70, 267-80, Yaliwan and Peli Association.

863 Allen, Bryant J[ames]. "The north coast region." In *A time to plant and a time to uproot*, edited by D. Denoon and C. Snowden. Port Moresby: Institute of Papua New Guinea Studies, 1981, pp. 105-27.

Includes the Peli Association.

New Guinea

864 Allen, Bryant J[ames]. "Pangu or Peli: Dreikikir open electorate." In *Prelude to Self-Government*, edited by D. Stone. Canberra: Australian National University, 1976, pp. 133-59.

865 Allen, Bryant J[ames]. *"The road was blocked so we tried another road."* Working Paper 15. Port Moresby: Department of Agriculture, 1979. Mimeo.
    Includes the Peli Association.

866 Aufenanger, Heinrich. "Heilbringer und Kulturheroen in Neuguinea." *Verbum* (Rome) 11 (1970): 189-95.
    By a Catholic missionary anthropologist.

867 Aufenanger, Henry. *The passing scene in northeast New Guinea (A documentation)*. Collectanea Instituti Anthropos, 2. St. Augustin-bei-Bonn: Anthropos Institut, 1972, 479 pp., illus., map.
    Pp. 2-4, the secret names of God; p. 247, myth of the two brothers; pp. 165-68, "beng-beng" money-seeking cargo cult behind Wewak in the early 1960s, and later disillusionment.

868 Aufinger, Albert. "Die Mythe vom Brüderpaar Kilibob und Manup auf den Yabob Inseln, Neuguineas." *Anthropos* 36-40, nos. 1-3 (1942): 45, 313-15.
    A Catholic missionary on the myth of the two brothers that lies behind many cargo cults.

869 Australia, Commonwealth of. *Reports to the Council of the League of Nations on the administration of the Territory of New Guinea*. Canberra: Commonwealth Government Printer, 1932-50.
    For 1930-31 (1932): p. 96, movement in Aitape district, 1931.
    For 1934-35 (1936): pp. 19-21, Marafi's movement, Morobe District [reprinted in *The South Seas in transition*, by W. E. H. Stanner (entry 480, pp. 59-61);
    For 1939-40 (1941): pp. 27-28, "Letup singsing" in Madang District.
    For 1948-49 (1950): p. 58, "mild" cargo cults in Sepik area, (and in Solus area of Bougainville) – "treated with sympathy and patience."

870 Baar, Wilhelm van. "Ein ganz eigentümlicher Vorgang." *Steyler Missionsbote* 59 (1931-32): 127-28.
    Kudju movement – quoted in G. Hoeltker (entry 970), p. 397.

871 Bader, Otto. "Im Dunkel des Heidentums." *Steyler Missionsbote* 63 (1935-36): 287-88.
The Black Kings movement in Uligan in 1935.

872 Bamler, G[eorg]. "Missionsstation Siassi, 1923 Januar bis June, [and] Juli bis Dez." *Neuendettelsauer Missionsblatt* 15, no. 12 [82, no. 12] (1925): 112-13.
Cargo ideology on the northeast coast.

873 Bamler, Heinrich. "Attitudes of the Lutheran Church in New Guinea towards cargo cult." Paper presented at Melanesian Institute Orientation Course, Mt. Hagen, 1971, 10 pp. Mimeo.
A sympathetic view of movements as basically sincere and religious, therefore capable of theological interpretation. By a German Lutheran missionary.

874 Bamler, Heinrich. "Cargo cults movements in the Highlands." Paper presented at Melanesian Institute Orientation Course, Mt. Hagen, 1971, 9 pp. Mimeo.
Both theoretical explanation and first-hand reports of movements in the 1950s, Okapa subdistrict, and in 1963 above the Markham valley.

875 Barnes, Helene, ed. *Niugini reader*. North Melbourne, Victoria: Australian Union of Students, 1972, 55 pp., illus., maps, tables.
See M. Weinstock (entry 1166) and J. Waiko (entry 1258).

876 Barr, [Kevin] John. "Spirit movements in the Highlands United Church." In *Point*. Series 3, *Religious movements in Melanesia today (2)*, edited by W. Flannery. Goroka: Melanesian Institute, 1983, pp. 144-54.

877 Bartholomaüs (Brother) [B. Kubitza]. "Die vier Propheten bei Wewak, Mittel-neuguinea." *Steyler Missionsbote* 60 (1932-33): 107-8. Reprinted in "The birth of a religious movement: A comparison of Melanesian cargo cults and early Christianity," by T. Aeerts, *Verbum SVD* 20, no. 4 (1979): 324
Republication of letter on the Black Kings prophets in 1931, and the Walman movements of 1931, by a Catholic missionary.

878 Bennett, Keith, and Smith, Lindsay. "A revival movement among the Telefomin Baptist Churches." In *Religious movements in Melanesia: A selection of case studies and reports*, edited by W. Flannery. Goroka: Melanesian Institute, 1983, pp. 127-46. Mimeo.

New Guinea

879 Bergmann, Gustav. "Boana." *Neuendettelsauer Missionsblatt* 26, no. 5 [93, no. 5] (1936): 34-36.
An apocalyptic movement in the Huon Peninsula, 1935-36; see extract in G. Eckert (entry 311), p. 30.

880 Bergmann, Gustav. "Eine papuanische Schwärmerei." *Neuendettelsauer Missionsblatt* 24, no. 4 [91, no. 4] (1934): 28.
A cargo cult in the Huon Peninsula in 1933; see extracts in G. Eckert (entry 311), pp. 29-30.

881 Bergmann, Gustav. "Von der Sattelberggemeinde, Jahresbericht 1931." *Neuendettelsauer Missionsblatt* 22, no. 7 [89, no. 7] (1932): 50.
On money-making and the Eemasang revival.

882 Bergmann, Heinrich Friedrich Wilhelm. *Vierzig Jahre in Neuguinea*. His daily diary mimeographed in 12 vols. for private circulation. Vol. 7, 248 pp., ca. January 1948.
Pp. 1-151, exact descriptions of new movements, especially pp. 32-151 on cargo cults in the Hube area, 1945-47.

883 Berndt, R[onald] M. "A cargo movement in the Eastern Highlands of New Guinea." *Oceania* 23, no. 1 (1952): 40-65; no. 2 (1952): 137-58; no. 3 (1953): 202-34.
Pp. 47-50, theory of cargo cults; pp. 56-65, movement around Kogu village; pp. 137-48, in adjacent areas; pp. 148-58, aftermath and conclusions; pp. 202-4, 22 texts as appendixes (with English translations of those in vernacular) including following patrol reports: no. 16 (p. 226), R. I. Skinner, 1947-48; no. 18 (pp. 227-30), Lieut. Ewing on "Religious revival," 1943; no. 19 (pp. 230-32), Lieut. Stevenson on "Preternatural cult," 1944-45; nos. 20 and 21 (pp. 232-33), D. S. Groves reports for 1947-48; no. 22 (p. 234), A. T. Timperley, 1948-49.

884 "'Bisnis' and cargo cults." *Bisnis Newsletter* (Department of Business Development, Port Moresby), no. 7 (August 1971), pp. 5-6. Reprinted as "Cargo: Government waging war on wishful thinking and the 'spirit' world." *Focus: New Guinea* (Port Moresby, Papua New Guinea News Service), no. 5 (September 1971), pp. 11, 18.
An attack on the Yangoru cult in East Sepik after the Mt. Turu episode.

885 "Bisschop contra Satan: Cargo-cult Australisch Nieuw Guinea." *Bijeen* (Hertogenbosch) (October 1972): 29-30, illus.
On Bishop Leo Arkfeld, an American.

886 Blood, N[eptune] B. N. "Extract of Report of patrol by Captain N. B. Blood, A.D.O. from Hagen to Ifitamin, in Australian New Guinea Administrative Unit." *Final report of activities*, 1 July 1945-23 June 1946, Appendix A, 7 pp.

On a "Great Pigs" movement with large cult houses in the Western Highlands, and his use of educational talks rather than force; later oral report in C. Simpson (entry 1110), pp. 256-57.

887 Blood, N[eptune] B. N. "Report on patrol to Bagasin area, Madang District, in Australian New Guinea Administrative Unit (Native Affairs)." *Report on activities*, January-February 1945, Appendix C, 10 pp.

Describes a cult movement led by Gomaip, and a police attack on it.

888 Brown, Paula B. "Chimbu tribes: Political organization in the Eastern Highlands District." *Southwestern Journal of Anthropology* 16, no. 1 (1960): 22-35. Reprinted in *Peoples and cultures of the Pacific*, edited by A. P. Vayda. Garden City, N.Y.: Natural History Press, 1968, pp. 451-85. [Paper presented at 34th Congress of the Australia and New Zealand Association for Advancement of Science, Perth, 1959.]

Cargo cults, passim.

889 Brown, Paula B. *The Chimbu: A study of change in New Guinea Highlands*. International Library of Anthropology. London: Routledge, 1973, 151 pp., illus.

"Cargo thinking," passim; "no fully developed cults in the Highlands."

890 Burman, Ben Lucien. "In N. G. they're still waiting for cargo." *Pacific Islands Monthly* 39, no. 1 (1968): 54-56, illus.

Includes a "bank" cult in the Western Highlands District, 1967.

891 Burridge, K[enelm] O[swald] L[ancelot]. "Cargo cult activity in Tangu." *Oceania* 24, no. 4 (1954): 241-54.

Theories and beliefs about a man "Mambu" who discovers the secret of the Europeans; in 1952, among the Riekans (one of the four Tangu groups).

892 Burridge, K[enelm] O[swald] L[ancelot]. *Mambu: A Melanesian millennium*. London: Methuen; New York: Humanities Press, 1960, xxiii + 296 pp., illus. 2d ed. New York: Harper & Row, 1970, pp. 250-

New Guinea

59. Reprinted in *Mythology: Selected readings*, edited by P. Miranda. Harmondsworth: Penguin Books, 1970, pp. 127-35.

A now-classic, sensitive study of Mambu's Black King movement of 1937 among the Tangu and later developments. Cargo movements operate through "myth-dreams" where the cargo symbolizes moral renewal and integrity.

893 Burridge, K[enelm] O[swald] L[ancelot]. "Racial tension in Manam." *South Pacific* 7, no. 13 (1954): 932-38.

The problems of Manam islanders in understanding whites and their resultant tendencies toward cargo cults.

894 Burridge, K[enelm] O[swald] L[ancelot]. *Tangu traditions*. Oxford: Clarendon Press, 1969, 538 pp., illus., maps.

Pp. 26, 28-36, cargo activity and Yali; pp. 334-37, 438-41, 454-57, 466-69, Tangu culture and Christianity.

895 Burton-Bradley, B[urton] G. "The New Guinea prophet: Is the cultist always normal?" *Medical Journal of Australia*, no. 1 (17 January 1970), pp. 124-29.

Surveys nine "abnormal prophets"; reviewed in *R. M. Bucke Memorial Society Newsletter-Review* (Montreal) 4, nos. 1-2 (1971): 60-61.

896 Burton-Bradley, B[urton] G. "Psychiatric implications of the New Guinea cargo cult." Paper presented at East-West Center Institute of Advanced Projects Seminar, Honolulu, June 1970, 10 pp. Mimeo.

897 Camp, Cheryl. "The Mt. Huron movement. The Peli Association and the New Apostolic Church." In *Point*. Series 2, *Religious movements in Melanesia today (1)*, edited by W. Flannery. Goroka: Melanesian Institute, 1983, pp. 78-93.

Yaliwan's "church," and Hawina's Peli Association's relations with a Canadian church that sends missionaries for brief visits and secures temporary mass responses, largely from Peli members; see entry 1089.

898 "Cargo cults for 'The good life.'" *Focus: New Guinea* (Port Moresby, Papua New Guinea News Service), no. 2 (May 1971), p. 23.

Early report on the Mt. Turu, Yangoru cultists; list of 17 movements in "the sorry history of cargo cults."

899 Catechist Training Centre, Maiwara. *Handbuk bilong culture-class*. Maiwara, Madang: The Centre, November 1972, 76 pp. In Pidgin.

Pp. 35-52, Kago kalt (advice to catechists on dealing with cultists; pp. 53 (i)-53 (vi), Mt. Hurun movement (in English). Copy at Melanesian Institute.

900 Cramb, George, and Kolo, Mapusiya. "Revival among Western Highlands/Enga Baptists." In *Point*. Series 3, *Religious movements in Melanesia today (2)*, edited by W. Flannery. Goroka: Melanesian Institute, 1983, pp. 93-112.

901 Davenport, William. Review of *Road belong Cargo*, by Peter Lawrence (entry 1025). *American Anthropologist* 68, no. 1 (1966): 236-38.

902 Dawia, Alexander. "A revival convention, Lumusa Baptist Church Baiyer River." In *Religious movements in Melanesia: A selection of case studies and reports*, edited by W. Flannery. Goroka: Melanesian Institute, 1983, pp. 121-23. Mimeo.

Lessons for the churches from the Baptist revival convention at Baiyer River; reply to criticisms of revival as disruptive.

903 De'Ath, Colin. "Cargo cults, millennial thinking, and salvation history." *Bikmaus: A Journal of Papua New Guinea Affairs, Ideas, and the Arts* (Boroko) 2, no. 1 (1981): 25-35.

On the "perennial" Yali cult.

904 De'Ath, Colin. "Christians in the Trans-Gogol and the Madang provinces." *Bikmaus II: A Journal of Papua New Guinea Affairs, Ideas, and the Arts* (Boroko) 2, no. 2 (1981): 66-88.

905 Dewdney, M. S. "The Maprik open electorate." In *The Papua-New Guinea elections, 1964*, edited by D. G. Bettison, C. A. Hughes, and P. van der Veur. Canberra: Australian National University, 1965, pp. 184, 190.

Cargo ideas in the elections: a Catholic catechist candidate who promised cargo; Bolgun's warnings against cargo instead of hard work.

906 Dollinger, Hans. "Kargokult in Neuguinea." *Lutherisches Missionsjahrbuch 1962*. Nurnberg: Bayerische Missionskonferenz, pp. 88-95.

On prophet Ku's cult at Kaliku, Madang District, 1956.

New Guinea

907 Eckert, Georg. "Der Goldbergbau in Deutsch-Neuguinea." *Koloniale Rundschau* (Berlin and Leipzig) (1936): 465-74.
P. 473, "Donkey" cargo movement, Huon Peninsula, 1935-36.

908 Eppelein, F. "Die Emasang-Bewegung (Aufräumungsbewegung) auf Neuguinea in ihrer Bedeuting für die Reichgottesarbeit daheim und draussen." *Freimund* (Neuendettelsau), no. 41 (8 October 1931), pp. 314-18.
The Eemasang revival.

909 Essai, Brian. *Papua and New Guinea: A contemporary survey.* Melbourne: Oxford University Press, 1961, 255 pp.
Pp. 52-56, cargo cults.

910 Evangelical Lutheran Church of New Guinea. "Riport bilong nambawan nasenal Luteran pasto konprens, 3-9 Februeri 1975." Edited by Peyandi Lepi. Lae: Evangelism department, ELCONG, 1975, 62 pp. Mimeo.
Pp. 33-39, report of S. Saurgaria's talk, including cargo cult; pp. 40-44, discussion. In Pidgin.

911 Fairbairn, I. J.; Fugmann, W.; and Sankoff, G. *Namasu: New Guinea's largest indigenous-owned company.* New Guinea Research Bulletin 28. Canberra and Port Moresby: New Guinea Research Unit, Australian National University, March 1969, 90 pp.
Pp. 2-3, cargo ideas (by Fugmann); pp. 74-75, cargo ideas (by Sankoff). In relation to a successful native marketing and supply service encouraged by the Lutheran Mission.

912 Faivre, Jean-Paul, and Sokoloff, Vera. "Mikloukho-Maklai (1846-1888): À l'occasion du centenaire de sa naissance." *Journal de la Société des Océanistes* 3 (1947): 93-102.
On first white contacts, as background to cargo ideas.

913 Feacham, Richard. "The Christians and the Enga '. . . misin i foulim mi!'" *New Guinea and Australia, the Pacific and South-East Asia* (Sydney) 8, no. 1 (1973): 36-44.
Critical of missions as largely responsible for cargo beliefs and other hindrances to development.

914 Feldt, Eric [Augustus]. *The Coast Watchers.* Melbourne: Oxford University Press, 1946, 425 pp., illus., maps.

Pp. 365-74, Yali's escape from the destruction of a coastwatching party destroyed by the Japanese, and how his version has been incorporated into the Yali legend.

915 Finney, Ben R[udolph]. "Bigfellow man belong business in New Guinea." *Ethnology* 7 (1968): 394-410. Reprinted in *Melanesia: Readings on culture area*, edited by L. L. Langness and J. C. Weschler. Scranton, London, and Toronto: Chandler Publishing Co., 1971, pp. 315-32.
   The success of business entrepreneurs in the Goroka area, as in the Gazelle Peninsula, as rational economic development; p. 407, contrast with cargo cults.

916 Finney, Ben R[udolph]. *Big-men and business: Entrepreneurship and economic growth in the New Guinea Highlands.* Canberra: Australian National University Press, 1973, 106 pp.
   Chap. 6 (pp. 123-45), "Preadaptions, preconditions and cargo cults," especially pp. 137-45, cargo cults and the Goroka people, with mention of Black Kings, Great Pigs, Ghost Wind, and Hine movements.

917 Fischer, Hans. "Cargo-Ideen." *Anthropos* 61, nos. 1-2 (1966): 49-97, illus., map.
   Pp. 49-55, introduction; pp. 56-97, Pidgin and German texts of his interviews concerning a cargo cult and cargo ideas among the Wampur of the lower Markham valley in 1965.

918 Flannery, Wendy. "All prophets: Revival movements in the Catholic and Lutheran Churches in the Highlands." *Catalyst* (Goroka) 10, no. 4 (1980): 229-57.
   Two Pentecostal-type movements.

919 Flannery, Wendy. "Bilip Grup." In *Point.* Series 3, *Religious movements in Melanesia today (2)*, edited by W. Flannery. Goroka: Melanesian Institute, 1983, pp. 155-93.
   The Bilip Grup or "Belief Group" from 1976 in Morobe Province, Warea River valley.

920 Flierl, Johann. *E-Emasang, die Erneuerungsbewegung in der Gemeinde Sattelberg (Neuguinea).* Allegemeine Missions-Studien, 11. Gütersloh: Bertelsmann, 1931.

New Guinea

921 Flierl, Johann. *E-Emasang; oder die wunderbare Heiligungsbewegung in inserer Lutheranischen Missionskirche auf New Guinea*. Taminda, South Australia: Auricht's Druckerei, 1932, 32 pp. English translation. *E-Emasang, or a marvellous movement of sanctification in our Lutheran Mission-Church, New Guinea*. N.p.: Board of the N. G. Mission, n.d., 39 pp.

922 Flierl, W[illi]. Declaration concerning cargo cult. Accepted by 5th Synod, Evangelical Lutheran Church in New Guinea, 5 October 1964.
Missionary Flierl's expanded English translation of the confessional statement he drafted in Kate, as reprinted by F. Steinbauer (entry 485), p. 107; see latter's p. 162 for criticisms. The Synod's official version is in Pidgin and is less severe.

923 Flierl, W[illi]. "New Guinea Ngic Nangâcnao Luther [*sic*] Qâjâpec *Mitigie fua ngeing Ewec Irec Binang*." Madang: Luthern Mission Press, 1962, 330 pp. + 8 pp., illus., map.
A history of Lutheran Mission New Guinea and the indigenous Lutheran Church; pp. 160-64, Eemasang revival 1927; pp. 217-24, Upikno movement. In the Kate language.

924 Fontius, Hanfried. *Mission – Gemeinde – Kirche in Neuguinea, Bayern und bei Karl Steck*. Erlanger Taschenbücher, 28. Erlangen: Verlag der Ev.-Luth. Mission, 1975, 258 pp., bib.
Pp. 17-19, 115, 123, 136, 160-61, 175, cargo cults.

925 Forge, Anthony. "Learning to see in New Guinea." In *Socialization: The approach from social anthropology*, edited by P. Mayer. London: Tavistock, 1970, pp. 269-91.
On the Abelam, Sepik District; p. 271, persistence of traditional *tamberam* cult and resistance to cargo ideas.

926 Fountain, Ossie C. "Religion and economy in mission station-village relationships." *Practical Anthropology* 13, no. 2 (March-April 1966): 49-58. Reprinted in *Catalyst* 2, no. 3 (3d quarter 1972): 33-48.
Pp. 36-37, cargo ideas; whole article is relevant; based on Virnum Mission, Sepik District coastal range.

927 Franke, Reiner. "Cargo-Kult und Christentum im Madang-Distrikt in Neuguinea." (Seminarbeit). St. Augustin: Anthropos Institut, 1966, 68 pp. Mimeo.

928 Frankel, Stephen. "Mass hysteria in the New Guinea highlands. A Telefomim outbreak and its relationship to other New Guinea hysterical reactions." *Oceania* 47, no. 2 (1976-77): 106-33.

"Epidemic hysteria" at Telefomin, 1973-74, similar to Vailala madness; followed by theoretical discussion.

929 Frerichs, A[lbert] C. "Vailala-Madness." *Lutheran Missionary* (Ohio, American Lutheran Church) 27, no. 5 (1947): 2.

930 Frerichs, Albert [C.], and Frerichs, Sylvia. *Utu conquers in New Guinea: A story of mission work in New Guinea*. Minneapolis: Augsburg Publishing House, 1957. 2d rev. ed. 1969, 160 pp., illus.

An outline of Madang District mission history; pp. 34-35, cargo beliefs and misunderstandings regarding whites.

931 Freund, A. P. H. "Papua New Guinea had cargo cults long before the white man came." *Post-Courier* (Port Moresby), 22 February 1976, p. 14.

Based on his forty years' experience, a Lutheran missionary describes cargo cults and their basis in traditional thought. The title is misleading.

932 Freund, Paul Joseph. "Social change among the Kasua, Southern Highlands, Papua New Guinea." Ph.D. dissertation (cultural anthropology), University of Iowa, 1977, 364 pp., illus.

Chap. 4 (pp. 206-43), eye-witness description of a brief cult prompted by comet Kohoutek; relation to political independence, missions, and migrant labour; stresses the creative responses of the Kasua and the neglect of mission influence by researchers.

933 Freund, Roland P. "Western innovations and Laiapu Enga values." Paper presented at 41st ANZAAS Congress, Adelaide, August 1969, 11 pp. Mimeo.

The effect on traditional political, economic, and religious values.

934 Freytag, Walter. *Die junge Christenheit im Umbruch des Ostens*. Berlin, 1938. English translation. *Spiritual revolution in the Far East*. London: Lutterworth Press, 1940, 264 pp.

English translation, pp. 50-51, the Eemasang movement, its context and significance.

New Guinea

935 Fugman, Gernot. "The Lutheran approach: A history of the Evangelical Lutheran Church of New Guinea." *Catalyst* 3, no. 2 (1973): 3-19.
Revivals and cargo cults among the congregations.

936 Fugmann, Wilhelm. *Junge Kirchen zwischen Steinzeit und Neuzeit: Reiseerlebnisse aus Neuguinea.* Neuendettelsau: Freimund Verlag, 1959, 64 pp., illus.
Lutheran missionary among the Hube. Pp. 25-28, "Mitiväter" and "Geldmütter" – local conceptions of money.

937 Fugmann, Wilhelm. *Mambu Jeremiah: Ein Kirchenfuhrer aus Papua-Neuguinea.* Neuendettelsau: Freimund Verlag, 1977, 56 pp.

938 Gerber, Horst. "The so-called cargo cult, a neo-animistic movement among the Hube (Part I)." Paper presented at Melanesian Institute Seminar on Adjustment Cults, Lae, 1976, 23 pp., map. Mimeo.
Detailed history of various cults among the Hube people from 1946 to 1970 and continuing.

939 Gerritsen, Rolf. "Aspects of political evolution of rural Papua New Guinea: Towards a political economy of terminal peasantry." Canberra: Department of Political Science, Research School of Social Sciences, Australian National University, 1975. Mimeo.
Dynamic community groups, universalist and idealist in objectives, seeking cultural regeneration as well as economic development; discussed also as inheritors of the cargo cult legacy.

940 Gesch, Patrick F[rancis]. "Cargo cult: The village-Christian dialogue." Paper presented at Melanesian Institute Seminar on New and On-Going Religious Movements in Melanesia, Goroka, November 1980, 8 pp.
The basic nature of religion as wonder at the unexpected, traced across local primal religion, cargo cults, and Christianity as a common basis for dialogue, with illustrations from the Mt. Hurun or Yaliwan movement.

941 Gesch, Patrick [Francis]. "The cultivation of surprise and excess in traditional village religion meeting the Western technological viewpoint in the Sepik of Papua New Guinea." In *Cargo cults and millenarian movements*, edited by G. W. Trompf. Religion and Society. Berlin: de Gruyter, Mouton Publishers, 1990, pp. 199-222.

942 Gesch, Patrick [Francis]. "Initiation and cargo cults: The Peli case." In *Point*. Series 2, *Religious movements in Melanesia today (1)*, edited by W. Flannery. Goroka: Melanesian Institute, 1983, pp. 94-102.

943 Gesch, Patrick [Francis]. *Initiative and initiation: A cargo cult-type movement in the Sepik against its background in traditional village religion*. Nettetal: Steyler Verlag, 1985, 353 pp. Also published in series Studia Instituti Anthropos, no. 33. St. Augustin: Anthropos Institut, 1985.
The published form of his 1982 dissertation.

944 Gesch, Patrick F[rancis]. "Initiative through initiation: A cargo cult-type movement in the Sepik against its background in traditional religion." Ph.D. thesis (religious studies), University of Sydney, 1982, 535 pp.
On the Yaliwan or Mt. Hurun movement, or the Peli Association; the New Apostolic Church in relation to this movement.

945 Gesch, Patrick F[rancis]. "National unity: Village style." Paper presented at Melanesian Institute Seminar on Adjustment Cults, Lae, 1976, 9 pp. Mimeo. Also presented at Melanesian Institute Orientation Course, 1976.
A Catholic missionary on the Yaliwan or Yangoro and the Peli movements.

946 Gibbs, Philip J. "The cult from Lyeima and the Ipilo." *Oceania* 48, no. 1 (1977): 1-25.
See M. J. Meggitt (entry 1049); the spread, changes and later history of the Ain cult, and contribution to success of missions.

947 Gibbs, Philip J. "Ipili religion past and present: An account of the traditional religion of the people of the Porgera and Paiela valleys of Papua New Guinea and how it has changed with the coming of Christianity." Diploma in Anthropology thesis, University of Sydney, 1975, 209 pp.
Pp. 150-60, the millenarian cult of Ain at Lyeimi from 1944, which M. J. Meggitt (entry 1049) reported to have failed by 1956, but which Gibbs (a Catholic missionary) believes prepared for the massive conversion of the Enga to Christianity.

948 Goerner, Karl. "Emanzipationsbewegung im Kargokultgewand?" *Zeitschrift für Mission* 8, no. 3 (1982): 169-74.
Women's emancipation in the Highlands.

New Guinea

949 Gore, Ralph Thomas. *Justice versus sorcery*. Brisbane: Jacaranda Press, 1965, 218 pp., illus.
Pp. 204-11, trial of Lagit for sacrificial murder 1961; by the trial judge.

950 Goro, E. "Kisim Mani na kago olsem wanem." *Niugini Luteran* 15 (July 1976): 6-9.

951 [Gottvater–Offenbarungen in Suain.] *Steyler Missionsbote* 58 (1930-31): 68-69.
A movement in the Sepik delta in 1930.

952 Guariglia, Guglielmo. *Prophetismus und Heilserwartungs-bewegungen als völkerkundliches und religionsgeschichtliches Problem*. Vienna: F. Berger, 1959, 332 pp.
Pp. 85-87, the 1914-28 Taro cult, the 1921 Timo and Eemasang movements in the Huon Peninsula – each movement classified.

953 Haberland, Eike. "Kulturverfall und Heilserwartung am oberen Korowori (Sepik District, Neuguinea)." *Sociologus*, n.s., 14, no. 2 (1964): 30-44, English summary.
A "negative instance" where cultural decline produced adaptation of myths and adoption of some Western ways but no cargo cults; explained as due to lack of ancestor cults and any belief in an after life.

954 Hanneman, Emil F. "Le culte du cargo en Nouvelle-Guinée." *Le Monde Non-chrétienne*, n.s., 8 (1948): 937-62.
A Lutheran missionary on the Kukuaik movement that began as an independent church.

955 Hanneman, Emil F. "The growth of culture. The Cargo cult and anthropology. A native Church and anthropology." Bumayong School, 1960, 10 + 6 + 6 pp. Mimeo.
First 6 pp. set, "The cargo cult and anthropology": the Madang area reactions to contact since 1870, including Letub, Yali, and Kukuaik; brief comparison with North American Indian Ghost Dance.

956 Harding, Thomas Grayson. "A history of Cargoism in Sio, northeast New Guinea." *Oceania* 38, no. 1 (1967): 1-23.
Lutub cult and Sio Pagan of 1959.

957 Harding, Thomas Grayson. "The Rai Coast open electorate." In *The Papua-New Guinea elections, 1964*, edited by D. G. Bettison, C. A.

Hughes, and P. van der Veur. Canberra: Australian National University Press, 1965, pp. 194-211.

Pp. 196, 211 include influence of cargoism; Stoi and Yali as two cultist candidates – their personal history; pp. 207-211, cargoism as of secondary importance in this election.

958 Harding, Tho[ma]s G[rayson], and Lawrence, Peter. "Cash crops or cargo?" In *The politics of dependence: Papua New Guinea, 1968*, edited by A. L. Epstein, et al. Canberra: Australian National University Press, 1971, pp. 162-217.

959 Harris, Marvin. *Cows, pigs, wars and witches: The riddles of culture.* London: Hutchinson, 1975, 276 pp.

Pp. 133-52, "phantom cargo": explanations of cults, using the Madang area and Yali movement (based on P. Lawrence, entry 1025) as the case study.

960 Hastings, Peter. *New Guinea: Problems and prospects.* 2d ed. Melbourne: Cheshire Publishing, 1973, 303 pp.

Pp. 26-30, 97-98, 104-7, 136, 151, 191, 202, cargo cults and millennial thinking.

961 Hawarry, William. "The Sepik youth movement." In *Tertiary students and the politics of New Guinea. Papers presented at the second seminar of Papua New Guinea tertiary students ... Lae ... August 1971.* Lae: PNG Institute of Technology, 1971, [3 pp.].

The founder of this antiwhite movement in 1969 interprets the recent cargo cult in the Sepik area as due to lack of social and economic development, for which he blames the government, the churches, and business enterprises.

962 H[egarty], D. [W.]. "Political chronicle, the Territory of Papua New Guinea." *Australian Journal of Politics and History* 17, no. 3 (1971): 454-60.

Pp. 458-59, Yangoro incipient cargo cult, East Sepik District, with former mission worker Yaliwan among the leaders.

963 Held, Helene. "Beginn und Fortgang der Missionsarbeit und der Erweckung in Neuguinea." Research paper, Seminar für missionarische Fortbildung, Kurs II, Bad Liebenzell-Monbachtel, 5 February 1983, 19 pp., illus. Xerox.

New Guinea

Various revivals and movements connected with the South Seas Evangelical Mission in the Sepik area – their presuppositions, features, and an evaluation (pros and cons listed).

964 Hempenstall, Peter J. "The reception of European missions in the German empire: The New Guinea experience." *Journal of Pacific History* 10 (1975): 46-64.
The pre-1914 period in New Guinea and the Bismarck Archipelago, with comparison of different missions; pp. 63-64, cargo cults as a continued form of resistance.

965 Henkelman, F. "Kukuaik: Story of the revival movement on Karkar Island, New Guinea." Lae: Lutheran Mission Archives, 1942, 27 pp. Ms.
Copied by Hans Wagner and used by J. F. Wagner (see Author Index).

966 Herrlinger. "Ein modernes Sittenbild." *Neuendettelsauer Missionsblatt* 16, no. 8 [93, no. 8] (15 August 1936): 82.
A cargo cult at Kajabit, Markham valley.

967 Hicks, H. and Hicks, B. "Revival . . . 3 years later: Orkana." *Light and Life* (Unevangelized Fields Mission), May 1977, p. 3.

968 Hitchen, John [Mason]. "Cross-cultural communication of the Gospel." In *God at work in New Guinea*, by K. W. Liddle, et al. Palmerston North, N.Z.: Gospel Publishing Society, [ca. 1970], pp. 25-37.
Pp. 31-32, cargoist interpretation of Genesis chap. 3.

969 Hoeltker, Georg. "Der Cargo-Kult in Neuguinea lebt noch." *Neue Zeitschrift für Missionswissenschaft* 18, no. 3 (1962): 223-26.

970 Hoeltker, Georg. "Die Mambu-Bewegung in Neuguinea: in Beitrag zum Prophetentum in Melanesian." *Annali Lateranensi* (Vatican City) 5 (1941): 181-219, bib. Reprinted in *Menschen und Kulturen in Nordost-Neuguinea: Gesammelte Aufsätze. Festschrift . . . Georg Höltker. . . .* Studia Instituti Anthropos, 29. St. Augustin bei Bonn: Verlag des Anthropos Instituts, 1975, pp. 360-398.
The first major study; by a Catholic missionary.

971 Hoeltker, Georg. *Menschen und Kulturen in Nordost-Neuguinea: Gesammelte Aufsätze. Festschrift . . . Georg Höltker. . . .* Studia Instituti Anthropos, 29. St. Augustin bei Bonn: Verlag des Anthropos Instituts, 1975, 414 pp.

Includes reprints of his "Die Mambu-bewegung . . ." (entry 970), pp. 360-98, and his "Schwärmgeister . . ." (entry 973), pp. 399-414.

972 Hoeltker, Georg. "Neues vom Cargo-Kult in Neuguinea." *Neue Zeitschrift für Missionswissenschaft* 19 (1963): 115.
A note on information from Fr. John Steirer, SVD, re movement in Wagital, 1962.

973 Hoeltker, Georg. "Schwärmgeister in Neu Guinea wahrend des letzen Krieges." *Neue Zeitschrift für Missionswissenschaft* (Beckenried) 2, no. 3 (1946): 201-16, bib. Abbreviated English translation. "How 'cargo-cult' is born: The scientific angle of an old subject." *Pacific Islands Monthly* (Sydney) 17, no. 4 (1946): 16, 70. Reprinted in *Menschen und Kulturen in Nordost-Neuguinea: Gesammelte Aufsätze. Festschrift . . . Georg Höltker.* . . . Studia Instituti Anthropos, 29. St. Augustin bei Bonn: Verlag des Anthropos Instituts, 1975, pp. 399-414.
Lists movements in Papua 1983-20, 1941, and in New Guinea 1921-43.

974 Hoeltker, Georg. "Zum 'Cargo-cult' in Neu Guinea." *Neue Zeitschrift für Missionswissenschaft* 20 (1964): 296.

975 Hofmann, G[eorg]. "Das Evangelium im Kampf mit dem Unglauben." *In Alle Welt* (Neuendettelsau), no. 4 (April 1949), pp. 2-3.

976 Hogbin, H[erbert] I[an Priestley]. "Native Christianity in a New Guinea Village." *Oceania* 18, no. 1 (1947): 1-33.

977 Hogbin, H[erbert] I[an Priestley]. *Transformation scene: The changing culture of a New Guinea village.* London: Routledge & Kegan Paul, 1951, xii + 362 pp., illus., maps.
Pp. 284-85, beliefs in magic and ritual and misunderstandings re whites underlie cults.

978 Hogg, Louise, and Robertson, Susan. "The Madang earthquake: Six weeks after." *Oceania* 41, no. 4 (1971): 298-311.
The variety of local explanations (grouped in terms of "omen" or "chastening"), including those of Christians and cargo cultists; Yali and his followers, passim.

979 Holl, Gotthilf. "Cargo-Hoffningen bei den Washkuk." Research paper, Seminar für Missionarische Fortbildung, December 1981, 13 pp. Photocopy.

New Guinea

A cargo movement among the Washkuk of east Sepik in 1978-80 – expectations of cargo accompanied by magical healings; in the Liebenzeller Mission area.

980 Horsfield, Don. "Cargo come on earth." *Outlook* (Christchurch, New Zealand) 80, no. 3 (1973): 12-13.

981 Horsfield, Don. "The Church in the Highlands." 1975, 6 pp. Typescript.
Revival in the Mendi Valley, Southern Highlands. On microfiche, the Centre, Selly Oak Colleges.

982 Hovey, Kev[in]. Term papers at School of World Mission, Fuller Theological Seminary 1979:
"New Life Forum: A description and communication analysis" [on use of the Genealogy Stick];
"Mowi 1977: Church planting or revival?";
"Yawehism: Monotheism or primary allegiance?";
"Christianity: Cultural form or primary allegiance?";
"The implications of juxtaposed world views to the effectiveness of missions: A case study from East Sepik Province, Papua New Guinea";
"Donors-Directors-Field strategies: A dynamic relation in historical perspective."
Spring Quarter:
"The anthropology of R. H. Codrington in the context of the emergence of missionary anthropology";
"Understanding cargoism . . .";
"Born brother – chosen friend";
"Evangelical ecumenics in action";
"Research methods and design: Sepik ancestors."

983 Hovey, Kev[in]. "Towards effective ministry in endemic cargo areas." In *Point.* Series 2, *Religious movements in Melanesia today (1)*, edited by W. Flannery. Goroka: Melanesian Institute, 1983, pp. 115-29.

984 Hovey, Kev[in]. "Understanding cargoism: Melanesia's challenge to the Church or the Church's challenge to Melanesia?" School of World Mission, Fuller Theological Seminary, course research paper, 1979, 35 pp.
By an Assemblies of God missionary on the Sepik River, New Guinea.

985 Hueter, D. "The battle for the abundant life: A brief study of the effect of economic development on the cargo cult and on church life." Paper presented at Lutheran Mission Wau Conference, January 1971. Madang: Lutheran Mission, 1971, 14 pp. Mimeo.

986 Hwekmarin, L.; Jamenan, J.; Lea, D.; Niniga, A.; and Wangu, M. "Yangoru cargo cult 1971." *Journal of the Papua New Guinea Society* 5, no. 2 (1971): 3-27.
By a professor of geography (Lea) and four students after visiting their home area and securing local information; pp. 18-27, appendices including myths built around various modern objects and Yaliwan himself, and notes on American and Japanese influences during World War II.

987 Inglis, Judy. Review of *Mambu: A Melanesian millennium*, by K. O. L. Burridge (entry 892). *Journal of the Polynesian Society* 70, no. 2 (1961): 381-84.

988 Inselmann, Rudolf. "The cargo cult, a hindrance to mission work," and conclusion. In "Changing missionary methods in Lutmis, New Guinea." Dissertation, Wartburg Seminary, Dubuque, Iowa, 1948, pp. 41-54. Mimeo.
The relevant part is "about the same" as his *"Letub"*. . . . (entry 989).

989 Inselmann, Rudolf. *"Letub" is a call for justice in the jungle of New Guinea*. Fort Collins, Colo.: The Mission Auxiliary of the American Lutheran Church [1945], 15 pp.
The cargo cult in Madang, 1940-45; the European responsibility for such beliefs; a popular and first-hand account.

990 Inselmann, Rudolf. "Letub: The cult of the secret of wealth." M.A. dissertation (missions), Hartford Seminary Foundation, 1944, 149 pp., unpublished except for limited ed. Wabag, New Guinea: Lutheran Mission. Mimeo.

991 Jacobsen, Werner. "Zwischen Cargo-Kult und Kirche." *Wort und Sendung: Beilage zum Rothenburger Sonntagsblatt*, no. 1 (January 1970), p. 1.
Reports from the Evangelical Lutheran Church of cults in two villages.

New Guinea

992 Jaeschke, Ernst. "New Guinea: Church in crisis?" *World Encounter* (Philadelphia, Lutheran Church) 11, no. 5 (1974): 25.
Report of a Leipzig Mission official in Germany of the influence of cargo and other ideas on the Evangelical Lutheran Church of New Guinea.

993 Julian, F.; Talmai, C.; and Sambui, M. "The popular appeal of religious movements: Personal testimonies." In *Point*. Series 3, *Religious movements in Melanesia today (2)*, edited by W. Flannery. Goroka: Melanesian Institute, 1983, pp. 194-204.

994 Kaima, Sam Tua. "The rise of money-cults in Wantoat." *Catalyst* (Goroka) 17, no. 1 (1987): 55-70.
Traditional factors at work in cargo cults in Morobe Province – the money cults from the late 1970s and their decline in the 1980s in the face of economic development.

995 Kale, Joan. "An investigation into the religious movement among the Kyaka Enga." University of Papua New Guinea, research report, 1975, 33 pp., appendix, map.
On the "revival" in the Baptist area in 1973.

996 Kale, Joan. "The religious movement among the Kyaka Enga." In *New Religious movements in Melanesia*, edited by C. Loeliger and G. Trompf. Suva: Institute of Pacific Studies, University of the South Pacific; University of Papua New Guinea, 1985, pp. 45-74.
A revival-type movement from 1973-74 accompanied by healing and "dream-given" hymns (see texts pp. 70-74), and using the translation of the New Testament in 1973 to "strengthen their faith" rather than "justify schism."

997 Karsten, Jan. "De droom van een Voek." *De Katholieke Missien* 82 (1961-62): 328-30.

998 Kasprus, Aloys. *The tribes of the Middle Ramu and the Upper Kwam rivers (North-east New Guinea)*. Studia Instituti Anthropos, 17. St. Augustin bei Bonn: Anthropos Instituts, 1973, 191 pp. + maps.
Pp. 180-82, "applications of the Melanesians' psychological traits to the cargo cults."

999 Kelly, Philip C. "Post war Manus." *Annals of Our Lady of the Sacred Heart* (Mendota, Ill.) 2, no. 4 (1948): 4-5, 24, illus.
P. 24, cargo cults.

1000 Keysser, Christian. *Gottesfeuer: Kurzgeschichte der Neuguinea Mission*. Neuendettelsau: Freimund Verlag, 1959, 62 pp.
    Especially pp. 26-44 on cargo cults.

1001 Keysser, Christian. *Eine Papuagemeinde*. Kassel: Barenreiter Verlag, 1929, 249 pp.; 2d rev. and enl. ed. Neuendettelsau: Freimund Verlag, 1950, 336 pp. English translation. *A people reborn*. Pasadena: William Carey Library, 1980, 306 pp.
    1950 ed., pp. 294-95, a Hube area movement.

1002 Keysser, Christian. "Religiöse Schwärmerein." *Neuendettelsauer Missionsblatt* 96, no. 2 (1939): 13.

1003 Kirchoff, Ernst. "Zwischen Güterkult und Entwicklungshilfe." *In Alle Welt* (Neuendettelsau), October 1966, pp. 153-55, illus.
    On the Yali movement on the Rai coast.

1004 Kiriba, F. "How Yali met the spirit." *Poroman* (Lae, Military Cadet School, Igam Barracks), November 1970, [2 pp.].
    As told to the author by an uncle who is a Yali follower.

1005 Kirk, Malcolm S. "Change ripples New Guinea's Sepik River." *National Geographic* 144, no. 3 (1973): 354-81, illus.
    Pp. 354-63, on Yaliwan and the Peli Association.

1006 [Kirschbaum, Francis.] "Die Ernte am Sepik reift." *Steyler Missionsbote* 60 (October 1932-33): 11-12.
    A Christian awakening in the Sepik delta in 1932. See extract in G. Eckert entry 311), p. 35.

1007 Klein, Rhyall. "Deluded people without hope." *Challenge* (Australian Lutheran Mission Annual), edited by J. G. Strelan, 1967, pp. 29-32.

1008 Knight, Michael. "The Peli ideal: An evaluation of the theology of the Peli Association." *Catalyst* (Goroka) 5, no. 4 (1975): 3-22.
    An important historical, descriptive and analytical account – by an Australian Catholic seminarian.

1009 Kong, Skae. "Wealth delusions." In *New Guinea Lutheran* 8 (November 1969): 16.

New Guinea

1010 Konogle, Botingu, et al. "Ripot bilong ol Filadalfia." Paper presented at New and On-Going Religious Movements in Melanesia, Melanesian Institute Seminar, Goroka, 1980, pp. 1-2. Mimeo.

1011 Koroma, J. "Cargo cult emerges on Karkar." *Weekend Nuis* 6/72, 14 May 1983, p. 1.

1012 Kowalak, Wladysklaw. "Matras Yaliwan, lider kultu cargo w prowincji Sepik Wschodini." In *Dzialalnosc Institutu Anthropos w Dziedzinie Lingwistyki, Etnologii i religioznawstwa*, edited by H. Zimonia. Materiaty i Studia Ksiezy Werbistow, 17. Pieniezno: 1980, pp. 117-25. English summary, pp. 125-26.

1013 Kriele, Ed. *Das Kreuz unter den Palmen: Die Rheinische Mission in Neu-Guinea*. Barmen: Verlag des Missionshauses, 1927, 200 pp., folding map.
Pp. 117, 122-24, 133, the Kilibob myth in the Astrolabe area.

1014 Krol, Tony, and Es, Simon. "Enga Catholics and the Holy Spirit movement." In *Point*. Series 3, *Religious movements in Melanesia today (2)*, edited by W. Flannery. Goroka: Melanesian Institute, 1983, pp. 137-43.
A Catholic report, with English appendix on hymn singing in Pumakos parish – beginning in 1973 within the Apostolic Church, growing but still within the Catholic Church in 1977; new Pentecostal features in 1978; decline and aftermath, 1980.

1015 Kubitza, Batholomew. "Cargo cult activities at Kaiep in the 1930s." *Oral History* (Papua New Guinea) 8, no. 2 (1980): 88-89. Reprinted from *Steyler Missionsbote* 60, no. 4 (1932-33): 79.

1016 Kuder, John. "Yali can not keep his promises." *Aakesin* (Madang, Lutheran Publishing House), no. 6 (1949), [1 p.].
By the Lutheran mission superintendent; a brief critical account of Yali, and defense of missions. This article led to Yali bringing a libel action against the Lutheran Mission; the Mission justified the statements, and subsequent administrative investigation led to Yali's six years' imprisonment.

1017 Kusuf, (Cadet). "Madang cargo." *Poroman* (Lae, Military Cadet School, Igam Barracks), [3 pp.].
An elementary essay, mainly on Yali.

1018 Laboi, Anton. "Cargo King." *Papua New Guinea Writing*, no. 6 (June 1972), 2 pp.

1019 Lacey, Roderic. "Tangu millennial ideology and ritual." Interdisciplinary Seminar paper, University of Wisconsin, June 1971, 32 pp. Mimeo.

1020 Lawrence, Fancy, and Lawrence Peter. "The Southern Madang regional electorate." In *Prelude to self-government*, edited by D. Stone. Canberra: Australian National University and University of Papua New Guinea, 1976, pp. 67-92, map.
   The cargo movement, dominating politics until 1968, now giving way to authentic political organization.

1021 Lawrence, Peter. "Cargo cult and religious beliefs among the Goria." *International Archives of Ethnography / International archive für Ethnologie* 47, no. 2 (1954): 1-20. Reprinted in *Melanesia: Readings on a culture area*, edited by L. L. Langness and J. C. Weschler. Scranton, South Carolina: Chandler Publishing Co., 1971, pp. 295-314.

1022 Lawrence Peter. "The fugitive years: Cosmic space and time in Melanesian cargoism and medieval European chiliasm." In *Millennialism and charisma*, edited by Roy Wallis. Belfast: Queen's University, 1982, pp. 285-315.

1023 Lawrence Peter. "Lutheran mission influence on Madang societies." *Oceania* 27, no. 2 (1956): 73-89.
   Pp. 85-89, cargo ideas.

1024 Lawrence Peter. "The Madang District cargo cult." *South Pacific* 8, no. 1 (1955): 6-13.
   Interpreted as reactions to Western contact since 1871; includes early revolts by the Jam up until 1914, the Letub cult 1940-42, Kaum's revolt of 1944, Pales' cult from 1945, and especially Yali's influence from 1945 in developing an anti-Christian cult.

1025 Lawrence, Peter. *Road belong cargo: A study of the cargo movement in the Southern Madang District, New Guinea*. Manchester: Manchester University Press; Atlantic Highlands, N. J.: Humanities Press; Melbourne: Melbourne University Press, 1964, 291 pp. Reprint. 1967. French translation. *Le culte du cargo*. Paris: Fayard, 1974, 346 pp. German translation of chap. 9 in *Religionsethnologie*, edited by C. A. Schmitz. Frankfurt, 1964. Abbreviated German translation of chap. 9 in

New Guinea

Aspekte der Entwicklungssoziologie, edited by R. Konig. Cologne: Westdeutscher Verlag, 1969, pp. 182-281. Original reprinted with new preface and postscript, 1971, 298 pp. Pidgin translation. *Rot bilong cargo*. Pos Mosby: Institut bilong PNG Stadis, 1986, 33 pp., illus., maps. A now classic study.

1026 Lawrence Peter. "Statements about religion: The problem of reliability." In *Essays presented to Ian Hogbin, Anthropology in Oceania*, edited by L. R. Hiatt and C. Jayawardena. Sydney: Angus & Robertson, 1971, pp. 139-54.

1027 Lawrence Peter. "The widening political arena in the Southern Madang District." In *The politics of Melanesia. ... 4th Waigoni Seminar ... 1970*, edited by M. W. Ward. Port Moresby: University of Papua and New Guinea, 1970, pp. 85-99.
    Pp. 90-97, "cargo prophets," especially Yali.

1028 Lea, David A. M. "Abelam land use and sustenance." Ph.D. dissertation (geography), Australian National University, 1964.
    Includes the Peli Association "as a widespread popular movement."

1029 Lehmann, Friedrich R[udolf]. "Of missionaries and cargo cult." *Pacific Islands Monthly* 18, no. 2 (1947): 58.
    An answer to criticisms of missions; mentions Yali and the Sepik area revival.

1030 Lehmann, Friedrich R[udolf]. "Of pinnaces and cargo cult and government's wasted funds." *Pacific Islands Monthly* 17, no. 9 (1947): 69.
    On Yali attacking cargo ideas, Sepik area; by a Catholic missionary.

1031 Lepani, C. "New Guinea's cargo cults." *Sunday Review*, 7 June 1971, p. 983.

1032 Lewis, Gilbert. *Knowledge of illness in a Sepik society: A study of the Gnau, New Guinea*. Monographs on Social Anthropology, 52. London: Athlone Press; Atlantic Highlands, N.J.: Humanities Press, 1975, 379 pp., illus.
    Pp. 133-34, brief reference to "Bengbeng" cargo cult among the Gnau in early 1950s, with spirit-possession phenomena, suppressed by the administration.

1033 Liddle, Kay W.; Tuck, Max; Hitchin, John [Mason]; et al. *God at work in New Guinea*. Palmerston North, New Zealand: Gospel Publishing Society, [ca. 1970?], 96 pp., map.

Pp. 22-23, cargo cults as examples of wrong conclusions drawn from wrong assumptions (by Liddle); pp. 31-32, an example of a cargoist interpretation of Genesis chap. 3 (from Hitchin).

1034 Lommel, Andreas. "Der Cargo-Kult in Melanesien: Ein Beitrag zum Problem der 'Europaïsierung' der Primitiven." *Zeitschrift für Ethnologie* 78, no. 1 (1953): 17-63.

Especially on the relation between the cult of the dead and cargo cults; Marafti Satan (Marafi/Marabi) movement, Markham valley, 1930s.

1035 Luck, G. C. "The problems of the Sepik: Progress v. cargo cultism; New Guinea head tax trouble again." *Pacific Islands Monthly* 29, no. 8 (1959): 69, 71, 73.

Cultic expressions of dissatisfaction among the Wapei and in the inland Wewak area to be met by economic development.

1036 Maahs, Arnold M. "A sociological interpretation of the cargo cult of New Guinea and selected comparable phenomena in other areas of the world." Ph.D. dissertation, University of Pittsburgh, 1956, 142 pp. University Microfilms, Ann Arbor, Michigan, 1956.

By a Lutheran chaplain later assistant to Lutheran bishop of New Guinea; first hand account of the Yali movement (pp. 43-72) from the mission's viewpoint, with new material (pp. 28-42).

1037 McCarthy, Dudley. *The fate of O'Loughlin: A novel*. Sydney: McGraw-Hill Book Company, 1979; London: Macdonald; New York: McGraw-Hill, 1980, 372 pp.

Fiction. Set in the Sepik area and includes a cargo-like movement late in the story; by a former patrol officer.

1038 McCarthy, Jack [John Desmond McCarthy]. *New Guinea Journeys*. Adelaide: Rigby, 1970, 235 pp., illus.

Chap. 6 (pp. 74-189), Journey into fantasy. By a journalist resident in Papua New Guinea since 1935.

1039 McDowell, N[ancy]. "A short note on the mythology of Yali." *Journal of the Polynesian Society* 91, no. 3 (1982): 449-52.

New Guinea

1040 McElhanon, K. A. "Current cargo beliefs in the Kubwum sub-district."
Oceania 39, no. 3 (1969): 174-86.
By a member of Summer Institute of Linguistics. No cargo cults
but many cargo ideas active in beliefs of church members after 40
years' mission work.

1041 McLaren, Peter Lee. "Religion and society in New Guinea, with special
reference to cults of the dead." M.A. thesis (anthropology), University
of London, London School of Economics, 1965.

1042 McLaren, Peter Lee. "Traditional and religious values in times of
change: A study of cultures in Madang District of Papua New Guinea."
Ph.D. thesis (anthropology), University of Sydney, 1972, 603 pp., maps.
Rereu village, Astrolabe Bay; especially chap. 5, traditional
concepts and change. Pp. 549-53, the secret power of Christianity; pp.
553-54, "Yali-ism"; pp. 571-73, "mouth" and "hand" cultures contrasted.

1043 McSwain, Romola. *The past and future people: Tradition and change in
a New Guinea Island.* Melbourne: Oxford University Press, 1977, 213
pp., maps. 2d ed. 1979, 246 pp., maps.
A valuable study of Karkar Island (1966-74) with extensive
reference to cargo cults and especially the Kukuaik cult, also Yali,
Letub, Kumoria, and Kevasob cults; pp. 169-82, the "intellectual
system" of the Karkar, with good account of Melanesian as against
Western ways of thought, and of cargoism persisting despite economic
and Christian development being above average.

1044 Mair, L[ucy] P[hilip]. *Australia in New Guinea.* London: Christophers,
1948, 238 pp. 2d ed. Carlton: Melbourne University Press, 1970, 254
pp.
Pp. 64-68, various movements.

1045 Matiabe, Aruru. "Revival movements 'beyond the ranges,' Southern
Highlands Province, Papua New Guinea." Paper presented at
Melanesian Institute Seminar on New and On-Going Religious
Movements in Melanesia, Goroka, November 1980, 9 pp. Mimeo.
In Koroba District, sparked by an Easter sermon in 1975.

1046 May, R[onald] J. "The view from Hurun: The Peli Association of the
East Sepik District." New Guinea Research Unit Discussion Paper no.
8. Boroko: The Research Unit, October 1975, 28 pp. Mimeo.

Its role in a broad political sense. Draft chapter of *Micro-nationalist movements in Papua New Guinea*, edited by R. J. May. Canberra: Australian National University, 1982.

1047 Mead, Margaret. *New lives for old–cultural transformation–Manus, 1928-1953*. London: Victor Gollancz, 1956, 548 pp.
Pp. 16-17, 42-, 101-2, 165-66, 188-215, 235, 373, various comments on cargo cults and the Paliau movement.

1048 Meggitt, M[ervyn] J. "The Ipili of the Porgera Valley, Western Highlands District." *Oceania* 28, no. 1 (1957): 31-55, map.
P. 54, a pig-killing cult accepted from the Taro Enga in 1953, through the effects of new knowledge.

1049 Meggitt, M[ervyn] J. "The Sun and the Shakers: A millenarian cult and its transformations in the New Guinea Highlands." *Oceania* 44, no. 1 (1973): 1-37; no. 2 (1973): 109-26.
Ain's cult among the Enga from 1944.

1050 "Das Menschenopfer von Garegut bei Sok." *Stadt Gottes* (Missionszeitschrift für die Katholische Familie), nos. 7-8 (1962): 362ff.
The human sacrifice of Garegut in 1961 as a local form of the necessary sacrifice which Jesus provided for the whites.

1051 Mihalic, Francis. "Cargo unlimited: Bishop Arkfeld confronts New Guinean leaders." *Catholic Weekly* (Surry Hills, Sydney), 3 June 1971, p. 2.
An S.V.D. missionary's report of a discussion between a Catholic bishop and Daniel Hawina Wavingian, "main organizer of Yaliwan's movement."

1052 Mitchell, William E. "A new weapon stirs up old ghosts." *Natural History* 82, no. 10 (1973): 74-84.
New rites and morality in the "Wape shotgun cult" of the 1960s in the Sepik river basin.

1053 Morauta, Louise. *Beyond the village: Local politics in Madang, Papua New Guinea*. London School of Economics Monographs on Social Anthropology, 49. London: Athlone Press; Atlantic Highlands, N.J.: Humanities Press; Canberra: Australian National University Press, 1974, 194 pp., maps.

New Guinea

Pp. 36-49, 137, cargo cults, especially their influence on recent political development; Yali, Yakob, Kaumip, Letub, Owro, and Tagarab cults mentioned.

1054 Morauta, Louise. "National parties and local-level politics: A view from Madang." In *Prelude to self-government*, edited by D. Stone. Canberra: Australian National University and the University of Papua New Guinea, 1976, pp. 93-113, map.
On the division between Yali cargoists and Lutheran Christians, corresponding to support for the Pangu and United parties respectively, with the latter candidate winning.

1055 Morauta, Louise. "The politics of cargo cults in the Madang area." *Man* 7, no. 3 (1972): 430-47.
Functions of cargo cults in achieving intervillage unity at the expense of village divisions; Yali cult as main example.

1056 Morren, George E. B., Jr. "A small footnote to the 'Big Walk': Environment and change among the Miyanmin of Papua New Guinea." *Oceania* 52, no. 1 (1981): 39-65.
Pp. 56-59, beginnings of "development," and Amusep's cargo-like movement without cultic dimensions.

1057 Munster, Judith. "A band of hope." *Point* (Goroka), no. 2 (1975), pp. 132-46.
Pp. 144-46, misunderstandings of a new women's self-development organization, Wok Meri, as a potential cargo cult.

1058 "Name change for Peli cult." *Post-Courier* (Port Moresby), 28 November 1972, p. 10.

1059 New Guineaite [pseud.]. "Disturbed natives: Recent events on the Rai coast of New Guinea." *Pacific Islands Monthly* 17, no. 12 (1947): 49-50.
On Yali's movement.

1060 Nilles, John. "The Kuman of the Chimbu region, Central Highlands, New Guinea." *Oceania* 21, no. 1 (1950): 64-65.
The first cargo cult among the Kuman, a Papuan group, with rapid spread to two centers but no details.

1061 Nilles, John [Johann]. "The Kuman people: A study of cultural change in a primitive society in the Central Highlands of New Guinea." *Oceania* 24, no. 1 (1953): 1-27; no. 2 (1953): 119-31.

P. 129, the "Black Mission," a temporary semi-independent prophet movement.

1062 Nita, Yaka. "Holi Spirit movement." Paper presented at Melanesian Institute Seminar on New and On-Going Religious Movements in Melanesia, Goroka, November, 1980, 2 pp. Mimeo.
By a Lutheran from Matianda valley. Enga Province, Kandep region; the movement from June 1979.

1063 Noss, J[acobus] M. "Cargo cult in Madang District." Melanesian Institute Orientation Course, Vunapope, 1969-70, 30 pp. Mimeo.
A comprehensive survey, by a Catholic missionary.

1064 Noss, J[acobus] M. "Cargo cult in the Madang District." Melanesian Institute Orientation Course, Bomana, 1971-72, 7 pp. Mimeo.
On Yali's movement.

1065 O'Donnell G[us] C. *Time expired: Authentic New Guinea*. Sydney: Leksand Press, 1967, 232 pp.
Fiction. Cargo references pp. 39-40, 45-48; a typical form without historical reference.

1066 Oertel, [Fritz]. "Kajabit." *Neuendettelsauer Missionsblatt* 22, no. 8 [89, no. 8] (15 August 1932): 63; 23, no. 7 [90, no. 7] (15 July 1933): 53; 24, no. 4 [91, no. 4] (15 April 1934): 27.
The Markham valley apocalyptic movement, 1932-33; see extracts in G. Eckert (entry 311), pp. 28-29.

1067 Oertel, [Fritz]. "Kajabit 1934." *Neuendettelsauer Missionsblatt* 26, no. 2 [93, no. 2] (20 February 1936): 11-13.
The Marafi movement at Kajabit, Markham valley, 1933-36; see use made in G. Eckert (entry 311), pp. 29-30.

1068 Os, B. van. "Moord voor de bisschop." *De Katholieke Missien* 82 (1961-62): 331-32.
Lagit's ritual murderous attack in 1959 near Alexishafen.

1069 Osborne, Kenneth B. "A Christian graveyard cult in the New Guinea highlands." *Practical Anthropology* 17, no. 1 (1970): 10-15. Reprinted in *Religious movements in Melanesia: A selection of case studies and reports*, edited by W. Flannery. Goroka: Melanesian Institute, 1983, pp. 116-20. Mimeo.

New Guinea

Among the Enga Baptists in 1967; its origins, cult leader Pyanjuwa, dreams and visions, similarity to cargo cults, and value for the churches.

1070 *Pacific Islands Monthly*. Various items as follows:
"Fanaticism: outbreak of religious mania in New Guinea," 3, no. 5 (1932): 46 [prophets in the Black Kings movement near Aitape];

"Fanaticism reported," 7, no. 1 (1936): 68; German translation in *Neuendettelsauer Missionsblatt* 26, no. 11 [93, no. 11] (15 November 1936): 112 [awaiting the second coming of Christ, on the Rai coast];

[News item] 17, no. 11 (1947): 50 [cargo cults in the Finschafen area];

"Disturbed natives: Recent events on the Rai coast of New Guinea," 17, no. 12 (1947): 49-50;

"Restless Sepik natives, adherents of 'cargo-cult,'" 18, no. 7 (1948): 62;

[News item] 18, no. 8 (1948): 50 [cargoism in the hinterland of Finschafen];

"Case history of Yali, New Guinea's first native leader," 20, no. 10 (1950): 33, 35 [a critical account of Yali; comments on the national dearth of adequate leaders];

"They still believe in cargo cult," 20, no. 10 (1950): 85, illus. [includes photo of cult house built to resemble an aeroplane];

"Cargo cults in Kainantu," 26, no. 11 (1956): 55;

"Of cargo cults and witchcraft," 42, no. 6 (1971): 22;

"Faith can move mountain markers," 42, no. 8 (1971): 16-17 [the Yangoro cult focused on Mt. Turu (Hurun), Sepik area];

"Cargo to politics," 42, no. 9 (1971): 134 [cultists who removed markers from Mt. Turu and formed a Peli (Eagle) Association for political action];

"Investment club," 43, no. 4 (1971): 42, illus. [Maga Nuginta, cult leader imprisoned at Mt. Hagen after a red box money-multiplying operation].

1071 *Papua New Guinea: House of Assembly Debates* 3, no. 6 (1972): pp. 552-53.
The member for Maprik seeking government help to deal with the Peli Association and cargoism in the Sepik area in general.

1072 Pech, Rufus. "Myth dream and drama: Shapers of a people's quest for salvation ('Illustrated by the devolution of the myth of the Two Brothers, Manub and Kilibob, in New Guinea')." M.S.Th. thesis, Trinity Lutheran Seminary (Columbus, Ohio), 1979, 269 pp.

Changes in the myth from precontact times, ending in 1886, to the 1970s and in different areas. Pp. 167-69, Eemasang movement; pp. 169-73, Upikno's revival; pp. 173-77, division within the Lutheran community over the alleged withholding of secret knowledge; pp. 177-80, Mambu, the Black King; pp. 180-85, Letub cult; pp. 185-90, Kukuaik revival; pp. 102-8, Yali.

1073 Penglase, N[athaniel]. "Report January/September 1942 (Ramu District)." *War Diary* (Australian New Guinea Administrative unit [ANGAU]) 1, no. 8 (September 1942): 45 (Appendix).

Pp. 3-4, "religious outbreaks" at Bogia under a police sergeant, and at Milkuk under Togolap, a police deserter, with Kalibob as the spirit worshipped.

1074 Peoples, James G. "From cargo cults to politics: The transformation of the Yali cult." In *Adaptation and symbolism: essays in social organization, presented to Sir Raymond Firth*, edited by K. A. Watson-Gegeo and S. L. Seaton. Honolulu: University Press of Hawaii for East-West Center, 1978, pp. 49-68.

1075 Peppelenbosch, P. G. N. Rijkdom. "Het geheim der blanken." *Mondiaal* (Groningen) 1 (1970): 32-37.

The secret of the whites' wealth.

1076 Peters, Johan. "Cargo-cults in Nieuw-Guinea: Een Bijdrage tot interpretatie." Licentiaat in de morele en religieuze wetenschappen, Katholieke Universitet te Leuven, 1971, 273 pp., bib. (pp. 240-70). Mimeo.

1077 Philosooph, H. [Shan]. "A note on the election and cargo cult in a West Sepik village." In *Prelude to self-government*, edited by D. Stone. Canberra: Australian National University and the University of Papua New Guinea, 1976, pp. 160-67, map.

Cargo cult at Puang village south of Lumi in 1957, stopped by imprisonment of leaders; cargo ideas dominated the elections, despite absence of the Peli Association and the rejection of cargoism by the elected candidate.

1078 Pilhofer, D. Georg. "Die Erneuerungsbewegung in der Sattelbergge-meinde." *Nürnberger Missionsblatt* 89, no. 1 (1932): 4-6, illus.; 89, no. 2 (1932): 18-22, illus.

New Guinea

1079 Pilhofer, D. Georg. *Die Geschichte der Neuendettelsauer Mission in Neu-guinea*. Vol. 2, *Die Mission Zwischen den beiden Weltkriegen mit einem Überblick über die neue Zeit*. Neuendettelsauer: Freimund Verlag, 1963, 312 pp., plates.
Pp. 183-88, cargo cults; by a Lutheran missionary.

1080 Pilhofer, D. Georg. "Syncretistische Kulte und säkularistische Strömmungen unter den Papua." *Evangelische Missions Zeitschrift*, n.s. 6, no. 5 (1932): 11-22.
Survey of Upikno's movement, 1933-36, in the Huon Peninsula.

1081 Ploeg, Anton. "Some indigenous views on the social and economic development of Papua New Guinea." *Journal of the Papua and New Guinea Society* 5, no. 1 (1971): 47-62.
Cargo versus "bisnis."

1082 Plutta, Paul, and Flannery, Wendy. "'Mama Dokta': A movement in the Utu Area, Madang Province." In *Religious movements in Melanesia: A selection of case studies and reports*, edited by W. Flannery. Goroka: Melanesian Institute, 1983, pp. 27-38. Mimeo.

1083 Prendergast, P[atricia] A[nn]. "A history of the London Missionary Society in British New Guinea (1871-1901)." Ph.D. dissertation (history), University of Hawaii, 1968, 520 pp.
Pp. 411-20 on cults.

1084 Price, A[rchibald] Grenfell. *The challenge of New Guinea; Australian aid to Papua progress*. Sydney: Argus & Robertson, 1965, 180 pp., illus.
Pp. 16, 39-40, 101, cargo cults.

1085 Radford, Robin. "Burning the spears: A 'Peace Movement' in the eastern highlands of New Guinea, 1936-1937." *Journal of Pacific History* 12, no. 1 (1977): 40-54.

1086 Rappaport, Roy Abraham. *Pigs for the ancestors: Ritual in the ecology of a New Guinea people*. New Haven and London: Yale University Press, 1967, xx + 311 pp., plates, map.
P. 9, a cult in the early 1940s among the Tsembaga before arrival of any whites.

1087 Read, K[enneth] E. "A recent 'cargo' situation in the Markham Valley, New Guinea." *Southwestern Journal of Anthropology* 14, no. 3 (1958): 273-94.

And see his further references to his papers on the Ngarawapum in *Oceania*.

1088 Reay, Marie O[live]. *The Kuma: Freedom and conformity in the New Guinea highlands*. Melbourne: Melbourne University Press for Australian National University; Cambridge: Cambridge University Press, 1959, 222 pp.

Pp. 23-24, 135, 287, 194-202, 205, cargo cults among the Kuma and in Wahi valley in 1953-55 and 1949.

1089 "Report of a visit to Papua New Guinea by District Apostle Kraus and Apostle Wagner, July 1979." *Canada District News* (Waterloo, Ontario), December 1979.

The New Apostolic Church; see entry 897.

1090 Robin, Robert W. "An 'end of the world revival' at Erave, Papua New Guinea." *Yagl-Ambu: Papua New Guinea Journal of Social Science and Humanities* 8, no. 1 (March 1981): 52-66, bibl.

A movement in Southern Highlands Province, 1973-75, influenced by a missionary of the Asia Pacific Christian Mission and his preaching.

1091 Robin, Robert W. "The presence, influence and effects of Christian missions on the people of the Southern Highland Province, Papua New Guinea." Ph.D. dissertation (psychology), University of Papua New Guinea, 1980.

1092 Robin, Robert W. "Revival movement hysteria in the Southern Highlands of Papua New Guinea." *Journal for the Scientific Study of Religion* 20, no. 2 (1981): 150-63.

Among the Huli people during the Tari revival fostered by "fundamentalist overzealous missionaries" in 1975-76, but less evident in more recent cargo movements.

1093 Robin, Robert W. "Revival movements in the Southern Highlands Province of Papua New Guinea." *Oceania* 52, no. 4 (1982): 320-43.

1094 Rowley, Charles D. "Book belong Lawrence." *New Guinea and Australia, the Pacific and South-East Asia* 1, no. 2 (1965): 84-86.

An extensive summary of Peter Lawrence's *Road belong cargo* (entry 1025), and of its "five stages of cargo belief" up to that of Yali.

New Guinea

1095 Ruhen, Olaf. *Land of Dahori: Tales of New Guinea.* London: Macdonald, 1957, 255 pp. Reprints. London, Sydney, etc.: Horwitz Publications, 1947 and 1966, 278 pp.

Pp. 138-51 (pp. 144-60 in 1966 ed.), "the village of phantom shps" – imaginative reconstruction of an actual cargo cult.

1096 Ruhen, Olaf. *Mountains in the clouds.* Adelaide: Rigby, 1963, 240 pp., illus., map. Sydney: Horwitz (Horwitz Australian Library), 1968, 240 pp.

Chap. 13 (pp. 197-211), popular summaries of many movements, with substantial extracts from provincial officers' reports: D. S. Grove (1947, on Kaimantu); R. J. Stevenson (1944, near Markham); Haviland (1943, Ramu district).

1097 Rule, M., and Rule, J. "Revival . . . 3 years later: Lake Kutubu." *Light and Life* (Unevangelized Fields Mission), May 1973, pp. 2-3.

1098 Sagom, Petrus. "The secret of Mount Turu." *Kanimbieh* (Brandi High School, East Sepik District), 1971, p. 21.

1099 Salisbury, R[ichard] F[rank] [Roswell]. "An indigenous New Guinea cult." *Kroeber Anthropological Society Papers,* no. 18 (1958), pp. 67-78.

1100 Salisbury, R[ichard] F[rank] [Roswell]. *From Stone to Steel: Economic consequences of a technological change in New Guinea.* Melbourne: Melbourne University Press, 1962, 237 pp.

On the Siane peoples, Goroka area (sixteen tribes with a non-Melanesian language); pp. 114, 121, briefly on cargo cults; pp. 123-39, on direct white contacts and practices re wealth.

1101 Saurgaria, Sorum. "Tok bilong kago kalt: Kain kain lotu na bilip bilong ol tumbuna." In *Riport bilong . . . ,* edited by Peyandi Lepi. Lae: Evangelical Lutheran Church of New Guinea, 1975, pp. 38-39.

A pastor's statement on cargo cults, with reference to Yali, as in the report of a church conference. In Pidgin.

1102 Schardt, Ronald F. "The power of God versus cargo cult." *Lutheran* (Adelaide) 4, no. 2 (1970): 10-13, illus.

Detailed report by a missionary on the Finonga cargo movement, 1968-69, Erap area, Markham valley, and how it was dealt with.

1103 Schindbeck, Markus. "Cargo-bewegung, Tradition und Migration: Sozio-Ökonomische Veränderungen bei den Sawos von Gaikorobi, Sepik-Gebiet, Papua-neuguinea." *Paideuma* 30 (1984): 275-98.

Cargo movements after World War II and in 1957 as ways to get whites' wealth, later replaced by shops but still with cargo ideas; mission education as contributing to this new form of cargo cult.

1104 Schmitz, Carl-A[ugust]. *Wantoat: Art and religion of the Northeast New Guinea Papuans.* The Hague and Paris: Mouton & Co., 1963, 159 pp., illus.

Pp. 60-61 background to development of cults once inequalities of wealth are discovered in the outside world.

1105 Schwab, Ignaz. "Der Koch des Teufels: Die Yerumot-Bewegung amd Keram River in Neuguinea." *Steyler Missionsbote* 65 (1937-38): 236-37.

The "Second-Coming-of-Christ" movement in 1936, on Rai Coast.

1106 Schwab, Ignaz. "Report of the Keram native king." *Pacific Islands Monthly* 15, no. 2 (1944): 16.

The Yerumot cargo cult, 1944.

1107 Schwarz, Guido. "The Catholic fellowship in the Mt. Hagen area." In *Point.* Series 3, *Religious movements in Melanesia today (2),* edited by W. Flannery. Goroka: Melanesian Institute, 1983, pp. 72-92.

A local Catholic missionary reporting a revival or "Spirit" movement within the Catholic Church, owing to Melanesian initiative by layman Andrew Dokta, from 1978.

1108 Scorza, David. "Classification of Au myths." *Practical Anthropology* 29, no. 5 (1972): 214-18.

Pp. 216-17, origin or cargo cult ideas and their expression in incipient myths invented by the old men; West Sepik area.

1109 Silate, P. "Yali's cargo cult: Comments on old secrets and new developments." In *Melanesian religion: Collected essays,* edited by G. W. Trompf. Suva: Institute of Pacific Studies, forthcoming.

1110 Simpson, Colin. *Adam in plumes.* Sydney, London, etc.: Angus & Robertson, 1954. 2d ed. 1955, 268 pp., illus., maps.

Pp. 254-57, Ninji's cargo movement near Mt. Hagen about 1940; also N. B. Blood's oral version of the Great Pigs cult in 1946 – see N. B. Blood (entry 886).

New Guinea

1111 Simpson, Colin. *Plumes and arrows: Inside New Guinea*. Sydney: Angus & Robertson, 1962, 405 pp. Reprint of selections from *Adam with arrows* (Sydney, London, etc.: Angus & Robertson, 1953; repr. 1958), *Adam in plumes* (Sydney, London, etc.: Angus & Robertson, 1955, 168 pp., illus., maps.), and *Islands of men* (Sydney, London, etc.: Angus & Robertson, 1955). 4th reprint. 1971, 421 pp.

   Pp. 290-91, cargo cult of the "Black King" form in Mt. Hagen area about 1940, suppressed by the leader's arrest; general account of such cults.

1112 Skae, Kong. "Wealth delusion." *New Guinea Lutheran* (Madang) 8 (November 1969): 16.

   Brief report on cargo movements in Kaiapit circuit, with comment as a Christian.

1113 Smith, Michael F. "From heathen to atheist: Changing views of Catholicism in a Papua New Guinea village." *Oceania* 51, no. 1 (1980): 40-52.

   P. 49, brief reference to failure of cargo expectations on Kairiru Island, Sepik coast.

1114 Somare, Michael [Thomas]. *Sana, an autobiography of Michael Somare*. Milton, Queensland: Jacaranda Press; Port Moresby: Nuigini Press, 1975, 152 pp.

   Pp. 84-85, brief account (by a former prime minister) of Yaliwan (i.e. Peli movement), including Somare's own part in handling the situation.

1115 Steinbauer, Friedrich. "Die 18 Jahreskonferenz der Lutherische Mission in Neu-Guinea (27.1 to 6.2.1964)." *Nachrichten der Evangelische Lutherische Kirche in Bayern* 19, no. 7 (1964): 108-11.

1116 Steinbauer, Friedrich. "Hinweise auf die Cargo-Kulte." *Nachrichten der Evangelische Lutherische Kirche in Bayern* 24, no. 1 (1969): 7-8.

1117 Steinbauer, Friedrich. *So war's in Tarabo*. Neuendettelsau: Freimund-Verlag, 1969, 210 pp., illus., map.

   On the Lutheran Mission at Tarebo, Eastern Highlands; p. 36, cargo movements in 1952, and pp. 83-84, in 1964.

1118 Steinbauer, Friedrich. "Der Traum vom Glück: Anpassung und in Cargo-Kulten von Papua Neuguinea." In *Theologische Beiträge aus*

Papua Neuguinea, edited by H. Bürkle. Erlangen Taschenbücher 43. Erlangen: Verlag der Evang.-Luth. Mission, 1978, pp. 123-35.

1119 Stent, W[illiam] R. "Aspects of the transition from a subsistence to a market economy in the Abelam, PNG." Ph.D. thesis (economics), LaTrobe University, 1979.
Includes an account of the Peli Association.

1120 Stent, W[illiam] R. "An interpretation of a cargo cult." *Oceania* 47, no. 3 (1977): 187-219.
Incorporates new material on the continuing Peli Association with that in entries 1121, 1122, and 1123.

1121 Stent, W[illiam] R. "An interview with a cargo cult leader [Confidential]." LaTrobe University, Economics Department Discussion Paper no. 3/73, 1973, 47 pp. Mimeo.
In 1973, East Sepik District, in a Peli Association (Yangoro cult) village; a former agricultural officer learns of the money-doubling attempts of a local literate cult leader, revealing money as still a magical object in the Ambelam world view.

1122 Stent, W[illiam] R. *The Peli Cargo cult – an Interpretation. Parts I and II.* LaTrobe University, Economics Department Discussion Paper no. 17/73, 1973, 57 + 3 pp., bib. Mimeo.
Part I, pp. 1-21, theories of causes; pp. 21-46, origins and recent attitudes of the Peli Association; pp. 46-57, Peli not a crisis cult but a "pre-crisis" normal reaction to economic problems.

1123 Stent, W[illiam] R. "A Sepik entrepreneur – a personal account." LaTrobe University, Economics Department Discussion Paper no. 4/73, 1973, 28 pp. Mimeo.
See entries 1121 and 1122. Such small-scale entrepreneurs effect the transition to a more rational understanding of modern economic activities.

1124 Stephen, Simon. "The 'Skin Guria' movement in the Buang Area, Morobe Province." In *Religious movements in Melanesia: A selection of case studies and reports*, edited by W. Flannery. Goroka: Melanesian Institute, 1983, pp. 1-11. Mimeo.

1125 Stoltz, M[ichael]. "Bericht über Sio für 1919." *Neuendettelsauer Missionsblatt* 11, no. 3 (1921): 9-10; no. 4, (1921): 13; 15, no. 12 (1925): 111.

New Guinea

Cargo ideas on the northeast coast.

1126 Stone, David, ed. *Prelude to self-government.* Canberra: Australian National University Press, for Research School of Pacific Studies and University of Papua New Guinea, 1976, 547 pp.
See B. J. Allen (entry 864), F. and P. Lawrence (entry 1020), L. Morauta (entry 1054), and H. Philsooph (entry 1077).

1127 Strathern, Andrew J. "Cargo and inflation in Mount Hagen." *Oceania* 41, no. 4 (1971): 255-65.
A cult in the early 1940s, based on information gathered in 1967.

1128 Strathern, Andrew J. *Ongka: A self-account by a New Guinea big-man.* New York: St. Martin's Press, 1979, 162 pp.

1129 Strathern, Andrew J. "The Red Box money-cult in Mount Hagen, 1968-71." *Oceania* 50, no. 2 (1979): 88-102; no. 3 (1979): 161-75.

1130 Strauss, Hermann. "Der Cargokult." In *Junges Neuguinea: Ein Informationsbuch,* edited by W. von Krause. Neuendettelsau: Freimund Verlag, [1970?], 240 pp., illus., maps.
A handbook, with passing references to cults; pp. 140-57 reprint of H. Strauss (entry 1132).

1131 Strauss, Hermann. "Die Geldzauberei." *Neuendettelsauer Missionsblatt* 29, no. 5 [96, no. 5] (1939): 38.
A movement in the Western Highlands; from the missionary's annual report for 1937.

1132 Strauss, Hermann. "Der Wandel in Neuguinea, III." *Evangelische Missions Zeitschrift,* n.s. 9, no. 4 (1952): 108-16.
P. 106, Cargo cults in Ogelbeng, by a long-term Lutheran missionary.

1133 Sturtevant, Steve. "Hearts ablaze with revival in Papua New Guinea." *Herald of His Coming* (Los Angeles, Gospel Revivals, Inc.) 40, no. 3 (1981): 11. Reprinted from *Mission Messenger* (Summerfield, Fla., Evangelical Bible Mission).
Mission-promoted revivals which exhibit an independent momentum, as seen by a missionary involved.

1134 Sumit. "Some sidelights on Yali: Can he be regarded as 'cargo cult' or mischievous influence?" *Pacific Islands Monthly* 21, no. 2 (1950): 45-47.

Report of meeting Yali, hearing his story, and also the favourable opinions of patrol officers and Catholic missionary, John Wold.

1135 Tamoane, Matthew. "Kamoai of Dararap and the legend of Jari." In *Prophets of Melanesia*, edited by G. W. Trompf. Port Moresby: Institute of Papua New Guinea Studies, 1977, pp. 174-211, map.

By a grandson of traditional prophetess Kamoai (d. 1964), who was possessed at Dararap by Jari, but had no cult.

1136 Taru, Lincoln. "Cult movements at Lumi." *Oral History* 4, no. 3 (1976): 59-60.

Three movements started in the 1940s by men who had travelled: Molou (d. 1964) and Deni (b. about 1925) with spirit possession and cargo aspects; and Yanepei (about 1920-1974) an ex-church leader with a more Christian movement about 1950 and cargo hopes; all served prison sentences and Yanepei was nearly elected to the House of Representatives of 1964.

1137 Teske, Gary. "The Holi Spirit movement among Enga Lutherans." In *Point*. Series 3, *Religious movements in Melanesia today (2)*, edited by W. Flannery. Goroka: Melanesian Institute, 1983, pp. 113-26.

A Lutheran missionary on a new movement from 1979; detailed descriptions of possession, dreams, healings, prophets and relation to the Church and to local religion.

1138 Teske, Gary. "Worship the Father in Spirit and in Truth." In *Point*. Series 3, *Religious movements in Melanesia today (2)*, edited by W. Flannery. Goroka: Melanesian Institute, 1983, pp. 240-52.

1139 Thomas, Gordon. "A plea for better regulation of mission activities in New Guinea." *Pacific Islands Monthly* 6, no. 4 (1935): 25-26.

Black Kings movement near Aitape mentioned during discussion of mission effects on natives, and with reference to League of Nations Permanent Mandates Commission 27th session reports, and queries there raised.

1140 Thompson, Rob. "The revival convention at Kainyamateta." In *Religious movements in Melanesia: A selection of case studies and reports*, edited by W. Flannery. Goroka: Melanesian Institute, 1983, pp. 123-26. Mimeo.

See also A. Dawia (entry 902).

New Guinea

1141 Todd, Ian A. *Papua New Guinea: Moment of truth*. Sydney: Angus & Robertson, 1974, 183 pp., illus., folding map.
Pp. 106-10, Yaliwan and Mt. Turu, quoting from journalist Ray Goodey's account of "scary rituals" and "absurd beliefs."

1142 Trompf, G[arry] W[inston]. "The effects of religious change on society." Humanities Foundation Course Lecture 21. University of Papua New Guinea, [1976], 6 pp. Mimeo.
Pp. 3-6, southern Madang district, especially Yali's modernizing and missionary movement to 1974.

1143 Trompf, Garry [Winston]. "The theology of Beig Wen, the would-be successor to Yali." *Catalyst* (Goroka) 6, no. 3 (1976): 166-74.
Yali's secretary-confidant and successor in 1975; two ways of salvation: through Christ for whites, through Yali for blacks.

1144 Trumbull, Robert. "New Guinea election: No one had to walk more than two days to reach a polling place." *New York Times Magazine*, 4 May 1972, pp. 32-33, 49-56.
Includes the election of Yaliwan to the House of Assembly in 1972.

1145 Valckx, Wim. "Roep om mensenoffers: Onrust in Australisch Nieuw-Guinea." *Bijeen*, October 1971, pp. 20, 45.
The call for human sacrifice.

1146 Vicedom, George F. *Church and people in New Guinea*. World Christian Books, 38. London: Lutterworth Press, 1961, 79 pp.
By a missionary-anthropologist. Pp. 58-62, cults among Evangelical Lutheran Churches: arising as a magical paganism and disciplined as apostates; winning these back to the Church; a literal form of salvation by prosperity, provoked by Western affluence.

1147 Vicedom, George F. "Kirche in Neiguinea unter Anfchtung." In *Deutsche Evangelische Weltmission. Jahrbuch 1952*. Hamburg: Verlag Deutschen Evangelischen Missions-Hilfe, 1952, pp. 53-61.

1148 Wabei, Turuk. "Kulubob." In *Two Plays from New Guinea*, edited by Patricia Healy. South Yarra, Vic.: Heinemann Educational Australia, 1970, pp. 46-69.
A Karkar (Madang) student points out that Kulubob legend predisposes people to read "cargo" into later events.

1149 Wacke, [Karl]. "Kalasa 1933." *Neuendettelsauer Missionsblatt* 24, no. 11 [91, no. 7] (1934): 55; 24, no. 11 [91, no. 11] (1934): 82-83.
Upikno's movement near Kalasa; extracts in G. Eckert (entry 311) p. 31.

1150 Wacke, Karl. "Missionsstation Kalasa." *Neuendettelsauer Missionsblatt* 15, no. 6 [82, no. 6] (1925): 45.
Cargo ideology on the northeast coast.

1151 Wacke, Karl. [Report.] *Neuendettelsauer Missionsblatt* 14, no. 5 [81, no. 5] (1924): 24.
The Timo movement of 1920-22 on the Huon Peninsula.

1152 Wagewa, Manuel, and Kovingre, Otto. "Kago kult: As bilong kago kult." *Point* (Goroka), no. 1 (1974), pp. 74-80.
Two Roman Catholic catechists discuss (in Pidgin) cargoism against the background of traditional cultures and recent changes; English summary, p. 80.

1153 Wagner, Hans. "Anfechtung und Sieg in Ulap." *In Alle Welt* (Neuendettelsau), February 1949, p. 2.

1154 Wagner, Hans. *Bericht ueber meine Selepet koma Reise vom 21 Juli-11 August 1947: Beobachten über den Cargo-cult*. Lae: Lutheran Mission, 1947, 6 pp.

1155 Wagner, Hans. "A field study of the Bongu Buged Circuit (Madang)." Lae: Lutheran Mission New Guinea, 1963, 90 pp. Mimeo.
In *Mission Archives*, Netherlands Reformed Church, Oegstgeest. Pp. 16-17, 33-35, cargoism; pp. 49-59, general account of cargoism and the Paliau movement; pp. 59-74, Yali movement, Bongu Bugud area; pp. 75-85, analysis and conclusions; pp. 88-89, summary from P. Lawrence (entry 1023).

1156 Wagner, Hans. "Der Lügenprophet." *In Alle Welt* (Neuendettelsau), December 1950, p. 186.

1157 Wagner, Herwig. "Auf der Suche nach dem heilen Leben." In *Heisses Land Niugini: Beiträge zu den Wandlungen in Papua Neuguinea*, edited by R. Italiaander. Erlangen: Verlag der Evang.-Luth. Mission, 1974, pp. 197-215.

New Guinea

1158 Wagner, Herwig. "'Cargo,' Hoffnung auf eine neue Welt?" *Breklumer Sonntagsblatt* 93, no. 28 (1968): 225-26.
On a renewal movement.

1159 Wagner, [Johan] Friedrich. "Der Cargo Kult des Luluai Menigiong von Imom." *Weltmission Heute* (Stuttgart) 37-38 (1968): 5-19. Reprinted in *Nachchristliche Bewegungen in Neuguinea und Brasilien; ein Studienhefte*, edited by E. Dammann. Stuttgart: Evangelische Missionsverlag, 1968, pp. 5-19.
The *luluai* of Imon in the Timbe area, Morobe Province, began a movement in 1964 which involved many Lutheran Christians.

1160 Wagner, [Leonhard]. "Wareo." *Neuendettelsauer Missionsblatt* 22, no. 9 [89, no. 9] (1932): 66-67, illus.
Eemasang renewal movement; see extract in G. Eckert (entry 311), p. 35.

1161 "Waiting for that cargo." *Time* (New York) 19 July 1971, pp. 19-20, illus.
Mainly on Yaliwan and the Yangoro cult in 1971.

1162 Walcke, Alfred W. "Cargo." *Lutheran Mission essays, by missionaries of the Lutheran Mission, New Guinea*. Vol. 1. N.p.: Lutheran Mission, n.d., no pagination.
First essay, 5 pp., on cargo but not very perceptive.

1163 Walcke, Alfred W. "Who and/or what? An attempt to understand why so many New Guineans are so prone to cargo cultism, and some implications of the findings for education." M.A. thesis, University of Minnesota, 1967, 125 pp.
Pp. 16-22, main discussions and theories of cargo cults; Appendix 1 (pp. 91-108, + 3 pp. of photos), manifestations of a cult near Madang, by a long-serving American missionary.

1164 Walne, Victor. "Cargo cults and Americanism." *Living Church* (Milwaukee, Episcopal Church weekly) 162, no. 12 (1971): 10.
Cargo cult philosophy identified with that of materialistic Americans, as encouraged by American military supplies in World War II; by an Episcopalian missionary.

1165 Wedde, Peter. "Papua New Guinea approaches nationhood." *Outlook* (Christchurch, N.Z.), April 1975, pp. 15-16.
The Sepik cult of Yaliwan as overrated in overseas reports.

1166 Weinstock, Margaret. "Notes on the Sepik cargo cult." In *Niugini Reader*, edited by H. Barnes. North Melbourne, Victoria: Australian Union of Students, 1972, pp. 37-39.
Pp. 37-39, Yaliwan's cult in early 1972, and the Peli Association.

1167 Wheeler, Tony. *Papua New Guinea—A travel survival kit*. South Yarra, Victoria: Lonely Planet, 1979, 224 pp.
Pp. 16-17, cargo cults.

1168 Winnett, Bob, and May R[onald] J. "Yangoru-Saussia open: The disappearance of an 83 per cent majority." In *Electoral politics in Papua New Guinea: Studies on the 1977 National elections*, edited by D. Hegarty. [Port Moresby]: University of Papua New Guinea Press, 1983, pp. 255-67.
Peli Association and the election, with Yaliwan's 1972 election majority lost.

1169 Woll, Bert. "Report of visit to Papua New Guinea by District Evangelist Woll, February 1980." *Canada District News* (Toronto, New Apostolic Church) 1, no. 2 (1980): 31-35, illus.
The expansion of the New Apostolic Church, especially in the Wewak area, where Yaliwan's movement has been somewhat identified with the Church, although this is not mentioned.

1170 Worsley, Peter [Maurice]. *The trumpet shall sound: A study of "cargo" cults in Melanesia*. London: MacGibbon & Kee, 1957, 290 pp. 2d ed., enl., with supplementary bib. New York: Schocken Books, 1968, 300 pp.
Chap. 3 (pp. 49-74, 1968 ed.): early movements.

1171 Wüst, Hermann. "Was geschah an der Raiküste Neuguineas?" *Lutherisches Missionsjahrbuch . . . 1960.* (Bayerischen Missionkonferenz), pp. 70-76.
A Lutheran missionary on cargo cults.

1172 Yagas, Alos. "The Begesin [*sic*] rebellion and the Kein 'independence' movement: Preliminary analyses." In *New religious movements in Melanesia*, edited by C. Loeliger and G. Trompf. Suva: Institute of Pacific Studies, University of the South Pacific; University of Papua New Guinea, 1985, pp. 18-25.
Kaum's Bagasin revolt of 1944 in Madang Province.

New Guinea

1173 Young, Doug. "Pastoral responses to the Enga Holy Spirit movement." In *Point*. Series 3, *Religious movements in Melanesia today (2)*, edited by W. Flannery. Goroka: Melanesian Institute, 1983, pp. 224-39.

Papua (within Papua New Guinea)

This is the southeastern part of the whole island. Politically it was called British New Guinea (1884-1906) and was at first under the control of Queensland. From 1898 to 1975 it was under the Commonwealth of Australia, which changed the name to Papua in 1906. Papua joined the Trust territory of New Guinea to the north to form independent Papua New Guinea in 1975. Papua includes the following provinces: Western, Southern, Highlands, Gulf, Central, Northern, and Milne Bay (which includes the Trobriand and D'Entrecasteaux Islands and the Louisade Archipelago). The so-called Vailala Madness from 1919 is well studied, but earlier movements go back at least to prophet Tokeriu in 1893.

1174 Abel, Charles [William]. *Savage life in New Guinea: The Papuan in many moods.* London: London Missionary Society, 1902, 221 pp., illus.
Chap. 8 (pp. 104-28), this missionary's encounter with Tokeriu and his movement, including narrow escape not in F. W. Walker's account (entry 1216); photo of Tokeriu in jail. Written for children.

1175 Abel, Russell William. *Charles W. Abel of Kwato: Forty years in dark Papua.* New York and London: Fleming H. Revell, 1934, 255 pp., illus., maps.
Pp. 77-79, Tokeriu as encountered by a pioneer missionary.

1176 Aitsi, L. A. "Aisi Abia." Undergraduate paper, University of Papua New Guinea, 1974.
Cited in D. Fergie (entry 1199), p. 164, n. 34. On a member of the Inawai'a movement among the Mekeo, who claimed to be the power in the background.

1177 Allen, L. W. "The Purari Kompani." In *The Purari Delta: Background and progress in community development,* by the South Pacific Commission. Restricted issue as Social Development Notes, no. 7, November 1951. As Technical Paper 35. Noumea: The Commission, November 1952, pp. 1-11 + map.
An L.M.S. missionary on the Tommy Kabu movement, 1946-48.

1178 Allen, L. W. "The Purari Kompani: A brief report on the main happenings of 1946-48 in the Purari Delta of Papua." *South Pacific Commission Social Development Notes* (Sydney) 7 (Section 1) (1952): 1-13, map.

1179 Australia, Commonwealth of. *Report to the League of Nations on the administration of the Territory of New Guinea, 1922-23.* Canberra: Commonwealth Government, 1924.
P. 8, Section 18, on the Baigona cult.

1180 Barker, John H. "Protestants and Papuans: A sociological study of the London Missionary Society, Methodist and Anglican Missions in Papua, 1871 to 1930." M.A. thesis (anthropology), Victoria University of Wellington, 1979, 267 pp.
Pp. 190-203, millenarian movements as in Tokeriu and Vailala; Appendix, pp. 220-244A, anthropology and the missions – a valuable detailed survey.

1181 Barr, Kevin J. "Revivalism in the urban situation: Port Moresby." In *Religious movements in Melanesia: A selection of case studies and reports*, edited by W. Flannery. Goroka: Melanesian Institute, 1983, 201-10. Mimeo.

1182 Beaver, W. N. "Some notes on the eating of human flesh in the Western Division of Papua." *Man*, article 74, 14 (1914): 145-47.
P. 147, passing note on Baigona, as forbidding killing snakes.

1183 Belshaw, Cyril Shirley. "Recent history of Mekeo society. (Central Division of Papua)." *Oceania* 22, no. 1 (1951): 1-23.
Pp. 5-8, Filo movement, based on written accounts of the leaders and of the Sacred Heart missionary at the time.

1184 Berde, Stuart. "The impact of Christianity on Melanesian economy." *Research in Economic Anthropology* 2 (1979): 169-87, map, bib.
The "negative instance" of the Panaeati people, Louisade Archipelago, converted as Methodists and in no need of cults.

1185 British New Guinea [i.e., Papua]. *Annual Report on British New Guinea, Year 1893-1894.*
See under R. J. Kennedy entry 1212 and W. McGregor entry 1217.

1186 Bromilow, William E. *Twenty years among primitive Papuans*. London: Epworth Press & J. Alfred Sharp, 1929, 316 pp., illus.

P. 107, pioneer Methodist missionary, D'Entrecasteaux Islands, on a prophet in the early 1890s.

1187 Brown, Herbert A. "Social and political change among the eastern Elema (Papua)." Diploma in anthropology thesis, University of London, London School of Economics, 1956.

By a long-term L.M.S. missionary. Pp. 219ff., the "Christian Association" among the eastern Elema about 1950, a revival form. (Copy in University of P.N.G. Special Collection.)

1188 Calvert Lin[nie Bryant]. "A renewal movement in the United Church, Kapuna, Gulf Province." In *Religious movements in Melanesia: A selection of case studies and reports*, edited by W. Flannery. Goroka: Melanesian Institute, 1983, pp. 189-94.

1189 Chalmers, James, and Gill, W. Wyatt. *Work and adventure in New Guinea, 1877 to 1885*. London: Religious Tract Society, 1885, 324 pp., illus., maps. 2d ed. 1902, 313 pp.

P. 324, prophet movement in 1884 at "Discovery Bay (Wagawaga)," i.e. somewhere near Milne Bay.

1190 Chinnery, E[rnest] W[illiam] P[earson], and Haddon A[lfred] C[ort]. "Five new religious cults in British New Guinea." *Hibbert Journal* 15, no. 3 (1917): 448-63.

The Kava-Keva and Kekesi rites (Taro cult of Orakaiva), Baigona, Tokeriu, and German Wislin.

1191 Clint, A. "Report on the co-operative movement in the Northern District of Papua." Port Moresby: Department of Trade and Industry, 1950. Mimeo.

A failed Christian-encouraged movement, by the missionary who promoted it, 1948-50.

1192 Cochrane, Glynn. "Power, status, and the Vailala madness." D. Phil. thesis (social anthropology), University of Oxford, 1967.

See also entry 302.

1193 Cranswick, Geoffrey F., and Shevill, Ian W. A. *A new deal for Papua*. Melbourne: F. W. Cheshire; London: Wadley & Ginn, 1949, 159 pp., illus.

Pp. 87-93, the Anglican Church and new cults, especially the Assisi movement (mocked by missionary feigning hysteria), all regarded as apostasy, and largely due to whites' superiorities and Seventh Day Adventist teachings.

1194 Cruttwell, Norman. "Arks and idols in Papua: The story of a fight against sorcerors." *Church Times* (London), 17 November 1961, p. 8, illus.

1195 Cruttwell, Norman. "Gindat's temple." In *New religious movements in Melanesia,* edited by C. Loeliger and G. Trompf. Suva: Institute of Pacific Studies, University of the South Pacific and University of Papua New Guinea, 1985, pp. 98-100.
    A brief local cult based on a "temple" built by Gindat in Daga country in 1954, and demolished at the author's instigation.

1196 Cruttwell, Norman. "The 'Peroveta' cult in the Daga." In *New religious movements in Melanesia,* edited by C. Loeliger and G. Trompf. Suva: Institute of Pacific Studies, University of the South Pacific and University of Papua New Guinea, 1985, pp. 101-5.
    An end-of-the-world cult which made "arks" (longhouses) on hilltops in 1960, and two male and female images burnt by government.

1197 Cruttwell, Norman. "Some cargo cults in the Milne Bay province." Melanesian Institute Orientation Course, 8 January 1979, 7 pp. Mimeo.
    Eleven cults arising between 1940 and 1972 around Goodenough Bay "as experienced or told to" the author.

1198 Dakeyne, R. B. "Co-operatives at Yega." *Orakaiva Papers.* New Guinea Research Bulletin 13. Canberra and Port Moresby: New Guinea Research Unit, Australian National University, November 1966, pp. 53-68.

1199 Fergie, Deane. "Prophecy and leadership: Philo and the Inawai'a movement." In *Prophets of Melanesia,* edited by G. W. Trompf. Port Moresby: Institute of Papua New Guinea Studies, 1977, pp. 147-73.
    Including material secured by interviews with Filo in 1974.

1200 Fossen, A[nthony] B[elgrano] van. "The problem of evil in a millennial cult: The case of the Vailala Madness." *Social Analysis,* no. 2 (November 1979), pp. 72-88.

1201 Frerichs, A[lbert] C. "[The] Vailala madness." *Lutheran Missionary* (Columbus, Ohio, American Lutheran Church) 27, no. 5 (1947): 2, cover picture.

1202 Gill, W. Wyatt. [Report of visit early in 1884 to "New Guinea" by a London Missionary Society officer.] *Sunday at Home* (London), no. 1591 (25 October 1884), p. 688.

"At Dinner Island I heard of a heathen prophet(?) who was going about proclaiming new era, and admonishing his people to give up cannibalism, murder, adultery and theft." Possibly the first mention of a new movement in Papua.

1203 Groves, W. C., ed. "Community development in the Purari Delta." Community Development Review Paper 1. Port Moresby: Social Welfare Branch, Department of Education, 4 June 1951, 12 pp. Reprinted in *The Purari Delta*. Technical Paper 35. Noumea: South Pacific Commission, November 1952, pp. 31-24.

On the Tommy Kabu movement. See also L. W. Allen (entry 1177).

1204 Guariglia, Guglielmo. *Prophetismus und Heilserwartungs-bewegungen als völkerkundliches und religionsgeschichtliches Problem.* Vienna: F. Berger, 1959, 332 pp.

P. 8, Milne Bay prophet; pp. 82-104, various movements.

1205 Haddon, A[lfred] C[ort], ed. *Reports of the Cambridge Anthropological Expedition to the Torres Straits.* 6 vols. in 7. Cambridge: Cambridge University Press, 1901-35.

Vol. 1, pp. 46-48, a new cult from 1913, "German Wislin."

1206 Hess, Michael. "A religious movement in Eastern Milne Bay." In *Religious movements in Melanesia: A selection of case studies and reports*, edited by W. Flannery. Goroka: Melanesian Institute, 1983, 12-16. Mimeo.

A cargo movement in eastern Milne Bay, during evacuation of Australian administration in 1942, violently suppressed when the administration returned.

1207 Hill, Jack. "An analysis of the Vailala Madness and other cults in Papua." M. Phil. thesis, University of London, 1970, 310 pp.

Microfilm copy in University of P.N.G. library.

1208 Jawodimbari, Arthur. "Cargo: A play." In *Five New Guinea Plays*, edited by U. Beier. Port Moresby, South Melbourne, and Brisbane: Jacaranda Press, 1971, pp. 11-19.

Based on a movement in the area of the early Anglican mission, Northern District.

1209 Jojoga [Opeba], Willington. "The *peroveta* of Buna." In *Prophets of Melanesia,* edited by G. W. Trompf. Port Moresby: Institute of Papua New Guinea Studies, 1977, pp. 212-37, illus., map.

First-hand account of Genakuiya Opeiya, a contemporary Christian prophetess from Buna, near Popondetta.

1210 Keesing, Felix M. "The Papuan Orokaiva vs. Mt. Lamington: Cultural shock and its aftermath." *Human Organization* 11, no. 1 (1952): 16-22.

On the absence of any movement after the major volcanic eruption in 1951, although many cults arose in the past.

1211 Kekeao, Thomas H. "Vailala madness." *Oral History* (Boroko) 1, no. 7 (1973): 1-8.

By a descendent of participants (who uses some of their written records) and takes issue with F. E. Williams (entries 1267-1272).

1212 Kennedy, R[obert] J. "Report on the Eastern Division, 21 June 1894." In *Annual report on British* [later Papua] *New Guinea, Year 1893-1894.* London: Her Majesty's Stationery Office, 1894. Appendix S (Not printed in Colonial Office version, but included in *Imperial Parliamentary Papers: New Guinea,* vol. 3.).

P. 71, Tokeriu, whose arrest "almost stopped his work."

1213 Kila, Timo Ani; Gerega, Gno; et al. "The Geno Gerega movement. Two reports: Report A by T. A. Kila; report B by G. Gerega (as interviewed by Chris Kopyoto and interpreted by Karo Rupa)." In *New Religious movements in Melanesia,* edited by C. Loeliger and G. Trompf. Suva: Institute of Pacific Studies, University of the South Pacific and University of Papua New Guinea, 1985, pp. 113-18.

Gerega's movement, Hula area 1954-57, rejecting magic and teaching a strict morality.

1214 King, Cecil J. *Copland King and his Papuan friends: being a memoir of . . . Copland King.* Sydney: Australian Board of Missions [Anglican] 1934, 42 pp., illus., map.

Pp. 31-32, missionary King's comments on the Baigona cult. By his twin brother.

1215 Lacey, Roderic. "The 'Vailala Madness' as a millenarian movement." Interdisciplinary seminar paper, University of Wisconsin, 1971, 25 pp. Mimeo.

1216 Lutton, Nancy F[lorence]. "Larger than life: A biography of Charles Abel of Kwato." M.A. thesis (history), University of Papua New Guinea, 1979, 393 pp. (bib., pp. 362-93).
   Pp. 51-57, the encounter between Tokeriu and the two L.M.S. missionaries (C. Abel and F. W. Walker) with discussion of the discrepancies between their accounts.

1217 McGregor, W[illiam]. "Appendix C: Despatch no. 17 of 1893." *Annual report on British* [later Papua] *New Guinea, Year 1893-1894*. London: Her Majesty's Stationery Office, 1894, p. 12.
   On Tokeriu; extract in N. Lutton (entry 1216).

1218 Maher, Robert F[rancis]. *New men of Papua: A study in culture change.* Madison: University of Wisconsin Press, 1961, 148 pp., illus., maps.
   Pp. 55-77, Tommy Kabu's Kompani, as a secular movement.

1219 Maher, Robert F[rancis]. "The Purari River delta societies: Papua New Guinea, after the Tom Kabu movement." *Ethnology* 23, no. 3 (1984): 217-27.
   Only the Maipua people have shown cargo activity (in 1953, and intermittently since); the Tommy Kabu movement (with initial religious overtones) failed; no successor but amid general apathy small adaptations are occurring.

1220 Maher, Robert F[rancis]. "Tommy Kabu movement of the Purari delta." *Oceania* 29, no. 2 (1958): 75-90.
   Example of a "realistic" movement as alternative to cargo cults; pp. 89-90 note the failure of a cargo movement.

1221 Mair, Lucy [Philip]. Review of *New men of Papua: A study in culture change*, by Robert J. Maher (entry 1218). *Journal of the Polynesian Society* 70, no. 2 (1961): 381.

1222 Martha, Sister M. "The madness or cargo cult at Inauaia." Paper presented at Xavier Institute of Missiology, Port Moresby, 1969, 4 pp.
   Recollections of the 1940 Mekeo cult of Filo.

1223 Meakoro, Evera. "A pastor's response to the Kapuna renewal movement." In *Religious movements in Melanesia: A selection of case studies and reports,* edited by W. Flannery. Goroka: Melanesian Institute, 1983, pp. 195-200. Mimeo.

1224 Nevermann, Hans. "Die Südsee und der Kontinent Australien" In *Die Heutigen Naturvölker im Ausgleich mit der neuen Zeit,* edited by D. H. Westermann. Stuttgart: F. Enke, 1980.
Pp. 261-62, German Wislin and Vailala Madness.

1225 Noga, Bedero Geno. "The Mareva Namo cult." In *New religious movements in Melanesia,* edited by C. Loeliger and G. Trompf. Suva: Institute of Pacific Studies, University of the South Pacific and University of Papua New Guinea, 1985, pp. 92-97.
Started by Marewa Namo around 1920 in the Rigo subdistrict.

1226 Ogan, Eugene. Review of *"The Vailala Madness" and other essays,* edited by E. G. Schwimmer (London: C. Hurst, 1976). *American Ethnologist* 5, no. 2 (1978): 391-93.

1227 Opeba, Willington-Jojoga. "Prophets in traditional society." [Ca. 1976], 20 pp. Mimeo.
A course-work paper, University of Papua New Guinea, expanded into a conference paper as background of his 1977 essay on Jenny the *peroveta* or prophetess from Buna, who is his grandmother.

1228 Opeba, Willington-Jojoga. "Taro or cargo? – study of taro cult among the Orokaiva of the Northern Province." B.A. (Hons.) thesis, University of Papua New Guinea, 1976, 124 + 34 pp., maps.
Baigona and Taro cults as neither "cargo" nor millenarian, but as traditional responses to new situations. Chap. 3 (pp. 66-80), white men's interpretations; chap. 4 (pp. 81-122), his own interpretations, including case study of prophet Donoba (d. 1975). Appendix 1 (A) (4 pp.), interview with Donoba.

1229 Oram, N. D. "Rabia Camp and the Tommy Kabu movement, as Pt. I of Rabia camp, a Port Moresby migrant settlement." *New Guinea Research Bulletin* (Canberra and Port Moresby), no. 14 (January 1967), pp. 8-43, illus.

1230 *Pacific Islands Monthly.* Various items as follows:
"Vailala madness: A wave of religious fanaticism that swept Papua in 1919," 6, no. 5 (1935): 25 [summary account by Mollie Lett, as similar to current "Buka fanatacism"];

"Crazy natives: A strange outbreak in Gulf Division of Papua," 11, no. 8 (1941): 18 [the local magistrate on Filo's movement];

"'Mekeo Madness': Queer religious hysteria in Papua," 12, no. 4 (1941): 58 [Filo, her imprisonment and attempted triumphal return];

"Cargo cult unrest?" 26, no. 11 (1956): 70 [a "mild outbreak" from about 1950, Gulf District];

"Their cargo-cult wasn't anti-European," 30, no. 4 (1959): 136-37 [a cargo-type reaction on Goodenough Island after sudden economic deprivation];

"Mr. Tommy Kabu," 40, no. 11 (1969): 135 [obituary on the founder of the failed "new Men" cult, who died about 1955].

1231 Papua Government. "Kerema patrol report." CAO [Commonwealth Archives Office.], CPI [Records of the Papuan (previously British New Guinea) Administration]. Set 35, bundle 16, Kerema patrol reports. 15-24 September 1919; 20 March to 7 April 1922.

The first notices of the "Vailala Madness."

1232 Papua and New Guinea Government, Department of District Services and Native Affairs. "Cargo cult–Vailala Madness and other." *Papua and New Guinea Department of District Services, etc.* D.S. 14.6.9. Circular Instruction no. 37, 46/47, of 8 January 1947.

On recent religious cults, by H. I. Hogbin.

1233 Papua and New Guinea Government, Department of District Services and Native Affairs. "Native agitation and social unrest." *Papua and New Guinea Department of District Services, etc.* D.S. 1.1.1. Circular Instruction no. 50, 46/47, of 26 June 1947.

An outline of policy for the administrative approach to and treatment of cults.

1234 Papua [earlier, British New Guinea] Government. *Annual reports for Papua*:

1910-11, p. 93 [Baigona cult]; 1911-12, p. 14 [J. H. P. Murray], pp. 128-29 [A. E. Oelrichs];

1912-13, pp. 154-55 [C. King];

1914-15, p. 58 [E. W. P. Chinnery];

1919-20, pp. 29-30 ["Vailala Madness," by R. P. Oldham], pp. 62-63 [C. T. Wuth], pp. 116-18 [G. H. Murray (reprinted in F. E. Williams [entry 1271, pp. 71-71)];

1920-21, p. 46 [Boninia (1914) and Taro cults, C. T. Wuth], pp. 47-49 [Taro cults and Dasiga Giama's breakaway, L. A. Flint];

1924-25, p. 44 [L. A. Flint];

1937-38, pp. 35-36 [J. H. P. Murray];
1940-41, p. 21 [Filo's movement attack on Catholic Mission, W. H. H. Thompson].

1235 Parratt, John K[ing]. "Religious change in Port Moresby." *Oceania* 41, no. 2 (1970): 106-13.
Cargo cults as not urban; the appeal of Seventh Day Adventism and Baha'i, which Tommy Kabu joined.

1236 Prendergast, P[atricia] A[nn]. "A history of the London Missionary Society in British New Guinea (1871-1901)." Ph.D. dissertation (history), University of Hawaii, 1968, 520 pp.
Pp. 411-20, the Tokeriu movement in relation to L.M.S. missionaries.

1237 Reif, Adelbert. "Im Land der Papua." *Kosmos* (Stuttgart) 62, no. 11 (1966): 463-69, illus.
Includes cargo cults.

1238 Riley, E. Baxter. *Among Papuan headhunters.* Philadelphia: J. B. Lippincott Co.; London: Seeley, Service & Co., 1925, 1 + 316 pp., illus., maps.
Pp. 294ff., prophetism on Kiwai island, Fly River; pp. 297-98, pig-killing reaction to an earthquake, since their grunting caused it – but not a cult.

1239 Ritter, Hans. "Die Schlange in der Religion der Melanesier." *Acta Tropica* (Supplementum no. 3). Basel: Verlag für Recht und Gesellschaft, 1945, 128 pp.
Pp. 64-65, Baigona cult.

1240 Ryan, Dawn. "Christianity, cargo cults, and politics among the Toaripi of Papua." *Oceania* 40, no. 2 (1969): 99-118.

1241 Ryan, Dawn. "Social change among the Toaripi." M.A. thesis (anthropology), University of Sydney, 1965, 156 pp., maps.
The early contact period. Pp. 138-46, puzzlement over Christianity's failure to bring wealth, and resulting cults (e.g., Torea's from 1951, and others in 1960) – Poro's, and the Tapela girls' cult.

1242 Saville, W[illiam] J[ames] V[iritahitemauvil]. *In unknown New Guinea.* London: Seeley, Service & Co., 1926, 316 pp. Reprint. New York: AMS, 1979, 316 pp., illus., folding map.

Papua

By a scholarly missionary, on Mailu Island off the Papuan coast. Pp. 288-90, form of the Vailala Madness in the Mailu district.

1243 Schwimmer, Erik G. *Cultural consequences of a volcanic eruption experienced by the Mount Lamington Orokaiva.* A Comparative Study of Cultural Change and Stability in Displaced Communities in the Pacific, Report no. 9. Eugene, Oreg.: Department of Anthropology, University of Oregon, 1969, 228 + 8 pp., maps.
Pp. 85-89, co-operatives after World War II, with millenarian ideas; pp. 67-69, 128-31, on the inevitable cultural influence of a mission station.

1244 Schwimmer, Erik G. *Exchange in the social structure of the Orokaiva: Traditional and emergent ideologies in the Northern District of Papua.* London: C. Hurst & Co., 1973, 244 pp. New York: St. Martin's Press, 1974, 244 pp.
Chap. 4, Christianity interpreted in terms of the religious basis of local economics, and the relation to the millennial movements; see also pp. 34-36, 107, 218-19.

1245 Seligman, Charles Gabriel. *The Melanesians of British New Guinea.* Cambridge: Cambridge University Press, 1910, 766 pp.
Pp. 655-57, Tokeriu.

1246 Siikala, J. "The cargo proper in cargo cults." *Temenos* 15 (1979): 68-80, bib.
Christian transposition of a cargo cult in a Mekeo village.

1247 South Pacific Commission. *Histoire et progrès du développement communautaire dans le delta du Purari d'après Papouasie et Nouvelle-Guinea et L. W. Allen.* Noumea: S.P.C., 1952, 39 pp., map.
See also entries 1177-1178.

1248 Stephen, Michele. *Cargo cult hysteria: Symptom of despair or technique of ecstasy.* Occasional Paper 1. Bundoora: Research Centre for South West Pacific Studies, LaTrobe University, 1977, 16 pp. Mimeo.
Uses Philo and the Mekeo as the example.

1249 Stephen, Michele. "Continuity and change in Mekeo society." Ph.D. dissertation, Australian National University, 1974.
Includes "cultist ideas during World War 2."

1250 Stephen, Michele. "'Dreaming is another power': The social significance of dreams among the Mekeo of Papua New Guinea." *Oceania* 53, no. 2 (1982): 106-22.

1251 Taylor, Merlin Moore. *The heart of black Papua.* New York: Robert M. McBride & Co., 1926, 266 pp., illus.
P. 42, Baigona snake cult, Mambare district.

1252 Taylor, Merlin Moore. *Where cannibals roam.* London: Geoffrey Bles, 1924, 329 pp., illus. German translation. *Bei den Kannibalen von Papua.* Leipzig: F. A. Brockhaus, 1925, 280 pp., illus., map.
Pp. 46-47 (English version), travel writer's brief reference to Baigona as a form of "sorcery."

1253 Trompf, Garry [Winston]. "Bilalaf." In *Prophets of Melanesia*, edited by G. W. Trompf. Port Moresby: Institute of Papua New Guinea Studies, 1977, pp. 20-107, illus., map.
On Ona Asi, or "Bilalaf" (d. 1963), a Guyughe prophet in the highlands and his cult 1930-54, within a French Catholic mission area.

1254 Trumbull, Robert. "Leader of a cargo cult elected to Papua House." *New York Times*, 4 April 1972, p. 37.

1255 Vangeke, Louis. "Interview between [Catholic] Bishop Louis Vangeke (Bishop at Bereina) and Garry Trompf (Bereina 30/4/74) on . . . Filo of Inawaia and a general oral history of the Mekeo people." University of Papua New Guinea, Religious Studies course material, [1974], 5 pp., map. Mimeo.
Vangeke's unwitting encouragement of cargo ideas; Filo and her movement.

1256 Wagner, Roy. *Habu. The innovation of meaning in Daribi religion.* Chicago: Chicago University Press, 1972, 186 pp., illus.
Pp. 163ff., new cults in Papua.

1257 Wagner, Roy. "A talk of Koriki: A Daribi contact cult." *Social Research* 46, no. 1 (1979): 140-65.

1258 Waiko, J[ohn] D[ouglas]. "Cargo cults: The Papua New Guinea way." In *Nuigini Reader,* edited by H. Barnes. Melbourne: Australian Union of Students, 1972, pp. 43-50.
A development of his paper to the 6th Waigoni Seminar.

1259 Waiko, J[ohn] D[ouglas]. "Oro Oro: A history of the Binandere people." B.A. (Hons.) sub-thesis (history), University of Papua New Guinea, 1972, 104 pp., + bib.
By a Binandere member. Pp. 203-4, briefly on cargo cults as anticolonial protests.

1260 West, Francis. *Hubert Murray: The Australian pro-consul.* Melbourne: Oxford University Press, 1968, 296 pp.
P. 221, notes 76, 77; p. 229 – briefly on Vailala Madness as first reported by Kerema Patrol.

1261 Wetherell, David [Fielding]. "A history of the Anglican mission in Papua 1891-1942." M.A. thesis, Australian National University, 1970.
Pp. 160-71, Baigona cult.

1262 Wetherell, David [Fielding]. *Reluctant mission: The Anglican Church in Papua New Guinea, 1891-1942.* St. Lucia: University of Queensland Press, 1977, 430 pp., bib.
Chap. 6, cults and revivals: pp. 186-87, Baigona; pp. 187-90, Taro; p. 290, Bogari; pp. 290-192, Asisi; also pp. 4, 199. Scholarly accounts using primary sources.

1263 Weymouth, Ross Malcolm. "The Gogodala Society: Adjustment movements 1966-1981." In *Religious movements in Melanesia: A selection of case studies and reports,* edited by W. Flannery. Goroka: Melanesian Institute, 1983, pp. 39-51. Mimeo.

1264 Weymouth, Ross Malcolm. "The Gogodola Society: A study of adjustment movements since 1966." *Oceania* 54, no. 4 (1984): 269-88.
Pp. 279-83, cargo thinking from the 1950s; pp. 283-85, A. L. Crawford's attempt to encourage cultural revival since 1972; pp. 285-87, recent revival movements.

1265 Weymouth, Ross Malcolm. "The Gogodala Society in Papua and the Unevangelized Fields Mission, 1890-1977." Ph.D. thesis (social sciences), Flinders University, 1978, 402 pp.
Chap. 11, religion and culture 1967-77: pp. 233-241, Kesali's unsuccessful cult; pp. 327-33, cargo thinking and its place in primal world views; p. 341, "adjustment movements"; pp. 346-50, shallowness of recent "Gogodala cultural revival" led by a European; pp. 351-53, revival movements, especially at Pisi, influenced by Solomon Islands revival about 1973.

1266 White, Roger. "Family prayer movement at Imbongu, Ialibu, Southern Highlands." In *Religious movements in Melanesia: A selection of case studies and reports*, edited by W. Flannery. Goroka: Melanesian Institute, 1983, pp. 152-74. Mimeo.

1267 Williams, F[rancis] E[dgar]. *Bull-Roarers in the Papuan Gulf.* Anthropology Report 17. Port Moresby: Government of the Territory of Papua, 1936, 55 pp., illus.
    P. 49, Bull-roarer cult abandoned in the Vailala Madness.

1268 Williams, F[rancis] E[dgar]. *Orokaiva magic.* London: Oxford University Press, 1928, xxii + 231 pp., illus., map. Reprint. Oxford: Clarendon Press, 1969.
    Part 1 (pp. 3-101), the Taro cult.

1269 Williams, F[rancis] E[dgar]. "Scientists consider future of native races in Pacific." *Pacific Islands Monthly* 5, no. 7 (1935): 62-63.
    Considers mission influence, with Vailala madness as illustration; see entry 1270 for his full report.

1270 Williams, F[rancis] E[dgar]. "Some effects of European influence on the natives of Papua." *Report of the 22nd meeting, Australian and New Zealand Association for the Advancement of Science, Melbourne 1935*. Melbourne and Canberra: Australian and New Zealand Association for the Advancement of Science, 1939, pp. 215-22.

1271 Williams, F[rancis] E[dgar]. *The Vailala Madness and the destruction of native ceremonies in Gulf Division.* Anthropology Report 4. Port Moresby: Anthropological Society, 1923, xiii + 79 pp., illus., map. Reprint. Bobbs-Merrill Social Science Series, A-241. Reprinted in *"The Vailala Madness" and other essays*, edited by E. G. Schwimmer. London: C. Hurst, 1976, pp. 331-84, with introduction (titled "Love and the aeroplane") by the editor, pp. 38-41. Reprint. New York: AMS Press, 1978.
    The government anthropologist's now classic account of a cargo cult.

1272 Williams, F[rancis] E[dgar]. "The Vailala madness in retrospect" In *Essays presented to C. G. Seligman*, edited by E. E. Evans-Pritchard, et al. London: Kegan Paul, 1934, pp. 369-79. Reprinted in *"The Vailala Madness" and other essays*, edited by E. G. Schwimmer. London: C. Hurst, 1976, pp. 385-95.

1273 Worsley, Peter [Maurice]. *The trumpet shall sound: A study of "cargo" cults in Melanesia*. London: MacGibbon & Kee, 1957, 290 pp. 2d ed., enl., with supplementary bib. New York: Shocken Books, 1968, 300 pp. Chap. 4 (pp. 75-92), Vailala Madness.

1274 Young, Michael W. "Goodenough Island cargo cults." *Oceania* 42, no. 1 (1971): 42-57, bib.
       Cults from 1947 in Milne Bay District, especially Isekel's Wafiga cult, its three phases in 1959-60, and quick failure.

Solomon Islands

What had been the Solomon Islands Protectorate (Great Britain) from 1893 became an independent nation in 1978. The northernmost islands of Buka and Bougainville, which geographically and culturally cohere with the rest of Solomon Islands, were under German control from about 1885 to 1914, then administered by Australia, and are here treated as part of Papua New Guinea, to which they belong politically. The Christian Fellowship Church is the best-known movement (see the Particular Movements section at the end of the volume). Other major movements have been Marching Rule or Masinga and its offshoots, and Moro's movement.

1275 Allan, Colin H[amilton]. *Customary land tenure in the British Solomon Islands Protectorate*. Report, Special Lands Commission. Honiara: High Commissioner for the Western Pacific, 1957, 329 pp., + map.
       Pp. 51-52, 249, 253, Marching Rule; p. 250, Bulu movements; p. 252, Richard Fallowes form of Marching Rule.

1276 Allan, Colin H[amilton]. "An early Marching Rule letter by Nori of Waisisi, Are'are, Malaita. Manuscript XV." *Journal of Pacific History* 15, no. 2 (1980): 110-12.

1277 Allan, Colin H[amilton]. "Further Marching Rule documents: Manuscript XVI – Anaefolo of Uru and the Federal Council decision of 1951; Manuscript XVII – the Special Lands Commissioner's note on the Nggela people and Marching Rule, 1954." *Journal of Pacific History* 17, no. 4 (1982): 222-27.

1278 Allan, C[olin] H[amilton]. "'Marching Rule': A nativistic cult in the British Solomon Islands." *Corona* 3, no. 3 (1951): 93-100. Reprinted in *South Pacific* 5, no. 5 (1951): 79-85.

1279 Allan, Colin Hamilton. "The Marching Rule movement in British Solomon Islands Protectorate: An analytical survey." Diploma in Anthropology thesis, University of Cambridge, 1950.

The author was British Resident Commissioner in the New Hebrides Condominium in the 1970s.

1280 Allan, Colin H[amilton]. "Some Marching Rule stories." *Journal of Pacific History* 9 (1974): 182-86.

1281 Belshaw, C[yril] S[hirley]. *Changing Melanesia*. Melbourne: Oxford University Press, 1954, 198 pp., maps.

Pp. 112-13, the Fallowes movement on Ysabel, etc.; pp. 78, 79, 97, 109, 112-14, 132, Marching Rule.

1282 Belshaw, Cyril S[hirley]. *Island administration in the South West Pacific: Government and reconstruction in New Caledonia, the New Hebrides, and the British Solomon Islands.* London and New York: Royal Institute of International Affairs, 1950, 158 pp., maps.

Pp. 68, 74-75, 89, 126-29, Masinga Rule and cargo ideas – much of this appeared in "Native politics. . . ." (entry 1283).

1283 Belshaw, Cyril S[hirley]. "Native politics in the Solomon Islands." *Pacific Affairs* (Vancouver) 20, no. 2 (1947): 187-93.

Pp. 190-93, Marching or Masinga Rule.

1284 Bennett, Judith A. *Wealth of the Solomons: A history of a Pacific archipelago, 1800-1978.* Pacific Islands Monograph Series, 3. Honolulu: University of Hawaii Press, 1987, 531 pp., illus.

Pp. 259-64, R. Fallowes and "Chair and Rule" movement; p. 272, Santa Cruz cargo cult; p. 278-80, 283-84, La'aka cult of the Kwai (American rule sought); pp. 292-99, Marching Rule; pp. 299-301, Christian Fellowship Church; pp. 317-18, Moro's cult on Guadalcanal, 1957-58.

1285 Bogutu, Francis. "The impact of Western culture on Solomon Islands society: A Melanesian reaction." In *The history of Melanesia. . . . 2d Waigoni Seminar . . . 1968,* edited by K. S. Inglis. Port Moresby: University of Papua New Guinea; Canberra: Australian National University, 1969, pp. 549-56.

P. 549, Marching Rule briefly interpreted as a self-identification reaction.

Solomon Islands

1286 British Solomon Islands. *Report for the year 1970.* Honiara: British Solomon Islands Protectorate Government, 1971, 157 pp., illus., map.
P. 107, brief history of Marching Rule, similar to accounts in earlier and later reports.

1287 British Solomon Islands Protectorate, Advisory Council. "Statements by Resident-Commissioner on the Marching Rule movement in the Solomons." *Reports of Meetings* (Suva, Government Printer) (February 1947): 3; (November 1947): 1, 3-4; (September-October 1948): 3-4.

1288 Burrows, William. "The background of Marching Rule: Late Henry Kuper gives some curious Solomons history." *Pacific Islands Monthly* (Sydney) 20, no. 11 (1950): 37-38.

1289 Burt, Ben. "The Remnant Church: A Christian sect of the Solomon Islands." *Oceania* 53, no. 4 (1983): 334-46.

1290 "Canon Willie Masuraa." *Melanesian Messenger* (Taroaniara), Easter 1964, pp. 20-22.
On the founder of the Church Association within the Anglican Mission on South Malaita.

1291 [Caulton, Sydney] Gething (bishop of Melanesia). "Bishop's address to conference." *Southern Cross Log* (Sydney, [Anglican] Melanesian Mission), no. 32 [January 1951]: 10-15.
P. 13, comments on Marching Rule.

1292 [Caulton, Sydney] Gething (bishop of Melanesia). "The Marching Rule delusion." *Pacific Islands Monthly* 21, no. 1 (1950): 77, 79.
Text of a New Zealand broadcast by the Anglican Bishop of Melanesia, discussing the causes in a general way.

1293 Coaldrake, F. W. "The Church Association." *Melanesian Messenger* (Taroniara), August 1963, pp. 26-30.
The history, rules, and contribution of the Association.

1294 Coaldrake, F. W. *Flood tide in the Pacific: Church and community cascade into a new age.* Stanmore, N.S.W.: Australian [Anglican] Board of Missions, [ca. 1964], 96 pp., illus.
Pp. 34-43, Willie Masurah and the Church Association from 1949.

1295 Coastes, Austin. *Western Pacific Islands*. London: H.M.S.O., 1970, 349 pp.
    Pp. 292-96, Marching Rule.

1296 Corris, Peter [Robert]. *Passage, port and plantation: A history of Solomon Islands labour migration, 1870-1914*. Carlton: Melbourne University Press, 1973, 201 pp.
    Pp. 142-44, (p. 178, notes), Marching Rule.

1297 Davenport, William. "Two social movements in the British Solomons that failed and their political consequences. In *The politics of Melanesia. . . . 4th Waigoni Seminar . . . 1970*, edited by M. W. Ward. Port Moresby: University of Papua and New Guinea, 1970, pp. 162-72.
    "New Law," a secular movement, Santa Cruz Islands; pp. 166-71, the reforming "True Church of Kuper,"–healing, anti-white, and anti-mission, in eastern Solomons in 1959.

1298 Davenport, William, and Coker, Gulbun. "The Moro movement of Guadalcanal, British Solomon Islands Protectorate." *Journal of the Polynesian Society* 76, no. 2 (1967): 123-75, illus., bib. Reprint. Wellington: Polynesian Society, 1967, reprint series, 13, 53 pp.

1299 Dewey, A. "The Marching Rule and its anthropological perspective." Ph.D. dissertation (anthropology), Harvard University, 1950.

1300 Faifu, T[imothy]. "Who and whose child?" *Melanesian Messenger* (Taroniara), December 1965, pp. 18-25.
    P. 19, Marching Rule; otherwise on the Church Association of Malaita, which reflects the earlier Marching Rule, its origins and history; by a layman who participated in the first secret meetings in 1949.

1301 Fisk, Denis. "Islands where pagan gods fell to a modern 'miracle.'" *Pacific Islands Monthly* 47, no. 6 (1976): 48-49, 51, illus.
    P. 51, at Niupani on Rennell Island in October 1938, an excited "Niupani Madness" against the old gods in the course of considering the newly arrived Christian faith.

1302 Fowler, Wilfred. *This island's mine*. London: Constable, 1959, 240 pp., illus.
    Chap. 1 (pp. 23-55), The Missionary–probably based on the Fallowes movement of 1938-39; by a district officer.

Solomon Islands

1303 Fox, Charles E[lliott]. "A journey on Gela." *Southern Cross Log* (Sydney, [Anglican] Melanesian Mission), no. 26 (1 April 1948): 20-22.

    A veteran medical missionary's personal enquiry into Marching Rule on island of Gela – its merits and demerits, and the strength of indigenous Christianity.

1304 Fox, Charles E[lliott]. *Kokamora*. London: Hodder & Stoughton, 1962, 157 pp.

    Chap. 15 (pp. 127-35), Marching Rule, by a missionary who lived in Solomons from 1902. Has been called "the best primary source on Marching Rule" – a questionable judgment.

1305 Fox, Charles E[lliott]. *Lord of the Southern Isles: Being the story of the Anglican mission in Melanesia 1849-1949*. London: A. R. Mowbray & Co., 1958, 272 pp., illus.

    Pp. 176-77, Marching Rule, well-organized but "purely political," affecting ninety per cent of the people, excepting indigenous Anglican priests.

1306 F[ox], C[harles] E[lliott]. "A new Melanesian movement: The Church Association on Malaita." *Southern Cross Log* (London), February 1954, pp. 153-60. Also news item, pp. 145-46.

    Pp. 153-56, "how it started" and "what it means"; pp. 156-60, Rules of the Church Association. See also *Southern Cross Log* (entry 1363).

1307 Fox, Charles E[lliott]. *The story of the Solomons*. Taroaniara, British Solomon Islands: Diocese of Melanesia Publications, 1967, 98 pp., folding map, illus.

    P. 37, Christian Fellowship Church secession; the "Remnant Church," half-Christian, half-heathen, as a "native movement"; pp. 63-66, Marching Rule or Loa.

1308 Fullerton, Leslie Douglas. "From Christendom to pluralism in the South Seas: Church-State relations in the twentieth century." Ph.D. dissertation (religion), Drew University, 1969, 335 pp.

    Pp. 265-69, cargo cults.

1309 Great Britain, Colonial Office – British Solomon Islands. *Annual reports on the British Solomon Islands*. London: H. M. Stationery Office: for the year 1948 (1949), pp. 26-28, 34; for the years 1949-50 (1951), pp. 37-41; for the years 1951-52 (1953), p. 46.

    Reports on Marching Rule.

1310 Griffiths, Alison. *Fire in the Islands: The acts of the Holy Spirit in the Solomons*. Wheaton, Ill.: Harold Shaw Publishers, 1977, 108 pp., illus.

Pp. 137-41, Marching Rule and God's overrule; pp. 169-97, the Revival in the South Seas Evangelical Church, from the Maori evangelist Muri Thompson in 1970; pp. 199-204, the 1976 Revival.

1311 H. V. C. R. "Church Association on Gela." *Southern Cross Log* (London) 62, no. 1 (1955): 16-17.

1312 Hagesi, Robert. "Towards localization of Anglican worship in the Solomon Islands." B.D. thesis, Pacific Theological College (Suva), October 1972.

Pp. 69-70, Charles Kuper's "True Church" (1958-1971?); p. 70, "White-water-God" movement ca. 1963 on Malaita.

1313 Harwood, Frances H[ine]. "Intercultural communication in the Western Solomons: The Methodist Mission and the emergence of the Christian Fellowship Church." In *Mission, church, and sect in Oceania*, edited by J. A. Boutilier, et al. Association for Social Anthropology in Oceania, Monograph Series no. 6. Ann Arbor: University of Michigan Press, 1978, pp. 232-50.

1314 Healey, A. M. "Administration in the British Solomon Islands Protectorate." *Journal of Administration Overseas* 5 (1966): 194-204.

Pp. 200-202, Marching Rule, and Vouza's movement; otherwise useful as background.

1315 Hilliard, David L[ockhart]. "Colonialism and Christianity: The Melanesian mission in the Solomon Islands." *Journal of Pacific History* 9 (1974): 93-116.

Pp. 112-16, Rev. Richard P. Fallowes, ex-Melanesian Mission, founder of the Chair and Rule movement in 1939.

1316 Hilliard, David L[ockhart]. *God's gentlemen: A history of the Melanesian Mission, 1849-1942*. St. Lucia: Queensland University Press, 1978, 342 pp., illus., maps.

Pp. 221-185, the Santa Isabel movement in 1938-39 fostered by Fallowes, an English defector from the Melanesian Mission; pp. 185-87, the Danielites on Raga (North Pentecost), 1931-34.

1317 Hilliard, David L[ockhart]. "The South Seas Evangelical Mission in the Solomon Islands: The foundation years." *Journal of Pacific History* 4 (1969): 41-64.

Solomon Islands

P. 61, briefly on Marching Rule, and its leaders who were associated with the South Seas Evangelical Mission.

1318 Hogbin, [Herbert] Ian [Priestley]. *A Guadacanal society – The Kaoka speakers*. Case Studies in Anthropology. New York, etc.: Holt, Rinehart & Winston, 1964, 103 pp., illus.
Pp. 96-98, convenient summary of Marching Rule.

1319 Keesing, Roger M[artin]. "Antecedents of Maasina Rule: Some further notes." *Journal of Pacific History* 15, no. 2 (1980): 102-7.

1320 Keesing, Roger M[artin]. "Chiefs in a chiefless society: The ideology of modern Kwaio politics." *Oceania* 38, no. 4 (1968): 276-80.
Pp. 277-78, Marching Rule and the later Custom movement on Malaita.

1321 Keesing, Roger M[artin]. "Christians and pagans in Kwaio, Malaita." *Journal of the Polynesian Society* 76, no. 1 (1967): 82-100.
On the "drastic and formalized" separation between the two, with Marching Rule (pp. 88, 98) partly bridging the gap.

1322 Keesing, Roger M[artin]. "Politico-religious movements and anti-colonialism on Malaita: Maasina Rule in historical perspective" (Parts 1-2). *Oceania* 8, no. 4 (1977-78): 241-61; 49, no. 1 (1978-79): 46-73.

1323 Keesing, Roger M[artin]. "Still further notes on 'Maasina Rule.'" *Journal of the Anthropological Society of Oxford* 12, no. 2 (1981): 130-34.
Comment on B. Murdoch (entry 1347).

1324 Keesing, Roger M[artin], and Corris, Peter. *Lightning meets the west wind: The Malaita massacre*. Melbourne, etc.: Oxford University Press, 1980, 219 pp., illus.
Pp. 199-200, Maasina Rule.

1325 Keesing, Roger M[artin], ed. *Elota's story: The life and times of a Solomon Islands big man*. St. Lucia: University of Queensland Press, 1978, 202 pp., illus.
Pp. 20-23, 155-65, Masina Rule.

1326 Knuf, Joachim. "Zum Ursprung der "Marching Rule" – Bewegung im ehemaligen British Solomon Islands Protectorate." *Wiener Ethnohistorische Blätter* 19 (1980): 25-53.

Uses manuscript records of former administrative officers to trace specific roots for the movement in experimental schemes for native self-government.

1327 Laracy, Hugh M[ichael]. "Catholic missions in the Solomon Islands, 1845-1966." Ph.D. thesis, Australian National University, 1969.
Chap. 7 on Marching Rule, also Hahalis Welfare Society.

1328 Laracy, Hugh [Michael]. "Maasina Rule." In *Historical dictionary of Oceania*, edited by R. D. Craig and F. P. King. Westport, Conn.: Greenwood Press, 1981, p. 165.

1329 Laracy, Hugh M[ichael]. "Maasina Rule: Struggle in the Solomons." In *Race, class, and rebellion in the South Pacific*, edited by A. Mamak and A. Ali. Sydney and London: Allen & Unwin, 1979, pp. 93-107.

1330 Laracy, Hugh M[ichael]. "Marching Rule and the missions." *Journal of Pacific History* 6 (1971): 96-114.

1331 Laracy, Hugh M[ichael]. *Marists and Melanesians: A history of Catholic missions in the Solomon Islands*. Honolulu: University Press of Hawaii; Canberra: Australian National University Press, 1976, 211 pp., maps.
Chap. 7 (pp. 121-43) and pp. 135-38, 162, Marching Rule; p. 140, various short-lived cults.

1332 Laracy, Hugh M[ichael], ed. *Pacific protest: The Maasina Rule movement, Solomon Islands, 1944-1954*. Suva: Institute of Pacific Studies, University of the South Pacific, 1983, xiii + 206 pp., illus, maps.
Mainly documents from the original Western Pacific Archives, showing Marching Rule in search of "brotherhood" rather than of cargo, and as not primarily political; but see pp. 150-55 on cargoism; pp. 156-61, Matthew Belamataga's "Freedom movement" in a Roman Catholic context; pp. 162-76, Sisili's movement in the context of the South Seas Evangelical Mission.

1333 Lasaqa, I. Q. *Melanesian's choice: Tadhimboko participation in the Solomon Islands cash economy*. New Guinea Research Bulletin 46. Port Moresby: New Guinea Research Unit; Canberra: Australian National University Press, 1972, illus.
Pp. 49-51, Marching Rule; pp. 88-90, Jacob Vouza as spiritually powerful "big man"; pp. 218-19, mixed experience of trade stores.

Solomon Islands

1334 Latukefu, Sione. "The Methodist mission and modernization in the Solomon Islands." In *The history of Melanesia. . . . 2d Waigoni Seminar . . . 1968*, edited by K. S. Inglis. Port Moresby: University of Papua New Guinea; Canberra: Australian National University, 1969, pp. 305-15.
P. 34, Eto's movement.

1335 L[enormand], M[aurice]. "'Marching Rule' aux Îles Salomons" and "Le 'cargo cult' à Bougainville." *Études Mélanésiennes* (Noumea), n.s. 4 [2] (July 1949): 82-83.

1336 Li'iouou, E. *Term and time: Definite origins – the history of the world.* Honiara: Honiara Museum, 1979.
A Solomon Islands Member of Parliament tracing Solomon Islands descent from Ephraim; similar to the Lost Tribes of Israel theme elsewhere.

1337 Macdonald-Milne, Brian. *The Melanesian Brotherhood: Religious Co-operation in the Pacific Islands.* Suva, Fiji: University of the South Pacific, 1983, pp. 30-40.

1338 Maetoloa, Meshach. "The Remnant Church." In *Point.* Series 3, *Religious movements in Melanesia today (2)*, edited by W. Flannery. Goroka: Melanesian Institute, 1983, pp. 35-53.

1339 Maetoloa, Meshach. "The Remnant Church." In *New religious movements in Melanesia,* edited by C. Loeliger and G. Trompf. Suva: Institute of Pacific Studies, University of the South Pacific and University of Papua New Guinea, 1985, pp. 120-48.
History of the two branches, led by Kwaisulia and by Sisimia; p. 134, the latter and Marching Rule in 1944; theologies of both leaders discussed.

1340 "Marching Rule." *Southern Cross Log* (Sydney, Melanesian Mission), no. 30 (October 1950), p. 7.
News item on the waning of the movement.

1341 "Le 'Marching Rule' aux îles Salomon." *Études Mélanénesiennes* (Noumea), n.s., no. 4 [2] (July 1949): 82.

1342 "Martin Lo." *Time* (New York), 29 September 1947, p. 40.
One of the names of Marching Rule, here interpreted as Communist-inspired and waiting for the "day of deliverance" and the "cargo" from the U.S.

1343 Masuraa, William Atkin, and Faifu, Timothy. "Church Council of South Malaita." [Ca. 1949], 7 pp. Mimeo.

The first formulation of the Council's biblical basis, rules, practices, and aims, as drawn up by the founder and assistants. On microfiche, the Centre, Selly Oak Colleges.

1344 Melanesian Mission. *Na LEI Vetena tana 'Church Association': Ni Gela.* Traoaniara, British Solomon Islands: Melanesian Mission Press, 1954, 8 pp.

1345 Montauban, Paul. "Schwärmgeister auf den Salomonen." *Kreuz und Karitas*, May 1934, 137ff.

1346 "Moro: A festival emphasizing tradition and love." *British Solomon Islands News Sheet* (Honiara, Solomon Islands Information and Broadcasting Services), no. 20 [17-31] (October 1972?), pp. 9-12, illus.

Account of two "open days" for visitors, including white students and a Canadian TV team, to "clear up rumours" about the movement.

1347 Murdoch, Brian. "On calling other people names: A historical note on 'Marching Rule' in the Solomon Islands." *Journal of the Anthropological Society of Oxford* 11, no. 3 (1980): 189-96, bib.

Derives from "Marchant's Rule," the name of the Resident Commissioner when an experimental local government scheme was introduced pre-war, based on unpublished memorandum by D. G. Kennedy in 1967.

1348 Nicoll, J. F. "Navy showed the flag in British Solomons; did not participate in Marching Rule arrests." *Pacific Islands Monthly* 18, no. 3 (1947): 71.

Statement by the Acting High Commissioner for the Western Pacific, correcting misleading press reports on the role of the Navy.

1349 O'Connor, Gulbun Coker. "The Moro movement of Guadalcanal." Ph.D. dissertation (anthropology), University of Pennsylvania, 1973, 602 pp.

Pp. 298-305, 308-11, Marching Rule; pp. 305-8, Freedom movement of Belamatanga; pp. 333-37, Paeni's cargo movement 1958-60; Part 3 (pp. 310-531), the Moro movement, its ideology as a politico-economic movement, its relation with the Catholic Mission, the "Custom House" at Makaruka; p. 567, illustration of Moro's vision.

Solomon Islands

1350 O'Reilly, Patrick [Georges Farell]. "Les chrétientés mélanésiennes et la guerre." *Neue Zeitschrift für Missionswissenschaft* 3, no. 2 (1947): 106-17.
Pp. 111-12, cargo ideas and prophetism in the context of World War II.

1351 O'Reilly, Patrick [Georges Farell]. "Malaïta (Îles Salomon): Un exemple de revendications indigènes." *Missions Maristes d'Océanie [Missions des Îles]* (Paris), no. 15 [2] (September-October 1948): 149-52, illus.
The Marching Rule movement; based on conversations with Pere Simler, missionary on Malaita.

1352 O'Reilly, Patrick, and Sédès, Jean-Marie. *Jaunes, Noirs et Blancs: Trois années de guerre aux Îles Salomons*. Paris: Édition du Monde Nouveau, 1949, 294 pp., illus., maps.

1353 *O Sala Ususur*. Taroaniara: Melanesian Mission Press. [A church paper in Mota and English.]
References to the Church Association among Anglicans: no. 86, 1954, pp. 28-30 (Aims and Band of Consolation); no. 87, 1954, pp. 36-38 (Reports on the Association on Gela); no. 89, 1955, pp. 10-12 (The Association on Gela); St. Andrew's Tide, 1955, pp. 2-5 (Editorial on the Association, probably by C. E. Fox); no. 90, 1956, pp. 16, 19-20 (A priest's dream).

1354 *Pacific Islands Monthly*, as follows:
"'Masinga Lo': Anti-British native movement is sweeping over Solomons," 17, no. 3 (1946): 7 [the Anti-British but not anti-Christian movement under "Timothy George, Rex"; if European planters, etc., are not to return, the islands should be handed over to this this movement];
"Masinga Rule," 18, no. 1 (1947): 66 [on C. S. Belshaw's departure, and article on Marching Rule];
"'Marching Rule': First-hand notes on a strange social phenomenon in Solomons," 18, no. 4 (1947): 9;
"Marching Rule leaders on trial in B.S.I.," 18, no. 4 (1947): 64;
"Marching Rule leaders sent to gaol: Extraordinary movement in Solomons broken up by government," 18, no. 8 (1948): 29-30 [a detailed account of the twenty-five-day trial, and the reasons given for finding the movement illegal];

"'Marching Rule': Police raids on fortified villages in Solomons,"
19, no. 5 (1948): 44 [news item, with general account of the movement
from the government viewpoint];

"Marching Rule activities in Solomons," 18, no. 8 (1949): 32;

"'Marching Rule' is now nearly dead," 19, no. 12 (1949): 43 [the
opinion of Dr. C. E. Fox];

"B.S.I.P. called a 'tragic Mess,'" 20, no. 8 (1950): 28, 31 [on
Marching Rule];

"Marching Rule leaders out of gaol," 21, no. 1 (1950): 41;

"Money can't buy me love – and freedom either," 36, no. 4 (1965):
7 [on Moro's attempt in 1965 to buy independence from the
government];

"B.S.I. outlaws' manifesto comes to light," 45, no. 6 (1974): 7,
illus. [Maasina Rule's manifesto of the 1940s; claims Marching Rule
was not influenced by cargo ideas.

1355 Paia, Warren A. "Nationalism and the Solomon Islands." *Yagl-Ambu:
Papua New Guinea Journal of the Social Sciences and Humanities* (Port
Moresby) 1, no. 2 (1974): 97-116.

Pp. 104-5, Pokokoqoro and other movements (based on A. R.
Tippett, entry 1365); pp. 107-9, Marching Rule.

1356 Peterson, Nicolas. "The Church Council of South Mala (Malaita): A
legitimized form of Masinga rule." *Oceania* 36, no. 3 (1966): 214-30,
table.

Pp. 227-30, Appendix on Laws, rules, and promises. The Church
Council (Anglican) founded in 1949, later as the "Church Association,"
to legitimize Masinga Rule and combat effect on Church membership
by organizing own administration of secular activities (schools,
finances, etc.) on Biblical principles.

1357 "The Remnant Church." *Melanesian Messenger* (Taroaniara), Easter
1966, pp. 9-10.

Anglican Mission's understanding of the founder and nature of
the Remnant Church, as a warning to Anglicans.

1358 Ross, Harold M. *Baegu: Social and ecological organization in Malaita,
Solomon Islands.* Illinois Studies in Anthropology, 8. Urbana:
University of Illinois Press, 1973, 334 pp., illus., maps.

Sundry references to cargo cults and the older Marching Rule,
especially pp. 58-59, 64-66, 103-4, 191-92, 203, 206.

Solomon Islands

1359 Ross, Harold M. "Competition for Baegu souls: Mission rivalry on Malaita, Solomon Islands." In *Mission, church, and sect in Oceania*, edited by J. A. Boutilier, et al. Association for Social Anthropology in Oceania, Monograph Series no. 6. Ann Arbor: University of Michigan Press, 1978, pp. 163-200.

    Pp. 183-89, Marching Rule and its successor, the Custom movement, and the 1970-71 Revival in the South Seas Evangelical Church; pp. 195-96, Seventh Day Adventist success as in effect a "European-sponsored cargo cult."

1360 Saunana, John S. "The politics of subservience." In *Priorities in Melanesian development. . . . 6th Waigoni Seminar . . . 1972*, edited by R. J. May. Port Moresby: University of Papua New Guinea; Canberra: Australian National University, 1973. Reprint. 1974, pp. 429-36.

    Especially pp. 431-32, Marching Rule and Custom movements as "status-seeking ideologies."

1361 Scheffler, Harold W. *Choiseul Island social structure*. Berkeley: University of California Press, 1965, 322 pp.

    Pp. 20-29, the advent of missions; pp. 29-31, Christian Fellowship Church and Marching Rule; little cargoism on Choiseul.

1362 Scheffler, Harold W. "Final report: Revitalization movements in British Solomons." NSF GS 1217. 1 July 1966 to 20 September 1971. Department of Anthropology, Yale University, 35 pp. Mimeo.

    A comparative study, including the Christian Fellowship Church (pp. 3-4, 7-23), Marching Rule (pp. 23-26), Moro movement (pp. 26-29), and comparison of movements (pp. 29-31).

1363 *Southern Cross Log* [English edition] (London and Sydney):

    Some references to the Church Association on South Malaita among Anglicans: May 1955, pp. 45-46 (The Association on Gela, by C. E. Fox), pp. 46-48 (on Malaita, by W. A. Masuraa); August 1958, p. 62 (on Malaita).

1364 Taruna, Joseph. "Revival in the Kieta Circuit of the United Church, North Solomons Region." In *Religious movements in Melanesia: A selection of case studies and reports*, edited by W. Flannery. Goroka: Melanesian Institute, 1983, pp. 175-88. Mimeo.

1365 Tippett, Alan R[ichard]. *Solomon Islands Christianity: A study in growth and obstruction*. London: Lutterworth Press, 1967, 407 pp. 2d ed. William Carey Library, [1975?].

Chap. 14, comparative analysis of nativistic movements; chap. 15, the prophet; chap. 16, Etoism; chap. 17, theological analysis.

1366 White, Geoffrey M[iles]. "Big men and Church men: Social images in Santa Isabel, Solomon Islands." Ph.D. dissertation (anthropology), University of California (San Diego), 1978, 520 pp.

Pp. 230-40, missionary Fallowes and his Chair and Rule movement; pp. 246-52, Marching Rule, including an explicit cult and also Zalamana's Christian version among the A'ara. Notes, pp. 276-77.

1367 White, Geoffrey M[iles]. "Social images and social change in a Melanesian society." *American Ethnologist* 7, no. 2 (1980): 352-70.

Pp. 355-56, 364, Fallowes and the Fallowes or Chair and Rule movement, 1939; in general on the two types of "big men" – church or government leaders.

1368 Whiteman, Darrell L[averne]. "Marching Rule reconsidered: An ethnohistorical evaluation." *Ethnohistory* 22, no. 4 (1975): 345-74.

Worsley's interpretation as inadequate: missionaries, entrepreneurs and administrators elicited different attitudes; examines theories of intercultural interaction, where "deprivation of worth" is an important factor.

1369 Whiteman, Darrell L[averne]. *Melanesians and Missionaries*. Pasadena: William Carey Library, 1983, 559 pp., maps, bib.

A major study. Pp. 130-31, 187-88, Christian villages. Pp. 194-98, (notes, pp. 238-39), Melanesian Brotherhood; pp. 469-76, Brotherhood and Church Association rules; pp. 280-93 (notes, pp. 319-320), Church Association. Pp. 250-273 (notes pp. 304-17), 276-77, Marching Rule (see entry 1368). Pp. 205-11, 218-19 (notes pp. 241-42), missionary Fallowes and his movement. Pp. 274-80 (notes pp. 317-19), Melanesian movements.

1370 Wouters, A. [A. M.]. "La 'Marching Rule': Aspects sociologiques d'un mouvement politique et social aux Salomons méridionaux." *Social Compass* 6, no. 2 (1958): 45-55.

By a Catholic missionary.

1371 Wouters, A. A. M. "Marching Rule, un aspect du Cargo-cult (Îles Salomon)." In *Devant les sectes non-chrétiennes*, by the Muséum Lessianum. Louvain: Desclée de Brouwer, 1962, pp. 281-91.

Vanuatu (formerly New Hebrides)

This group of islands was known as the New Hebrides and was administered as a condominium jointly by Britain and France from 1906 until independence in 1980 under the new name. Its most notable new religious movements have been the Jon (or John) Frum and Nagriamel (associated with Jimmy Stevens), and the latter was involved in the revolt that threatened the new state at its birth.

1372 Allen, M[ichael] R[ichard]. "The establishment of Christianity and cash-cropping in a New Hebridean community." *Journal of Pacific History* 3 (1968): 25-46.

Aoba Island, northern Vanuatu, as about 1962; strong churches and no cargo cults, but occasional minor prophets, and strong belief that Americans took the local creator god to the U.S. to teach him all they know and he will return.

1373 Allen, M[ichael] R[ichard]. "Innovation, inversion and revolution as political tactics in West Aoba." In *Vanuatu: Politics, economics and ritual in island Melanesia,* edited by M. R. Allen. Sydney: Academic Press, 1981, pp. 105-34.

Pp. 126-28, early Christian period and prophets; pp. 128-31, Nagriamel.

1374 Allen, M[ichael] R[ichard]. "Report on Aoba." Edited by Caroline Leaney. Vila, New Hebrides: N.p., 1969, 246 pp. Mimeo.

Report to the British residency. Pp. 3, 141-43, background to cargoism; pp. 214-26, five cargo movements, 1955-61 on West Aoba.

1375 Attenborough, David. "The cargo cult and the great god Frum." South Seas Adventures, 2. *Sunday Times* (London), 24 April 1960, p. 5, illus.

A popular account of factors encouraging cargo cults; outline of the Jon Frum based on a visit to Ambrym.

1376 Barrow, G. L. "The story of Jonfrum." *Corona* 3, no. 10 (1951): 379-82.

Reflections from colonial service viewpoint. The background, 1848-1940, and the first "Jonfrum," Manehiri; subsequent "Jonfrums," including Neloiag in 1943, and the 1947 "flareup."

1377 Beasant, John. *The Santo rebellion: Imperial reckoning.* Honolulu: University of Hawaii Press, 1986, 172 pp., illus.

Includes Nagriamel.

1378 Bonnemaison, Joël. *La dernière île*. Librairie Les Fruits du Congo. Paris: Arléa/Orstom (Diffusion Le Seuil) 1986, 407 pp.
On Tanna. Chap. 12 (pp. 262-87), John Frum; chap. 13 (pp. 288-307), John Frum mythology; pp. 344 *et seq.*, Nagriamel and Jimmy Stevens in relation to the revolt of Tanna.

1379 Bonnemaison, Joël (text), and Hermann, Bernard (photos). *New Hebrides*. English translation. Les éditions du pacifique. Papeete: Les Éditions du Pacifique, 1975, 128 pp., col. illus.
A tourist book. Pp. 91-94, John Frum movement, with two good photos.

1380 Brunton, Ron. "The origins of the John Frum movement: A sociological explanation. In *Vanuatu: politics, economics and ritual in island Melanesia*, edited by M. R. Allen. Sydney: Academic Press, 1981, pp. 357-77.

1381 "A businessman's paradise." *Kakamora Reporter* (Honiara), no. 17 (July 1971). Reprint. *New Hebridean Viewpoints* (Lolowai), no. 1 (August 1971), [pp. 4-5].
On Nagriamel and expatriate developers.

1382 Calvert, Ken[neth]. "Cargo cult mentality and development in the New Hebrides today." In *Paradise postponed: Essays on research and development in the South Pacific*, edited by A. Mamak and G. McCall. Rushcutters Bay, N.S.W., and Oxford: Pergamon Press, 1978, pp. 209-24.

1383 Calvert, Ken[neth]. "Old Nambas dies, but not the cult." *Outlook* (Christchurch, N.Z.), 11 May 1968, p. 15.
On continuing Jon Frum groups.

1384 Calvert, Ken[neth]. "Revival sweeps the New Hebrides." *Outlook* (Christchurch, N.Z.), April 1975, pp. 10, 12, illus.
Editorial report of interview with K. Calvert, Presbyterian missionary; p. 10, improved relations of John Frum with the Presbyterian Church.

1385 Coates, Austin. *Western Pacific islands*. London: H.M.S.O., 1970, 349 pp.
Pp. 275-78 Jonfrum.

Vanuatu

1386 Eliade, Mircea. "Die Amerikaner in Ozeanien und der eschatologische Nacktkult." *Antaios* (Stuttgart) 3, no. 3 (1961): 201-14.
Translation from a French article – on the Naked cult of 1944-51.

1387 Fox, [Charles Elliott]. "Native fanatics: A new sect in New Hebrides." *Pacific Islands Monthly* 9, no. 8 (1939): 30. Reprinted from the *Southern Cross Log*.
The Danielites, with six villages among the bush people of Raga.

1388 Gourguechon, Charlene. "The decline of Jimmy Stephens' star." *Pacific Islands Monthly* 42, no. 7 (1971): 39-40.

1389 Griffin, John. "New Hebrides: French ambition, British pride – and now American dreams." *Pacific Islands Monthly* 42, no. 1 (1971): 38-44, illus.
P. 44, Jimmy Stevens and Nagriamel.

1390 Guariglia, Guglielmo. *Prophetismus und Heilserwartungs-bewegungen als völkerkundliches und religionsgeschichtliches Problem.* Vienna: F. Berger, 1959, 332 pp.
Pp. 114-20, eight movements summarized.

1391 Guiart, Jean [Charles Robert]. "L'après-guerre à Ambrym, Nouvelles Hébrides." *Journal de la Société des Océanistes* (Paris) 6 (1950): 238-41.
P. 238, Jonfrum movement as part of the situation on Ambrym.

1392 Guiart, Jean [Charles Robert]. "The co-operative called 'The Malekula Native Company': A borderline type of cargo cult." *South Pacific* (Sydney) 6, no. 6 (1952): 429-32, 439.
From 1939 on Malekula, spreading to Pentecost and Ambrym, and in 1951 moving from John Frum ideas towards politico-economic goals.

1393 Guiart, Jean [Charles Robert]. "Culture contact and the 'John Frum' movement on Tanna, New Hebrides." *Southwestern Journal of Anthropology* 12, no. 1 (1956): 105-16.

1394 Guiart, Jean [Charles Robert]. *Espiritu Santo (Nouvelles Hébrides).* L'Homme: Cahiers d'Ethnologie, de Géographie et de Linguistique, 2. Paris: Librairie Plan, 1958, 236 pp., illus., maps, bib.
Pp. 119-23, 217-19, critique of Presbyterian mission methods; pp. 148, 198-202, 206, Rongofuru's movement; pp. 202-3, Avu-Avu; pp.

203-4, Atori; pp. 204-7, reflections on the belief in the country of the dead.

1395 Guiart, Jean [Charles Robert]. *Grands et petits hommes de la montagne: Espiritu Santo*. Nouvelles Hébrides. New Caledonia: Institut Français d'Océanie, 1958, pp. 182-209.
    Pp. 182-209: pp. 183-87, Rongofuru movement; pp. 187-88, Avu-Avu; pp. 188-89, Atori; pp. 193-97, Naked cult.

1396 Guiart, Jean [Charles Robert]. "John Frum movement in Tanna." *Oceania* 22, no. 3 (1952): 165-77 (pp. 176-77, Appendix of two letters by natives.)
    A good history, suggesting a tendency to formation of a neopagan national theocracy.

1397 Guiart, Jean [Charles Robert]. "Le mouvement coopératif aux Nouvelles-Hébrides." *Journal de la Société des Océanistes* 12 (1956): 326-34.
    Pp. 327ff., Malekula Native Company, as alternative to cargoism; p. 333, briefly on a recent variation on the John Frum movement.

1398 Guiart, Jean [Charles Robert]. "Le mouvement 'Four Corners' à Tanna (1974)." *Journal de la Société des Océanistes* 31 (1974): 107-11.
    On the unsuccessful attempt of adventurer Fornelli to establish Tanna as an independent state allied to the United States of America, with his possible covert manipulation by John Frum leaders.

1399 Guiart, Jean [Charles Robert]. "New Hebrides: 'A gross mistake for Europeans to interfere.'" *Pacific Islands Monthly* 51, no. 4 (1980): 10-11.
    Interview with anthropologist J. Guiart, his comments on Nagriamel, its being used by whites and its own attempt to arrest decline by association with whites.

1400 Guiart, Jean [Charles Robert]. "Les Nouvelles-Hébrides avant l'indépendence." *Journal de la Société des Océanistes* (Paris) no. 54-55, [33] (March-June 1977): 93-103.
    P. 95, author's efforts on behalf of imprisoned John Frum leaders; p. 96, a recent independent Presbyterian Church under Pastor Solomon, southeast Ambrym; p. 96, repressive action.

Vanuatu

1401 Guiart, Jean [Charles Robert]. "Report of the native situation in the north of Ambryn (New Hebrides)." *South Pacific* (Sydney) 5, no. 12 (1952): 256-67.

1402 Guiart, Jean [Charles Robert]. *Un siècle et demi de contacts culturels à Tanna, Nouvelles Hébrides.* Publications de la Société de Océanistes, 5. Paris: Musée de l'Homme, 1956, 426 pp., illus., maps.
Pp. 151-221, John Frum; pp. 228-33, John Frum myth; pp. 406-15, appendix with important letters and reports on John Frum, especially pp. 411-15, missionary J. Bell's report to the Presbyterian Synod, 1941, describing causes and remedies, and seeking a sympthetic understanding; facing p. 128, map of John Frum villages on Tanna.

1403 Harrisson, Thomas [Harnett]. *Savage civilization.* London: Victor Gollancz, 1937, 461 pp.
Pp. 380-81, Ronovura's movement on Santo in 1923.

1404 Hillinger, Charles. "Island cult waiting for 'John Frum.'" *Los Angeles Times*, 10 August 1978, pp. 1, 6, 7, illus.
Outline history since chief Kahu's vision in 1939, through apparent fulfillment by American forces in 1942, and continuing hopes.

1405 Hours, B. "Leadership et cargo cult: L'irrésistible ascension de J. T. P. S. Moise." *Journal de la Société des Océanistes* 32, nos. 51-52 (1976): 207-31.
Life of Jimmy Moses, the leader.

1406 Hours, B. "Un mouvement politico-religieux néo-hébridais: Le Nagriamel." *Cahiers ORSTOM.* Série Sciences Humaines, 11, nos. 3-4 (1974): 227-42, illus., map.
Socioeconomic background, and cultural functions of Nagriamel, treated as a "neo-cargo" cult similar to Moro movement on Guadalcanal.

1407 Hume, Lynne. "Church and custom on Maewo, Vanuatu." *Oceania* 56, no. 4 (1986): 304-13.

1408 Humphreys, C. B. *The southern New Hebrides: An ethnological record.* Cambridge: Cambridge University Press, 1926, 214 pp.
Anthropologist on Tanna in 1926.

1409 Hutton, Ken. "Santo lawlessness follows official paralysis." *Pacific Islands Monthly* 51, no. 2 (1980): 10-11.

Includes Nagriamel and its illegal Radio Vanafu.

1410 Jackson, A. L. "Current developments in the Pacific: Towards political awareness in the New Hebrides." *Journal of Pacific History* 7 (1972): 155-62.

Pp. 158-60, Jimmy Stevens, his association with Church of Christ leader Abel Bani, and formation of Nagriamel from 1967.

1411 Jackson, Bud [A. L.] "The development strategy of a social movement." In *Priorities in Melanesian development. . . . 6th Waigoni seminar . . . 1972*, edited by R. J. May. Port Moresby: University of Papua New Guinea; Canberra: Australian National University, 1973, pp. 327-31.

On Nagriamel from early sixties as response to European encroachment on land.

1412 Kalkoa, A. G. "The political situation in the New Hebrides." In *The politics of Melanesia. . . . 4th Waigoni Seminar . . . 1970*, edited by M. W. Ward. Port Moresby: University of Papua and New Guinea, 1970, pp. 207-24.

Pp. 220-22, Nagriamel and Jon Frum, as "quasi-political" and "cargo cult" respectively.

1413 Kalkot, Singoleo Hanson Matas-. "Silou Dan: A movement on the island of Pentecost (Raca) in Vanuatu." In *New Religious movements in Melanesia*, edited by C. Loeliger and G. Trompf. Suva: Institute of Pacific Studies, University of the South Pacific; University of Papua New Guinea, 1985, pp. 149-62.

Daniel Tambi's movement in an Anglican context from the early 1930s – also known as "Silo ata Tambok" and "Silon Dan." See also Kele-Kele, Kalkot Matas.

1414 Kele-Kele, Kalkot Matas. "A political groundswell in the New Hebrides." *Pacific Islands Monthly* 45, no. 5 (1974): 42, 43, photo (of Jimmy Stevens).

Survey of various parties, including Nagriamel and its relation to the Church.

1415 Kele-Kele, Kalkot Matas, et al. *New Hebrides: The road to independence*. Edited by Christ Plant. Suva: Institute of Pacific Studies, University of the South Pacific, in association with South Pacific Social Sciences Association, 1977, 128 pp., illus., map.

Vanuatu

Pp. 32-33, 35-40 (by Jimmy Stevens), 88-92, 99, 101, 112 (with Jon Frum also), on Nagriamel; p. 210, Jon Frum; p. 124, Daniel Light and other movements.

1416 Lane, R. B. "The Melanesians of South Pentecost, New Hebrides." In *Gods, ghosts, and men in Melanesia,* edited by P. Lawrence and M. J. Meggitt. New York, Melbourne, etc.: Oxford University Press, 1965, pp. 250-79.
Pp. 277-78, relation to Christian missions, and absence of cults towards which these people are sceptical.

1417 Langdon, Robert. "Chief President Moses: A man with a message for 10,000 Hebrideans." *Pacific Islands Monthly* 40, no. 7 (1969): 23-25, illus.
Land reforms and patterns of social reform initiated by a cult-like society, Nagriamel.

1418 Lindstrom, Lamont C. [Monty Lindstrom, pseud.]. "Americans on Tanna: An essay from the field." *Canberra Anthropology* 2, no. 2 (1979): 37-46.
Local expectations from America, in John Frum context.

1419 Lindstrom, Lamont C. "Cargo cult, John Frum." In *Historical dictionary of Oceania,* edited by R. D. Craig and F. P. King. Westport, Conn., and London: Greenwood Press, 1981, p. 47.

1420 Lindstrom, Lamont C. [Monty Lindstrom, pseud.]. "Cult and culture: American dreams in Vanuatu." *Pacific Studies* (Laie, Hawaii) 4, no. 2 (1981): 101-23.
John Frum and Nagriamel, and the Phoenix Foundation.

1421 Lindstrom, Lamont C. "Knowledge of cargo, knowledge of cult truth and power on Tanna, Vanuatu." In *Cargo cults and millenarian movements,* edited by G. W. Trompf. Religion and Society Series. Berlin: de Gruyter, Mouton Publishers, 1990, pp. 223-43.

1422 Lini, Walter. *Beyond pandemonium – from the New Hebrides to Vanuatu.* Wellington: Asia Pacific Books, 1981, 64 pp., illus., map. Suva: Institute of Pacific Studies, University of the South Pacific.
A biography of the first Prime Minister, by his sister and others. P. 45 John Frum; pp. 47-50, Jimmy Stevens and Nagriamel.

1423 Luke, Harry [Charles]. *From a South Seas diary, 1938-42.* London: Nicholson & Watson, 1945, 255 pp., illus.

Pp. 203-4, briefly on Jon Frum; plate 75M, photo of Jon Frum. By a Governor of Fiji and British High Commissioner for the Western Pacific.

1424 Macdonald-Milne, Brian J., and Thomas, Pamela, eds., *Yumi stanap: Leaders and leadership in a new nation.* Suva: Institute of Pacific Studies, University of the South Pacific and Lotu Pasifika Productions, 1981, 135 pp., photos.

Pp. 46-52, Jimmy Stevens.

1425 McKee, Matthew. "Waiting for the skies to open." *Pacific Islands Monthly*, March 1989, pp. 26-27, 30, illus.

Popular historical outline of John Frum movement with descriptions of its annual February celebrations at Sulphur Bay, and the problem of the nearby Yassur volcano.

1426 Marsh, Don (narrator). "The surprising Gospels of John Frum: He who swept sin away." *Pacific Islands Monthly* 39, no. 10 (October 1968): 83-90.

An Englishman who "played in the John Frum band" narrates the stories of six individual members of the movement, together with his own interpretation.

1427 Martin, Pierre. "Les mouvements de John Frum et de Tieka: Deux faits sociaux totaux aux Nouvelles Hébrides." *Le Monde Non-Chrétien* 17 [n.s. 43-44] (July-December 1957): 225-65.

1428 Miller, J. Graham. "Naked cult in Central West Santo." *Journal of the Polynesian Society* 57 (1948): 330-41.

The first study, by a Presbyterian missionary.

1429 "Misleading story in New Zealand newspaper" ("Switzerland in the Pacific," in *New Zealand Herald,* 18 February 1976). Also as "Stori we i kamaot long niuspepa long niesilan." *New Hebrides News* (British Residency Information Office, Vila), no. 48 (8 March 1976), p. 2; *idem,* "Joint denial by B. R. C. and F. R. C.," p. 3 [the two Resident Commissioners' official reply].

1430 Muller, Kal. "Tanna awaits the coming of John Frum." *National Geograpahic* 145, no. 5 (1974): 706-15, illus.

Vanuatu

A brief outline, largely through comments on the color photographs.

1431 New Hebrides: Anglo-French Condominium. Biennial *Reports*. London: H.M.S.O. *For years 1955 & 1956* (1958), p. 11, official report on "custom" practices – typical of annual references to "revitalization" movements; *For years 1957 & 1958* (1960), pp. 3-4, Jon-frum movement on Tanna in a renewed "active phase" and successful control by the administration; *For years 1971 & 1972* (1974), pp. 99-101, Religion and custom – an outline including missions and churches, and briefly on John Frum and Nagriamel.

1432 *The New York Times index*. New York: New York Times Co., annually. See relevant names (e.g., 1980, p. 1571, Jimmy Stevens' revolt, same year).

1433 Nottage, Basil R. C. *New Hebrides calling*. Auckland: Mission Committee, Presbyterian Church of New Zealand, 1940, pp. 25-26. Pp. 25-26, comment on John Frum movement (not named) as allied to the "Vailala madness."

1434 "On a Pacific island, they wait for the G.I. who became a god." *New York Times*, 19 April 1970. John Frum.

1435 O'Reilly, Patrick [Georges Farell]. "'Jonfrum' is New Hebridean 'cargo cult'" (Parts 1-2). *Pacific Islands Monthly* 20, no. 6 (1950): 67, 69-70; 20, no. 7 (1950): 59-61, 63-65. English translation, with editorial introduction of entry 1436.

1436 O'Reilly, Patrick [Georges Farell]. "Prophètisme aux Nouvelles-Hébrides: Le mouvement John Frum à Tanna (1940-1947)." *Le Monde Non-Chrétien*, n.s. 10 (1949): 192-208. By a Catholic missionary who visited area in 1948 and collected all available evidence, verbal or written. For English version, see entry 1435.

1437 Parsonson, G[ordon] S. *The Gospel in the southern New Hebrides, 1893-1958*. Presbyterian Society of New Zealand, Annual Lecture, Dunedin, 1986. [Auckland: The Society, 1986], 16 pp. Pp. 12-16, John Frum origins on Tanna in land disputes and local conservatism rather than missionary mistakes as claimed by J. Guiart; vivid account of subsequent renewals.

1438 Paton, W. F. "The native situation in the north of Ambryn (New Hebrides)." *South Pacific* (Sydney) 6, no. 5 (1952): 392-96.
John Frum movement, ca. 1952, by a Presbyterian missionary, in criticism of Guiart's account in *idem* 5, no. 12 (March 1952).

1439 Plant, C. "The Nagriamel Federation: New country, old story." *Pacific Perspective* (Suva, Fiji) 6 (1977): 49-57.

1440 Poirier, Jean. "Les mouvements de libération mythique aux Nouvelles-Hébrides." *Journal de la Société des Océanistes* 5, no. 5 (1949): 97-103.

1441 Raffe, E. [Letter, 1 October 1924, to F. E. Williams – extract.] In *Orokaiva Magic*, by F. E. Williams. London: Oxford University Press, 1928. Reprint. Oxford: Clarendon Press, 1969, Appendix, 100-101.
A movement on Espiritu Santo under Ronovuro, 1914-23.

1442 Rentoul, Alexander. "John Frum: Origin of New Hebrides movement." *Pacific Islands Monthly* 19, no. 6 (1949): 31.
Letter to the editor by former temporary District agent on Tanna: on "Frum" as meaning "broom."

1443 Rice, Edward. *John Frum he come: A polemical work about a Black tragedy.* Garden City, N.Y.: Doubleday & Co., 1974, xxv + 262 pp., illus., map.
An American writer-photographer's first-hand account of the John Frum movement from a pro-Tannese viewpoint; pp. 60-113, racy reports of Melanesian movements; p. 113-20, Nagriamel; pp. 151-63, local opinions of John Frum; pp. 175-227, verbatim accounts by adherents; pp. 251-62, diary of events, especially administrative actions, 1940-57.

1444 Rubinstein, Robert L. "Knowledge and political process on Malo." In *Vanuatu: Politics, economics, and ritual in island Melanesia*, edited by M. R. Allen. Sydney: Academic Press, 1981, pp. 135-72.
Pp. 159-62, 169-71, Nagriamel and Jimmy Stevens.

1445 Ryman, Anders. "John Frum: Won't you please come home?" *Journey: Australian Geographical Magazine* (Dee Why West, N.S.W.) 9, no. 4 (1987-88): 78-93.
Members of the movement on Tanna waiting for the U.S. to save them from poverty.

Vanuatu

1446 Salmon, M. "Hebrides: A sorely troubled run-up to freedom." *Pacific Islands Monthly* 51, no. 7 (1980): 10-11.
The Jimmy Stevens troubles.

1447 Sawer, Marian, and Jupp, James. "The New Hebrides prepares for independence." *Current Affairs Bulletin* (Department of Adult Education, University of Sydney) 56, no. 11 (1980): 22-30, map.
Pp. 25b-26, the "custom" parties–John Frum, Nagriamel, and Kapiel; p. 26, Stevens illegally detaining a pastor, 1978-79.

1448 Shiffer, James. "John Frum and the Cargo cults." *Far East* (Magazine of Columban Fathers and Sisters), July-August 1983, pp. 3-7, illus.
Includes selections from Thomas Merton on cargo cults.

1449 Sope, Barak. "Decentralisation: A priority for political development in the New Hebrides." In *Priorities in Melanesian development. ... 6th Waigoni Seminar ... 1972*, edited by R. J. May. Port Moresby: University of Papua New Guinea; Canberra: Australian National University, 1973, pp. 83-88.
P. 87, briefly on John Frum and Nagriamel as primarily political, antigovernment movements.

1450 Sope, Barak. *Land and politics in the New Hebrides*. Suva: South Pacific Social Sciences Association, [1975], 60 pp., illus.
Pp. 22-23, John Frum and Nagriamel.

1451 "A spark, at last in the New Hebrides Council." *Pacific Islands Monthly* 41, no. 1 (1970): 26-29.
Pp. 28-29, the debate on Nagriamel and Stevens's recent activities.

1452 Stevens, Jimmy Moli. "The Na-Griamel [*sic*] viewpoint on the New Hebrides scene." *Pacific Islands Monthly* 48, no. 2 (1977): 16-17, photo.
Nagriamel's founder expounds its policy, attacks the national party, recognizes French assistance, and threatens independence for the northern islands.

1453 Stevens, Ross. "The New Hebrides politics simmering." *Outlook* (Wellington, N.Z.) 86, no. 1 (1979): 6-7, illus.
French political party manipulation of John Frum movement against the Vanuaaku party of New Hebrideans.

1454 Toa, Oscar Arthur. "Strange religion on Raga." *Melanesian Messenger* (Taroaniara), August 1965, pp. 23-26.

An independent Christian church formed by Daniel on Pentecost Island, anti-"custom" and pro-Anglican, but nationalistic and prophesying independence both religious and political.

1455 Trease, T. H[oward] van. "Frustrations of trying to 'guide' the unguidable." *Pacific Islands Monthly* 53, no. 8 (1982): 27-29.

Extracts from letters from the French Resident commissioners showing their use of Jimmy Stevens for political purposes.

1456 Trompf, G[arry] W[inston]. "Jimmy Stevens as betrayer of a faith." *Pacific Islands Monthly* (Sydney) 51, no. 11 (1980): 27, 33.

Nagriamel as a religious movement and parallel to Hehela Church and Christian Fellowship Church.

1457 Watters, R. F. [Roger Clare, pseud.]. "Prophet in Paradise." *New Zealand International Review* 5, no. 5 (1980): 21-22, illus.

A geographer interviewing Jimmy Stevens on Nagriamel in 1977.

1458 Whimp, Neal. *The Church in Vanuatu since 1945 with special reference to its role in the move to independence, 1980.* (Annual Lecture, 1981). N.p.: Presbyterian Historical Society of New Zealand, [1982?], 14 pp.

Pp. 1, 4, John Frum, Naked cult and "custom" movements; pp. 1, 4-5, 7, 12-13, Nagriamel and Stevens.

1459 Wilson, Bryan [Ronald]. *The noble savages: The primitive origins of charisma and its contemporary survival.* Berkeley and London : University of California Press, 1975, 133 pp.

Pp. 86-89, Jon Frum movement.

1460 Woodcock, George. *South Sea Journey.* London: Faber & Faber, 1976, 341 pp.

Pp. 218-43, Jon Frum and similar movements.

1461 Worsley, Peter [Maurice]. *The trumpet shall sound: A study of "cargo" cults in Melanesia.* London: MacGibbon & Kee, 1957, 290 pp. 2d ed., enl., with supplementary bib. New York: Schocken Books, 1968, 300 pp.

Pp. 146-69 (1968 ed.), various movements, pp. 153-60 on John Frum.

Micronesia

General (including Guam, Nauru, and various small states)

This term is used here in an older and wider geographical sense to include what have become Kiribati (formerly Gilbert Islands) and Tuvalu (formerly Ellice Islands). It also includes former elements of the United Nations Trust Territory (to U.S. 1947-81), which have formed four new states: Marshall Islands, Palau (Western Carolines), Federated States of Micronesia (Eastern Carolines), and Northern Marianas. Guam remains a U.S. Trust Territory, while Nauru became independent in 1968. The main documented movement is Modekne (or Modekngei) on Palau, and there are also two studies of reactions to typhoons as "negative instances."

1462 Aoyagi, Machiko. "The transformation of traditional religion: The influence of Christianity." In *The tribal world and its transformation*, edited by B. Singh and J. S. Bhandari. New Delhi: Concept Publishing, 1980, pp. 131-39.

Modekngei movement on Palau.

1463 Barnett, Homer G[arnett]. *Being a Palauan*. Case Studies in Cultural Anthropology. New York: Holt, Rinehart, & Winston, 1960, 87 pp., map.

Pp. 79-82, Palauan religion; pp. 83-85, Temudad's Modekne cult, its development under Ongesi and persecution first by the Japanese and then by Americans.

General

1464 Barnett, Homer G[arnett]. *Palauan society: A study of contemporary native life in the Palau islands*. Coordinated Investigation of Micronesian Anthropology, Report 20. 1949, 223 pp., maps. Reprint. Eugene: Department of Anthropology, University of Oregon, n.d.

Pp. 210-13, mission history; pp. 213-14, Ardial as a prophet; pp. 214-22, Modekne cult under Temudad and his successor Ongesi.

1465 Charles, Hubert E[lechues]. "Essays on Palau." M.A. project, School of World Mission, Fuller Theological Seminary, 1976, 164 pp.

Pp. 105-19, the testimony of an eye-witness to the "Palau Revival," 1955-57, initiated through actions of a missionary of the Bad Liebenzell Mission.

1466 Fey, Wilhelm. "Interview: Pastor Wilhelm Fey." *Micronesian Reporter* (Saipan, Mariana) 20, no. 2 (1972): 2-8.

Lutheran missionary Fey's work since 1933 in Palau; p. 3, the Modekngei religion as more political than religious.

1467 Force, Richard W. *Leadership and cultural change in Palau*. Museum Publication 882: Fieldiana: anthropology, 50. Chicago: Natural History Museum, 1960, 211 pp., maps, bib. (pp. 198-207).

P. 87, Modekngei movement as the only organized opposition to cultural change, among a people very receptive to change; leaders imprisoned and meeting places razed during the Japanese occupation.

1468 Kahn, Ely Jacques, Jr. *A reporter in Micronesia*. New York: W. W. Norton, 1966, 313 pp., illus.

Pp. 274-76, Pulo Anna's new religion, and Modekngei movement, 1912, later under Ongesi and continuing.

1469 Leonard, Anne P. "Spirit mediums in Palau: Transformations in a traditional system." In *Religion, altered states of consciousness, and social change*, edited by E. Bourguignon. Columbus: Ohio State University Press, 1973, pp. 129-77.

Pp. 140-59, Palau religion, possession and mediums, with two case studies of the latter; pp. 159-65, Modekngei and its mediums.

1470 Lessa, William A. "The social effects of typhoon Ophelia (1960) on Ulithi." *Micronesia* (Guam) 1, nos. 1-2 (1964): 1-47, illus., map. Reprinted in *Peoples and cultures of the Pacific*, edited by A. P. Vadya. Garden City, N.Y.: Natural History Press, 1968, pp. 330-79.

A "negative instance": Christianity was in fact enhanced by the typhoon, traditional tabus were undermined, and no new movement occurred.

1471 "Modekngei: The Palauan religion." *Micronesian Reporter* (Saipan, Mariana) 20, no. 1 (1972): 9-10.

A survey of the history and development of Modekngei, extracted from A. J. Vidich (entry 1477) and updated by the editor.

1472 Müller, Klaus W. "Die evangelische Missionsarbeit auf den Trukinseln: Eine missiologische Analyse." M.A. thesis, School of World Mission, Fuller Theological Seminary, 1979.

By a German missionary. Pp. 61-68, 71, Kanisio's movement in the Truk Lagoon, 1972; pp. 446-49, vernacular text and German trans. of the account given by Ebet, of the Evangelical Church at Moch.

1473 "Nauru friction: Political and religious." *Pacific Islands Monthly* 4, no. 6 (1934): 28.

Brief news item on inter-Catholic strife and the new Anglican Church of Nauru. An erroneous report, corrected in entry 1474.

1474 "Religious stir in Nauru: When High Chief Detudamo founded a new denomination." *Pacific Islands Monthly* 4, no. 11 (1934): 28-29.

Detudamo, trained as Methodist missionary in the U.S., found London Missionary Society had taken over the Methodist Mission and fomented unrest; after imprisonment rose high in the administration and then founded the Anglican Church of Nauru as a secession from the L.M.S.; subsequent strife led the Administration to prevent this development.

1475 Thompson, Laura [Maud]. "Crisis on Guam." *Far Eastern Quarterly* 6 (1946): 5-11.

Contrasts imposition of Spanish Catholicism followed by much cultural accommodation, with the imposition of U.S. navy rule without accommodation, producing a cultural crisis.

1476 Useem, John. *Report on Yap and Palau, Western Carolines*. Economic Survey of Micronesia, 6. Honolulu: U.S. Commercial Co., 1946, 124 pp.

Pp. 76-77, Modekngei on Palau–its theology and liturgy, an openly acknowledged mixture of "protective shamanism and Christian ideology."

General

1477 Vidich, Arthur J. "Political factionalism in Palau." Coordinated investigation of Micronesia Anthropology (CIMA). Report no. 23, June 1949.

> See section reprinted and updated in *Micronesian Reporter* (entry 1471)

1478 Yamashita, Antonio C. "Attitudes and reactions towards typhoon Karen in Guam (1962)." *Micronesia* (Guam) 2, no. 1 (1965): 15-23.

> People prayed, but there was no religious movement emerging – although little inquiry was made on this point; again, a "negative instance."

Kiribati (formerly Gilbert Islands)

The Gilbert and Ellice islands formed a British colony from 1916 until independence was achieved as two states, Kiribati and Tuvalu, in 1979 and 1980. The most notable recorded movement was known variously as Barane, God-the-Father, or Swords of Gabriel movement.

1479 "Amazing religious disturbance in Southern Gilberts." *Pacific Islands Monthly* 2, no. 12 (1932): 19.

> Quoting the Resident Commissioner's report from 1929-30 on Onotoa Island: Barane's movement, anti-Catholic and antigovernment.

1480 Baraniko, Mikaere; Tuam, Tangitang; and Tabokai, Nakibae. "Strife: The civil wars." In *Kiribati: Aspects of History*, edited by Alaima Talu, et al. Suva: University of the South Pacific; Kiribati Ministry of Education, Training, and Culture, 1984, pp. 44-64.

> P. 52, Tanako's Tioba (Jehovah) cult at war with the Christians in Tabiteuea North, 1879.

1481 Eastman, G. "Report on the work in the southern and central islands, Onotoa." In *Progress: The Decennial Report, 1920-1930*, of the Gilbert Islands and Nauru Mission, Central Pacific. Beru, Gilbert Islands: Rongorongo Press (London Missionary Society) 1931, pp. 31-35.

> The Swords of Gabriel movement and how missionaries dealt with it.

1482 Engelhardt, Heinrich. "Gilbert-Insulaner sterben für ihren heiligen Glauben." *Hiltruper Monatshefte* 50 (April 1933): 115-17.

> God-the-Father movement from a Catholic viewpoint; see extracts in G. Eckert (entry 311), p. 32.

1483 Geddes, W. H. "Tabiteuea North: Its social and economic organization." Ph.D. thesis (geography?), Victoria University of Wellington, 1977.
Includes the Tabiteuea wars with the Tioba cult in 1879-80.

1484 Gilbert and Ellice Islands Colony. *Gilbert and Ellice Islands Colony: Report for 1929-1930*. Colonial Reports – Annual. No. 1564. London: H. M. Stationery Office, 1932, 34 pp., map.
Pp. 31-33, religious disturbances on Onotoa Island in 1930 – the God-the-Father movement.

1485 Grimble, Arthur [Francis]. *A pattern of islands*. London: John Murray; New York: W. Morrow, 1952, 246 pp.
Pp. 90-98, God-the-Father movement and its suppression. By a former Resident Commissioner who had to deal with the movement.

1486 Guariglia, Guglielmo. *Prophetismus und Heilserwartungs-bewegungen als völkerkundliches und religionsgeschichtliches Problem*. Vienna: F. Berger, 1959, 332 pp.
Pp. 123-24, movement on Onotoa.

1487 Ieuti, Teeruro. "The Kiribati Protestant Church and the new religious movements, 1860-1985." B.D. thesis, Pacific Theological College (Suva), 1987.

1488 L[ehmacher], G. "Südsee. Vikariat Gilbertinseln. Katholikenverfolgung (Gilbert Islands)." *Die Katholischen Missionen* 61, no. 8 (1933): 218.
Barane's anti-Catholic movement on Onotoa.

1489 Maude, H[arry] C., and Maude, H[onor] E. "Tioba and the Tabiteuean wars." *Journal of the Polynesian Society* 90, no. 3 (1981): 307-36.
On the neoprimal Tioba (Jehovah) cult in the 1870s and the Protestant attack on it – a detailed historical study from unpublished materials.

1490 Maude, H[onor] E. "The Swords of Gabriel: A study in participant history." *Journal of Pacific History* (Canberra) 2 (1967): 113-36.
The Barane movement in 1930, not consciously antigovernment and did not become a cargo cult; arrested in mid-development and collapsed.

Polynesia

General (including various small islands)

This wide-ranging cultural area extends from Hawaii in the north to the New Zealand Maoris in the south, and to Easter Island (part of Chile) in the east. It also includes certain "Polynesian outliers" such as Rennell and Bellona Islands and Tikopia, which geographically are in Solomon Islands' area. Most movements have been on the larger islands and especially among the New Zealand Maoris. While a few have had cargo features this has not been so characteristic as in the Melanesian area. In more recent times independent churches formed by secessions have been more common.

1491 Burridge, Kenelm [Oswald Lancelot]. *New heaven, new earth: A Study of millenarian activities*. Pavillion Series: Social Anthropology. Oxford: Blackwell, 1969, 191 pp.
      Chap. 3-4, for Polynesian examples–Hauhas, Siovili, Cooks Islands prophetess.

1492 Daws, Alan Gavan. "Polynesian religious revivals: A study with background." M.A. thesis, University of Hawaii, 1960, 140 pp.
      Pp. 69-98, Hawaiian revivals; pp. 99-119, Samoan "Great Awakening"; otherwise relates these to revivals in the U.S. (Jonathan Edwards) and other Western societies.

1493 Firth, Raymond. "The theory of 'cargo cults': A note on Tikopia." *Man*, article 142, 55 (September 1955): 130-32.
      No cargo cults in Tikopia, but two rumors regarded as "prototype cargo cult phenomena"–"The goods of Pa Fenumera," and an

General

apocalyptic movement related to a threatened hurricane; cult behavior occurs but does not develop into movements.

1494 Keesing, Felix M[axwell]. *The South Seas in the modern world.* International Research Series. New York: John Day Co. for Institute of Pacific Relations, 1941, 391 pp., illus. Reprint. London: Allen & Unwin, 1942. Rev. ed. New York: John Day Co., 1945, xxiv + 391 pp., illus. Reprint. 1946.

P. 230, a Samoan chief with incipient cargo ideas; pp. 235-38, Hawaiian traditional revival, with passing reference to a number of movements.

1495 Koskinen, Aarne A. *Missionary influence as a political factor in the Pacific Islands.* Finnish Academy of Sciences Series. Helsinki: N.p., 1953, 163 pp.

Pp. 101-3, "Semi-heathen heresies in the Pacific." A doctoral dissertation.

1496 Lanternari, Vittorio. "Culti profetici Polinesiani." *Studi e materiali di storia delle religioni* 28, no. 2 (1957): 55-78.

Similar to material in entry 1497, 1963.

1497 Lanternari, Vittorio. *The religions of the oppressed: A study of modern messianic cults.* English translation. London: MacGibbon & Kee, 1963, xx + 343 + xiii pp.; New York: A. A. Knopf, 1963, xvi + 286 pp. Reprint. New York: Mentor Books, 1965, xvi + 286 pp.

Chap. 6 (Mentor, pp. 191-210), messianic movements–Tuka, Mamaia, Hapu, Siovili, Kanito, Hau Hau, and Ringatu.

1498 Monberg, Torben. "Crisis and mass conversion on Rennell Island in 1938." *Journal of the Polynesian Society* 71 (1962): 145-50.

A "Polynesian outlier" in Solomon Islands; a temporary outbreak of millennialism, destroying goods, breaking tabus, etc.

1499 Morrell, William P[arker]. *Britain in the Pacific Islands.* Oxford: Clarendon Press, 1960, 454 pp.

Pp. 56-57, Joe Gimlet's "Jovelites"; pp. 57-59, 60, Mamaia, and the founder, Teau.

1500 Mühlmann, Wilhelm Emil. "Polynesische Beispiele." In *Chiliasmus und Nativismus*, edited by W. E. Mühlmann. Berlin: Reimer (1961) 1964, pp. 191-95.

1501 Parsonson, Gordon S. "The literate revolution in Polynesia." *Journal of Pacific History* 2 (1967): 39-57.

P. 55, Mamaia; p. 57, note 118, John Frum member, on the hidden Bible.

1502 Pritchard, William T[homas]. *Polynesian reminiscences, or life in the South Pacific Islands*. London: Chapman & Hall, 1866, xii + 428 pp., illus. Facsimile reprint. Papakura, N.Z.: Southern Reprints, 1985.

Pp. 203-4, early sailors' or "vagabond" religious sects; pp. 205-6, Siovili in Fiji.

1503 Routledge, Mrs. Scoresby [Katherine]. *The mystery of Easter Island: The story of an expedition*. London: Sifton Praed & Co., 1919. 2d ed. 1920, 404 pp., illus., map.

Chap. 11 (pp. 140-49), "a native rising" – prophetess Angata and her death, with photo (fig. 30); pp. 205-9, entry into the wider world, and Christianization.

1504 Schulze-Maizier, Friedrich. *Die Osterinsel*. Leipzig: Insel-Verlag, [1926], 238 pp., illus., maps.

Pp. 164-70, prophetess Angata and the nativistic revolt of 1914 on Easter Island.

1505 Siikala, Jukka. *Cult and conflict in tropical Polynesia: A study of traditional religion, Christianity and nativistic movements*. F. F. Communications, 233. Academia Scientiarum Fennica, 1981, 308 pp.

1506 Tippett, Alan Richard. *People movements in Southern Polynesia: Studies in the dynamics of Church-planting and growth in Tahiti, New Zealand, Tonga, and Samoa*. Chicago: Moody Press, 1971, 288 pp.

See index, "nativistic movement," especially Hau Hau, John Frum, Kingites (King movement), Mamaia, Marching Rule, Pai Marire, Ratana, Ringatu, Taro cult.

1507 Turner, George. *Nineteen years in Polynesia: Missionary life, travels, and researches in the islands of the Pacific*. London: John Snow, 1861, 548 pp., illus.

Pp. 104-6, religions of white runaway sailors, etc.; pp. 106-9, Samoan millennial cult, perhaps Siovili.

1508 Williamson, Robert Ward. *Essays in Polynesian ethnology*. Edited by R. Piddington. Cambridge: Cambridge University Press, 1939, 373 pp.

General

1509 Williamson, Robert Ward. *Religion and social organization in central Polynesia*. Edited by R. Piddington. Cambridge: Cambridge University Press, 1937, 340 pp. Reprint. New York: AMS Press, 1976.

Cook Islands and Tokelau or Union Islands

These islands, along with Niue, have been under the control of New Zealand since 1901, and became a self-governing external territory in 1965. The Tokelaus have been part of New Zealand since 1948. There have been a number of villages seceding from the L.M.S. or Congregational Churches, and one recorded cargo-type movement under a prophetess, Kapuvai.

1510 Beaglehole, Ernest. *Social change in the South Pacific, Raratonga, and Aitutaki*. London: George Allen & Unwin, 1957, 268 pp.
      Pp. 96-99, Raratongan "military style drinking organization" as a "nativistic movement" in reaction to James Chalmers' mission, but finally incorporated in the latter; p. 195, Amuri Free Church on Aitutaki; p. 197, earlier secession villages on Rarotonga and Aitutaki.

1511 Boardman, David W. "Religion as a factor in the adjustment of immigrants." *Social Compass* 26, no. 1 (1979): 73-85.
      The Tokelau community in Wellington, New Zealand.

1512 Crocombe, Ronald G[ordon]. "A modern Polynesian cargo-cult." *Man*, article 28, 61 (1961): 40-41.
      Prophetess Kapavai on Cook Islands from 1947, but short-lived.

1513 Gray, Joseph David. "A history of Raratonga, 1800-1883." 2 vols. Ph.D. thesis (history), University of Otago, 1975, xi + 581 pp.
      Pp. 456-57, a semimilitary nativistic cult reacting against missionary Chalmers in 1874.

Hawaii

After having continued, through various vicissitudes, as an independent kingdom through the nineteenth century, Hawaii was annexed by the U.S. in 1898 and admitted as a state within the Union in 1959. Although it now contains most of the races and religions of the world, our concern is confined to those new movements deriving from the independent response of Hawaiian Polynesians to the Christian or other major religious traditions. Other new religions in Hawaii stem from non-Polynesian immigrants, but many new healing cults combine divergent cultural influences.

1514 "Aiea's Calvary Church of the Pacific, built almost entirely by members, to hold 1st services." *Honolulu Advertiser*, 22 July 1978, p. B2.

1515 Aiona, Darrow Lewis. "The Hawaiian Church of the Living God: An episode in the Hawaiian's quest for social identity." M.A. thesis, University of Hawaii, 1959, 124 pp.
    On the Ekalesia O Ka Mauna O Oliveta (Mount Olivet Church) in Waikanae, Oahu, also known as the Church of the True, or the Living, God founded by Mrs. Ellen Ling about 1943. On microfiche, the Centre, Selly Oak Colleges.

1516 Alexander, W. D. "A statement of facts relating to politics during Kalakaua's reign." In *Report of the Committee on Foreign Relations, House Executive Document 47, U.S. Senate, 53rd Congress, 2nd Session.* Vol. 2. Washington: Government Printing Office, 1894.
    P. 658, Kalakaua's Temple of Science. On microfiche, the Centre, Selly Oak Colleges.

1517 "Aus allen Erdteilen." *Globus* (Braunschweig) 14 (1868): 379-84.
    P. 384, prophet Kaoni whose revolt was suppressed.

1518 Beaglehole, Ernest. *Some modern Hawaiians*. University of Hawaii Research Publications, 19. Honolulu: University of Hawaii Press, 1939, 175 pp.
    Pp. 79-81, 86, Kalakaua's Hale Naua society, 1886; pp. 83-88, nativistic religions, based on S. Dibble (entry 1524), J. J. Jarves (entry 1532), and the *Polynesian* (entry 1548); pp. 84-87, a prophet in 1867, and the Living God Church.

1519 Bicknell, James. *Hoomanamana – idolatry*. Kalakaua's Hawaii, 1874-1891. Part 2, No. 1. N.p., [188?], 12 pp.
    A pamphlet by a missionary (?) on King Kalakaua's nativistic revival.

1520 Blackman, William Fremont. *The making of Hawaii: A study in social evolution*. New York: Macmillan, 1899, 266 pp.
    Pp. 88-91, on the 1880s pagan reaction.

1521 Brown, J[ohn] Macmillan. *People and problems of the Pacific*. Vol. 2. London: T. Fisher Unwin, 1927, 297 pp. Reprint. New York: AMS Press, 1976.

Hawaii

Pp. 53-54, the brief Hapu cult as a new "magical religion" proclaiming an imminent catclysmic judgment.

1522 Burrows, Edwin G[rant]. *Hawaiian Americans: An account of the mingling of Japanese, Chinese, Polynesian, and American cultures*. New Haven: Yale University Press, 1947, 228 pp. Reprint. Hamden, Conn.: Archon Books, 1970.

Pp. 148-67, a general survey quoting primary sources and including Pele, Hapu, Kalehua ("Leno"), Hoana, Kalakaua, independent churches, and Wahiawa Stones.

1523 Dibble, Sheldon. *History and general views of the Sandwich Islands Mission*. New York: Taylor & Dodd, 1839, 268 pp.

Pp. 107-10, on this missionary's suppression of the Hapu cult.

1524 Dibble, Sheldon. *A history of the Sandwich Islands*. Lahainaluna, Hawaii: Press of the Mission Seminary, 1843, 451 pp., map.

Pp. 280-82, the Hapu Cult built around a deceased prophetess.

1525 Dunstan, J. Leslie. "The churches in Hawaii." *Social Process in Hawaii* (University of Hawaii) 16 (1952): 34-39.

Protestant churches only: their relation to family life, variety, ignorance of Christianity, lack of social influence, and including independent churches of Hawaiian origin.

1526 Engle, Murray. "The 'healing' stones." *Honolulu Star-Bulletin*, 13 November 1977, p. C-3.

At Wahiawa.

1527 Hale Naua. *Constitution and bylaws of the Hale Naua or Temple of Science. Ancient secret society of the Order of Nauas or Order of the Temple of Science*. San Francisco: Bancroft Co. (Printers), 1890, 41 pp.

King Kalakaua's revival, 1881-.

1528 Hale Naua. "*Kumukanawai*." Honolulu: Paiia Ma Ka Halepai o Ka Elele, 1887, pp. 1-9.

In Hawaiian: published by the Hale Naua or Temple of Science secret society.

1529 "He Hoomana Pegana ma Hawaii Nei, Oia Na Kipi" [A pagan sect in Hawaii, the Rebels]. *Ke Alaula* (Hawaii), December 1868, p. 2, col. 3. Reprinted in *Kukini 'Aha'ilono* [Carry on the news]: *Over a century of native Hawaiian life and thought from the Hawaiian language newspapers of 1823-1948* ... , edited by R. Johnson. Honolulu: Topgallant Publishing Co., 1976, pp. 310-11.

On prophet Kaona's movement 1867-68. Hawaiian text and English trans.

1530 Hormann, Bernhard L. "Towards a sociology of religion in Hawaii." *Social Process in Hawaii* (University of Hawaii) 25 (1961-62): 58-66, bib.

The great religious diversity and interaction. P. 59, Church of the Living God; p. 60, Japanese nativistic movements.

1531 Jabbour, Millard E. "The sect of Tensho-Kotai-Jingu-Kyo: The emergence and career of a religious movement." M.A. thesis, University of Hawaii, 1958, 128 pp.

The "Dancing Goddess" religion, a new form from Japan.

1532 Jarves, James Jackson. *History of the Hawaiian or Sandwich Islands*. Boston: Tappan & Dennet, 1843, 407 pp.; London: Edward Moxon, 1843, 377 pp. 2d ed. Boston: J. Munroe & Co., 1844, 407 pp. 3d ed. Honolulu: C. E. Hitchcock, 1847, 240 pp. 4th ed. Honolulu: H. M. Whitney, 1872, 242 pp.

P. 262 (1843 and 1844 U.S. eds.), p. 240 (U.K. ed.), Hapu cult, 1825-.

1533 Kaonohiokala. *Kakuaokalani: The foundation of Heaven. Principles of Hawaiian religion. Ho'omanamana, "How to make reality of Divine power."* Edited by John Douglas Low. 1971, 33 pp.

A sophisticated reformulation of traditional religion, "arranged according to the teachings of Kaonohiokala, a High Priest of the Twentieth Century."

1534 Kawai'i, Abraham. [Several papers on *kahuna* beliefs and practices.] Honolulu: Institute of Pacific Wisdom, 1979-81, illus.

A sophisticated form of primal religious practice and teaching.

1535 Kealanahele, K[ahu] E[dward] I[opa]. *Religious Freedom of Kahoolawe*, 6 February 1980, 16 + 2 pp.

A primal religious revival and its assistance by the U.S. Navy to reestablish after its sacred island had been bombed; by "a Christian minister."

Hawaii

1536 Keesing, Felix Maxwell. *Hawaiian homesteading on Molokai.* University of Hawaii Research Publications, 12. University of Hawaii Publications, 1, no. 3, January 1936, 133 pp., illus.

Pp. 109f., statistics for number of families who are Mormon, Congregational, Catholic, Ke Akua Ola (Church of the Living God) – 22, Apostolic, Christian Science, and Seventh Day Adventist.

1537 Kolarz, W. "The melting pot in the Pacific." *Social Process in Hawaii* (University of Hawaii) 19 (1955): 23-26.

P. 26, religions as both dividing and uniting factor; "religious oddities" – Church of the Latter Rain (Chinese), Association for Absolute Victory (Hisshokai), House of Growth (Seich-no-Ie), Mormons.

1538 Korn, Alfons L. *News from Molokai: Letters between Peter Kaeo and Queen Emma, 1873-1876.* Honolulu: University Press of Hawaii, 1976, xlv + 345 pp.

Pp. xxii-xxvi, Kaeo and prophetess Hua and other Hawaiian elements; pp. 278-79, Queen Emma's syncretism of Anglican and native elements; pp. 182-83 et passim, prophetess Hua.

1539 Kraus, Bob. "Lono Hawaiian rites attract 200 at base." *Sunday Star Bulletin and Advertiser* (Honolulu), 12 October 1980, 2 pp., illus.

1540 Kuykendall, Ralph Simpson. *The Hawaiian kingdom.* Vol. 2, *1854-1874, Twenty critical years.* Vol. 3, *1874-1983, The Kalakaua dynasty.* Honolulu: University of Hawaii Press, 1953. Reprint. Vol. 2, 1967.

Vol. 2, pp. 105-6, "nativistic religions," with summary account of Kaona's church, 1868; vol. 3, note on p. 345, the Hale Naua society, with quotations from its constitution.

1541 Lebra, Takie Sugiyama. "An interpretation of religious conversion: A millennial movement among Japanese Americans in Hawaii." Ph.D. dissertation (sociology), University of Pittsburgh, 1967, 461 pp.

On the "Dancing Religion," Tensho.

1542 Lind, Andrew N. [*sic.*] "Religious diversity in Hawaii." *Social Progress in Hawaii* (University of Hawaii) 16 (1952): 11-19.

P. 13 lists some forty types of churches; pp. 14-15, Asian religions (including Seich-no-Ie or House of Growth); pp. 15-19, students' reports on their own family religious situations.

1543 Lind, Andrew W. [*sic.*] "Some types of social movements in Hawaii." *Social Progress in Hawaii* (University of Hawaii) 7 (November 1941): 5-14.

A survey, including the "Great Awakening" of 1836-38 (pp. 6-7), Kaona's revolt of 1868, syncretist and messianic antiwhite movements (pp. 13-14).

1544 Lum, Henry, and Miyazawa, M. "An abortive religious cult." *Social Progress in Hawaii* (University of Hawaii) 7 (November 1941): 20-24.

Based on the sacred stones of Wahiawa, in 1919, and appealing to all ethnic groups.

1545 Man Kwong Au. Foreword to *Social Process in Hawaii* (University of Hawaii) 7 (November 1941): 2-4.

Comments on the articles on social movements in Hawaii, the special theme of this issue, including those of A. W. Lind (entry 1543) and D. Thompson (entry 1556).

1546 Mulholland, John Field. *Hawaii's religions*. Honolulu: Kamehameha, 1961. Rev. ed. *Religions in Hawaii*. Rutland, Vt. and Tokyo: C. E. Tuttle Co., 1970, 344 pp.

Pp. 221-25, 240-41, independent churches.

1547 "The once Hawaiian sacred stone Mecca is now silent place." *Star-Bulletin* (Honolulu), 10 October 1931.

On the demise of the Oahu island healing cult focused on an ancient cluster of boulders.

1548 [On Prophetess Kalehua.] *Polynesian*, n.s. 1, no. 34 (12 January 1845): 137. Reprinted in *Some modern Hawaiians*, by E. Beaglehole. University of Hawaii Research Publications, 19. Honolulu: University of Hawaii Press, 1939, pp. 84-85.

1549 Opsahl, Amanda. "The master of the mana." *Sandwich Islands Monthly*, February 1978, pp. 21-23, illus.

On "kahunas" or spiritual leaders: Emma de Fries, Abram Kakai'i (Institute of Pacific Wisdom), and Ella Wise Harrison (Church of the Living God).

1550 Parke, William C[ooper]. *Personal reminiscences of William Cooper Parke, Marshall of the Hawaiian Islands, 1850-1884: Rewritten and arranged by his son, William C. Parke*. Cambridge, Mass.: [Harvard] University Press, 1891, 107 pp.

Hawaii

Pp. 99-106 J. Kaona's millennial movement, 1867-68, on the island of Hawaii; described from the police viewpoint as "religious fanatic and rebel."

1551 Ralston, C. "Early 19th century Polynesian millennial cults and the case of Hawaii." *Journal of the Polynesian Society* 94, no. 4 (1985): 307-31.

1552 Rosa, Antone. "Hale Naua." Mimeo.
Second address at annual meeting of the Hale Naua or Temple of Science, on 4 February 1889, by the vice-president of the Scientific Section of Hale Naua, on various geological and astronomical matters, together with descriptive report of the meeting, its rites, members, and dance following. Selections on microfiche, the Centre, Selly Oak Colleges.

1553 "Sacred stones at Wahiawa drew big crowds in 1927." *Honolulu Advertiser*, 31 January 1939.
Includes account of the associated legends.

1554 Sierksma, Fokke. *Een nieuwe hemel en een nieuwe aarde*. The Hague: Mouton, 1961, 312 pp.
Chap. 1 (pp. 13-37), "Goodbye Hawaii" – acculturation with no large-scale messianic reactions, but some nativistic and syncretist responses.

1555 Synder, Patricia Jean. "Folk healing in Honolulu, Hawaii." Ph.D. dissertation (anthropology), University of Hawaii, 1979, 247 pp.
Studies 35 healers from 8 ethnic groups, with clients crossing ethnic boundaries and various religious contexts.

1556 Thompson, David. "The Filipino Federation of America Incorporated: A study in the natural history of a social institution." *Social Process in Hawaii* (University of Hawaii) 7 (November 1941): 24-35.
Pp. 32-33 on the Federation of Hawaii. See further in the Philippines section of *Bibliography of New Religious Movements in Primal Societies*, vol. 4, *Europe and Asia*, by Harold W. Turner (Boston: G. K. Hall & Co., in press 1990).

New Zealand

Although the country was not annexed by Britain until 1841, Christian missions, which began in 1814, early elicited a major response from the

Maori people and the first new religious movements appeared in the 1820s. There have been over fifty distinguishable movements, large or small, but the main ones have been the Hau Haus; Pai Marire; Parihaka of the prophet Te Whiti; Ringatu, founded by Te Whiti; and in the twentieth century, the Ratana Church, named after its founder and stemming from the 1918 epidemic. The last two movements have their own special materials in the Particular Movements section at the end of the volume, but also feature in many of the items in the national section.

1557 A. F. G. "Rua's part in Maori's last affray." *Weekly News* (Auckland), no. 3717 [83] (3 March 1937): 7 + illus., p. 44.
    Good photos of Rua and wives; summary of the 47-day trial in Auckland Supreme Court.

1558 A., E. A. "An enchanted mountain for the Maori messiah." *Otago Daily Times* (Dunedin), 12 December 1979.
    Reviews of J. Binney et al. (entry 1590) and P. J. Webster (entry 1988)–both on prophet Rua.

1559 Alexander, James Edw[ard]. *Bush fighting illustrated by remarkable actions and incidents in the Maori war in New Zealand.* London: Sampson Low, Marston, Low & Searle, 1873, 326 pp., illus., map. Facsimile reprint. Christchurch: Capper Press, 1973.
    Pp. 211-15, Pai Marire religion and early Hau Hau military encounters.

1560 Andrews, C. Lesley. "Aspects of development: The Maori situation 1870-1890." M.A. thesis (history), University of Auckland, 1968, 177 pp., maps.
    Pp. 131-41, surveys the prophets in some seven movements, as reflecting group identity, millenarian hopes and kinship relations as much as socioeconomic deprivation, and both products and catalysts of social change.

1561 Aporo. "Maori warrior's book of dreams." *Te Ao Hou* (Wellington), no. 40 (September 1962), pp. 38-40, illus.
    Selection from drawings of visions seen in dreams, in the notebook of a Hau Hau warrior killed in 1867 (Turnbull library.)

1562 Arthur, Peter Neil. "Te Whiti and the land: Case study in attitudes and opinions of Taranaki settlers on native policy, 1878-1882." B.A. (Hons.) thesis (history), Massey University (Palmerston North), 1975, [3] + 34 + [7] pp.

New Zealand

Chap. 2, Te Whiti's and government actions as narrated in the press; chap. 3 analyses this material and suggests Te Whiti represented for the settlers, resistance to progress.

1563 Ausubel, David P. "The Maori: A study in resistive acculturation." *Social Forces* 39, no. 3 (1961): 218-27.

On the withdrawal from acculturation for some seventy years after the defeats in the wars of 1860-72, discussed in relation to revitalization movements, although none mentioned; theoretically useful.

1564 Ausubel, David P. *Maori youth*. New York: Holt Rinehart, 1965, 221 pp.

Pp. 102-3, "adjustment cults."

1565 B., P. C. "A chapter on pai marire: The new religion of the Maoris." *Fraser's Magazine*, no. 43 [72], (October 1865): 423-38. Reprinted in *Good Words* (Edinburgh) 1 (October 1865): 726-32. Reprint. *Wanganui Chronicle*, 24 January 1866, p. 3. Reprint. *Daily Southern Cross* (Auckland) 9, 10, and 11 January 1866. French translation, with additional note by A. de Viguerie, "Le Pai Maririsme à la Nouvelle Zélande (Étude sur la nouvelle religion du Maorisme)." *Revue Britannique* (Paris), 1865, pp. 337-61.

Pp. 426-38, Te Ua, Pai Marire sermons, rituals, conversions, the murder of Volkner, and reasons for rise of Pai Marire. "A very intelligent account" by the Presbyterian chaplain to the Imperial troops.

1566 Babbage, Stuart Barton. *Hau Hauism: An episode in the Maori Wars, 1863-1864*. Wellington: A. H. & A. W. Reed, 1937, 89 pp., illus., maps.

Based on the literature. Originally a thesis.

1567 Barker, Ian Rewi. "The connexion: The Mormon Church and the Maori people." M.A. thesis (history), Victoria University of Wellington, 1967, 157 pp.

Pp. 5-6, 40, Paora Potangaroa's abortive movement; pp. 9-10, "the challenge of Ratana"; pp. 24-28, Mormon identification of Maoris with the Israelites; pp. 48-49, Te Whiti and Te Kooti rejection of Mormons; pp. 28-36, appeal of Mormons to Maoris.

1568 Barsanti, Ottavio. *I Protestanti tra i selvaggi della Nuova Zelanda ossia storia del Pai Marire*. Turin: P. di G. Marietti, 1868, 283 pp.

Extensive account of origin and practice of Pai Marire, regarded as due to Protestant influence; Barsanti headed the Franciscans in New Zealand 1851-65; information probably from Fr. Garavel.

1569 Bassett, Judith. Review of *Ask that mountain . . .* , by Dick Scott (entry 1903). *New Zealand Journal of History* 9, no. 2 (1975): 189-92.
Review article, highly critical, and correcting some perspectives.

1570 Bathurst, K[eith] O[rton]. "The Hauhau movement: A study in social, abnormal and religious psychology." M.A. thesis (philosophy), University of New Zealand (Canterbury University College), 1940, 124 pp., illus.
Stresses the cultural normality of the seemingly bizarre and pathological, especially Te Ua's personality and experience, and the rituals.

1571 B[aucke], W[illiam]. "Maori-Pakeha: Te Whiti's estimate." *Supplement to the New Zealand Herald* (Auckland), no. 20845 (11 April 1931), p. 1.
Baucke's last article on Te Whiti.

1572 Baucke, William [W. B. Otorohanga, pseud.]. *Where the white man treads.* 2d rev. ed. Auckland: Wilson & Horton, 1928, 313 pp., photo.
Various articles from the *Auckland Herald* and the *Auckland Weekly News*: pp. 163-67, 191-92, Te Whiti; pp. 207-11, "A twentieth century tohunga"; pp. 265-68, "A final word on tohungaism."

1573 B[aucke], W[illiam]. "Where the white man treads. Te Whiti: 'In memoriam.'" *Supplement to the New Zealand Herald* (Auckland), no. 13,609 [44] (30 November 1907), p. 1.
Obituary containing material withheld until Te Whiti's death.

1574 Baucke, William [W. B. (Te Kuiti), pseud.]. "Wit and wisdom of Te Whiti." *Huia* (Auckland), no. 1 (December 1903), p. 71.
Based on his second visit of several days in 1903; author was son of Moravian missionaries.

1575 Beach, Harlan P. *A geography and atlas of Protestant missions*. Vol. 1, *Geography*. New York: Student Volunteer Movement, 1901, 571 pp.
Pp. 176-77, "Hau-Hau superstition," as "grossest immorality," by Maoris who saw themselves as the true Israelites.

1576 Beeching, Jack. *An open path: Christian missionaries, 1515-1914.* London: Hutchinson, 1979, 325 pp., maps.

New Zealand

> Pp. 179-80, Pai Marire described in the sensational way that is not uncommon.

1577 Begg, Alison. "Early Maori religious movements ... the reactions of the Maoris to the Christian gospel up until 1860." M.A. thesis (history), University of Otago, 1974, 211 pp.

> A major study with extensive use of archival materials.

1578 Belich, James. *The New Zealand wars and the Victorian interpretation of the race problem.* Auckland: Auckland University Press; Oxford: Oxford University Press, 1986, 350 pp.

1579 Bell, James MacKintosh. *The wilds of Maoriland.* London: Macmillan & Co., 1914, 253 pp., illus., map.

> Pp. 115-17, 119-31, account of a visit to Maungapohatu and Rua.

1580 Bennett, Enid, and Donovan, Peter, eds. *Beliefs and practices in New Zealand: A directory.* Massey University Religious Studies Department, 1980, 175 pp.

> Pp. 97-98, Maramatanga transtribal movement, with healing; pp. 121-22, Ratana Church; pp. 131-32, Ringatu; pp. 159-60, Unification Church.

1581 Benton, Eric. "There's nothing new about a beehive for New Zealand." *Hawke's Bay Herald-Tribune,* 7 June 1965, p. 7, illus.

> Rua and his temple, with photos.

1582 Best, Elsdon. *Tuhoe: The children of the mist.* 2 vols. Memoirs of the Polynesian Society, 6. New Plymouth: Board of Maori Ethnological Research, 1925. Facsimile reprint (2 vols. in 1). Wellington: A. H. & A. W. Reed, 1972, 1211 pp.

> Pp. 578-81, Hauhau "craze"; p. 1029, Ringatu.

1583 "Big day for Maori Church." *Outlook* (N.Z. Presbyterian Church), May 1977, pp. 20-21.

> Announcing forthcoming opening of Maori Synod's new meeting house, with historical background of the relations between prophet Rua, and the Ringatu religion, and the early Presbyterian missionaries.

1584 Binney, Judith [Mary Caroline (Musgrove)]. "Christianity and the Maoris to 1840: A comment." *New Zealand Journal of History* 3, no. 2 (1969): 143-65.

Small initial impact, then wave of conversions, followed by rival religious movements hostile to Europeans; pp. 156-57, Matamata Christian community.

1585 Binney, Judith [Mary Caroline (Musgrove)]. *The legacy of guilt: A life of Thomas Kendall*. [Auckland]: Oxford University Press for Auckland University Press, 1968, 220 pp., illus.
Pp. 63, 148 note 114, Papahurihia.

1586 Binney, Judith [Mary Caroline (Musgrove)]. "Maori oral narratives, Pakeha written texts: Two forms of telling history." *New Zealand Journal of History* 21, no. 1 (1989): 16-28.
Uses the Ringatu traditions concerning Te Kooti to discuss the relation of oral history to mythology, and to changes in the course of time; p. 27, comment on the Maramatanga movement related to the Roman Catholic Church.

1587 Binney, Judith [Mary Caroline (Musgrove)]. "Maungapohatu revisited; or how the government underdeveloped a Maori community." *Journal of the Polynesian Society* 92, no. 3 (1983): 353-92, illus.
Detailed account of the history, buildings, and inhabitants of Rua Kenana's "New Jerusalem," and of successive government failures to see the potential for development and to assist with roads and capital.

1588 Binney, Judith [Mary Caroline (Musgrove)]. "Myth and explanation in the Ringatu tradition: Some aspects of the leadership of Te Kooti Arikirangi Te Turuki and Rua Kenana Hepetipa." *Journal of the Polynesian Society* 93, no. 4 (1984): 345-98.

1589 Binney, Judith [Mary Caroline (Musgrove)]. "Papahurihia: Some thoughts on interpretation." *Journal of the Polynesian Society* 75, no. 3 (1966): 321-31.

1590 Binney, Judith [Mary Caroline (Musgrove)]; Chaplin, Gillian; and Craig, Wallace. *Mihaia: The prophet Rua Kenana and his community at Maungapohatu*. Wellington: Oxford University Press, 1979, 208 pp., illus.
A major study in the form of a photographic essay.

1591 Bracken, Thomas [Paddy Murphy, pseud.]. *Paddy Murphy's budget*. Dunedin: MacKay, Bracken & Co., 1880, 94 pp.
Pp. 73-75, "Misther Murphy visits Tay Whitty" (1880) – "much excruciating wit at 'Tay Whitty's [i.e., Te Whiti's] expense."

New Zealand

1592 Brathwaite, Errol [Freeman]. *The companion guide to the North Island of New Zealand.* Auckland and London: Collins, 1970, 462 pp., illus.
Pp. 156, 315, Ringatu; pp. 184-86, Te Ua, Hau Hau and Pai Marire – what is told to tourists; pp. 197-98, Parihaka.

1593 Bres, Pieter H[endrik] de. "The contribution of Maori religious movements to religion in New Zealand." *Exchange* (Leiden), no. 22 [8] (April 1979): ii + 36 + 36 pp., Addenda. Reprinted in *Religion in New Zealand Society*, edited by B. J. Colless and P. Donovan. Palmerston North: Dunmore Press, 1980, pp. 31-48.

1594 Bres, P[ieter] H[endrik] de. "Maori religious affiliation in a city suburb." In *Conflict and promise: Essays on the Maori since colonisation*, edited by I[an] H[ugh] Kawharu. Wellington: A. H. & A. W. Reed, 1975, maps, pp. 144-66.
Based on his 1971 book (entry 1596).

1595 Bres, Pieter H[endrik] de. "Maori religious movements in Aotearoa." In *Religion in New Zealand society*, edited by B. J. Colless and P. Donovan. Palmerston North: Dunmore Press, 1980, pp. 31-55.
Uses J. Wach's categories (cognitive, cultic, communal) for analysis.

1596 Bres, Pieter Hendrik [de]. *Religion in Atene: Religious associations and the urban Maori.* Memoirs of the Polynesian Society, 37. Wellington: Polynesian Society, 1971, 95 pp.
Abbreviated and revised version of his 1967 thesis (entry 1597); pp. 10-13, 19-24, 29-30, same subjects.

1597 Bres, Pieter Hendrik de. "The religious affiliation and religious behaviour of the New Zealand Maori: A sociological study of the religious life of Maoris in a suburban area." M.A. thesis (anthropology), University of Auckland, 1967, 222 pp.
Pp. 49-66, 71-72, Ratana, Maori Evangelical Fellowship, Ringatu and Absolute Established Maori Church members.

1598 Brookes, Edwin Stanley. *Frontier life: Taranaki, N.Z.* Auckland: H. Brett, 1892, 203 pp.
Pp. 36-45, by surveyor who visited Parihaka; anti-Maori viewpoint.

1599 Broughton, Ruka. "The Maramatanga Christian Society." *Te Ao Hou* (Wellington), June-July 1980, pp. 37-38. In Maori, with English translation.

Text of action song composed in 1940 by Mrs. Phyllis Luke (Uruhete) of the Maramatanga Christian Society; history of the latter; its leaders, especially Te Rua Hoani Te Uawiri Hakaraia and his wife.

1600 Brown, Helen. "Rua's 'Union Jack' flag sold for $2600 – Maoris fail in their bid"; "A 'brother in Christ.'" *Press* (Christchurch), 7 January 1982, illus.

Bought by the Urewera National Park Board, against Tuhoe people bidding; attempted history of the flag, and general account of Rua.

1601 Brown, J[ohn] Macmillan. *Peoples and problems of the Pacific.* 2 vols. London: T. Fisher Unwin, 1927, illus. Reprint. New York: J. H. Sears, 1927. Reprint. New York: AMS Press, 1976.

Pp. 53-54, Hau Hau as a "mongrel religion."

1602 Buck, Peter [Henry]. "The Taranaki Maoris: Te Whiti and Parihaka. In *Papers and addresses read before the Second Annual Conference of the Te Aute Students' Association December 1897.* Napier: 1898, pp. 7-12. Reprinted in *Te Rangi Hiroa,* edited by J. B. Condliffe. London: Whitcombe & Tombs, 1971, pp. 40-45.

Description and criticism of Parihaka after Buck's visit as a young Te Aute College student.

1603 Buddle, Thomas. "Letter [on the King movement] to Col. Thomas Gore Browne, 28 June 1861." In *Appendices to the Journals of the House of Representatives,* New Zealand Government, 1861, E-1H. Reprinted in *Transplanted Christianity: Documents . . . of New Zealand church history,* edited by A. K. Davidson and P. J. Lineham. Auckland: College Communications, 1987, pp. 128-29.

1604 Buddle, Thomas. *The Maori King movement in New Zealand, with a full report of the native meetings held at Waikato, April and May 1860.* Auckland: "New Zealander" Office, 1860, 72 pp. Reprint. New York: AMS Press, 1979.

Pp. 22-26, "Professed principles in action" – "Christianity, love and law."

1605 Buller, James. *Forty years in New Zealand.* London: Hodder & Stoughton, 1878, 503 pp., illus., map.

New Zealand

A notable Wesleyan missionary. Part 3, chap. 12 (pp. 343-52), "Apostasy": on Te Ua and Riemenschneider.

1606 Burdon, R[andall] M[athews]. *New Zealand notables.* First series. Christchurch: Caxton Press, 1941, 140 pp.
Pp. 71-104, Te Whiti's movement.

1607 Bush, Ernest E. "Origins of the King movement." *Journal of the Tauranga Historical Society,* no. 54 (August-September 1975), pp. 6-9.

1608 Bush, R. S., et al. "Reports from officers in native districts." *Appendix to the Journal of the House of Representatives,* 1876, G-1. Wellington: Government Printer, 1876, pp. 2, 3, 5, 8, 10, 19, 22-23, 32, 35.
The Government interpreter and others reporting on the "Morning Star" faith of the King movement.

1609 Butt, E. A. "Meeting house of the Hau Haus. History in deserted village." *Weekly News* (Auckland), no. 5070 (25 January 1961), p. 8., illus.
At village of Maringa te Karaka, 12 miles from Mangapehi, erected by Pao Miere.

1610 Butterworth, G. V. "A rural Maori renaissance? Maori society and politics 1920 to 1951." *Journal of the Polynesian Society* 81, no. 2 (1972): 160-95.
Pp. 164-65, Kingitanga; pp. 165-67, 179-80, 182, Ratana.

1611 Campbell, Gordon. "Rua: 'myth dream' and history." *New Zealand Listener* (Wellington), no. 2081 [93] (24 November 1979): 66, 70-71, illus.
Interview with P. J. Webster on his study 1979 of Rua (entry 1988).

1612 Carleton, Hugh [Francis]. *The life of Henry Williams, Archdeacon of Waimate.* 2 vols. Auckland: Upton & Co., 1874-77. Rev. ed. Wellington: A. H. & A. W. Reed, 1948, 328 pp., illus.
Vol. 2 (original ed.), pp. 346-49, Hau Haus.

1613 Carr-Gregg, Charlotte. "The changing situation of prisoners of war during 19th century warfare in New Zealand." *Oceania* 51, no. 3 (March 1981): 161-80.
Pp. 167, 174-79, brief references to the King movement, Hau Hau, Ringatu, and Pai Marire.

1614 Caselberg, John. *The voice of the Maori: A culture conflict anthropology.*
Christchurch: Nag's Head Press, 1969, 55 pp. (miniature).
P. 36, a prayer of Te Kooti, reprinted from W. Colenso (entry
2164); pp. 42-45, sayings of Te Whiti, reprinted from G. W. Rusden
(entry 1889).

1615 Caselberg, John, ed. *Maori is my name: Historical writings in
translation.* Dunedin: John McIndoe, 1975, 152 pp.
P. 110, Te Kooti's prayer, reprinted from W. Colenso (entry
2164); pp. 127-39, extracts from various source on Te Whiti, Tohu, and
Parihaka.

1616 Church Missionary Society. *The murder of the Rev. C. S. Volkner in
New Zealand.* London: Church Missionary House, 1865, 32 pp.
Contains the diaries of S. A. Levy and T. S. Grace, and journals
and letters of the Bishop of Waiapu (William Williams), etc.

1617 Church Missionary Society. [Various letters on Papahurihia.]
Missionary Register (London).
July 1835, p. 309 (Yate); September 1835, p. 428 (Williams); July
1836, pp. 336-37 (King). See C. J. Parr (entry 1838).

1618 Church of the Seven Rules of Jehovah. *The Church of the Seven Rules
of Jehovah.* Masterton: E. H. Waddington (Printer), 1902, 74 pp.
Bible verses arranged to explain words in the Rule, why
sacraments not used, various prayers, explanation of the Kingdom from
Adam to Edward VII (with linking genealogies), and of Maori
authority from Taane to Sir James Carroll, etc.

1619 Church of the Seven Rules of Jehovah. *National prayer.* Masterton: M.
P. Co., 1918, 4 pp.
Prayers "for the soldiers," for victory and for peace within the
year, all with biblical content and in the manner of the Anglican Book
of Common Prayer.

1620 Clark, Charlton. "Te Miringa te Kakara will rise again." *Tu Tangata*
(Wellington, Maori Affairs Department), no. 11 (April 1963), pp. 23-
25, illus.
On the meeting house, Te Miringa te Kakara, of the Pao Miere
movement at Te Hape near Benneydale, with various versions of its
history.

New Zealand

1621 Clark, Paul John Abbott. *Hauhau: The Pai Marire search for Maori identity.* Wellington: University of Auckland Press, 1975, 186 pp., illus., map.

Based on "Prophet of peace: Te Ua and the Pai Marire 1862-66," MA thesis (history), University of Auckland, 1974.

1622 Clover, Gary Allan Malcolm. "Christianity among the South Taranaki Maoris, 1840-53: A study of the Wesleyan Mission at Waimate South." M.A. thesis (history), University of Auckland, 1973, 216 pp.

The Ngatiruanui and Ngarauru tribes: pp. 114-15, syncretistic developments; pp. 116-19, 180, Warea Tapu cult and cargo ideas; p. 163, Wesleyans who became Hau Haus.

1623 Cody, Joseph Frederick. *Man of two worlds: Sir Maui Pomare.* Wellington: A. H. & A. W. Reed, 1953, 161 pp., illus.

Pp. 17-20, 68-69, 83-85, 88, Te Whiti; pp. 58-67, new types of *tohunga* (e.g., p. 64, a woman, and one using the New Testament as magic); p. 94, the Parewanui headquarters of Mere Rikiriki's Wairua Tapu (Holy Ghost) movement in 1911; pp. 133-35, Ratana.

1624 [Cognet, Père]. "La révolte Maori de 1863, récit vécu d'un épisode millénariste." *Bulletin. Société d'Études Historiques de la Nouvelle Calédonie,* no. 46 (1981), pp. 49-64.

1625 Committee of Ngatiawa, Whakatohea, Urewera, Taranaki. "Letter to the Office of the Government, Auckland, 6 March 1865." *Appendices to the Journals of the House of Representatives.* Wellington, 1865, E-5, pp. 9-10. Reprinted in *Transplanted Christianity: Documents ... of New Zealand church history,* edited by A. K. Davidson and P. J. Lineham. Auckland: College Communications, 1987, p. 142.

Hau Hau justification of Volkner's murder, by British deceptions and atrocities; exchange of prisoners offered.

1626 Cowan, James. *The adventures of Kimble Bent: A story of wild life in the New Zealand bush.* London: Whitcombe & Tombs, 1911, xxi + 336 pp., map. Reprint. Christchurch: Capper Press, 1975.

Chap. 3, the Hau Hau camp, with *niu* pole rites; chap. 5, Te Ua; chap. 7, life with the Hau Haus; chap. 8, the Hau Hau Council town; chap. 11, Hau Hau war rites; et passim on Hau Hau campaigns – as told by a white captive of the Hau Haus. Also p. 331, his invitation to heal the sick at Parihaka.

1627 Cowan, James. *Fairy folk tales of the Maori.* 2d ed. Wellington:
Whitcombe & Tombs, 1930, 173 pp.
P. 71, Pao Miere as "an offshoot of Pai Marire"; its cruciform
meeting-house.

1628 Cowan, James. "Famous New Zealanders, no. 19: Te Whiti of
Taranaki, the story of a patriot and peacemaker." *New Zealand Railway
Magazine* (Wellington) 9, no. 7 (1934): 17-19, 21, illus.
Cowan met Te Whiti in 1904 and was deeply impressed by him.

1629 Cowan, James. *Hero stories of New Zealand.* Wellington: Harry H.
Tombs, 1935, 288 pp., illus.
Pp. 207-11, Rev. Samuel Williams' encounters with Hau Hau
apostles; pp. 236-46, Te Whiti.

1630 Cowan, James. *The Maori yesterday and today.* Auckland, etc.:
Whitcombe & Tombs, 1930, 266 pp., illus., map; a revised version of
his *Maoris of New Zealand* (Christchurch: Whitcombe & Tombs,
1910), xxiv + 365 pp., illus.
Pp. 63-68, 80-83, 200, 261-62, brief accounts of modern religious
movements including Pao Miere of the mid-1970s and a visit to Te
Whiti – with Maori texts and English trans. of prayers.

1631 Cowan, James. *The New Zealand wars: A history of the Maori
campaigns and the pioneering period.* Vol. 1, *1845-1864.* Vol. 2, *The
Hauhau Wars, 1864-1872.* Wellington: Government Printer, 1922-23, xx
+ 549 pp., illus., maps. Reprint. Vol. 1, 1955, 471 pp.; vol. 2, 1956, 560
pp., illus.
Vol. 2 (1956), pp. 237-38, the King movement journal *Te Hokioi*,
its press and editor; vol. 2, Hau Hau, passim, but especially chap. 1, Pai
Marire; chap. 7, Volkner's death; chap. 43, includes Te Whiti and
Parihaka; p. 548, Rua Kenana and his arrest. A classic account.

1632 Cowan, James. "Rua the prophet." *World Wide Magazine* 38 (1916):
229-39, illus.

1633 Craig, Dick. *South of the Aukati line.* Te Kuiti: N.p., 1962, pp. 69-79.
Te Mahuki's Tekau-ma-rua movement capture of land surveyors
in the King country in 1883. The "aukati line" formed the barrier
around King country.

1634 Craig, E[lsdon] W[alter] G[rant]. *Man of the mist: A biography of
Elsdon Best.* Wellington, etc.: A. H. & A. W. Reed, 1964, 247 pp., illus.

New Zealand

Pp. 120-21, Best's experiences and criticisms of Rua and his movement; p. 28, Best in the Parihaka raid, 1881; by his grandnephew, using Best's unpublished papers.

1635 Craig, Elsdon [Walter Grant]. "Religious life of the Auckland Maori." *Te Ao Hou* (Wellington), no. 27 [7], no. 3 (1959): 56-57.
P. 56, briefly on Ringatu attending interdenominational services; p. 57, Ratana, with at least 10 ministers, an Easter convention, and services in the Maori community centre.

1636 Crawford, John Coutts. *Recollections of travel in New Zealand and Australia.* London: Trubner & Co., 1880, 468 pp., maps, illus.
Pp. 353-54, superficial remarks about Hau Hau.

1637 Cresswell, John C[harles] M[arshall]. *Maori meeting houses of the North Island.* Auckland: P.C.S. Publications, 1977, 131 pp. + 31 pp. of plates, illus.
Pp. 70, 76, prophet Rua's meeting houses (but see J. Binney et al. (entry 1590), p. 196, n95 for corrections); p. 110, Ratana meeting houses and other buildings at Ratana Pa and at Raetihi.

1638 Croumbie-Browne, S. *The raid on Parihaka.* N.p.: Edwards & Green (Printers), [1881?], 3 pp.
Sent by author to Sir George Grey, Governor.

1639 Cruikshank, George. *Robert Graham, 1820-1885: An Auckland pioneer.* Wellington: A. H. & A. W. Reed, 1940, 157 pp., portrait.
Pp. 78-86, Graham at the wreck of the "Lord Worsley" negotiating with Maoris including Te Ua and Te Whiti, who appears in a favorable light.

1640 Dale, William Sydney James. "The influence of Christianity on the Maoris of New Zealand: A study of the impact of Western religion on a non-western people." M.A. thesis, Yale University.
Pp. 173-211, Hau Hau apostasy; pp. 228-33, "the great Ratana movement" – a rather naive account.

1641 Dalton, B. J. Review of *Studies of a small democracy*, edited by R. Chapman and K. Sinclair (Hamilton, N.Z.: Blackwood & Janet Paul, for the University of Auckland, 1963, 288 pp.; reprint, 1965). *Journal of the Polynesian Society* 73, no. 3 (1964): 351-53.
The King movement.

1642 Dansey, Harry [Delamere Barter]. "Fifty years after Rua's arrest . . . 'It shouldn't have happened.'" *Auckland Star*, 2 April 1966, illus.
Interview with one of the police party which arrested Rua.

1643 Dansey, Harry [Delamere Barter]. "Maori's emotional need, and the role of the tohunga." *Auckland Star*, 27 October 1962.
The traditional, and the contemporary, faith-healing tohunga–the latter usually a member of one of the new religious movements; many on the East Coast (mostly Ringatu).

1644 Dansey, Harry [Delamere Barter]. "Simple humble folk, all of us." *Auckland Star*, 24 October 1964, illus.
A Maori account of Te Aka Rapana's Absolute Established Maori Church in Northland–first at Te Tii and now at Tinopai under his nephew.

1645 Dansey, Harry [Delamere Barter]. *Te Raukura: The feathers of the Albatross: A narrative play in two acts*. [Auckland]: Longman Paul, [1974], 63 pp.
A play for the Auckland Festival, 1972; on Te Ua Haumene and Te Whiti-o-Rongomai. On the research involved, see *The Auckland Star*, 6 April 1972, Hau Hau play meant much research.

1646 Davidson, Allan K., and Lineham, P. J., eds. *Transplanted Christianity: Documents illustrating aspects of New Zealand church history*. Auckland: College Communications, 1987, 369 pp.
Reprints of texts; see at various authors included.

1647 Dickinson R[owland]. *Rising fish: Catching trout from Taupo to the Bay of Plenty*. Christchurch: Whitecombe & Tombs, 1956, 111 pp., illus., map.
Pp 86-91, a fisherman's encounter with Rua, late in the latter's life, and his visit to Maungapohatu, with two uncanny experiences. Photo of Rua as old man, facing p. 78.

1648 Dollimore, Edward Stewart, comp. *The New Zealand guide*. Dunedin: H. Wise & Co. (N.Z.), 1962, p. 981.
Pp. 435-36, Rua's Maungapohatu; pp. 604-5, Parihaka; p. 63, Ratana Pa–historical outlines.

1649 *Dominion* (Wellington), 24 February 1937; 5 March 1937; 28 April 1937; 21 July 1951.
On Kenana Rua.

New Zealand

1650 Donne, T[homas] E[dward]. *The Maori past and present.* London:
Seeley Service & Co., 1927, 287 pp., illus.
Pp. 208-11, Maori reactions to Christianity, including Pai Marire.

1651 Downes, T. W. "A *tuahu* on the Whanganui river." *Journal of the
Polynesian Society*, no. 146 [37] (1928): 165-68, illus.
The Pai Marire ritual flagstaff, with photo of the pole at
Arimatia.

1652 Duffy, Alex Edward. "The Church of the Seven Rules of Jehovah."
Research essay, Victoria University of Wellington, Department of
Anthropology, October 1973, 38 pp. Typescript. Also Maori version, 38
pp.
Begun in the Wairarapa ca. 1895 to 1897 by Simon Patete and
Taiaiwhio Te Tau. Written by a Maori clergyman.

1653 Dumont d'Urville, Jules Sebastian César. *Voyage au Pole Sud . . . 1837
. . . 1840. . . .* 4 vols. Paris: Gide, 1842-53.
Vol. 4 reported to include Hongi Hika's new rituals.

1654 Elder, John Rawson. *The history of the Presbyterian Church of New
Zealand, 1840-1940.* Christchurch: Presbyterian Bookroom, [1940], 464
pp., illus.
Pp. 252-68, the Maori Mission in relation to Rua, Ringatu, and
Ratana, especially on the latter two as cults.

1655 Elmberg, John-Erik. *Morgondagens Öar.* English translation. *Islands of
tomorrow.* London: Rupert Hart-Davis; Toronto: Clarke Irwin & Co.,
1956, 255 pp., illus., maps.
Swedish traveler's visit to Maungapohatu. Pp. 242-43, a
Ruatahuna Maori's memories of Rua and his arrest; pp. 249-51, Te
Kooti–legends of his burial place and his powers.

1656 Elsmore, Bronwyn Margaret. "According to the Scriptures–the
influence of the publication of the Christian Scriptures in Maori on
Maori religious movements." Ph.D. dissertation (religious studies),
Victoria University of Wellington, 1986, 412 pp.
A study of some sixty movements from 1830s to 1920, grouped in
four periods and phases: 1830-50 (early reactions), the 1850s (the
healers), 1860-1900 (prophetic period), 1900-20 (Maori Christian
Churches). See also her 1985 book (entry 1658).

1657 Elsmore, Bronwyn [Margaret]. *Mana from heaven: A century of Maori prophets in New Zealand.* Tauranga: Moana Press, 1989, 398 + 17 pp., illus., maps.
   Revised version of her doctoral dissertation (entry 1656).

1658 Elsmore, Bronwyn Margaret. *Like them that dream.* Tauranga: Tauranga Moana Press, 1985, 189 pp., illus.
   The first book-length survey of new religious movements among the Maori, with some dozen main examples, set in the context of the effects of missionaries and settlers.

1659 Elsmore, Bronwyn Margaret. "Te Hahi o te Kohititanga Marama (The religion of the reflection of the moon): A study of the religion of Te Matenga Tamati." M. Phil. thesis (religious studies), Massey University, 1983, 120 pp.
   The Kohiti religion in the Wairoa area late 19th century, as a fulfilment of the Ringatu faith.

1660 Elvy, W[illiam] J[ohn]. *Kei puta te Wairau. A history of Marlborough in Maori times.* Christchurch, etc.: Whitcombe & Tombs, 1957 [i.e., 1958], 120 pp., illus.
   Pp. 96-99, chief Taniora, and briefly on his later foundation of "his own religion called 'The Seven Rules of Jehovah.'"

1661 [Excerpts on the death of Te Whiti.] *Budget* (Dunedin), 23 November 1907, pp. 29-30, 47, illus.
   Pp. 29-30, Te Whiti's life, death, funeral, teachings and influence, but little on Parihaka; p. 47, "Death of Te Whiti" (by W. F. Gordon) on death and funeral. All articles show a not unsympathetic settler's attitude to "this noted Maori chief."

1662 Fieldhouse, D. K. "Sir Arthur Gordon and the Parihaka crisis, 1880-1882." *Historical Studies* (Melbourne) 10 (1961): 49.
   A reappraisal of Rusden's (1883) account, based on contemporary documents.

1663 Findlay, G[eorge] G[illanders], and Holdsworth, W[illiam] W[est]. *The history of the Wesleyan Methodist Missionary Society.* Vol. 3. London: J. A. Sharp, 1921, 483 pp.
   Pp. 241-42, King movement; p. 244, Hau Hau as a Christian heresy.

New Zealand

1664 Finlayson, Roderick. "The everlasting miracle." In *Speaking for ourselves*, edited by F. Sargeson, Christchurch, N.Z.: Caxton Press, 1945, pp. 17-22.

A fictional story of Monday, an erstwhile Maori prophet, converted from loose living by a vision, and his attempt at walking on the water.

1665 Firth, Josiah Clifton. *Nationmaking: A story of New Zealand, savagism v. civilization*. London: Longmans, Green & Co., 1890, 402 pp.

Pp. 4-5, Hauhaus and the King movement, with a prayer in Maori and English translation; pp. 35-37, detailed description of Tamihana's Christian village of Peria, in 1856, by one of the first settlers on Matamata plains.

1666 "Flags of early New Zealand – No. three: Te Kooti's 'whip.'" *New Zealand Home Journal* (Christchurch), June 1958, p. 7, with drawing.

The history of Te Kooti's flag, 51 ft. by 4 ft., with symbols – crescent, cross, star, Mt. Egmont, and bleeding heart (Maori sufferings).

1667 Foster, B[ernard] J[ohn]. "Rua Tapunui Hepetipa, or Kenana Rua Hepetipa (1869-1937)." In *Encyclopaedia of New Zealand*. Vol. 3. Wellington: Government Printer, 1966, pp. 1316-1332a.

1668 Foster, B[ernard] J[ohn]. "Te Mahuki Manukura." In *Encyclopaedia of New Zealand*. Vol. 2. Wellington: Government Printer, 1966, pp. 377b-378a.

1669 Foster, B[ernard] J[ohn]. "Te Whiti-o-Rongomai or Erueti Te Whiti. c. 1830-1907." In *Encyclopaedia of New Zealand*. Vol. 3. Wellington: Government Printer, 1966, pp. 655b-656b.

1670 Fowler, Leo. "A new look at Te Kooti." *Te Ao Hou* (Wellington), no. 20 [5, no. 4] (1951): 17-19; no. 21 [6, no. 1] (1957): 18-22.

1671 Fox, William. *The war in New Zealand*. London: Smith Elder & Co., 1860. Reprint. 1866. Reprint. Christchurch: Capper Press, 1973, 268 pp.

Pp. 125-43 on Pai Marire; Fox was Colonial Secretary and Native Minister in the 1860s, and a "Maori-phile."

1672 G., S. W. "Rua – Urewera messiah of the Maori." *Hawke's Bay Herald-Tribune* (Napier), 17 November 1979, illus.

Review summarizing P. J. Webster (entry 1988) on Rua.

1673 Gadd, Bernard. "The teachings of Te Whiti O Rongomai, 1831-1907."
Journal of the Polynesian Society 75, no. 4 (1966): 445-57, bib.

1674 Gadd, Bernard. "Three religious faiths." *Te Ao Hou* (Wellington), no.
53 (1965), pp. 50-51.
Ringatu, Hauhau, Te Whiti.

1675 Geering, L[loyd] G[eorge]. "The church in the New World." *Landfall*,
March 1966, pp. 24-30.
Pp. 28-29, Ratana.

1676 Gibson, Tom. *The Maori wars: The British army in New Zealand.*
Nineteenth-Century Military Campaign Series. Hamden, Conn.: Shoe
String Press; London: Leo Cooper, 1974, 271 pp., illus.
Pp. 131-36, Te Ua and the Hau Haus, pp. 157-59, 247, Hau Haus
in the military conflict – a view typical of whites.

1677 Gifford, W[illiam] H[enry], and Williams, H. Bradney. *A centennial
history of Tauranga.* Dunedin and Wellington: A. H. & A. W. Reed for
the Tauranga Centennial Committee, 1940, 351 pp. Reprint.
Christchurch: Capper Press, 1976.
Pp. 165-69, two "false prophets" in the Tauranga district in 1849
reported by A. N. Brown, Anglican missionary – a woman, and a boy,
Te Witu, with New Testament passages to proclaim a cataclysmic
introduction to a millennium.

1678 Gisborne, William. *The colony of New Zealand, its history, vicissitudes,
and progress.* London: E. A. Petherick & Co., 1888. 2d ed. 1891, 360
pp., maps.
P. 146, "Pai Marire or Hau Hau" faith was "worse than heathen
superstition."

1679 Gluckman, L. "Kereopa, the psychodynamics of a 19th century
murder." *New Zealand Medical Journal* 63 (1964): 486-91.
Explains Kereopa's "barbarous" conduct in terms of his culture
and situation; by a psychiatrist.

1680 Goldman, Lazarus Morris. *The history of the Jews in New Zealand.*
Wellington: A. H. & A. W. Reed, 1958, 272 pp.
Chap. 11, the "Maori wars," especially the Levy brothers on Hau
Haus and Volkner's murder, and on Te Kooti.

New Zealand

1681 Good, Norman. "A wonderful journey into the wilderness." *Journal of the Auckland-Waikato Historical Societies* 22 (April 1973): 9-12. Reprinted from *Alpine Sport*, 1935.
Record of journey by an Auckland lawyer in 1934. Pp. 10-12, Rua's village as in 1935.

1682 Gordon, Mona [Clifton]. *Those days, those men*. Christchurch: Pegasus Press, 1975, 159 pp., illus.
Pp. 72-73, King Tawhiao and Christianity; pp. 92-107, Tamihana (photo) and especially pp. 94-96, 104, vivid popular accounts of his Christian villages, based on primary sources.

1683 Gorst, J[ohn] E[ldon]. *The Maori King or the story of our quarrel with the natives of New Zealand*. London and Cambridge: Macmillan & Co., 1864, 409 pp. Reprint. Hamilton: Paul's Book Arcade; London: Oxford University Press, 1959, 284 pp. Facsimile reprint. Christchurch: Capper Press, 1975.
An accurate and understanding account of the nationalist movement. Pp. 319-20 (1959 ed., pp. 206-7), the more religious aspects.

1684 Gorst, J[ohn] E[ldon]. *New Zealand revisited: Recollections of the days of my youth*. London: Sir Isaac Pitman & Sons, 1908, 336 pp., illus.
Chap. 8 (pp. 115-41), Tamihana, et passim, especially pp. 129-30 on his religious activities.

1685 Grace, John Te Herekiekie. *Tuwharetoa: The history of the Maori people of the Taupo district*. Wellington: A. H. & A. W. Reed, 1959. Reprint. 1966, 567 pp., illus.
Chap. 53, Volkner and the Hau Haus; chap. 57 (pp. 442-57) and pp. 426-28, the King movement; chap. 60, Hau Hau and Pai Marire; chaps. 61-62, Te Kooti; pp. 502-4, Pao Miere in the 1880s.

1686 Grace, Thomas S[amuel]. *A pioneer missionary among the Maoris 1850-1879: Being the letters and journals of Thomas Samuel Grace*. Edited by S. J. Brittan, G. F., C. W., and A. V. Grace. Palmerston North, N.Z.: G. H. Bennett, [1928], 341 pp.
Pp. 60, 66-67, Wairuarua movement or "Tapu heresy," 1855-56; pp. 134-49, Hau Hau and Volkner; pp. 285-87, reflections on various movements.

1687 Great Britain, Army, Quarter Master-General (Deputy) in New Zealand (Gamble). *Journals ... 24.12.1861-7.9.1864*. London: War

Office, 1864, xxi + 128 pp., maps (no. 0238). 4th addendum, 8.1.1865-
7.3.1865, 6 pp., illus. (no. 0238-IV).
P. 147 On Te Ua and Pai Marire religion as peacemakers.

1688 Greenwood, William. *Riemenschneider of Warea*. Wellington: A. H. &
A. W. Reed, 1967, 152 pp., illus.
On a Lutheran who worked with the Wesleyans among the
Taranaki Maoris at Warea from 1846 until the wars forced him out in
the 1860s. Pp. 18, 86-87, his relations with Te Whiti and Tohu, whom
he taught the Scriptures as youths at Warea.

1689 Greschat, Hans-Jürgen. *Mana und Tapu: Die Religion der Maori auf
Neuseeland*. Beiträge zur Kulturanthropologie. Berlin: Dietrich Reimer
Verlag, 1980, 247 pp., illus., map. English translation by R. Rivers (in
preparation).
Chap. 8 (pp. 136-60), Papahurihia, Te Ua, Te Whiti, and Rua;
chap. 9 (pp. 162-81), Te Kooti and Ringatu; chap. 10 (pp. 183-203),
Ratana; pp. 214-19, relevant notes and references.

1690 Grey, George. "Proclamation." *New Zealand Gazette*, no. 14 (29 April
1865), p. 129. Reprinted in *Pai Marire and the Niu at Kwanui*, by Evelyn
Stokes. Occasional Paper 6. Hamilton: University of Waikato Centre
for Maori Studies and Research, April 1980, p. 59.
The Governor's banning of "Pai Marire or Hau Hau" on 22 April
1865.

1691 "Guardians of the peace: Te Whiti and Tohu," and "The death of Tohu
of Parihaka." *Maori Record* (Normanby, Taranaki) 1, no. 7 (1906): 5; 2,
no. 22 (1907): 83-84.

1692 Guariglia, Guglielmo. *Prophetismus und Heilserwartungs-bewegungen
als völkerkundliches und religionsgeschichtliches Problem*. Vienna: F.
Berger, 1959, 332 pp.
Pp. 74-75, Hau Hau; p. 79, Hokianga Bay movement.

1693 Gudgeon, Tho[ma]s Wayth. *The defenders of New Zealand*. ...
Auckland: H. Brett, 1887, 620 pp., illus.
Pp. 313-16, the government attack on Parihaka, "dealing with a
bloodthirsty fanatical crew of savages" [*sic*, for peaceful Parihaka!]; pp.
370-73, Tamehana's routing of Hau Haus and death of their prophet.

New Zealand

1694 Gudgeon, Thomas W[ayth]. *Reminiscences of the war in New Zealand.*
London: Sampson Low, Marston, Searle & Rivington, 1879, 372 pp.,
illus.
Chap. 4 (pp. 23-26), origin and progress of Hau Hau religion;
chap. 5 (pp. 27-31), early Hau Hau campaign; chap. 7 (pp. 40-47),
deaths of Volkner and Falloon; et passim on Hau Hau and Te Kooti
military campaigns.

1695 Gudgeon, W[alter] E[dward]. *The Maori, his customs and folklore.*
Privately printed, [1905 or 1907?], [268 pp.]
Collected reprints, mainly from the *Journal of the Polynesian
Society,* as in entries 1697 and 1697; pp. 1-26, Maori superstition; pp. 1-
24 (separate pagination), Maori religion; he was in charge of the N.Z.
Police, 1887-90, and chaired the first meeting of the Society.

1696 Gudgeon, W[alter] E[dward]. "Maori religion." *Journal of the
Polynesian Society,* no. 55 [14] (September 1905): 107-30. Reprinted in
The Maori, his customs and folklore. Privately printed, [1905 or 1907?].

1697 Gudgeon, W[alter] E[dward]. "Maori superstition." *Journal of the
Polynesian Society,* no. 56 [14] (December 1905): 167-92. Reprinted in
The Maori, his customs and folklore. Privately printed, [1905 or 1907?],
[26 pp. (no serial pagination, but represents pp. 102-27 of these
collected articles)].
Pp. 168-69, on the meaning of the Bible being kept secret; pp.
171-76, Hau Hau; pp. 176-77, Te Kooti; pp. 177-78, Te Whiti; p. 179,
Ani Kaaro as prophetess; pp. 179-81, Rimana Hi as prophetess.

1698 Gudgeon, W[alter] E[dward]. "The tohunga Maori." *Journal of the
Polynesian Society* 16 (1907): 63-91.
Pp. 70-71, 74, Te Kooti as a wizard rather than a *tohunga*; pp. 74-
75, Papahurihia, as a "genuine *tohunga*"; p. 83, a Hau Hau prophet; all
set in extensive account of *tohungas* and their powers.

1699 Hamilton, Lila [May]. "The affair at Opotiki." *New Zealand's Heritage*
(Wellington) 3, no. 32 (1972): 874-78, illus.
On Volkner's killing, well illustrated.

1700 Hamilton, Lila [May]. "Christianity among the Maoris: The Maoris and
the Church Missionary Society's mission, 1814-1868. Ph.D. thesis
(history), University of Otago, 1970, 405 pp., maps.
Pp. 134-38, 143-44, 157-59, Papahurihia; pp. 315-17, Maori
fascination with the Old Testament; pp. 317-25, deviations and

syncretisms; pp. 325-26, King movement; pp. 326-39, Te Ua and Pai Marire.

1701 Hamilton, Lila [May]. "The followers of the prophet." *New Zealand's Heritage* (Wellington) 3, no. 32 (1972): 869-73, illus.

Good survey of Te Ua and Pai Marire, with fine illustrations.

1702 Hamilton-Browne, G. *Camp-fire yarns of the Lost Legion.* London: T. Werner Laurie, [1913], 381 pp., illus.

A rather highly colored account by a British colonel; chap. 2 (pp. 53-72), how Matene (a Pai Marire) failed to convert the lower Wanganui area; chap. 4 (pp. 84-91), a Hau Hau martyr; chaps. 3, 6, 14, military engagements with Hau Haus.

1703 Hamilton-Browne, G. *With the lost legion in New Zealand.* London: T. Werner Laurie, [1911], 397 pp., illus.

A military viewpoint. Pt. 1, chap. 2, Hau Haus; Pt. 2, chaps. 2, 8, Te Kooti, and see index for Te Ua, and Pai Marire.

1704 Hammond, T[homas] G[odfrey]. *In the beginning: The history of a mission.* Hawera: W. A. Parkinson & Co., 1915, 113 pp. Reprint. Auckland: Epworth Bookroom, 1915. 2d ed. (with foreword by T. A. Joughlin, pp. 7-8), 1940, 116 pp., illus.

P. 8, his visit to Ratana to avoid a split; pp. 106-7, prophet Tohu on the detention of Bishop Selwyn and Parihaka; by a veteran Methodist missionary intimate with both places.

1705 Hammond, T[homas] G[odfrey]. "Raumati Te Pomakariri." *Newsletter of Patea Historical Society*, 3 December 1976 [i.e., 1975].

A Taranaki prophet ca. 1870-80s at Whenuakwa, near Patea, who encouraged return to Christianity.

1706 Harawira, P. A. "Peterehema, Kaihota" [Bethlehem, Homewood]. *Matuhi Press* (Masterton), no. 7 [28] (October 1903): 9-10.

In the journal of the Church of the Seven Rules of Jehovah; its building called "Mount Moriah" at Homewood, Wairarapa.

1707 Harrop, A[ngus] J[ohn]. *England and the Maori wars.* London: New Zealand News; Christchurch: Whitcombe & Tombs, 1937, 423 pp., illus., map.

See index for many references to Te Ua, Hau Hau, Te Kooti, and the King movement.

New Zealand

1708 "Hau-Hau." *All the Year Round: A Weekly Journal Conducted by Charles Dickens* (London), n.s., no. 627 [26] (4 December 1888): 151-57.

A sympathetic description, critical of the British handling of Te Kooti, etc., and based on personal knowledge.

1709 "Hauhauism, or the new superstition called Tariao." *Te Wananga*. Reprint. *Bay of Plenty Times*, 2 September 1876.

1710 "The Hau Hau outbreak: How Von Tempsky fell." *Press* (Christchurch), 3 February 1894.

An extract, in Turnbull Library, under "Maori disturbances, etc., 1881-1919"–includes account of Hau Hau worship around *niu* pole, and prophet's revelations.

1711 Hawthorn, H[arry] B[ertram]. "The Maori: A study in acculturation." American Anthropological Association Memoirs, 64. *American Anthropologist* 46, no. 2:2 (1944), 130 pp.

P. 14, "Revivalist-rational" sects continue to grow. "Maoris' own sects" as unifying, and assisting change.

1712 Head, Lyndsay F. "Te Ua and the Hauhau faith in the light of the Ua Gospel notebook." M.A. thesis, University of Canterbury, 1983.

1713 Hight, James. "New Zealand." In *The Cambridge History of the British Empire*. Vol. 7, Part 2. Cambridge: Cambridge University Press, 1933, 309 pp.

Pp. 56-58, missions and Pai Marire; pp. 132-39, "Maori wars," Hau Haus and the King movement.

1714 Hinch, D. W. "General elections in Taranaki, 1879-1884." M.A. thesis (history), Victoria University of Wellington, 1968, ix + 272 pp., + folding map.

An outline of influence of the Parihaka affair on elections in 1879 (pp. 38-39) and 1881 (pp. 103-10), making full use of the Taranaki Press, and showing public and candidates' attitudes towards Parihaka to be more moderate than is often suggested.

1715 Hogg, C. "Real Rastaman fights back." *New Zealand Times*, 3 March 1986.

Hensley Dyer, Jamaican Rastafari living in Auckland, complaining that Maori trouble-makers are being labeled as Rastas who are not true followers of the religion.

1716 Hohepa, Patrick Wahenga. *A Maori community in Northland.* University of Canberra Anthropology Department Bulletin 1, 1964, 99 pp. Wellington: A. H. & A. W. Reed, 1970, 142 pp., maps. Originally a Ph.D. thesis (anthropology), University of Auckland, 1964 (earlier form, M.A. thesis, 1961, 183 pp.).

Pp. 45-49, revival of Papahurihia in Waima in the 1890s.

1717 Holt, Edgar. *The strangest war: Story of the Maori wars 1860-1872.* London: Putnam, 1962, 301 pp., illus., prints.

1718 Honore, Abraham. "Mission town among the Maoris." *Evangelist* 2, no. 6 (1870): 167-70.

Pp. 167, 169-70, a Maori missionary's discussions (political and theological) with Hau Haus, and the paucity of the latter in the Manawatu.

1719 Honore, [Abraham]. "Work among the Maoris in the north." *Evangelist* 7 (1 April 1875): 7.

An intelligent and reasonable Maori missionary's visit to Parihaka; and description of Te Whiti as "false prophet," a "great influence for evil," with "his head full of scripture but . . . none of it in his heart."

1720 Houston, John. *Maori life in old Taranaki.* Wellington: A. H. & A. W. Reed, 1965, 224 pp., illus.

Pp. 156-59, Te Ua and Pai Marire; chap 27 (pp. 167-71), Parihaka.

1721 Howe, K[erry] R[oss]. "The Maori response to Christianity in the Thames-Waikato area, 1833-1840." *New Zealand Journal of History* 7 (1973): 28-46.

Asserts Maori response was not due to cultural disruption, but positively to the new and exciting ideas of Christianity, e.g. Heaven and Hell ideas, literacy; pp. 43-45, new syncretisms.

1722 Howe, K[erry] R[oss]. "Missionaries, Maoris, and 'civilization' in the Upper Waikato 1833-1863: A Study in culture contacts with special reference to the attitudes and activities of the Reverend John Morgan of Otawhao." M.A. thesis (history), University of Auckland, 1970, 272 pp.

Pp. 27-30, rejects dislocation, deprivation, etc., theories for acculturation of the Maori; pp. 34-36, Papahurihia and similar early prophets; p. 55, Matamata and Otawhao Christian villages; pp. 181-85,

Christian influences on the King movement, to which Morgan was consistently hostile.

1723 Hunt, Brian W. *Zion in New Zealand: A history of the Church of Jesus Christ of Latter-Day Saints in New Zealand 1854-1977.* Temple View: Church College of New Zealand, 1977, 110 pp., illus.

Pp. 9, 11, early Maori prophecies concerning whites; pp. 55, 57, relations between Mormons and Ratana.

1724 Hunt, C. G. "Maringa Te Kakara village." *Journal of the Polynesian Society* 68, no. 1 (1959): 3-7, plan. See replies by Pei Te Hurunui [Jones] and by W. Hugh Ross in *Journal of the Polynesian Society* 68, no. 4 (1959): 393-94 and 394-96, respectively.

Includes the cruciform building, of uncertain use, built by two priests of the Pao Miere cult, an "offshoot of Pai Marire." Jones denies this, seeing it as part of the Io cult. Ross calls the village by a name now lost, Toroa, gives 1880s as date of building, and describes another temple building two kilometers away where a girl (prophetess?) in the tower listened through a hatch to her followers below–reminiscent of Rua Kenana.

1725 [Illustrated news reports of the current police action against prophet Rua.] *Weekly News* (Auckland) 6 April 1916, p. 20 (text), pp. 42-43 (photos); 13 April 1916, pp. 17, 20 (text), pp. 41-44, 46, 48 (photos).

Shows the police rather than the Maoris, but has several photos of Rua and his son Whatu, and of his wives.

1726 Irvine, Jean. "Maori mysticism in the north." In *Dialogue on religion: New Zealand viewpoints, 1977,* edited by P. Davis and J. Hinchcliffe. Auckland: N.p., [1978?], pp. 6-10.

P. 3, Ratana; pp. 9-10, Papahurihia and Nakahi cult.

1727 Irvine, Jean. *Township of Rawene.* [Rawene, Northland]: The author, 1977, 119 pp., illus., maps.

Chap. 8, Kotahitanga (unity), covers a widespread movement which includes pp. 69-71 and 89-90, reactions to Christianity and the Bible, and material on Atua Wera, Papahurihia, Nakahi, and Huai (as various names of one movement), also Aperahama and Kotahitanga; local oral tradition and manuscript sources are drawn upon.

1728 Irvine, R[obert] F[rancis], and Alpers, O[scar] T[horwals] J[ohan]. *The progress of New Zealand in the century.* Nineteenth Century Series.

Toronto and Philadelphia: Linscott Publishing Co.; London and Edinburgh: W. & R. Chambers, 1902, 460 pp.

Pp. 300-306, the "Parihaka fiasco"; pp. 410-41, Parihaka, with its modern developments, and P. Buck's visit in 1896.

1729 Irwin, James. *An introduction to Maori religion*. Bedford Park, South Australia: Australian Association for the Study of Religions, 1984, 85 pp., illus.

Pp. 44, 68, Pai Marire; pp. 45-46, Wahi Tapu cult.

1730 Irwin, James. "The mana-tapu-noa concepts in Maori religion from the beginning of the nineteenth century." M.Litt. thesis (religion in primal societies), University of Aberdeen, 1976, 189 pp.

Chap. 5 (pp. 100-120), surveys six new religious movements, 1840-1920, with *mana* and *tapu* ideas continuing but the *tohunga* becoming more of a healer; Ratana Church was the exception in rejecting both *mana* and the *tohunga*.

1731 Irwin, James. "The role of religious mediators in a multicultural society." *Journal of the Whakatane and District Historical Society* 23, no. 1 (1975): 24-34.

Includes the King movement, Te Whiti, Te Kooti, and the Young Maori Party.

1732 Irwin, James. "Some Maori responses to the Western form of Christianity." In *Religion in New Zealand*, edited by C. Nicol and J. Veitch. Wellington: Victoria University of Wellington, Religious Studies Department and Combined Chaplaincies, 1980, pp. 53-75. Enl. ed. 1983.

Pp. 59-63, 70-71, various movements.

1733 Jackson, Michael. "Literacy, communications and social change: The Maori case, 1830-1870." M.A. thesis (anthropology), University of Auckland, 1967, 233 pp.

Pp. 10-21, relevance of cargo cult theory; pp. 76-81, Whare Wananga probably a postcontact development; p. 196, Tamihana's Matamata Christian village; pp. 202-9, Whare Wananga as a "spiritual counterpart" of the King movement; pp. 209-14, Hau Hau, as similar to cargo cults; pp. 214-15, Ringatu: all considered as innovative syncretistic movements.

1734 Jackson, Michael. "Literacy, communications and social change: The Maori case, 1830-1870." In *Conflict and promise: Essays on the Maori*

New Zealand

since colonisation, edited by I. H. Kawharu. Wellington: A. H. & A. W. Reed, 1975, pp. 27-54.

P. 38, new cult leaders and the printed word; pp. 22-24, the King movement.

1735 Jacobs, Henry. *Colonial Church Histories: New Zealand*. . . . New York: E. and J. B. Young & Co.; London: Society for Promoting Christian Knowledge, [1887], 484 pp., illus.

Pp. 286-88, Hau Hau, with extended quotation of the section on Hau Hau in Bishop Selwyn's address to the 3d. General Synod of the Church of England in New Zealand, 1865.

1736 Johansen, J. Prytz. *Studies in Maori rites and myths*. Historisk-filosofiske Meddeleser ungivet af Det Kongelige Danske Videnskakernes Selskab 37:4. Copenhagen: Ejnar Munksgaard, 1958, 201 pp., bib.

Pp. 36-62, summarizes opinion as to whether the cult of Io was of pre-European origin or not.

1737 [Johnson, John.] "Notes from a Journal." *New Zealander* (Auckland), no. 162 [3] (18 December 1847): 2.

Dr. Johnson's visit to Tamihana's Christian village at Matamata, 1846.

1738 Jones, Pei Te Hurunui. "Maori kings." In *The Maori people in the nineteen-sixties: A symposium*, edited by E. G. Schwimmer. Auckland: Blackwood & Janet Paul, 1968 [i.e., 1969], pp. 132-73.

The only detailed study of the King movement up to the 1960s, by a participant-observer, but religious aspects dealt with only incidentally.

1739 Kawharu, I[an] H[ugh], ed. *Conflict and promise: Essays on the Maori since colonisation*. Wellington: A. H. & A. W. Reed, 1975, 219 pp., maps.

See essays by M. Jackson (entry 1734), D. P. Lyons (entry 1772), G. Z. Misur (entry 2181), and P. H. de Bres (entry 1594).

1740 Keesing, Felix M[axwell]. "The changing Maori." Memoirs of the Board of Maori Educational Research, 4. New Plymouth: Thomas Avery & Sons, Printer, 1928, 198 pp., illus.

Pp. 49-51, Hau Hau and Te Ua, Titokowaru, Te Kooti, Rua, Ratana; pp. 142-51, religious life and census statistics; pp. 146, 148, Rua; pp. 149-50, Ratana.

1741 Kernot, [Clifton] B[ernard] [Joseph]. "Parihaka revisited." *New Zealand Listener* (Wellington), no. 2046 [91] (24 March 1979): 28-29, illus.; no. 2051 [91] (28 April 1979): 24, 34, illus.

Two reviews of the exhibition "Parihaka" of paintings by Maori artist Selwyn Muru on the Te Whiti-Parihaka-Bryce themes, using almost the same text and illustrations in the second article!

1742 Kernot, [Clifton] B[ernard] [Joseph]. *People of the four winds.* Wellington: Hicks Smith & Sons, 1972, 80 pp.

Pp. 27-29, religious affiliations in Pukekohe borough at 1961, including Ratana and healing *tohungas*.

1743 Kerry-Nicholls, J[ames] H[enry]. *The King country, or, explorations in New Zealand.* 2d ed. London: Sampson Low, Marston, Searle & Rivington, 1884, 379 pp., illus. Facsimile reprint. Christchurch: Capper Press, 1974.

Pp. 276-80, Hauhau religion, with "Te Kooti's lament" and a Hauhau hymn (English translation).

1744 King, John. "Perversion of the Gospel by some." *Missionary Register*, July 1836, p. 336.

A C.M.S. missionary's report on Papahurihia and his "foolish ceremonies."

1745 King, Michael. *Being Pakeha: An encounter with New Zealand and the Maori situation.* Auckland: Hodder & Stoughton, 1985, 215 pp., illus.

Pp. 120-24, 166, the Parihaka community divided between followers of Te Whiti and Tohu and the disastrous effects on the author's TV film-making in 1974; repercussisons in 1985. Pp. 200, 202, briefly on King, Ratana, and Ringatu movements.

1746 King, Michael. "Ngakahikatea." *New Zealand Listener* (Wellington), no. 1863 [79] (16 August 1975): 18-20, illus.

Life of Ngakahikatea Whirihana (d. 1974), who knew and followed Tawhiao and remained a Pai Marire member; Pai Marire beliefs articulated.

1747 King, Michael. *Te Puea [Herangi]: A biography.* Auckland, London: Hodder & Stoughton, 1977, 331 pp., illus.

On the remarkable Maori "Princess" (d. 1952) who embraced a modern form of Pai Marire faith; see index for Pai Marire, Parihaka, Ringatu, Ratana (which she opposed); pp. 99-101, the 1918 epidemic.

New Zealand

1748 King, Michael, ed. *Tihe Mauri Ora: Aspects of Maoritanga*. London: Methuen, 1978, 111 pp.
See essays by R. Mahuta (entry 1784), M. Raureti (entry 2141), and W. Tarei (entry 2198).

1749 [King Movement.] *Te Hokioi e Rere Atu na* (Ngaruawahia).
The King Movement newspaper, "The War Bird," edited by Patara Te Tuhi, mission-educated cousin of King Potatau; provoked the Government paper *Te Pihoihoi Mokemoke*, edited by James Gorst, and seized by the Maoris after four issues in 1863.

1750 Kitchin, Philip. "Life through Rasta eyes." *H. B. Herald-Tribune* (Hastings, N.Z.), 14 September 1985, illus.
An extended interview with two Hastings Rastafari Maori young men, explaining their beliefs and practices, correcting the false image common among whites.

1751 K[ohere], R[eweti] T[uhorouta] M. "He tohunga pakeha." *Te Pipiwharauroa* (Gisborne), no. 74 [April 1904], pp. 1-2.
On American religious movements, especially that of J. A. Dowie, and Maori movements – Paomiere, Tariao, Pai Marire, Ringatu mentioned.

1752 Kohere, Reweti T[uhorouta M.]. *The story of a Maori chief: Mokena Kohere and his forbears* [*sic*]. Wellington: A. H. & A. W. Reed, 1949, 109 pp., illus.
P. 8, how Mokena Kohere opposed the Hau Haus, forgave those who joined them, and opposed government land confiscations; pp. 60-62, critical account of Hau Hau incantations, wtih text and translation. By a Maori clergyman.

1753 "Kowhiti logs lie waiting for an unknown prophet." *Daily Telegraph* (Napier), 10 December 1964, illus.
Article by staff reporter on Te Mahenga Tamati's totara logs on a beach near Wairoa, brought for his planned Kowhiti temple.

1754 Lambert, Thomas. *The story of old Wairoa, East Coast District, North Island New Zealand; or Past, present, and future*. Dunedin: Coulls Somerville Wilkie, 1925, 801 pp., illus.
Chaps. 18-19, Te Kooti: pp. 476-500, Te Ua, earlier Hau Hau history and Hau Haus on the East Coast.

1755 Lanternari, Vittorio. "Culti profetici polinesiani." *Studi e Materiali di Storia della Religioni* (Bologna) 28, no. 2 (1957): 55-78.
Pp. 71-76, Maori movements (largely based on F. Vaggioli (entry 1973).

1756 Lanternari, Vittorio. *The religions of the oppressed: A study of modern messianic cults.* English translation. London: MacGibbon & Kee, 1963, xx + 343 + xiii pp.; New York: A. A. Knopf, 1963, xvi + 286 pp. Reprint. New York: Mentor Books, 1965, xvi + 286 pp.
Pp. 200-208 (Mac Gibbon & Kee edition), Maori movements. See R. Firth's critical comments in *Current Anthropology* 6, no. 4 (1965): 450, and Lanternari's reply, p. 461.

1757 "The last Maori trouble in New Zealand." *Illustrated London News*, no. 2230 [80] (28 January 1882): 76, 78, and p. 77 as illustrations.
An illustrated report of the government invasion of Parihaka and arrest of Te Whiti and Tohu, together with historical background.

1758 Latourette, Kenneth Scott. *A history of the expansion of Christianity.* Vol. 5. *The great century in the Americas, Australasia and Africa, A.D. 1800-A.D. 1914.* London: Eyre & Spottiswoode; New York: Harper & Brothers, 1943, 525 pp. + maps.
Pp. 183-84, Maori religious movements, with references.

1759 Laughton, J[ohn] G[eorge]. *From forest trail to city street: The story of the Presbyterian Church among the Maori people.* Christchurch: Presbyterian Bookroom for the Maori Synod, 1961, 100 pp.
Pp. 16-17, prophet Rua–the author knew him intimately. P. 36, Hau Hau and Ringatu in Opotiki area.

1760 [Laughton, John George]. "The Ringatu and Ratana cults." In *The History of the Presbyterian Church of New Zealand*, by J. R. Elder. Christchurch: Presbyterian Bookroom, 1940, pp. 265-68.

1761 Laurenson, Geo[rge] I. *Te Hahi Weteriana: Three half centuries of the Methodist Maori Missions, 1822-1972.* Proceedings of the Wesley Historical Society of New Zealand, 27, nos. 1-2. Auckland: Wesley Historical Society, 1972, 272 pp., illus.
Pp. 32, 48, 90-91, 152-53 (later conversion), Papahurihia; pp. 174-75, 184-85, 189-90, 197-98, 230, Te Whiti and Parihaka; pp. 180, 206, 210, 216, 218, 219-20 (Methodist-run school), Ratana movement–as superintendent of Methodist Maori Missions, the author knew him well.

New Zealand

1762 Leach, Marjorie Cecilia (Sister M. St. Florienne). "Wiremu Tamihana: a study in Maori staesmanship." M.A. thesis (history), University of New Zealand (Auckland), 1932.

1763 Ledger, James. *Pen and ink sketches of Parihaka and neighbourhood, with scenes of Maori life.* Dunedin: Fergusson & Mitchell, [1881], 12 leaves.
Parihaka village, and food brought to prisoners; by a private in the South Canterbury contingent.

1764 Lehmann, F[riedrich] R[udolf]. "Prophetentum in der Südsee." *Zeitschrift für Ethnologie* 66, (April 1934): 261-65, illus.
P. 264, Hau Hau; pp. 264-65, Te Kooti–both in the context of Polynesian prophetism. Based on J. Cowan (entry 1630).

1765 Lehmann, F[riedrich] R[udolf]. "Prophetismus in der Südsee." *Christentum und Wissenschaft* 10 (1934): 56-68.
P. 68, prophetess Maria in 1885, based on *Globus* (entry 1878).

1766 Leitch, Madeline Lilian. "Te Kooti." M.A. thesis, University of New Zealand (Wellington), 1927. [Not deposited.]

1767 Lennard, L. Maurice. "The trial of Rua Kenana." *Historical Review: Journal of the Whakatane and District Historical Society* 11, no. 2 (1963): 55-61.

1768 Lindauer, Gottfried. *Maori Paintings: Pictures from the Partridge collection of paintings by Gottfried Lindauer.* Edited by J. C. Graham. Wellington: A. H. & A. W. Reed, 1965, 117 pp. + colored plates.
P. 74 and plate, Wiremu Tamihana; p. 86 and plate, Te Ua.

1769 Love, Ralph Henerley Ngatata. "Policies of frustration: The growth of Maori politics; the Ratana/Labour era." Ph.D. thesis (political science), Victoria University of Auckland, 1977, 566 pp.

1770 Lusk, Hugh. "Maori Mahommedanism." *Fortnightly Review* (London) 2 (15 August to 1 November 1865): 731-37.
Pp. 731-32, rise of the King movement; pp. 733f., Pai Marire founded by "a Christianized *tohunga*"; sundry analogies with Islam are suggested.

1771 Luxford, John A. "Parihaka–its surroundings and its inhabitants." *New Zealand Wesleyan* (Christchurch) 11, no. 11 (1881): 248-49.

A favorable report of visit to Parihaka in September 1881 by the Methodist minister of Opunake.

1772 Lyons, Daniel Patrick. "An analysis of three Maori prophet movements." In *Conflict and promise: Essays on the Maori since colonisation*, edited by I. H. Kawharu. Wellington: A. H. & A. W. Reed, 1975, pp. 55-79.
A shorter form of entry 1773.

1773 Lyons, Daniel Patrick. "An analysis of three Maori prophets." M.A. thesis (anthropology), University of Auckland, 1970, 247 pp.
Pp. 35-68, Papahurihia; pp. 69-138, Te Ua; pp. 139-98, Te Whiti.

1774 Lyons, Daniel Patrick. "Parihaka rebellion in New Zealand." In *Race, class, and rebellion in the South Pacific*, edited by A. Mamak and A. Ali. Sydney and London: Allen & Unwin, 1979, pp. 107-13.

1775 Lyons, Edward. "Te Kooti; priest and warrior and founder of the Ringatu Church." M.A. thesis, University of New Zealand (Auckland), 1932.

1776 M. K. A. "He whakaatu mo te tahi kotiro" [Information about a particular girl]. *Matuhi Press* (Masterton), no. 17 (6 January 1904), p. 9.
On Simon Patete, originator of the Church of the Seven Rules of Jehovah, healing a dying girl.

1777 MacDonald, Robert. *The Maori of New Zealand*. Minority Rights Group Report no. 70. London, 1985, 16 pp., maps, bib.
Brief references to Maori prophet movements, pp. 9-10.

1778 McDonald, Rod. *Te Hekenga. Early days in Horowhenua.* Compiled by E. O'Donnell. Palmerston North: G. H. Bennett & Co., [1929], 207 pp., illus.
"The Drifting" or "The Passing Away." Pp. 104-13, a settler's experience of Maori religion and its continuance after conversion; pp. 116-25, Hau Haus, (pp. 124-25, Motai, a local Hau Hau prophet with his "Twelve Apostles"); pp. 184-86, Te Whiti.

1779 McDonnell, Thomas. *Maori history, being a native account of the Pakeha-Maori wars in New Zealand*. Auckland: H. Brett, n.d. Reprinted in *The defenders of New Zealand* . . . , edited by T. W. Gudgeon. Auckland: H. Brett, 1887, pp. 493-556.

New Zealand

Based on Kowhai Ngutu Kaka's narratives. Pp. 521-23, Hau Hau religion; pp. 528-29, role of Hau Hau priests in war; pp. 531-32, Volkner's death. By a soldier/civil servant and good Maori linguist.

1780 McIntyre, W[illiam] David, ed. *The journey of Henry Sewell 1853-1857.* Vol. 1, *February 1853-May 1854.* Vol. 2, *May 1854-May 1857.* Christchurch: Whitcoulls, 1980, 1:510 pp.; 2:371 pp.; index.

Prophet movement of Tamaiharoa, Anglican church warden near Kaiapoi, beginning about 1853 and becoming separate in the 1860s.

1781 Mackay, Jessie. *The spirit of the Rangatira and other ballads.* Melbourne: George Robertson & Co., 1889, 111 pp.

Pp. 30-33, "The Charge of Parihaka"–a satirical parody of "The Charge of the Light Brigade," referring to government invasion of Parihaka, reprinted in D. Scott (entry 1903), p. 118; pp. 32-33, "Departure of the Timaru volunteers for Parihaka."

1782 Mackay, Joseph Angus. *Historic Poverty Bay and the East Coast, N.I., N.Z. . . . a Centennial memorial. . . .* Gisborne: J. A. Mackay, 1949, 471 pp., map, illus.

Chap. 25, "Under the Hau Hau banner"; chap. 26, Te Kooti's imprisonment and escape; chaps. 27-33, campaigns against Te Kooti; chap. 34 (pp. 299-304), Te Kooti's own history.

1783 McMaster, Nita Marie. "Te Whiti and the Parihaka incident." M.A. thesis (history), University of New Zealand (Wellington), 1945, 161 pp. (bib. pp. 151-61).

Pp. 1-45, origins of the movement in land disputes; detailed accounts of Te Whiti, his village and its destruction. Uses secondary sources and the Parliamentary papers and has useful comments on the bibliography.

1784 Mahuta, Robert. "The Maori King movement today." In *Tihe Mauri Ora*, edited by M. King. London: Methuen, 1978, pp. 33-41.

With a modern form of Pai Marire, as the official religion, friendly relations with Ringatu and peace made with the Ratana movement.

1785 Maloney, G. J., and Neil, William. "The Rua expedition." *Historical Review: Journal of the Whakatane and District Historical Society* 11, no. 2 (1963): 62-71, illus.

Maloney's account extracted from *N.Z.: Police Journal*, November 1937; Neil's account appeared as an interview by Annabell

Ross in *Daily Post* (Rotorua), 5 September 1962. Both were policemen engaged in the expedition to arrest Rua.

1786 Manchester, Anne. "Partners in Christ: Ringatu born in bondage." *Crosslink* (Wellington, Presbyterian and Methodist Churches) 3, no. 4 (1989): 16, 14, illus.

Outline history of Te Kooti and Ringatu and of recent relations with the Presbyterian Church; more detailed account of close relations between Presbyterian missionary John Laughton and prophet Rua, self-styled successor to Te Kooti.

1787 Maning, F[rederick] E[dward] [originally under pseud., A Pakeha Maori]. *Old New Zealand ... together with a history of the war in the north of New Zealand.* ... Edited by T. M. Hocken. Originally *The war in the north.* London and Auckland, 1863. 2d ed. 1864. Many subsequent editions under later title, e.g., London: R. Bentley & Son, 1884, xxiv + 278 pp. Australian ed. 1893, 278 pp. London and Christchurch: Whitcombe & Tombs, 1906, 1922, 1948, 1956, etc.

1906 ed.: pp. 245, 275-78, 282, 302, Te Atua Wera (Papahurihia) and his part in Heke's wars; opp. p. 277, photo of Te Atua Wera.

1788 "A man of high principle." *New Zealand Listener* (Wellington), no. 1552 [59] (6 December 1968): 62-63, illus.

On Te Whiti.

1789 "Man who moved mountains: Tokaanu-Taupo 1889-1967." *Zealandia* (Auckland) 32, no. 43 (16 March 1967): 15, portrait.

Includes Father Adrian Langerwerf, Catholic priest, and his booklet Te Whaka O Hata Petera (The ship of Peter) against Ratana when it spread in his district.

1790 Maori Evangelical Fellowship. "Constitution." N.p., [1960?], 5 pp. Mimeo. Also Whangarei, N.Z.: Calder Print, 1960.

1791 Maori Evangelical Fellowship. *Maori Christian*, April 1975; July 1979.

Journal, bimonthly, of the fairly independent Maori church.

1792 "Maoris give away property and fast at madman's prediction of world's end." *New York Times*, 23 September 1934, p. 8E, col. 2. Summarized in *The Ghost Dance*, by W. LaBarre. Garden City, N.Y.: Doubleday & Co., 1970, pp. 233-34.

Announcement of the end of the world at Waitarata in 1934.

New Zealand

1793 "The Maori troubles in New Zealand." *Aborigines Friend* (London), n.s., no. 13 (April 1882), pp. 453-63.

1794 "The march on Parihaka" [News dispatch from Pungarehu, 5 November 1881]. *Lyttelton Times*, 7 November 1881.
Bryce's entry into Parihaka.

1795 Martin, (Lady) Mary Ann. *Our Maoris*. London: Society for Promoting Christian Knowledge, 1884, 220 pp., illus. Facsimile reprint. Auckland: Wilson & Horton, [1970].
Pp. 35-36, account of a *tohunga's* challenge to Tamihana's Christian faith through a whistling seance with a Maori god.

1796 Martin, T. J. "Maramatanga movement – Onga Hau E Wha." In *Beliefs and practices in New Zealand*, edited by E. Bennett and P. Donovan. Massey University Department of Religious Studies, 1980, pp. 97-98.

1797 Matangi, Rawiri [pseud.]. "Te Whiti, the prophet of Parihaka." *New Zealand Times*, 29 March 1899, p. 2. Reprinted in *Speeches and Documents on New Zealand History*, edited by W. D. McIntyre and W. J. Gardner. Oxford: Clarendon Press, 1971, pp. 158-62.
A description of Parihaka as a model Europeanized village, and of Te Whiti's policies.

1798 Matheson, A. H. "Matiu Tahu; tohunga and Christian teacher." *Journal of the Tauranga Historical Society*, no. 49 (1973): 23-33.

1799 Meade, Herbert George Philip. *A ride through the disturbed districts of New Zealand*. . . . Edited by R. H. Meade. London: John Murray, 1870. 2d ed. 1871, 375 pp., illus.
Pp. 32, 37, 121, 123-24, and especially 126-29, 141-43 on Hau Haus, from his experiences of capture, and of their worship.

1800 Metge, [Alice] Joan. *The Maoris of New Zealand*. London: Routledge & Kegan Paul, 1967, x + 245 pp.
Chap. 4: Maoris and Maori culture today.

1801 Mikaere, Buddy [Piritihana]. *The Maiharoa and the Promised Land*. Auckland: Heinemann, 1988, 159 pp., illus.
Pp. 39-45, Kaingarara movement in Taranaki and its influence on the South Island Kai Tahu people; pp. 56-62, Te Ua and Hauhaus; pp. 64-66, Te Whiti; otherwise a balanced, detailed study of prophet Te

Maiharoa and his Arowhenua movement in relation to government and the land problem.

1802 Mikaere, Piritihana. "Hipa Te Maiharoa–A South Island response to the loss of land." *Te Karanga* 1, no. 3:21. Also as lecture to the Canterbury Maori Studies Association–shortened version, 1986 [1985?], 5 pp.

On the Arowhenua religious movement from 1866 under Te Maiharoa–its migration to Omarama and then to Korotuaheka in 1879.

1803 Miller, Harold [Gladstone]. *New Zealand*. London: Hutchinson, 1950, 155 pp.

Good references to Maoris and Christianity, and the Maori land wars; pp. 62-71, 93, on the King movement.

1804 Miller, Harold [Gladstone]. *Race conflict in New Zealand 1814-1865*. Auckland: Blackwood & Janet Paul, 1966, xxvii + 238 pp., illus.

Pp. 118-21, Hau Hau; p. 218, texts on Hau Hau; the King Movement, passim (see index), but pp. 51-52, 54, 181-84 on religious features.

1805 Mitcalfe, Barry. *Maori poetry: The singing word*. Wellington: Price Milburn for Victoria University Press, 1974, 209 pp., illus.

Pp. 109-15, Pai Marire songs; pp. 118-20, Te Kooti songs; pp. 210-15, Parihaka songs; pp. 138-39, Ratana songs; pp. 186-88, music in the prophet movements.

1806 Mitcalfe, Barry. "Maori song." *Polynesian Studies* (Wellington), no. 5, (1968), pp. 1-97 [defective numbering]. Mimeo.

P. 16, preservation of Maori song and chant in the prophet movements; pp. 57-61, Pai Marire chants with notes; pp. 64ff., Parihaka songs; p. 65 + 2 pp., cult of Io.

1807 Mitcalfe, Barry. *Nine New Zealanders*. Christchurch: Whitcombe & Tombs, 1963, 72 pp., + illus.

Pp. 51-59, Te Whiti.

1808 Mitcalfe, Barry. "Te Whiti-O-Rongomai." *Te Maori* (Wellington) 4, no. 4 (1970): 8-9, 11, illus.

Songs and sayings of Te Whiti from Taranaki Museum mss.

New Zealand

1809 Mol, J[ohannis] J. "The religious affiliations of the New Zealand Maoris." *Oceania* 35, no. 2 (1964): 136-43.

Includes statistics of Ringatu, Ratana, and Mormons, with discussions of various affiliations.

1810 Morgan, J. [Letter to C. W. Richmond, 10 May 1859.] Alexander Turnbull Library. Richmond-Atkinson Papers. Additional letters, 1859-1860, Acc. 77-253. Reprinted in *Transplanted Christianity: Documents . . . of New Zealand church history*, edited by A. K. Davidson and P. J. Lineham. Auckland: College Communications, 1987, pp. 127-28.

Summarizes his opinion of the current position in the King movement, and advises strong government action.

1811 Morley, William. *A history of Methodism in New Zealand*. Wellington: McKee & Co., 1900, 510 pp., illus.

P. 62, possession and messianism in the early 1830s; pp. 163-64, 166, Hau Hau; pp. 172-73, syncretistic *tohunga* healers in the 1880s, with followers (reprinted in *Religious organization among the Maoris of New Zealand after 1860*, by Ann Judith Gibson [entry 2173] pp. 46-47); p. 173, a prophetess, and Te Whiti; p. 179, Ani Karo; p. 181, Te Whiti.

1812 Morrell, W[illiam] P[arker]. *The Anglican Church in New Zealand: A history*. Dunedin: Anglican Church of the Province of New Zealand, 1973, 277 pp.

Pp. 78, 81, 84-85, Hau Hau; pp. 106-7, Te Whiti; p. 126, Ringatu; pp. 174-75, Ratana in relation to the Anglican Church.

1813 Morton, A[rchibald] W[entworth]. *Wiremu Tamihana.* [Sydney: D. S. Ford, Printer], [1963], 4 pp., portrait.

On William Thompson as a Christian, including references to his Christian village.

1814 Morton, H[enry] B[ruce]. *Recollections of early New Zealand*. Auckland: Whitcombe & Tombs, [1925], 176 pp., illus.

Pp. 104-7, atrocities against the Hau Haus.

1815 *Mr. J. C. Firth's visit to the King natives at Orahiri*. Auckland: Daily Southern Cross, 1869, 19 pp. [Reprinted from the *Daily Southern Cross*, June? 1869.]

Pp. 4-5, the Hauhau welcome, with description of religious service, and texts of a prayer and a hymn in Maori and English.

1816 "The native insurrection"; " The new superstition." *Southern Monthly Magazine* (Auckland), no. 24 [3] (February 1865): 373-75.
On Pai Marire.

1817 Nelson, Theo Bagge. "The religion of Pai Marire and its later developments." M.A. thesis, University of New Zealand (Wellington), 1932. [not deposited].

1818 Newman, Jacqui. "European masters and Maori messiahs." *Polynesian Studies*, no. 2 (1967), pp. 46-54.
Surveys Hau Hau, Ringatu and Ratana.

1819 "New Zealand fanaticism." *Nautical Magazine and Naval Chronicle* 34 (August 1865): 406-13; (September): 460-71; (December): 639-40.
August issue, magistrate J. White to Governor Grey on evils of Pai Marire and the tenets of Te Ua, and on Volkner's murder; September issue: pp. 409-11, Volkner's murder, p. 412, Maori opposition to Hau Hau, pp. 462-71, settler Graham's eulogy of the Maoris and criticism of land confiscation policies.

1820 New Zealand Government. *Appendices to the Journal of the House of Representatives*. Wellington: Government Printer. Various reports and references as follows:
1862, E-9, no. 2, p. 5 [report by Resident Magistrate T. H. Smith on a 'Sacred Runanga' (Maori Council) at Tauranga, with rules based on the Mosaic code, in which Wiremu Tamihana showed an interest. Included as example of independent establishment on the new Christian basis].
Papers on Pai Marire and Hauhau, also Papahurihia:
1864, E-8, pp. 1-13, Pai Marire [no. 5 (pp. 3-4) is extract from *Taranaki Herald*, "The new Maori faith," with Maori texts]; 1864, E-8A, 1 p., Pai Marire; 1865, E-4, pp. 3-43 [papers on "the Hau Hau superstition" from both Europeans and Maoris (some in Maori)]; 1865, E-5, pp. 3-19 [papers on "murder of Rev. C. F. Volkner by Hau Hau fanatics," from Maoris (some in Maori) and Europeans (including local residents)]; report of interview between R. C. Mainwaring and William Thompson [28th September 1865]; 1865, E-14, no. 2, pp. 2-3; 1868, A-4, 38 pp. [p. 5, brief outline of Hauhauism by W. N. Searancke, resident magistrate, Waikato; p. 11, outline of Hauhauism and Papahurihia by T. M. Clarke; p. 23, brief mention of E. M. Williams, Resident Magistrate, Waimate, on comparison of Hauhaus and Papahurihia; pp. 26-29, Appendix A, on Pai Marire worship (texts of songs) and vocabulary – all in Maori with English translations]; 1876, Paper G-1, p.

New Zealand

19 [resident magistrate S. von Sturmer at Hokianga, reporting death of Papahurihia at Omanaia, 3rd November 1875, "after 12 years useful service as Warden of Police"].

Papers on Te Whiti and Parihaka, 1876-86:

1876, G-1, p. 35, [district officers' reports]; 1879, G-7, 1 p., [interviews between Te Whiti and the Hon. the Native Minister]; 1882, A-8, pp. 1-11, [Governor Gordon's report to Colonial Office (1881)], pp. 12-18 [his correspondence with Premier Hall and Colonial Office over differences of viewpoint]; 1882, A-8A, 1 p., [correction of clerical error in above]; 1882, A-8B, pp. 1-2, [Government proclamation of October 1881 on Parihaka]; 1882, G-1, pp. 8-13, [six reports by R. Parris on Te Whiti by district officers]; 1882, H-14, pp. 1-4, [Annual Report, N.Z. Constabulary, including full report of Commander, Taranaki Colonial Forces (pp. 2-4)]; 1883, A-4, pp. 1-31, [the controversy between the Governor and his Ministers over Parihaka]; 1883, A-8 (for 5), pp. 1-4, [Sir H. Robinson to Colonial Office on Te Whiti]; 1883, G-1, p. 5 [arrest of surveying party]; 1885, G-2A, no. 13, pp. 11-12 [Dr. P. J. O'Carroll in Parihaka settlement]; 1885, G-4, p. 5, [Parihaka threatening attitudes]; 1885, G-8, [1 page, speeches of Te Whiti and Tohu at Parihaka 29 June 1885]; 1885, G-8A, 1 p., [Maori meeting at Parihaka 20-29 June 1885]; 1886, G-1, p. 19 [Report no. 13 of April 1886, by W. Rennell, on Te Whiti's influence.]; 1892, G-3, p. 4 [Wilkinson to Native Department; Te Mahutu's imprisonment].

Papers on the King Movement in the more religious aspects:

1876, Paper G-1, pp. 1-11, 19, 21-23, 25. [district officers' reports]; 1876, Paper G-4A, no. 1, pp. 1-2 [more reports]; 1882, G-4A, pp. 3-4, [resident magistrate R. S. Bush on Tawhiao's meeting at Whatiwhatihoe, May 1882.].

Reports from Dr. Maui Pomare:

1907, H-31, pp. 54-56 [Pp. 54-55, prophet Rua; p. 54, followers of Te Whiti and Tohu; pp. 55-56, a woman *tohunga*, Hikapuhi, 1905-9, and a kind of neoprimal movement; p. 55, white "charlatan seers"–all hostile reports from the Maori doctor, Maui Pomare, as health officer.

1821 New Zealand Government. *Parliamentary debates*. Vol. 41. 1882.

Portions of the debate on the West Coast Peace Preservation Bill, 30 May 1882, included as examples of attitudes to Te Whiti: pp. 142-43 (Mr. John Sheehan, Timaru), pp. 150-54 (Mr. William Montgomery, Akaroa), pp. 154-55 (Mr. John Stevens, Rangitiki).

1822 New Zealand Government. "Rex v. Rua." *Gazette Law Reports*, 3 November 1916, pp. 658-60.

Official reports of the summing up by Supreme Court judge at the trial of prophet Rua in Auckland, 1 August 1916–and asserting that Rua's arrest, on 4 February 1916, cannot be justified.

1823 New Zealand Government. "Tohunga suppression bill." *New Zealand Parliamentary Debates* 139 (1907): 510-25 (19 July 1907). P. 519 reprinted as "Te Rua," in *Transplanted Christianity: Documents . . . of New Zealand church history*, edited by A. K. Davidson and P. J. Lineham. Auckland: College Communications, 1987, pp. 166-67.

Pp. 510-12, Sir James Carroll, in moving the bill, on prophet Rua as a retrogressive *tohunga*, quoting white opinions from the *Whakatane County Press*, and from Elsdon Best; pp. 514-15, Hau Haus and Te Whiti; pp. 518-19, Apirana Ngata on Rua, his claims as successor of Te Kooti, and disastrous effects of his prophecies of King Edward VII's arrival; pp. 521-22, Parihaka; pp. 517, 525, Rua.

1824 New Zealand West Coast Commission. *Reports of the Royal Commission appointed . . . under "The Confiscated Lands inquiry and Maori Prisoners Trials Act, 1879."* Wellington: Government Printer, 1880, 91 pp. + appendixes (various paginations), maps. Reprinted in *Appendices to the Journal of the House of Representatives*, 1880, G2, 91 pp. + appendixes.

P. 4, Katene of Weriweri on Te Whiti and Te Ua; pp. 6-7, the Commissioner's comments on Te Whiti, with Maori replies; p. 33, further criticism of Te Whiti; pp. 70-71, peaceful removal of white surveyors' camps; p. 72, Parihaka Maori's not selling land. Appendix A, pp. 9-12, interview with Te Whiti; Appendix A, Part 2, pp. 1-2, correspondence on Parihaka.

1825 Ngata, Apirana [Turupu]. "Waikato of a hundred taniwhas." *Te Ao Hou* (Wellington), no. 18 [5, no. 2] (May 1957): 18-21. Translation of Waikato Taniwha-rau in *Te Pipiwharauroa*, no. 32 (October 1900): 8-9 and no. 33 (November 1900): 2.

Ngata, at age twenty-five, reported on the state of the King country; pp. 19-20, the effects of Hauhau seen in the abandoning of the Anglican Church for forty years.

1826 Nihoniho, H. T[uta]. "Karakia Ruuri Tuawhitu." *Te Pipiwharauroa* (Gisborne), no. 74 (April 1904), pp. 3-4; no. 76 (June 1904), p. 10 (with editorial note by Rev. R. T. M. Kohere).

"Worship of the Seventh Rule"–of the Church of the Seven Rules of Jehovah: critical of this new body claiming to be the church for all

New Zealand

Maoris, when they already have the Church of England; this was an
Anglican journal.

1827 O'Connor, P. S. "The recruitment of Maori soldiers, 1914-18." *Political
Science* (Wellington) 19, no. 2 (1967): 48-83.
P. 77, brief reference to revival of Hauhau ritual by Waikato
Maoris when pressed into war service.

1828 Ogilby, J. P. "Facts about New Zealand." *Overland Monthly and Out
West Magazine* (San Francisco) 9 (September 1872): 247-51.
Pp. 249-50, Hauhaus in Hawke's Bay; a traveler's superficial
impression.

1829 Oliver, W[illiam] H[osking]. *The Oxford History of New Zealand.*
Oxford: Clarendon Press; Wellington: Oxford University Press, 1981,
xiii + 572 pp.
Pp. 38-39, Papahurihia (by J. M. R. Owens); pp. 188-89, Te Whiti
and Rua (by M. P. K. Sorrensen); pp. 293-95, Ratana (by M. King).

1830 Oliver, W[illiam] H[osking]. *The story of New Zealand.* London: Faber
& Faber, 1960, 301 pp., illus.
Pp. 89-92, 256-57, Pai Marire; pp. 254-57, Te Whiti and the King
movement – convenient summaries but little on religion.

1831 Oliver, W[illiam] H[osking], and Thomson, Jane M. *Challenge and
response: A study of the development of the Gisborne East Coast Region.*
Gisborne: East Coast Development Association, 1971, 251 pp.
Pp. 34, 46, white and Maori millennialism; p. 49, a new "spiritism"
in 1857-58; pp. 86-91, Hau Haus and Pai Marire; pp. 172-73, Te
Tataia's revival of 1883, Te Kooti and his religion.

1832 Orbell, Margaret, ed. *Maori poetry: An introductory anthology.*
Auckland: Heinemann Educational Books (N.Z.), 1978, 104 pp.
P. 59, Song sung in imprisonment in Mt. Eden prison by Rua
Kenana; pp. 93-94, editor's commentary; for corrections of
transcriptions of names, also of text and translation, see Judith Binney,
et al. (entry 1590), p. 195, n. 64.

1833 *Otago Witness* (Dunedin), no. 3240 (19 April 1916), p. 42.
Photos of the capture of Rua Kenana, including Rua and his son,
and his large flag like a Union Jack, inscribed: "Kotahi te ture. Mo Nga
Iwi e Rua. Maungapohatu" [One law for the two peoples].

1834 Owens, John [M. R.]. "Papahurihia." In *The Oxford history of New Zealand*, edited by W. H. Oliver. Oxford: Clarendon Press; Wellington: Oxford University Press, 1981, pp. 38-39.

1835 Owens, John [M. R.]. "Religious disputation at Whangaroa, 1823-27." *Journal of the Polynesian Society* (Wellington) 79, no. 3 (1970): 288-304.
   Methodist missionaries and Maoris discussing god, devil, dreams, hell, Jesus, etc. – as example of cultural interaction.

1836 Palmer, G. Blake. "Tohungaism and Makutu." *Journal of the Polynesian Society* 63, no. 2 (September 1954): 147-63.
   Pp. 148-49, 154, faith-healing and Papahurihia and "Blackout" movements; good for background.

1837 Palmer, John Bruce. "Maori religious movements." In *Encyclopaedia of New Zealand*. Vol. 2. Wellington: Government Printer, 1966, 458a-460a.

1838 Parr, C. J. "Before the Pai Marire." *Journal of the Polynesian Society* 76, no. 1 (1967): 35-46.

1839 Parsonson, Ann [Rosemary]. "'He whenua te utu'" (the payment will be land). Ph.D. dissertation (history), University of Canterbury, 1978.
   Includes the King movement, and therefore the Tariao faith.

1840 Parsonson, Ann [Rosemary]. "Parihaka – a triumph of Maori spirit." *New Zealand's Heritage* (Wellington) 49 [4] (1972): 1352-57, illus.
   A scholarly account of the clash with the government, 1880-81.

1841 Parsonson, A[nn Rosemary]. "The pursuit of Mana." In *The Oxford History of New Zealand*, edited by W. H. Oliver. Oxford: Clarendon Press; Wellington: Oxford University Press, 1981, pp. 140-67.
   P. 143, Wahi Tapu or Kaingarara movement, 1857; p. 154, King movement; pp. 157-59, Hau Hau and Te Kooti; pp. 159-60, Te Ua and Pai Marire; p. 160, Ringatu.

1842 Parsonson, Ann [Rosemary]. "Te Mana o te Kingitanga Maori: A study of Waikato-Ngatimaniapoto relations during struggle for the King country, 1878-1884." M.A. thesis (history), University of Canterbury, 1972, ix + 188 pp.
   Pp. 87-88, the Tariao movement introduced by Tawhiao about 1876.

New Zealand

1843 Parsonson, Ann [Rosemary]. "Te Whiti–the protector of his people." *New Zealand's Heritage* (Wellington) 49 [4] (1972): 1360-63, illus.

1844 Patete, Haimona [Simon], et al. "Te hui ki Mataikona." *Te Puke ki Hikurangi* (Greytown) no. 9 [16] (July 1900): 5-6.
"The meeting at Mataikona." A special meeting of the Church of the Seven Rules of Jehovah; by the originator of the Church, in Maori.

1845 Payne, (Mr.). "Arrival of the schooner Rifleman from Poverty Bay." *Wellington Independent*, no. 2710 (23 July 1868): p. 4.
The account by the ship's chief officer of Te Kooti's escape from Chatham Islands and the subsequent casting of a man overboard. Many reports of Hauhau campaigns, passim.

1846 Payton, E[dward] W[illiams]. *Round about New Zealand, being notes from a journal of three years' wandering in the Antipodes.* London: Chapman & Hall, 1888, 368 pp., map, illus.
Pp. 293-95, 297-98, Parihaka and Te Whiti–a traveler's cynical account; p. 152, Te Kooti.

1847 Pearce, G[ilbert] L[lewelyn]. *The story of the Maori people.* Auckland and London: Collins, 1968, 164 pp., illus. 2d enl. ed., 1980.
Pp. 77-81, the rise of Hau Hau and Te Kooti's campaigns, pp. 92-95, Te Kooti and his influence on Maui Pomare; pp. 125-28, Ratana–popular summaries.

1848 Perry, Leslie W. G. "The history of the Maori King Movement until the Taranaki War." M.A. thesis, University of New Zealand (Auckland University College), 1921.

1849 Peterson, G. R. H. "Old Bay of Plenty." *New Zealand Methodist Times*, 28 March 1936.
Includes summary account of "Hauhauism and Volkner's murder–an example of the common understanding in the Church; by a Methodist minister.

1850 Phillipps, William John. *Carved Maori houses of the eastern districts of the North Island.* Wellington: Dominion Museum, 1944. Reprinted from *Records of the Dominion Museum* 1 (October 1944): 61-119.
P. 83, Te Matenga Tamati's planned Kowhiti temple.

1851 Phillipps, W[illiam] J[ohn]. "The cult of Nakahi." *Journal of the Polynesian Society* 75, no. 1, (1966): 107-8.

Derived from Papahurihia's cult; Nakahi (serpent of Genesis 3); later transformations at end of 19th century. See also "Blackout cult."

1852 Polack, J[oel] S[amuel]. *Manners and customs of New Zealanders.* . . . Vol. 2. London: James Madden & Co.; Hatchard & Son, 1940, 304 pp. Facsimile reprint. Christchurch: Capper Press, 1976.

P. 237, brief reference to Papahurihia's "new religion"–fuller account in entry 1853.

1853 Polack, J[oel] S[amuel]. *New Zealand, being a narrative of travels and adventures between the years 1831 and 1837.* 2 vols. London: Richard Bentley, 1838, 403 pp. and 441 pp., illus. Facsimile reprint. Christchurch: Capper Press, 1974.

Vol. 2, pp. 63-64, Papahurihia cult as "some new idolators"; "sounds like a rehash of Yate"; by a British trader, 1831-37, sympathetic to Maoris.

1854 Pomare, Maui [Wiremu Piti Naera]. [Integration by the middle of the twentieth century?] *Auckland Star*, 14 February 1907, p. 5. Reprinted in *Speeches and Documents on New Zealand History*, edited by W. D. McIntyre and W. J. Gardner. Oxford: Clarendon Press, 1971, pp. 174-75.

A medical doctor of the "Young Maori Party" in criticism of prophet Rua (and the King Movement) as retarding progress.

1855 Pomare, Maui [Wiremu Piti Naera]. *Legends of the Maori.* Vol. 2. Wellington: H. H. Tombs, 1930, 285 pp., illus.

Pp. 175-80, Te Whiti's use of the Old Testament to show that Maoris were descended from the lost tribes of Israel; mainly on the love-story of a warrior of Parihaka; p. 245, Pomare's oration on Te Whiti at 1907 mourning ceremonies.

1856 Pope, Diana, and Pope, Jeremy. *Mobil New Zealand travel guide: North Island.* Wellington: A. H. & A. W. Reed, 1973, 266 pp., illus., map.

Pp. 64-65, Parihaka; pp. 154-55, Ratana Pa; pp. 73-74, 138-40, Hau Hau, Te Kooti and Ringatu; pp. 199, 246-47, Rua–interesting popular summaries for visitors.

1857 Porter, J. P. "The cult of Io: The Rarotongan version." *Journal of the Tauranga Historical Society*, no. 36 (April 1969): 29-32.

As developed before the great migration, by some exceptionally thoughtful *tohunga*.

New Zealand

1858 Porter, J. P. "Io Matua Kore." *Journal of the Tauranga Historical Society*, no. 34 (August 1968), pp. 25-29.
 Supporting the view of the Io cult as ancient, but expanded by Te Matorohanga.

1859 Porter, J. P. "The lore of the Whare Wananga." *Journal of the Tauranga Historical Society*, no. 39 (April 1970), pp. 5-13.
 The cult of Io, with survey of the literature and the various views; by a supporter of the precontact view.

1860 Porter, J. P. "The Maori supreme God, Io." *Whakatane Historical Review*, no. 17 (1969), pp. 83-85.
 As precontact or "modern"?

1861 Porter, [Thomas William Rose]. *History of the early days of Poverty Bay: Major Ropata Wahawaha.* . . . Gisborne: Poverty Bay Herald Co., 1923, 556 pp., illus.
 Pp. 8-19, Pai Marire and the early Hau Hau fighting, including Te Kooti and the escape from the Chatham Islands. By a military officer.

1862 Porter, [Thomas William Rose]. "Te Kooti Rikirangi: The real story of the rebel leader, with an account of the Maori fanatic religions, Pai Marire, Ringa-tu, and Wairua Tapu." *Auckland Star*, Supplement, 28 February to 27 June 1914, pp. 16-17.
 Probably similar to a series of articles on Te Kooti in the *Otago Daily Times* 1914. Sources not given, but these influential articles are used by T. Lambert (entry 1754), J. Cowan (entry 1631) and B. M. Elsmore (entry 1656).

1863 Presbyterian Church of New Zealand. *Proceedings of the [Annual] General Assembly.* Reports of the Committee variously named Maori Missions, Home and Maori Missions, and Missions, (including reports of individual stations and missionaries), with sundry references to Ringatu or Hauhau, prophet Rua (especially by J. G. Laughton) and Ratana, between 1917 and 1941 (each *Proceedings* published in the year following the Assembly):
 1917, pp. 133, 137-38; 1919, 66-67, 103, 105 (Rua);
 1920, pp. 87-89 (Ringatu and Rua);
 1921, pp. 121-22, 133 (Ratana), pp. 126-28, (Ringatu and Rua; reprinted in *Transplanted Christianity: Documents . . . of New Zealand church history*, edited by A. K. Davidson and P. J. Lineham [Auckland: College Communications, 1987], p. 168);

1922, pp. 124-25, 129, (Ringatu and Rua);

1923, pp. 100, 107-11 (Ringatu), p. 106, (Ratana);

1924, pp. 121, 124 (Rua); 1925, pp. 79, 92 (Ratana);

1926, pp. 69, 82 (Ratana), pp. 74-79 (Ringatu);

1927, pp. 74-75, 87 (Ratana), pp. 76-77, 80, 82-83 (Ringatu);

1928, p. 92 (Ratana), pp. 96-97 (Rua);

1930, p. 140 (Ringatu); 1937, pp. 93-94 (Rua's funeral); 1941, p. 87 (Ringatu);

1964, pp. 253a-260a (on Maori history and relations with whites), p. 258a, (passing reference to Ringatu and Ratana);

1965, pp. 430a-439a (reports including reprint of J. G. Laughton's paper, "Maoritanga" on the nature of Maori culture).

1864 Price, A[rchibald] Grenfell. *White settlers and native peoples: An historical study of racial conflicts in United States, Canada, Australia and New Zealand.* Melbourne: Georgian House; Cambridge: Cambridge University Press, 1950, 232 pp., illus., maps. Reprint. Westport, Conn.: Greenwood Press, 1972, 232 pp.

Pp. 168-70, "cults of despair" – Te Ua and Hau Hau, Ringatu, Ratana and Rua; pp. 194-95, general interpretation.

1865 "The prophet Rua Tapunui Hepetipa." *New Zealand Herald*, 20 April 1908, p. 7. Reprinted in *Speeches and Documents on New Zealand History*, edited by W. D. McIntyre and W. J. Gardner. Oxford: Clarendon Press, 1971, pp. 175-78.

An account of Rua's modernizing village of Maungapohatu and its "tabernacle" or "house of parliament."

1866 "The prophet Te Whiti and the Parihaka stronghold." *Graphic* (London), no. 624 [24] (12 November 1881): 386-487, 497, illus.

Report of the arrest of Te Whiti; quotation from a letter of Miss Mary B. Dobie, with a favorable account of her visit to Parihaka; three drawings of Te Whiti and Parihaka.

1867 Rakena, Ruawai D. *The Maori response to the Gospel: A study of Maori-Pakeha relations in Methodist Maori Mission from its beginnings to the present day.* Proceedings, Wesley Historical Society (Auckland, N.Z.) 25, nos. 1-4 (August 1971). Reprinted and issued separately by the Society as 2d ed., February 1972, vi + 40 pp., photo of author, 2 figures.

Pp. 28-30, independent religious movements, with special reference to Methodist-Ratana relations and their failure. By the

New Zealand

Maori assistant-superintendent, Home and Maori Mission Department.

1868 Ramsden, Eric. *Marsden and the Missions: Prelude to Waitangi*. Sydney: Angus & Robertson, 1936, 295 pp.
Chap. 8: The followers of the Red God: pp. 160-74, Papahurihia, the prophet cult.

1869 Ramsden, Eric. *Rangiatea: The story of the Otaki Church, its first pastor, and its people*. Wellington: A. H. & A. W. Reed, 1951, 351 pp.
Incidental references to Ringatu, Te Whiti, Hau Hau (see index); pp. 305, 309, 315, more fully on Ratana.

1870 Rangihaua, John; Karetu, T. S.; Melbourne, Syd; and Milroy, Jim. "Mission at Maungapohatu. Rua and the Maori Millennium." *New Zealand Listener* (Wellington), no. 2090 [94], (2 February 1980): 60-61, illus.
A composite review from a Maori viewpoint, critical of the forcing of Rua's movement into anthropological models and of the limited area of Tuhoe life covered.

1871 Reed, A[lexander] W[yclif]. *The impact of Christianity on the Maori people*. Wellington: A. H. & A. W. Reed, 1955, 38 pp.
Pp. 23-24, Lieut. T. McDonnell's report to Resident Busby on chief Pi, convert to Papahurihia, 1830s; pp. 30-31, reprint of W. Morley's account (entry 1811) of Kaitoke, leader of Papahurihia cult.

1872 Reed, A[lfred] H[amish]. *From East Cape to Cape Egmont. On foot at eighty-six*. Wellington: A. H. & A. W. Reed, 1962, 108 pp., illus.
Pp. 196-201 (appendix C), by Shirley Anderson, Wanganui 1962: The Parihaka affair (a good summary); pp. 201-4, The Parihaka chants (appendix D): two chants in Maori with English translations.

1873 Reed, A[lfred] H[amish]. *The story of New Zealand*. Wellington: A. H. & A. W. Reed, 1945, 535 pp., illus. Rev. ed. London: Phoenix House, 1955, 335 pp. Reprint. Wellington and Sydney: A. H. & A. W. Reed, 1974, 337 pp. Reprint. London: Collins, 1975.
Chap. 4 (1945 ed., pp. 334-47), Hau Hau, with Te Ua as "a crazy tohunga" and Te Kooti a "foolish new religion"; p. 346, Parihaka – a popular history that is out of keeping with his other works.

1874 Reed, A[lfred] H[amish]. *Walks in Maoriland byways*. Wellington: A. H. & A. W. Reed, 1958, 374 pp., illus., maps.

Pp. 323-24, general outline of Te Kooti affair; brief description of ruinous remains at Parihaka.

1875 Reeves, William Pember. *The long white cloud: Ao Tea Roa*. London: George Allen & Unwin, 1898. 3d ed., enl., 1924, 382 pp., illus., map. 4th ed. 1930.

Pp. 211-13, "a very brief inaccurate but interesting attempt to describe and explain Hauhauism"; pp. 225-26, brief account of Te Whiti, based on an official visit to Parihaka as Minister of Labour in 1895.

1876 Reischek, Andreas. *Yesterdays in Maoriland. New Zealand in the 'Eighties*. Life and Letters Series. Whitcombe & Tombs, 1930. Reprint. 1952, 312 pp., illus. London: Jonathan Cape, n.d.

Chap. 9, Maori *versus* pakeha (the King Movement – based on information from Wahanui, *ariki* and priest, and Tawhiao: pp. 141-47, religious aspects, including Te Na (i.e., Te Ua) and Pai Marire; by an Austrian scientist long resident in New Zealand and intimate with the Maoris.

1877 "Remote temple last relic of mystic cult: Set in heart of King Country." *Taranaki Daily News*, 14 September 1951.

The Pao-miere cruciform meeting house at Te Tiroa.

1878 [Report on prophetess Maria Pangari.] *Globus* (Braunschweig) 48, no. 1 (1885): 16.

Highly distorted report, probably compiled by the editor, R. Kiepert, of a movement at Hokianga Bay in 1885.

1879 "Report on the trial of Rua Kenana, cross examination of Tohu by J. A. Tole, Crown Prosecutor." *New Zealand Herald*, 7 July 1916. Reprinted in *Transplanted Christianity: Documents . . . of New Zealand church history*, edited by A. K. Davidson and P. J. Lineham. Auckland: College Communications, 1987, p. 167.

1880 Richards, E[va] C., ed. *Diary of E. R. Chudleigh, 1862-1921, Chatham Islands*. Christchurch: Simpson & Williams (Printers), 1950, 474 pp., illus.

Pp. 223-27, escape of the Hau Haus, being the diary for 4 July to 2 August 1868; also reference to support for Te Whiti's refusal to pay dog tax in 1889.

New Zealand

1881 Rickard, Lawrence Sandston. *Tamihana, the kingmaker*. Wellington: A.
H. & A. W. Reed, 1963, 200 pp., illus., bib. pp. 192-94.
Pp. 36-37, 41-46, 53-53, 165, Tamihana and his Christian villages
at Tapari (Matamata) 1838, and Peria 1846 (latter based on J. E. Gorst
[entry 1683] and J. C. Firth [entry 1665]); his seances with Maori gods;
pp. 156-59, his attitude to Hau Hau.

1882 Riseborough, Hazel. *Days of darkness: Taranaki, 1878-1884*. London:
Allen & Unwin, 1989, 267 pp., illus.
The first major academic history of the Parihaka community,
from a pro-Maori viewpoint; based on a Massey University Ph.D.
dissertation.

1883 Ritchie, James [Ernest] (text) and Westra, Ans (photos). *Maori*.
Wellington: A. H. & A. W. Reed, 1967, 231 pp., illus.
Pp. 153-55, outline of Ringatu and Ratana, treated as forms of
Christian church.

1884 Roberts, C[yril[J[ohn], comp. *Centennial history of Hawera and the
Waimate Plains*. Hawera: Hawera County Council, et al., 1939, 395 pp.,
illus.
Chap. 8 (pp. 78-88), Parihaka and peace–from the settler
viewpoint.

1885 Rogers, Lawrence M. Review of *Mihaia: The prophet Rua Kenana*. . . . ,
by J. Binney et al. (entry 1590). *Outlook* (Wellington), August 1980, pp.
28-29.
By a retired principle of the former Presbyterian Maori
Theological College.

1886 Rowan, [Marion] [Ellis]. *A flower hunter in Queensland and New
Zealand*. London: John Murray, 1898, xivi + 272 pp., illus., map.
Pp. 193-94, Hau Haus and Te Kooti; pp. 216-19, report of a visit
to Parihaka (extract reprinted in D. Scott (entry 1903, p. 171). By an
Australian traveler.

1887 "Rua Kenana and the King who never came." *Church and Community*
(Christchurch, N.Z.), 1973, n. p. [5-9], illus.
Based on P. J. Webster (entry 1989).

1888 Rusden, G[eorge] W[illiam]. *Aureretanga: Groans of the Maoris*.
London: William Ridgway, 1888, 178 pp. Reprint. Cannons Creek:
Hakaprint, 1974. Facsimile reprint. Christchurch: Capper Press, 1975.

Pp. 43f., defense of Te Kooti in Parliament, and by Bishop Selwyn in the House of Lords; pp. 87, 109-41, the Parihaka affair and its political repercussions, by a Maoriphile.

1889 Rusden, G[eorge] W[illiam]. *History of New Zealand.* 3 vols. Melbourne: George Robertson; London: Chapman & Hall, 1883. 2d ed. Melbourne and London: Melville, Mullen & Slade, 1895.

Vol. 2, chaps. 12-16, passim on Hau Hau and Te Kooti, especially pp. 318-32, 352-61, 452-55, 526-28 on religious features; vol. 3, pp. 240-42, 259-65, 270-82, 301-9, 318-21, 332-35, 350-61, 389-431, 444-54, Te Whiti.

1890 Ryburn, Hubert J. *Te Hemara. James Hamlin, 1803-1865: Friend of the Maoris.* Dunedin: The author (J. McIndoe, Printer), 1979, 151 pp.

P. 114, "Papahurihiahism" – reference by this C.M.S. missionary in a letter of 1853.

1891 Rylance, Patricia A. "Sir Arthur Gordon and the Parihaka crisis: The wrong man, the wrong place, the wrong time." B.A. (Hons.) long essay, University of Otago, 1972, vii + 124 pp.

Chaps. 3-4, detailed clear examination of the Parihaka crisis, attempting to see both sides, especially pp. 38-45 on Sir Arthur Gordon's views of Te Whiti and Maoris; pp. 45-51, Te Whiti, pp. 48-53, European reactions to Te Whiti.

1892 St. John, [J. H. Herbert]. *Pakeha rambles through Maori lands.* Wellington: Robert Burrett (Printer), 1873, 212 pp.

P. 58, Wiremu Tamihana's high moral standard; p. 94, influence of "Hau Hau fanaticism"; p. 156, Volkner's murder; Hau Hau, passim.

1893 Salmond, Anne. *Hui: A study of Maori ceremonial gatherings.* Wellington: A. H. & A. W. Reed, 1975, 220 pp., maps.

Marae rituals: pp. 28, 197, Ratana gatherings; pp. 200-202, Ringatu; pp. 202-3, Parihaka's two maraes; pp. 203-7, King movement gatherings.

1894 Satchell, William. *The greenstone door.* Auckland, etc.: Whitcombe & Tombs, 1914, etc., 400 pp. Auckland: Golden Press, 1973, 400 pp.

An historical novel set in the time of the Waikato war: pp. 322-25, Wiremu Tamihana; no other relevant material.

New Zealand

1895 Saunders, Alfred. *History of New Zealand from the discovery . . . in 1642 to 1893*. 2 vols. Christchurch: Smith, Anthony Sellers & Co., 1896, 1:467 pp.; 2:558 pp. Reprint. 1899.

A shrewd and liberal account of the Parihaka period – its personalities and events – by a member of the House of Representatives. See vol. 2 (history from 1861), chap. 73 (pp. 453-68), arrest and imprisonment of Te Whiti.

1896 Scholefield, Guy Hardy, ed. *A dictionary of New Zealand biography*. 2 vols. Wellington: Department of Internal Affairs, 1940.

Useful outlines on various prophets: see vol. 1, entries on Rua Kenana and Te Kooti; vol. 2, on Ratana, J. C. Riemenschneider, and Te Whiti and Tohu, Titokowaru in relation to Parihaka, Tohu, Te Ua, Wiremu Tamihana in the King movement, Te Whiti – each with sources.

1897 Scholefield, Guy H[ardy]. *Newspapers in New Zealand*. Wellington: A. H. & A. W. Reed, 1958, 287 pp.

Pp. 258-59, history of the King movement's newspaper and the Government's opposition paper 1861-63; p. 250, the Ratana fortnightly, *Te Whetu Marama o Te Kotahitanga*, from 1924.

1898 Schultz-Ewerth, Erich [Bernard Theodor]. *Erinnerung an Samoa*. Berlin: August Scherl, 1926, 171 pp., illus.

P. 47 on Rua and his German sympathies in 1917. By a German governor of Samoa.

1899 Schwimmer, Erik [Gabriel], ed. "The aspirations of the contemporary Maori." In *The Maori people in the nineteen-sixties: A symposium*. Auckland: Blackwood & Janet Paul, 1968 [i.e., 1969]; London: C. Hurst; New York: Humanities Press, pp. 9-64.

Pp. 49-56, religious life, including "messianic churches" and imported millennial groups compared; Ratana, etc.

1900 Schwimmer, Erik [Gabriel]. "The cognitive aspect of cultural change." *Journal of the Polynesian Society* 74, no. 2, (1975): 149-81.

Further aspects of the Mormon Maori village of North Auckland, where a revitalization occurred in 1959: analysis of Mormon Maori religious thought; p. 173, Ratana healers; pp. 168-77, coexistence of the *mana* concept.

1901 Schwimmer, Erik Gabriel. "Mormonism in a Maori village: A study of social change." M.A. thesis (anthropology and sociology), University of British Columbia, 1965, 165 pp., maps, tables.

The isolated settlement of Whangaruru, North Auckland. A valuable account of the affinities and differences between Mormonism and Maoris, especially sections on religious life (pp. 79-104) and "bipolar value system" (pp. 105-30). Mormonism as reconstruction, as compared with Ratana and Ringatu which "continue the millennial dream" (p. 152.).

1902 Schwimmer, Eric [*sic*] [Gabriel]. *The world of the Maori.* Wellington: A. H. & A. W. Reed, 1966, 160 pp., illus.

Pp. 112-13, various movements; pp. 114-16, doctrine of Io; pp. 117-21, Hau Hau and Ringatu; pp. 121-25, Maori revival factors–Io doctrine, Te Kooti, lost tribes of Israel theory, etc.; pp. 147-49, Ratana.

1903 Scott, Dick [Richard George Scott]. *Ask that mountain: The story of Parihaka.* Auckland: Heinemann Educational Books (N.Z.); Southern Cross Books, 1975, 216 pp., illus., map.

A new work from more extensive written and oral sources, replacing the 1954 version, *Parihaka Story.* Also pp. 19-24, 28, 32, 154-55, Hauhau; pp. 30f, King Movement; pp. 77, 133, 178-79, Te Makuta's movement; pp. 199f., Ratana; for Te Whiti's religion see especially pp. 18, 37-38, 58, 74. A lavish, revised edition.

1904 Scott, Dick [Richard George Scott]. *Parihaka story.* Auckland: Southern Cross Books, 1954, 160 pp., illus. Russian translation by N. A. Butinov, with introduction, 1957.

Pp. 5-59, the Maori movement at Parihaka under Te Whiti from 1862; a popular account, but based on documents of the period. This was the first New Zealand book to be translated into Russian, probably because of its anti-imperialism, anticolonialism potential.

1905 Seffern, W. H. J. "Parihaka–its past and present aspect." *New Zealand Graphic and Ladies Journal* (Auckland) 18, no. 21 (1897): 629-30, illus.

1906 Selwyn, George Augustus. *Charge to Synod.* Christchurch, 26 September 1865.

In same year as Volkner's murder, contains bitter criticism of Te Ua and Hauhaus, by the pioneer Anglican bishop. See extract in B., P. C., *Fraser's Magazine* October 1865, pp. 436f. (entry 1565).

New Zealand

1907 Servant, Louis-Catherin. *Customs and habits of the New Zealanders, 1838-42.* Translated by J. Glasgow. Edited by D. R. Simmons. Foreword by E. R. Simmons. Wellington: A. H. & A. W. Reed, 1973, 84 pp., illus., maps, plates, etc.

    Pp. 56-57, Papahurihia. By a Marist missionary. Reviewed in detail by J. Kennedy in *Journal of the Polynesian Society* 83, no. 4 (1975): 398-400, and shown to depend on W. Yate .

1908 Sewell, Henry. *The New Zealand native rebellion.* Auckland: The author, 1864, 51 pp. Reprint. Dunedin: Hocken Library, facsimile no. 14, 1974.

    A letter to Lord Lyttelton. See p. 30 on Te Atua Wera (Papahurihia) and his son as among the King movement Maoris.

1909 Shortland, Edward. *Traditions and superstitions of the New Zealanders with illustrations of their manners and customs.* London: Longman, Brown, Green, Longmans & Roberts, 1854. 2d ed. 1856, xi + 316 pp. Reprint. Christchurch: Capper Press, 1980, 316 pp.

    Pp. 84-89 (2d ed.), conversations and experiences with Wiremu Tamihana, including a seance with whistling and speech from an *auta* – by a profound Maori scholar; pp. 120-25, early reactions to Christianity, relevant as background.

1910 Shrimpton, A[rnold] W[ilfred], and Mulgan, A[lan] E. *Maori and Pakeha: A history of New Zealand.* Limited ed. Auckland and London: Whitcombe & Tombs, 1921. 2d ed. 1930, 452 pp.

    Pp. 242-45, 312-13, Te Whiti and Hau Hau.

1911 Simmons, D[avid] R[oy]. *Iconography of Maori religion.* Iconography of Religions, vol. 2, no. 1. Leiden: E. J. Brill, 1986, vii + 33 pp., 21 pp. of plates.

    Some illustrations are of new movements.

1912 Simmons, David [Roy], and Biggs, Bruce. "The sources of 'The lore of the Whare-Wananga.'" *Journal of the Polynesian Society* 79, no. 1 (March 1970): 22-42.

    Volume 1 appears to represent an authentic *tohunga* tradition; volume 2 is a late compilation from many sources, whose value is uncertain.

1913 Simpson, Terry. "The Pakeha missionary, the Maori prophet, and Maungapohatu." *Historical Review: Bay of Plenty Journal of History* 35, no. 2 (1987): 106-11, photo.

Presbyterian missionary John Laughton's relations with Rua Kenana and the Urewera people, 1918-37.

1914 Simpson, Tony. "Rua the prophet." *New Zealand's Heritage* (Wellington) 75 [5] (1973): 2084-85, 2088-90, illus.

A sympathetic outline, with a balanced account of his arrest and trial.

1915 Sinclair, Karen Phyllis. "Maramatanga: Ideology and social process among the Maori of New Zealand." Ph.D. dissertation (anthropology), Brown University (Rhode Island), 1976, 347 pp., map.

Maramatanga as a religious movement, maintaining Maori identity while adjusting to change; studied in Levin, Ohakune, Wanganui, Taihape, Hastings, Rotorua, Waitangi and Auckland. Chap. 4, Maori prophetess; chaps. 5-9, and map p. 12, on this movement, which draws on the prophetic heritage and embraces elites from the Catholic Church and Maori organizations in a nominally Catholic context.

1916 Sinclair, Keith. *The origins of the Maori wars*. Wellington: New Zealand University Press, 1957. Reprint. 1961-62, 297 pp., illus., maps.

King movement, passim (see index); pp. 77-78, Hau Hau; W. Tamihana (see index).

1917 Sinclair, Keith. *William Pember Reeves, New Zealand Fabian*. Oxford: Clarendon Press, 1965, 356 pp., illus.

Pp. 219-20, Reeves' visit to Te Whiti at Parihaka in 1885.

1918 Sinclair, Keith, and Harrex, Wendy. *Looking back: A photographic history of New Zealand*. Wellington: Oxford University Press, 1978, 240 pp., illus.

Pp. 44-45, 53, Pai Marire and Hau Hau; p. 53, Tariao faith; pp. 53-56, Parihaka; pp. 60-62, Rua; pp. 62-64, mostly photographs familiar in other publications, with very brief text.

1919 Sissons, Jeffrey. "Te mano o te waimana: Tuhoe history of the Tauranga valley [Urewera ranges]." Ph.D. thesis (anthropology), University of Auckland, 1984, 218 pp.

Includes Rua Kenana and the "Israelites" of Maungapohatu.

1920 Smith, Jonathan Z. *Imagining religion: From Babylon to Jonestown*. Chicago: University of Chicago Press, 1982, 165 pp.

New Zealand

Chap. 5, on the Maori high god, Io, and pp. 79-89 (notes, pp. 152-55), "syncretistic religious movements"–King movement, Te Ua, Pai Marire and Io cult.

1921 Smith, Norman. *The Maori people and us.* Wellington: A. H. & A. W. Reed for Maori Purposes Fund Board, 1948, 232 pp.
Pp. 187-90, Te Whiti and Parihaka, Te Kooti and Pai Marire; pp. 169-70, Te Ua Haumene; sympathetic outlines by a member of the Department of Maori Affairs.

1922 Smith, R. W. "Rua Kenana." *Historical Review. Journal of the Whakatane and District Historical Society* 11, no. 3, (1963): 171.
A letter, on Rua and a *tohunga* in rivalry over healing a barren woman.

1923 Smith S[tephenson] Percy, trans. *The Lore of the Whare-wananga: Teachings of the Maori College on religion, cosmogony and history.* Part 1, *Te Kawae-runga, or things celestial.* Memoirs of the Polynesian Society, vol. 3. New Plymouth: W. T. Avery for the Polynesian Society, 1913, 193 pp., + index, illus.
The Io cult; see D. Simmons and B. Biggs (entry 1912) for critique.

1924 Smith S[tephenson] Percy. *Maori wars of the nineteenth century: The struggle of the northern against southern Maori tribes prior to . . . 1840.* [1st ed., with slightly different title, 1904.] New enl. ed. Christchurch: Whitcombe & Tombs, 1910, 490 pp., illus. Reprint. New York: AMS Press, 1976. Reprinted from the *Journal of the Polynesian Society.*
Pp. 314-15, Te Toroa's new religion with "Wheawheau" as God, and Te Toroa's death, probably in 1824.

1925 "Some typical friendlies: Ropata Wahe Wahe and Renata Kawepo." *Weekly Press and Referee* (Christchurch), 14 June 1894.
Extract on Hau Hau, and Te Kooti *mana* as prophet, in Turnbull Library under "Maori disturbances, etc., 1881-1919."

1926 Sorrenson, M[aurice] P[eter] K[eith]. "The changing face of Maori society." *New Zealand's Heritage* 49 [4] (1972): 1345-51, illus.
A sympathetic account of "Maori forms of Christianity" as part of the response to defeat in the wars of the 1870s-1880s–Ringatu, Te Whiti, Tariao, Te Mahuki, Pareha and Maria Pungare.

1927 Sorrenson, M[aurice] P[eter] K[eith]. "Land purchase methods and their effect on Maori population 1865-1901." *Journal of the Polynesian Society* 65, (1956): 183-99.

See especially on Taraio and Parihaka.

1928 Sorrenson, M[aurice] P[eter] K[eith]. *Maori and European since 1870: A study of adaptation and adjustment.* New Zealand History Topic Books. Auckland and London: Heinemann Educational Books, 1967, viii + 44 pp., illus.

Pp. 11-13, King movement; pp. 13-15, Te Whiti; pp. 27-30, Ratana – reliable convenient summaries.

1929 Sorrenson, M[aurice] P[eter] K[eith]. "The Maori King movement: A reply to B. J. Dalton." *Journal of the Polynesian Society* 74, no. 1 (1965): 70-75.

1930 Sorrenson, M[aurice] P[eter] K[eith]. "The Maori King movement, 1858-85." In *Studies in a small democracy: Essays in honour of Willis Airey,* edited by K. Sinclair and R. Chapman. Hamilton: Blackwood & Janet Paul, for the University of Auckland, 1963, pp. 33-55. Reprint. 1965.

Pp. 52-53, brief comment on Tariao faith.

1931 Sorrenson, M[aurice] P[eter] K[eith]. "The politics of land." In *The Maori and New Zealand politics: Talks from a N.Z.B.C.* [New Zealand Broadcasting Corporation] *series with additional essays,* edited by J. G. A. Pocock. Auckland: Blackwood & Janet Paul, 1965, pp. 21-45.

Summarizes his M.A. thesis of 1955.

1932 Sorrenson, M[aurice] P[eter] K[eith]. "The purchase of Maori lands, 1865-1892." M.A. thesis (history), Auckland University College, 1955, 246 pp.

Includes detailed account of the Parihaka affair's relation to land problems – valuable as background rather than on Parihaka itself, but presents impressive picture of Te Whiti.

1933 Sorrenson, M[aurice] P[eter] K[eith]. "Te Whiti and Rua." In *The Oxford History of New Zealand,* edited by W. H. Oliver. Oxford: Clarendon Press; Wellington: Oxford University Press, 1981, pp. 188-89.

1934 Stack, James W[est]. *Koro.* Christchurch, etc.: Whitcombe & Tombs, 1909, 109 pp.

New Zealand

Pp. 51-53, Tamaiharoa's new movement, South Canterbury, and Koro's opposition to it; pp. 80-81, Koro's reconversion of the Port Levy seceders; pp. 102-4, Hau Hau and Te Whiti.

1935 Stack, James W[est]. *Notes on Maori Christianity ... Read before the Church meeting ... Christ College Library, Canterbury ... October 30th, 1874.* Christchurch: The Press (Printers), [1874], 6 pp.
P. 3, an understanding view of Hau Hau and Te Kooti, and their identification with Israel; p. 4, Anglican Maoris prone to rebel; p. 6, reprint of a Hau Hau song, with comments.

1936 Stafford, D[onald] M. "Po-takato: A form of religion founded on the rupee." *New Zealand Numismatic Journal* 11, no. 4 (1964): 169-70.
Tariao, a new religion with Christian elements founded by Himiona (Simeon) at Maketu, Bay of Plenty, in the 1880s.

1937 Stafford, D[onald] M. *Te Arawa: A history of the Arawa people.* Wellington: A. H. & A. W. Reed, 1967, x + 573 pp., illus.
Pp. 388-92, Te Ua and Hau Hau hostilities with the Arawa.

1938 Stirling, Eruera, and Salmond, Anne (narrator). *Eruera: The teachings of a Maori elder.* Wellington: Oxford University Press, 1980, 288 pp., illus., map.
Pp. 127-39, Ratana as healer; pp. 190-95, author's successful negotiations at Parihaka in 1956 on behalf of the government.

1939 Stock, Eugene. *The story of the New Zealand mission. ...* London: Church Missionary Society; Nelson, N.Z.: New Zealand Church Missionary Association Depot, 1913, 78 pp., illus. Rev. ed. *The history of the Church Missionary Society in New Zealand.* Wellington: New Zealand Church Missionary Society, 1935, 68 pp., illus.
Pp. 40-43 (in 1935 ed., pp. 42-45), Hau Haus and Tamihana–brief popular outline; p. 49 (p. 51), passing disparaging reference to Te Whiti.

1940 Stokes, Evelyn. *Pai Marire and the Niu at Kwanui.* Occasional Paper 6. Hamilton: University of Waikato Centre for Maori Studies and Research, April 1980, 62 pp., illus., bib.
The *niu* was the ritual flagstaff of Pai Marire; extensive use of the *Appendices to the Journal of the House of Representatives*, 1860-73, and illustrations from Turnbull Library resources.

1941 Stout, Robert. "Governor Gordon and the Maoris, a chapter of New Zealand history." *Melbourne Review* 8 (January-October 1883): 164-85.

Pp. 168-70, a fair-minded account of political and military history, showing Te Whiti as a prophet of peace and temperance, and as a hero in future Maori history.

1942 Stout, Robert. "Political parties in New Zealand." *Melbourne Review*, no. 17 [5, no. 1] (1880): 56-79.

Pp. 73-74, the King movement as a political problem; pp. 74-75, a detached view of Te Whiti.

1943 Stuart, Alexander. *Sir George Grey, his friends and foes: A political satire.* Christchurch: Lyttelton Times Office, 1882, 12 pp.

P. 7, part of this satirical poem is in defense of Te Whiti and critical of Bryce, reprinted in D. Scott (entry 1903), p. 131.

1944 Sutherland, I[an] L[orin] G[eorge]. *The Maori situation.* Wellington: Harry H. Tombs, 1935, 123 pp.

Pp. 31-32, sympathetic reference to the main religious movements as attempts to have a faith of their own, but psychologically as "group neurosis."

1945 Sutherland, I[an] L[orin] G[eorge], ed. *The Maori people today: A general survey.* London: Oxford University Press for New Zealand Institute for International Affairs, 1940, 449 pp.

See pp. 336-73, essay by Sutherland and A. Ngata, "Religious influences."

1946 Taipo [pseud.]. "A dusky Dowie." *Life* (Melbourne), 1 December 1908, pp. 495-500, illus.

By an early visitor to prophet Rua's village, describing his house, and buildings for worship and for council meetings, and the emphasis on physical and ritual cleanliness. "Dowie" (not explained) is John Alexander Dowie, widely-known founder of the Christian Catholic Apostolic Church in Zion in 1896 in Chicago – a healing and adventist church, later with a holy community, Zion City, Illinois, which probably provides the point of comparison.

1947 Takao, Tame. "Warm welcome from Maori Churches." *Outlook* (Wellington, N.Z.) 91, no. 3 (1984): 27.

Report by the current Moderator of the Presbyterian Church of New Zealand on his official visits, first to the Ringatu community at Te

New Zealand

Mapou, Te Teko, Bay of Plenty, and later to Ratana Pa – and the warm reception in both cases.

1948 Tamihana, Wiremu [Te Waharoa]. [The election of a Maori King, 1858.] *Southern Cross*, 3 and 6 August 1858. Reprinted with editorial comment by Keith Sinclair in *The Maori King*, by J. E. Gorst. Hamilton and Auckland: Paul's Book Arcade, 1959, pp. 265-74. Also in *Speeches and Documents on New Zealand History*, edited by W. D. McIntyre and W. J. Gardner. Oxford: Clarendon Press, 1971, pp. 125-31.

Includes the biblical sanctions and texts quoted in various speeches.

1949 Tamihana, Wiremu [Te Waharoa]. [Letter to the Governor. Ngaruawahia, 7 June 1861.] Wellington: *Appendices to the Journals of the House of Representatives* 1861, E-1B, p. 19. Reprinted in *Transplanted Christianity: Documents ... of New Zealand church history*, edited by A. K. Davidson and P. J. Lineham. Auckland: College Communications, 1987, pp. 219-30.

On the King movement.

1950 Taonui, Aperahama. *Nga Kupu a Aperahama*. Dargaville: [no information].

The sayings of Aperahama Taonui, successor to Te Atua Wera as leader of the Nakahi movement – "a very old much worn book of them printed in Dargaville, a rare and much-prized possession of a Hikutu elder." As seen by J. Irvine (entry 1727), p. 96.

1951 Taylor, Alan. "Sacred cult temple." *Te Awatea* (New Zealand Maori Theatre Trust) 1, no. 4 (1973): 34-35, illus.

The history and current state of the cruciform temple of the Pao Miere cult, built in the 1880s, at Te Tiroa, Rangitoto ranges, its relation to the Io and Hauhau Pai Marire cults, and the King movement.

1952 Taylor, Alan, and Taylor, W. A. (illustrator). *The Maori builds: Life, art and architecture from moahunter days*. Christchurch and London: Whitcombe & Tombs, 1966 [i.e., 1967], 80 pp., illus.

Pp. 44-45, the Pai Marire temple at Te Tiroa; pp. 62-63, Rua's temple, 1908 – text and large line drawings of each.

1953 [Taylor, David M.] "New member of W.C.C." *Church and Community* (Christchurch, N.Z.) 26, no. 9 (1969): 10 (and photos, p. 8).

The Kimbanguist Church in Africa, and possible implications for Maori equivalents, by the General Secretary of the National Council of Churches in N.Z.

1954 Taylor, Richard. *The past and present of New Zealand; with its prospects for the future*. London: Wm. Macintosh, 1868, 331 pp., illus.
P. 41, Papahurihia; pp. 41-43, Warea cult; pp. 59-61, Wahi Tapu. By a missionary.

1955 Teague, Bernard. "Israel in Wairoa." *New Zealand Listener* (Wellington), no. 2016 [89] (19 August 1978): 48-49, illus.
On Te Matenga Tamati and his temple-building plan, Wairoa district.

1956 Te Kooti. [Unpublished notebook.] Alexander Turnbull Library. Maori MS, vol. 3, MS.DAV. Translated by George H. Davis. N.d. Reprinted in *Transplanted Christianity: Documents . . . of New Zealand church history,* edited by A. K. Davidson and P. J. Lineham. Auckland: College Communications, 1987, pp. 162-63.
Claims to be his notebook found on the battlefield. His prophetic call on 21 February 1867, and vision of a heavenly being, reported in biblical language.

1957 Te Rangi Hiroa [Buck, Peter Henry]. *The coming of the Maori.* Wellington: For Maori Purposes Fund Board by Whitcombe & Tombs, 1949, 548 pp., illus. 2d ed. South Pasadena: P. D. & I. Perkins, 1950, 580 pp., illus.
Bk. 4, chap. 5, pp. 531-35, critique of cult of Io; also pp. 443-44 on the Io cult.

1958 Te Tau, Pani. "E Kupu ruarua nei. . . ." *Matuhi Press* (Masterton), no. 44 (13 July 1904): 1-2.
"This is just a word. . . ." The editor, wife of the founder of the Seven Rules of Jehovah, replying to criticisms.

1959 Te Ua, Te Kani. "Spiritualism and Maori beliefs: The love of the Whare-Wananga." In *Echoes of the Pa. Proceedings of the Tairaiohiti Maori Association for 1932*. Gisborne: The Association, 1933, pp. 38-54.
Pp. 41-46, Whare Wananga, its construction and use, its *tohungas,* priestesses and second grade teachers; p. 52, alleged "spirit duel" with Bishop Selwyn; p. 53, Tawhiao's killing of wizards.

New Zealand

1960 Te Ua Haumene. "Te Ua Haumene, Ua Rongopai." Auckland Public Library, Grey Collection. Chapter 2, 13 January 1863. English translation by Lyndsay Head. GNZMMSS1. Reprinted in *Transplanted Christianity: Documents . . . of New Zealand church history*, edited by A. K. Davidson and P. J. Lineham. Auckland: College Communications, 1987, pp. 139-40.

1961 Te Ua Haumene. "Ua Rongopai [Gospel of Te Ua]." Selections printed as Appendix 1, in *'Hauhau': The Pai Marire search for Maori identity*, by P. Clark. Auckland: Auckland University Press, 1975, pp. 113-31.

Te Ua's prophetic message as "corrected" by Sir George Grey and freshly translated for this appendix, from Te Ua's manuscript notebook.

1962 Te Whiti. "Speech to his followers at Pungarehu." *New Zealand Herald*, 18 October 1881, p. 5. Reprinted in *Transplanted Christianity: Documents . . . of New Zealand church history*, edited by A. K. Davidson and P. J. Lineham. Auckland: College Communications, 1987, p. 165.

1963 "Te Whiti, poropiti." *Te Pipiwharauroa* (Gisborne), no. 74 (April 1904), p. 5.

An Anglican Maori magazine–on the prophet Te Whiti, in Maori.

1964 Thomson, Jane. "The Roman Catholic Mission in New Zealand, 1838-1870." M.A. thesis (history), Victoria University of Wellington, 1966, 256 pp.

Pp. 209-17, 228-29, Hau Haus and the mission.

1965 Thorne, Margaret Cheston. "The Kingmaker: The part played by Wiremau Tamihana (Tarapipi) Te Waharu in the King Movement, 1856-1866." M.A. thesis, University of New Zealand (Canterbury University College), 1929, 194 pp., illus., map.

1966 Tiesmeyer, L[udwig]. *Eine Deutsche Missionsarbeit auf Neu-Seeland. Lebensgeschichte des Missionars J. F. Reimenschneider*. Bremen: W. Balette & Co., 1875, 142 pp. [in Gothic type].

On the Lutheran missionary who taught Te Whiti and Tohu; especially chaps. 6-14, on his Warea period.

1967 Tippett, A. R. *People movements in Southern Polynesia*. Chicago: Moody Press, 1971, 288 pp.

Pp. 68-72, Hau Hau, Te Kooti, Ringatu.

1968 Treagar, Edward. "The Pai-Marire word *Hau.*" *Journal of the Polynesian Society* 13 (1904): 194.
A brief note.

1969 Triggs, W. H. "The Maori Mecca and its prophets." *Centennial Magazine* (Sydney) 2, no. 7 (1890): 516-22, illus.
The attitude towards Parihaka, Te Whiti, and Tohu is typical of the settlers and the Government as represented by Bryce. Useful factual information on Parihaka and the prophets, with good black-and-white drawing of the village.

1970 Tucker, H[enry] W[illiam]. *Memoir of the life and episcopate of George Augustus Selwyn, D.D., Bishop of New Zealand 1841-1869; and Bishop of Lichfield, 1867-1878.* Vol. 2. London: William Wells, Gardner, 1879, vi + 393 pp.
Pp. 196-201, 108, Te Ua and Hauhaus; the rescue of Mr. Grace; tolerant explanation of Hauhaus and Volkner's murder.

1971 "Two poles preserve Maori history." *Wanganui Chronicle*, 14 March 1970, p. 17, illus.
Two totara-wood *niu* poles of the Hau Hau faith at Opatu South on Mr. O. F. Burn's property, now also a national reserve.

1972 Umbra [pseud.]. "Pai Marireism and popery identified." Letter, 22 September 1865, 1 p.
In Grey Collection, Auckland Public Library. Critical of Pai Marire as "a mongrel sort of Maori idealism and Popish sacerdotal system."

1973 Vaggioli, Felix. *Storia della Nuova Zelanda.* Vol. 2. Parma: Tipografia Vesc. Fiaccadori, 1896, 548 pp., illus.
Pp. 356-457 on Hau Hau history; pp. 506-19, Te Whiti; pp. 533-35, Te Kooti and Te Whiti. The author, an Italian historian, was Catholic priest in Gisborne in 1880.

1974 Vennell, C. W., et al. *Centennial history of the Matamata Plains.* Wellington: Whitcombe & Tombs for Matamata County Council, 1951, 318 pp., map, illus.
Pp. 24-39, Tamihana; pp. 53-53, description of Peria pa, drawn from Firth (entry 1665).

New Zealand

1975 Volkner, C. S. [Letter to Governor Grey, 16 February 1864.] National Archives [New Zealand], G 13/3, 89. Reprinted in *Transplanted Christianity: Documents . . . of New Zealand church history*, edited by A. K. Davidson and P. J. Lineham. Auckland: College Communications, 1987, p. 141.

Asking Grey to treat as confidential the information on the "disturbed state of the natives" passed on in letters.

1976 Waikato and Taranaki Museums. *Te Whiti O Rongomai of Parihaka as seen by his contemporaries*. Hamilton: Waikato Museum, 1973, 14 pp., illus.

An exhibition guide book of sketches, a photograph of Te Whiti, and texts describing this Maori prophet.

1977 Walker, R. J. "The genesis of Maori activism." *Journal of the Polynesian Society* 93, no. 3 (1984): 267-81.

Pp. 270-71, the King movement, Pai Marire, Te Kooti, Parihaka, and Rua Kenana as forms of active protest; pp. 274-75, 278-79, Ratana's alliance with and divorce from the Labour party.

1978 Walsh, (Archdeacon). "The passing of the Maori." *Transactions of the New Zealand Institute* 40 (1907): 154-75.

An address on the state of the people, with (p. 167) severe criticisms of Parihaka, by an Anglican clergyman.

1979 Ward, Alan [Dudley]. "Law and enforcement on the New Zealand frontier, 1840-1893." *New Zealand Journal of History* 5, no. 2 (1971): 128-49.

Pp. 137-40, 147-48, the King movement and its revivals in 1890s.

1980 Ward, Alan D[udley]. "The origins of the Anglo-Maori wars: A reconsideration." *New Zealand Journal of History* 1, no. 2 (1967): 148-70.

P. 157, King Movement and missionaries; pp. 166-67, prophets Rua and Te Whiti.

1981 Ward, Alan [Dudley]. *A show of justice: Racial "amalgamation" in nineteenth century New Zealand*. Auckland: Auckland University Press; London: Oxford University Press, 1973, 382 pp.

Pp. 98-101, Wiremu Tamihana; pp. 167-69, 224-29, Te Ua and Pai Marire, and King movement; pp. 279-80, 284-85, Te Whiti and Parihaka.

1982 Ward, Alan [Dudley]. "Toa and Tumuaki: Contrasting leadership in the early King movements." *Te Maori* (Wellington) 1, no. 2, (Spring [1969]): 47-49, 51, 59, illus.

Wiremu Tamihana and Rewi Maniapoto – little on the Tawhaio faith itself; p. 47, Tamihana's efforts at a new Christian *kianga* with new codes.

1983 Ward, John P. *Wanderings with the Maori prophets, Te Whiti and Tohu . . . from 1882 until . . . 1883.* Nelson, N.A.: Bond, Finney & Co., 1883, 136 pp.

As custodian of the prophets, during their exile from Parihaka.

1984 Ward, Robert. *Life among the Maoris of New Zealand. . . .* Edited by T. Lowe and W. Whitby. London: G. Lamb; Toronto: W. Rowe, 1872, 472 pp.

By the first Primitive Methodist minister in New Zealand. Pp. 320-25, W. Tamihana and Potatau I; chap. 12 (pp. 440-48), "the Pai Marire delusion"; chap. 13 (pp. 449-57), war with the Hau Haus.

1985 "The war in New Zealand." *Brett's Auckland Almanack*, 1877, pp. 47-67.

Pp. 61-62, "Hau Hau fanaticism"; pp. 65-66, Te Kooti, escape from Chatham Islands, and his new religion.

1986 Watkins, June E. "Messianic movements: A comparative study of some religious cults among the Melanesians, Maori, and North American Indians." M.A. thesis (anthropology), University of Sydney, 1951.

1987 Webster, John. *Reminiscences of an old settler in* Australia and New Zealand. Christchurch: Whitcombe & Tombs, 1908, vi + 294 pp., illus.

Pp. 259ff, 261, a friend of Papahurihia describes a seance in 1845 at Omanaia.

1988 Webster, Peter J. *Rua and the Maori millennium.* Wellington: Price Milburn & Co. for Victoria University Press, 1979, 328 pp., illus.

An anthropologist's study of Rua and his community at Maungapohatu.

1989 Webster, Peter J. "When the King comes to Gisborne – a Maori millennium in 1906." *Historical Review: Journal of the Whakatane and District Historical Society* 15, no. 1 (1967): 46-59.

On prophet Rua and Maungapohatu.

New Zealand

1990 White, John. "Lectures on Maori customs and superstitions." In *Appendices to the Journal of the House of Representatives,* 1861, E – No. 7, 1-48.

Pp. 9-10, cult of a high god, Maru, in Wanganui area, with some Christian features; pp. 19-21, "Nakahi" and other seers showing some Christian influence; p. 21, "another imposter named Papahurihia." White grew up in Hokianga in close contact with those influenced by Papahurihia, but his reliability has been questioned.

1991 Whiteley, John. *Prophetic letter by the late Rev. John Whiteley who was murdered at the White Cliffs, 13 February 1869.* New Plymouth: Taranaki Herald Office [1869?], 1 p.

Written to *The Watchman* concerning the Hau Hau war and the British Government attitude towards it in withdrawing troops and so encouraging the Hau Haus.

1992 Wilkinson Geo[rge] B. "Rua's five widows." *Journal of the Tauranga Historical Society,* no. 63 (August 1979), p. 10.

Brief report of a Maori request for five forms for widow's pensions for Rua's wives.

1993 Williams, F[rederick] W[anklyn]. *Through ninety years: Life and work among the Maoris of New Zealand, 1826-1916.* Auckland, etc. Whitcombe & Tombs, [1940]. 360 pp.

Pp. 196-97, Hau Hau religion; pp. 198-205, 210-25, Hau Hau campaigns; pp. 268-69, comments on Hau Hau religion and its failure; pp. 236-41, Te Kooti and his religion; pp. 251-55, quoting W. L. Williams (entry 2002) on Ringatu religion.

1994 Williams, Henry (archdeacon of Waimate). *The early journals of Henry Williams.* . . . Edited by L. M. Rogers. Christchurch: Pegasus Press, 1961, 524 pp., illus., map.

Pp. 354, 377-78, 387-88, 396, 400, 402-3, passing references to those who spoke for or followed Papahurihia; pp. 461, 463-65, encounter with Wiremu Neira and his "troops."

1995 Williams, Henry. "Tares sown among the wheat." *Missionary Register* (London), September 1835, p. 428.

On Nakahi or Papahurihia, making "Maoris twofold more the children of Satan." By a C.M.S. missionary.

1996 Williams, Herbert W[illiam]. "The reaction of the Maori to the impact of civilization." *Journal of the Polynesian Society* 44 (1935): 216-43.

Brief outline of new religious movements on p. 241–rather incidental. Paper read before Wellington Philosophical Society, 22 May 1935.

1997 Williams, John A[drian]. *Politics of the New Zealand Maori: Protest and co-operation, 1891-1909*. N.p.: Oxford University Press for the University of Auckland, 1969, 204 pp., illus.

Pp. 29-30, 37-40, 63, 143, Parihaka and Te Whiti; pp. 40-47, King movement; p. 131, woman *tohunga*; pp. 132-34, Rua; pp. 160-62, Ratana.

1998 [Williams, Thomas Coldham.] *The Manawatu purchase completed, or the Treaty of Waitangi broken*. London and Edinburgh: Williams & Norgate; Wellington: New Zealand Times Office, 1867, 72 pp.

P. 22, brief reference to Hauhauism; pp. 70-72, English translation of letter from Wiremu Tamihana describing his peacemaking and his large church.

1999 Williams, W[ilfred] G[aster], ed. *The child grew: The story of the Anglican Maori mission*. 2d ed. Wellington: A. H. & A. W. Reed, 1949, 76 pp., illus.

P. 48, Te Ua, Hauhau, Te Whiti, Ringatu–very simple incidental accounts. No mention of Ratana.

2000 Williams, William. *Christianity among the New Zealanders*. London: Seeley, Jackson & Halliday, 1867, 384 pp., illus.

Pp. 128, 336-74, Te Ua and Hauhau; by an Anglican Bishop of Waiapu.

2001 Williams, W[illiam] J[ames]. *Centenary sketches of New Zealand Methodism*. Christchurch: Lyttelton Times Co., 1922, xv + 327 pp., illus.

Pp. 143-45, Hauhauism–the deaths of Volkner and John Whiteley, from a missionary viewpoint.

2002 Williams, W[illiam] L[eonard]. *East Coast (N.Z.) historical records*. Gisborne: Poverty Bay Herald Office [posthumously published], 1932, 92 pp.

An Anglican bishop's contemporary account of the political and religious upheavals during the Maori wars.

New Zealand

2003 Williams, William Temple, ed. *Pioneering in New Zealand: Life of Venerable Archdeacon Samuel Williams.* Published for private circulation only, 1929, 215 pp., illus.
Pp. 150-55, Samuel Williams's encounters with Hau Hau prophets; pp. 158-65, his contributions to military defeat of Hau Haus in the Napier area in 1866.

2004 Wilson, Beatrice Alice. "The Hauhaus and Te Kooti: An episode in the history of New Zealand." M.A. thesis, University of New Zealand (Auckland), 1921, [86 pp.].

2005 Wilson, Bryan R[onald]. *Magic and the millennium: A sociological study of religious movements of protest among tribal and third-world peoples.* London: Heinemann Educational Books; New York: Harper & Row, 1973, 547 pp. Reprint. Frogmore, St. Albans: Granada Publishing, Paladin Books, 1975, 547 pp.
Pp. 247-52, (and index), Te Ua and Hau Hau; pp. 397-401 (and index), Ringatu; pp. 402-3, Ratana; pp. 246-48, King Movement.

2006 Wilson, [George Hamish] Ormond. "The Maori supreme god Io." *Whakatane Historical Review*, no. 17 (1969), pp. 135-36.
Discusses C. Kingsley-Smith's views, and see latter's reply, *idem* no. 17, 1969, pp. 80-83.

2007 Wilson, [George Hamish] Ormond. "Papahurihia, first Maori prophet." *Journal of the Polynesian Society* 74, no. 4 (1965): 473-83.
Based on primary sources.

2008 Wilson, John Alexander. *Missionary life and work in New Zealand, 1833-1862: Being the private journal of the late Rev. John Alexander Wilson.* Edited by C. J. Wilson. Auckland: (Star Office, Printer), for private circulation, 1889, 114 pp., illus.
Reports on Hauhau from first-hand contact. Pp. 96-99, Tamihana at his Christian village, Peria, in 1861; description of village and school.

2009 Wilson, John Alexander. *The story of Te Waharoa in three parts: A chapter in early New Zealand history.* Auckland: Daily Southern Cross Office, 1866, 63 pp.
P. 43, "a series of religions adapted to the generation professing it"; Te Waharoa was W. Tamihana's father: p. 62, Tamihana as successor chief and a Christian.

2010 Winiata, Maharaia. *The changing role of the leader in Maori society: A study in social change and race relations.* Auckland: Blackwood & Janet Paul, 1967, 192 pp., photo of author, map, illus.

Pp. 61-66, 82-86, 100, King movement; pp. 67-71, Hau Hau; pp. 71-76, 119, 123-45, 140-41, 153, Ringatu; pp. 95-101, 112, 122-25, 140-41, 157-60, Ratana; pp. 96, 98, Nakahi cult; pp. 119-22, Mormon church.

2011 Winiata, Maharaia. "The charismatic leaders." In *Traditional Maori leadership and race relations.* Adult Education Discussion Course. Lecture no. 6. Auckland: Adult Education Department, University of Auckland, [1960?], 10 pp.

Hauhau and Ringatu of Te Kooti.

2012 Winks, Robin W. "The doctrine of Hau-Hauism." *Journal of the Polynesian Society* 62, no. 3 (1953): 199-236.

2013 Worger, William H[ewlett]. "Te Puea, the Kingitanga and Waikato." M.A. thesis (history), University of Auckland, 1975, 208 pp., illus., maps.

Pp. 44, 57-59, support for Princess Te Puea from Rua's people; p. 77, effect of 1918 epidemic; pp. 104-6, Te Puea's religious attitude as a Pai Marire member; p. 130, Ratana; pp. 171-78, political rivalry between King and Ratana movements.

2014 Wright, Harrison M. *New Zealand, 1769-1840: Early years of the Western contact.* Harvard Historical Monographs, 42. Cambridge, Mass.: Harvard University Press, 1959, 229 pp.

Chap. 9 (pp. 166-83), The Christian Maori. Pp. 177-78, Papahurihia. Very useful as background for all Maori movements.

2015 Yate, William. *An account of New Zealand and the formation and progress of the Church Missionary Society's mission in the northern island.* London: R. B. Seeley & W. Burnside, 1835, 320 pp. Reprint. Shannon: Irish University Press, 1970, xxi + 320 + viii pp.

Pp. 220-22, Papahurihia's cult.

2016 Yate, William. "Artifices of the enemies of missions." *Missionary Register* (London), 1835, p. 309.

A C.M.S. missionary reporting on Papahurihia and his Sabbatarianism.

Samoa (including American Samoa)

The Samoan Archipelago has become divided between American Samoa (a dependency of the U.S. since 1900) and independent Samoa. The latter was controlled by Germany (1899-1914), and then administered by New Zealand until independence in 1962. The whole archipelago is treated as one for our purposes. The movements range from the Siovili cult of the 1830s, reflecting the early influence of Christian missions, to the more recent secessions that form small independent churches.

2017 Ablon, Joan. "The social organization of an urban Samoan community." *Southwestern Journal of Anthropology* 27, no. 1 (1971): 75-96, bib.
On secessions among immigrants to the Pacific coast of the U.S.

2018 Buzacott, Aaron, and Sunderland, J. P. *Mission life in the islands of the Pacific: Being a narrative of the life and labours of Rev. A. Buzacott, missionary of Raratonga, for some time co-worker with the Rev. John Williams.* . . . London: J. Snow, 1866, xxii + 288 pp.
Pp. 126-27, "sailor religions," and Siovili or Joe Gimlet.

2019 Cain, Horst. "Die Konsequenz der Mission für die Erforschung der autochthonen Religion im heutigen Samoa." *Baessler Archiv*, n.s. 24, no. 2 (1976) [appeared 1977]: 301-51, bib.
Pp. 306-7, Siovili.

2020 Churchward, William B[rown]. *My consulate in Samoa: A record of four years' sojourn in the Navigators Islands.* . . . London: Richard Bently & Son, 1887, 403.
Pp. 204-5, "an idolatrous sect called 'Feather-Worshippers'" in the Line Islands – feathers on sticks in imitation of Catholic paraphernalia.

2021 Crawford, Ronald James. "The Lotu and the Fa'asamoa: Church and society in Samoa, 1830-1880." Ph.D. thesis (history), University of Otago, 1977, xiii + 454 pp.
Siovili passim; pp. 284-89, Tutuila revival of 1839.

2022 Daws, Alan Gavan. "The great Samoan awakening of 1839." *Journal of the Polynesian Society* 70, no. 3 (1961): 326-27.

2023 Dumont d'Urville, Jules Sebastian César. *Voyage au pole sud . . . 1837 . . . 1840.* 4 vols. Paris: Gide, 1842-53.
Vol. 4, pp. 106-7, Siovili (not named) and his new religion.

2024 Freeman, J[ohn] D[erek]. "The Joe Gimlet or Siovili cult: An episode in the religious history of early Samoa." In *Anthropology in the South Seas*. Essays presented to H. D. Skinner, edited by J. D. Freeman and W. R. Geddes. New Plymouth: Thomas Avery & Sons, 1959, 185-200.
  Siovili as a spirit medium in a syncretistic and millennial cult.

2025 Gilson, R[ichard] P[hilip]. *Samoa 1830-1900: The politics of a multicultural community.* Melbourne: Oxford University Press, 1970, 457 pp., maps.
  Pp. 72-87, cults, and see index for Siovili, Mamaia, and sailor sects; pp. 109-14, Tutuila revival.

2026 Guariglia, Guglielmo. *Prophetismus und Heilserwartungs-bewegungen als völkerkundliches und religionsgeschichtliches Problem.* Vienna: F. Berger, 1959, 332 pp.
  Pp. 75-76, Siovivi (for Siovili).

2027 Holmes, Lowell D. "Cults, cargo and Christianity: Samoan responses to Western religion." *Missiology* 8, no. 4 (October 1980): 471-88.
  Pp. 477-78, sailor cults; pp. 478-80, Joe Gimlet and Siovili cult; pp. 480-81, cargo cults; pp. 482-84, the "Great Awakening."

2028 Inglis, D. J. "Reasons for the acceptance of Christianity in Western Samoa in 1830." In *Dialogue on religion: New Zealand viewpoints 1977*, edited by P. Davis and J. Hinchcliff. Auckland: N.p., [1978?], pp. 10-14.
  P. 11, sailor sects; pp. 11-13, Siovili.

2029 Inglis, D. J. "The Siovili cult." In *Religious studies in the Pacific,* edited by J. Hinchcliff, et al. Auckland: Colloquium Publishers, Auckland University, 1978, pp. 37-44.

2030 Kotchek, Lydia. "Ethnic visibility and adaptive strategies: Samoans in the Seattle area." *Journal of Ethnic Studies* (Bellingham, Wash.) 4, no. 4 (1974): 29-38.
  Pp. 33-34, Four Samoan churches in Seattle.

2031 Monfat, Antoine. *Les premiers missionaires des Samoa.* Lyon and Paris: Librairie Catholique Emmanuel Vitte, 1923, 335 pp., illus.
  Pp. 146-47, Joe Gimlet or Siovili, obtaining his name from Dumont D'Urville, and ultimately joining the Methodist Church.

Samoa

2032 Ta'ase, Elia Tulifau. "Beyond Samoan Christianity: A study of the Siovili cult and the problems facing the Church in Samoa today." B.D. thesis, Pacific Theological College, Suva, 1971, xi + 150 pp., bibl.

Uses unpublished papers by W. N. Gunson (1971) and P. F. Sunia (1968).

2033 Tiffany, Sharon W. "The land and titles court and the regulation of customary title successions and removals in Western Samoa." *Journal of the Polynesian Society* 83, no. 1 (1974): 35-57.

Pp. 48-49, and n36, an independent church founded in American Samoa and with some 1,400 members on Tutuila and Upolo islands, and a small continuation in 1970.

2034 Tiffany, Sharon W. "The politics of denominational organization in Samoa." In *Mission, church, and sect in Oceania*, edited by J. A. Boutilier, et al. Association for Social Anthropology in Oceania, Monograph Series no. 6. Ann Arbor: University of Michigan Press, 1978, 423-56.

Pp. 427-28, Siovili; pp. 449-51, a secession from the L.M.S. congregtion and subsequent litigation.

2035 Tully, James. "The day of the spirit healer." *Pacific Islands Monthly* 51, no. 2 (1980): 14f.

Digest of a report in *New Zealand Medical Journal* by Dr. Michael Short and Dr. Patricia Kinloch, on the successful treatment of a young Samoan boy in Hutt Hospital, New Zealand, by a Samoan spirit healer.

2036 Watters, R. F. "The transition to Christianity in Samoa." *Historical Studies: Australia and New Zealand*, no. 32 [8] (May 1959): 392-99.

Society and Tuamotu Islands (French Polynesia)

These islands, together with the Marquesas Islands, form French Polynesia, having been acquired by France from 1842 on. The Mamaia movement of the 1830s in Tahiti has been extensively studied; other movements have taken the form of secessions, with varying degrees of orthodoxy, from the mission-connected churches, including the Mormons, who had missions in the Pacific very early in their own history. Tiurai was a notable prophet-healer who died in the 1981 epidemic.

2037 Buck, Peter H[enry]. *Vikings of the Pacific*. (Originally as *Vikings of the Sunrise*, 1938). Chicago: University of Chicago Press, 1959, pp. 88-90.

Pp. 88-90, the Arioi Society of the Oro cult – a new development within primal religion on Raiatea and thence outwards to Tahiti, etc.

2038 Caillot, Augustus Charles Eugène. *Histoire des religions de l'Archipel Paumotu*. Paris: E. Leroux, 1932, 144 pp., illus.

Pp. 133ff., Tupa's religion; pp. 143-44, the Hio Hio (Whistlers).

2039 Caillot, Augustus Charles Eugène. *Les Polynésiens orientaux au contact de la civilisation*. Paris: Ernest Leroux, 1909, 291 pp. + 92 plates.

Pp. 33-34, 38-40, Kanito (a secession from the Mormons); p. 38, passing reference to Moutons (Mamoe) cult in Tuamotu, and to the Whistlers, and the Israelites.

2040 Danielsson, Bengt E[llerik]. *Work and life on Raroia: An acculturation study from the Tuamotu group, French Oceania*. Uppsala: Almqvist & Wiksells, 1953; London: George Allen & Unwin, 1956, 244 pp., illus., maps.

Pp. 86-88, early Mormon missions; pp. 100-101, Kanito cult, and the Israelites.

2041 Davies, John. *The history of the Tahitian mission: 1799-1830*. Edited by Colin W. Newbury. New York: Cambridge University Press for Hakluyt Society, 1961, 392 pp.

Pp. 254-56, 328-31, Mamaia; p. xxxvi, Arioi Society.

2042 Driessen, H. A. H. "Outriggerless canoes and glorious beings: Pre-contact prophecies in the Society Islands." *Journal of Pacific History* 17, no. 1 (1982): 3-28.

2043 Ellis, William. *Polynesian researches during a residence of nearly eight years in the Society and Sandwich Islands*. 2 vols. London, 1829. 2d ed. London: Fisher Son & Jackson, 1831. London: H. G. Bohn, 4 vols., 1853. New York: J. & J. Harper, 1833. Reprint of 1st ed. London: Dawsons of Pall Mall, 1961.

Vol. 2, pp. 130-32, missionary account of the Arioi Society in traditional religion adopting Christianity in Tahiti in the 1820s.

2044 Guariglia, Guglielmo. *Prophetismus und Heilserwartungs-bewegungen als völkerkundliches und religionsgeschichtliches Problem*. Vienna: F. Berger, 1959, 332 pp..

Pp. 73-74, Mamaia in Tahiti; p. 125, Ivi-Atua on Easter Island.

Society and Tuamotu Islands

2045 Gunson, W[alter] N[eil]. "An account of the *Mamaia* or visionary heresy of Tahiti, 1826-1841." In Pacific Science Association, *Abstracts of Symposium Papers, Tenth Pacific Science Congress*. Honolulu: Pacific Science Association, 1961, pp. 72-73.

A good summary of the "first nativist movement of the millenarian or cargo-cult type to appear [in] the Pacific."

2046 Gunson, W[alter] N[eil]. "An account of the Mamaia or visionary heresy of Tahiti, 1826-1841." *Journal of the Polynesian Society* 71, no. 2, (1962): 209-44.

Treated as millennial and healing movement. See also R. G. White (entry 2061) for glossary and texts.

2047 Gunson, W[alter] N[eil]. *Messengers of grace: Evangelical missionaries in the South Seas 1797-1860*. Melbourne: Oxford University Press, 1978, 437 pp., illus., maps.

Mamaia, passim, but more fully treated in his 1962 article (entry 2046).

2048 Henry, Teuira. *Ancient Tahiti, based on material recorded by J. M. Orsmond*. Bernice P. Bishop Museum Bulletin 48. Honolulu: B. P. Bishop Museum, 1928, 651 pp., illus.

Pp. 230-41, Arioi Society as a performing society of scholars and actors many of whom later became Christians.

2049 Jaspers, Reiner. *Die Missionarische Erschliessung Ozeaniens ... in Ozeanien bis 1855*. Mission Studies and Documents, 30. Munster Westfallen: Aschendorffsche Verlagsbuchhandlung, 1972, 288 pp., maps.

P. 126, Mamaia.

2050 Kent, Graeme. *Company of Heaven*. Nashville, N.Y.: Thomas Nelson, 1972, 230 pp., illus.

P. 86, Teau, an L.M.S. deacon, led a secession in 1839 on Tahiti, as "Jesus Christ"; p. 87, Queen Pomare IV joined Mamaia in 1830.

2051 Levy, Robert I[saac]. "Personal forms and meanings in Tahitian Protestantism." *Journal de la Société des Océanistes*, no. 25 [15] (December 1969): 125-26.

Village Christianity on the island of Huahine; p. 126, Kanito (as the Reorganized Church of Jesus Christ of Latter Day Saints), with 24 members; p. 126, brief report of a schism in the early 1960s, largely healed by 1964, as example of what is probably a not uncommon event.

2052 Levy, Robert I[saac]. *Tahitians: Mind and experience in the Society Islands*. Chicago: University of Chicago Press, 1973. Reprint. London: 1975, 547 pp., illus., maps.

Pp. 16, 19, 50, 53-54, 505, Teiva's church by secession from the village Protestant church.

2053 Lovett, Richard. *The history of the London Missionary Society: 1795-1895*. Vol. 1. London: Oxford University Press, 1899, 832 pp.

Pp. 297-98 on Mamaia, as an "outbreak of fanaticism," based on Darling's letter of 25 December 1827.

2054 "Missions." *South Asian Register*, no. 4 (December 1828), pp. 334-58.

Mamaia in Tahiti as persecuted by the "higher powers" – based on information from sea captains Kent and Henry.

2055 Moerenhout, Jacques-Antoine. *Voyages aux îles du Grand Océan*. 2 vols. Paris: A. Bertrans, 1837. 2d ed. Paris: A. Maisonneuve, 1942, 1:574 pp.; 2:520 pp.; map. Reprint. 1959, 1120 pp.

Vol. 1, pp. 479-84, inspired prophets; pp. 485-503, Arioi Society and Oro cult, origin, organization, practices, and aims. Vol. 2, pp. 219-316, Arioi festivals; pp. 501-5, Teau as founder of Mamaia in Tahiti.

2056 Mühlmann, W[ilhelm] E[mil]. *Arioi und Mamaia: Eine ethnologische, religionseziologische und historische studie über Polynesische Kultbunde*. Weisbaden: F. Steiner Verlag, 1955, 169 pp.

Pp. 25-26, 223-44, 246, the Mamaia in Tahiti, 1828, as successor to Arioi sect; banned in 1833.

2057 Mühlmann, W[ilhelm] E[mil]. "Les mouvements polynésiens." In *Messianismes révolutionnaires du tiers monde*, edited by W. E. Mühlmann. Paris: Éditions Gallimard, 1968, pp. 147-51.

2058 Stevenson, Robert Louis. *In the South Seas: A footnote to history*. Works, vol. 16. New York: Scribners, 1892, 591 pp. Reprint. London: Chatto & Windus, 1900, 343 pp. London: W. Heinemann, et al., 1922. Numerous other printings.

Vol. 16, pp. 234-38, the Tuamotu Whistlers about 1890; pp. 231f., the Israelites and Kanito.

2059 "Tiurai's mana: Tahitian who worked miracles." *Pacific Islands Monthly* (Sydney) 8, no. 4 (1937): 41-42.

On Tiurai (ca. 1855-1918) a Catholic prophet-healer at Punaauia in Tahiti, who died from exhaustion in the 1918 "influenza" epidemic.

Society and Tuamotu Islands

2060 [Various reports on Mamaia or "visionary heresy," especially on Island of Maupiti.] *Missionary Register* (London, Church Missionary Society).
E.g.: 1829, p. 310; 1830, p. 45; 1831, p. 310; 1832, pp. 98-99; 1833, pp. 100-101.

2061 White, Ralph Gardner. "An account of the Mamaia: Glossary and texts." *Journal of the Polynesian Society* 71 (1962): 244-53.
See also W. N. Gunson (entry 2046) for main article.

Tonga (Friendly Islands)

This is the only surviving independent Polynesian kingdom. After being a British protectorate from 1900 it became an independent member of the Commonwealth in 1970. A Methodist form of Christianity is predominant, with the Free Wesleyan Church of Tonga as a notable secession encouraged by a white missionary, S. W. Baker. The Red Coat movement of the 1960s has been a more synthetist development by a prophetess. Some new forms of Tongan churches began to appear among immigrants to New Zealand in the 1970s.

2062 Arntz, D. P. "Religion and its effects on social cohesion in an emerging community." *Kroeber Anthropological Society Papers* 57, no. 8 (1978): 20-39.
On Tongans in the United States.

2063 Beaglehole, Ernest, and Beaglehole, Pearl. *Pangai, village in Tonga.* Wellington: Polynesian Society, 1941, 145 pp.
1931 census statistics: Free Wesleyan Church of Tonga, 58%; Free Church of Tonga, 16%; Church of Tonga, 10%. Nothing on Baker as such.

2064 Carter, G. G. *A family affair. Proceedings of the Wesley Historical Society of New Zealand* 28, nos. 3-4 (1973). Auckland: The Society, 1973, 245 pp. + 21 unnumbered pages.
Pp. 20-30, Shirley Baker, Jabez Watkins and the Free Wesleyan Church – in an "official" history of New Zealand Methodist overseas missions.

2065 Crosby, E. E., comp. *The persecutions in Tonga, as narrated by onlookers and now taking place, 1886.* London: William Clowes & Sons (Printers), 1886, 74 pp.

Baker's treatment of members of the original Wesleyan Church, and others, as reprinted from fourteen journals published in London, Australia, and New Zealand, by a Wesleyan missionary in Tonga.

2066 Farmer, Sarah Stock. *Tonga and the Friendly Islands, with a sketch of their mission history.* London: Hamilton Adams & Co., 1855, 427 pp., illus.
Pp. 240-51, the Tongan revival of 1834.

2067 Gunson, [Walter] Neil. "Visionary experience and social protest in Polynesia: A note on 'Ofa Mele Longosai." *Journal of Pacific History* 8 (1973): 125-32.
The "Red Coat" movement of 'Ofa Mele Longosai, a prophetess assisting the expression of social protest from the 1960s.

2068 Hodgkinson, Penny. "Strife at the top in Tonga's F.W.C." *Pacific Islands Monthly* 51, no. 5 (1980): 15, illus.
Between president and secretary of Free Wesleyan Church.

2069 Korn, Shulamit R. Deckter. "After the missionaries came: Denominational diversity in the Tonga Islands." In *Mission, church, and sect in Oceania,* by J. A. Boutilier, et al. Association for Social Anthropology in Oceania, Monograph Series no. 6. Ann Arbor: University of Michigan Press, 1978, 500 pp. Reprint. University of America Press, 1984, pp. 395-422.

2070 Latukefu, Sione. *Church and state in Tonga: The Wesleyan Methodist missionaries and political development, 1822-1875.* Honolulu: University Press of Hawaii; Canberra: Australian National University Press, 1974, 302 pp.

2071 Rutherford, Noel. *Shirley Baker and the King of Tonga.* Melbourne: Oxford University Press, 1971, 220 pp., illus.
S. W. Baker, Methodist secessionist, founder of the Free Church of Tonga (1885). Pp. 126-38, the "Tongan Reformation."

2072 Rutherford, Noel, ed. *Friendly Islands: A history of Tonga.* Melbourne: Oxford University Press, 1977, 297 pp.
Pp. 128-29, 265, the 1834 revival (by S. Latukefu); pp. 167-69, 197-99, Methodist secession and reunion (by A. H. Wood and E. W. Ellem).

Tonga

2073 Shumway, Eric B. "Tonga." In *Historical dictionary of Oceania*, edited by R. D. Craig and F. P. King. Westport, Conn., and London: Greenwood Press, 1981, pp. 291-92.

2074 Thomson, Basil Home. *The diversions of a prime minister.* (A sketch of the history of Tonga.) London: Wm. Blackwood & Sons, 1894, 407 pp.
    Baker, ex-Wesleyan missionary, Prime Minister of Tonga and in Free Church of Tonga, passim, but especially pp. 4-7.

2075 Waterhouse, Jabez B. *The secession and persecution in Tonga.* Sydney: Wesleyan Book Depot, 1886, 101 pp.
    The origins of the Free Church of Tonga under Baker, the treatment of the continuing Wesleyan Church, and the dealings between the Australasian Wesleyan Methodist Missionary Society and the Tonga government—a condensation of articles by Waterhouse in the Sydney *Weekly Advocate* updated from unpublished sources, and the report of the deputation to Tonga from the New South Wales and Queensland Methodist Conference.

2076 Wood, A[lfred] Harold. *Overseas missions of the Australian Methodist Church.* Vol. 1, *Tonga, Samoa.* Melbourne: Aldersgate Press, 1975.
    Pp. 163-64, the Free Church secession, 1885; pp. 216-25, Queen Salote and reunion; p. 256, sailor cults, but nothing on Siovili. An official Methodist history.

Particular Movements

Christian Fellowship Church (Solomon Islands)

This is the best known and largest ongoing movement in Solomon Islands, founded in New Georgia in the late 1950s by Silas Eto, a catechist within the Methodist Mission. The Mission was regarded as having fallen away from the true teaching of John Wesley, although J. F. Goldie, its founder, continued to be held in high regard. This movement has been the subject of extensive study by Esau Tuza, himself a Solomon Islander; relations with the churches were improving in the 1980s. Other material will be found in items in the main Solomon Islands section.

2077 Carter, G[eorge] G[ilmour]. *A family affair. Proceedings of the Wesley Historical Society of New Zealand* 28, nos. 3-4 (1973). Auckland: The Society, 1973, [245 + 21 pp.]

Pp. 134-40, 153, Silas Eto's Christian Fellowship Church in relation to missionary Goldie, and his failure to have the New Testament translated into Roviana.

2078 Chesher, Richard H. "Holy Mama, Solomon's prophet ... built a paradise for his people." *Pacific Islands Monthly* 49, no. 7 (1978): 18-20, illus., and color photo on cover.

A vivid and enthusiastic account.

2079 Eto, Silas. "A native chief takes stock." *Open Door* (Auckland) 29, no. 3 (1949): 4, illus.

Christian Fellowship Church

A letter when Eto was still a mission teacher, to the New Zealand Methodist Church, with recommendations for strengthening the Church.

2080 Glass, Vickie. "20 years of Holy Mama's Church." *Pacific Islands Monthly* 51, no. 11 (1980): 25. Reprinted from a report in *Solomons News Drum*.

2081 Groves, W. C. "A model village: Menakasapa, New Georgia." *Open Door* (Auckland, N.Z., Methodist Church) 19, no. 1 (1940): 3-4, 8, illus.
A government education adviser's report on a Methodist mission village, which was later renamed Paradise by Eto.

2082 Harwood, Frances H[ine]. "The Christian Fellowship Church, a revitalization movement in Melanesia." Ph.D. dissertation (anthropology), University of Chicago, 1971.

2083 Harwood, Frances H[ine]. "Paradise found: A chronicle of fieldwork in the Solomon Islands." *Vassar Quarterly* (Fall 1970): 7-11.

2084 Methodist Church of New Zealand. *Minutes of the Annual Conference.*
1960, p. 151, noting the spread of erroneous "new way" of Silas Eto; p. 150, Christian Fellowship Church formed during the year, and drop in Methodist adherents by 1,000, mostly in Roviana circuit; 1963, p. 145, Etoism lessened, but Hahalis Welfare Society attracting Methodists and Catholics.

2085 Tippett, Alan R[ichard]. *Solomon Islands Christianity: A study in growth and obstruction.* London: Lutterworth Press, 1967, 407 pp. 2d ed. William Carey Library, [1975?].
Chap. 16, Etoism.

2086 Tuza, Esau [Taqasabo]. "Cultural suppression? Not quite!" *Catalyst* (Goroka) 7, no. 2 (1977): 106-26.
Advent of the Methodist mission and its effects; pp. 14 *et seq.*, Eto as a "son" of pioneer missionary Goldie.

2087 Tuza, Esau [Taqasabo]. "The demolition of church buildings by the ancestors." In *The Gospel is not Western: Black theologies from the southwest Pacific*, edited by G. W. Trompf. Maryknoll, N.Y.: Orbis Books, 1987, pp. 67-89, illus.
The Christian Fellowship Church–the place of its founder, his contributions in art and church buildings, relation to the ancestors and

local culture, experience of religious ecstasy in relation to Methodist "heart-warming," its more recent worship; Appendix, pp. 87-88, CFC Order of Service.

2088 Tuza, Issau [Esau] [Taqasabo]. "The emergence of the Christian Fellowship Church: A historical view of Silas Eto, founder of the Christian Fellowship Church." M.A. dissertation (history), University of Papua New Guinea, 1975 (submitted 1976), 274 pp., illus., maps.

2089 Tuza, Esau [Taqasabo]. "Overseas Churches and the Christian Fellowship Church." In *Point*. Series 4, *Religious movements in Melanesia today (3)*, edited by W. Flannery. Goroka: Melanesian Institute, 1984, pp. 209-35.

2090 Tuza, Esau [Taqasabo]. "Paternal acidity." *Pacific Islands Monthly* 50, no. 1 (1979): 8-9.
      A reply to G. G. Carter's letter, October 1978, on the Christian Fellowship Church.

2091 Tuza, Esau [Taqasabo]. "The rise of Eto: An historical perspective." B.A. (Hons.) subthesis, University of Papua New Guinea, 1974.

2092 Tuza, Esau [Taqasabo]. "Silas Eto of New Georgia." In *Prophets of Melanesia*, edited by G. W. Trompf. Port Moresby: Institute of Papua New Guinea Studies, 1977, pp. 108-46, map.
      Eto interpreted as a prophet; substantial treatment of Goldie's influence on Eto.

2093 Tuza, Esau [Taqasabo]. "Silas Eto, the 'Holy Mama' and the Christian Fellowship Church." *Melanesian Journal of Theology* 1 (1985): 71-77.

2094 Tuza, Esau [Taqasabo]. "Towards indigenization of Christian worship in the Western Solomons." B.D. thesis, Pacific Theological College (Suva), 1970, 107 pp.
      Includes the Christian Fellowship Church.

Ratana (New Zealand Maoris)

This is the largest independent Maori movement, founded by Wiremu Ratana (1873-1939), a Methodist farmer, after the 1918 world influenza epidemic. He rejected traditional Maori religion and sought return to Jehovah, and moral reform. After early cooperation with the churches, he

Ratana

formed the Ratana Church in 1925, with headquarters at Ratana Pa and some 25,000 members by the 1970s. For a period all four Maori seats in Parliament were held by Ratana members. Despite friendly dealings with individuals, especially Methodists, there has been little desire for relations with the Christian churches. The main history has been that of J. McL. Henderson; accounts by Maori writers are found in items by M. Winiata (see entries 2010 and 2011 under Polynesia: New Zealand) and by the journalist Harry Dansey; note also the material by the Ratana Church.

2095 A. V. "The Ratana Movement: Some sidelights specially written for *The Month* (Auckland) 1925-26." Reprinted from *Month* (Auckland), 15 September 1925, p. 15; 20 October 1925, p. 24; 17 November 1925, p. 12; 15 December 1925, p. 15; 19 January 1926, p. 31.
Five articles produced as a pamphlet; skeptical remarks aimed at Catholic readers.

2096 Anglican Church. Bishop' pastoral letter on the Ratana schism. *Yearbook and Report of the Proceedings of the First Session of the 23rd Synod, 1925*, 31-32. Reprinted in *Transplanted Christianity: Documents . . . of New Zealand church history*, edited by A. K. Davidson and P. J. Lineham. Auckland: College Communications, 1987, pp. 170-71.

2097 Anglican Church/Church of England, Diocese of Waiapu. *Yearbook of the Diocese of Waiapu, 1925*. Napier: The Diocese, 1926.
Pp. 29-32, the setting up of a commission to consider Maori self-expressions; and the "Ratana schism," with the Pastoral Letter describing Ratana attitude to the Churches, and excommunicating those who participate in the Ratana ordinances.

2098 Beaglehole, Ernest, and Beaglehole, Pearl. *Some Modern Maoris*. Educational Research Series, 25. Wellington: New Zealand Council for Educational Research, 1946, 350 pp.
In Kowhai township. Pp. 206-9, Ratana, including case studies and relations with other churches.

2099 Bennett, Enid, and Donovan, Peter, eds. *Beliefs and practices in New Zealand: A directory*. 2d ed. Massey University, Religious Studies Department, 1980, pp. 21-122.

2100 Bolitho, Hector Henry [Rongoa Pai, pseud.]. *Ratana: The Maori miracle man. The story of his life; the record of his miracles!* Auckland: Geddis & Blomfield, [1921] 46 pp.

2101 Bush, Dick. "Ratana Pa: Move for unity among Maoris." *Waikato Times*, January 1967.

2102 Butterworth, Graham. "The Ratana movement." *New Zealand Heritage* 79 [6] (1973): 2185-89, illus.

2103 Carmichael, (Lieut.-Col.). *Ratana the healer. A visit to his Pah. Personal experiences of Lieut.-Col. Carmichael.* Greymouth: Greymouth Evening Star, 1921, 12 pp. Reprinted from *Evening Star*, 15 April 1921.
Reported from a lecture by a Salvation Army officer.

2104 Caton, Eric. "A report on the Maori population of Dunedin." Practical exercise by a Theological Hall student for Presbyterian Maori Synod, Dunedin, April 1968, 85 pp. Typescript.
Pp. 54-56, Ratana adherents, et passim. Copy at Knox College, Dunedin.

2105 Dale, William Sydney James. "The influence of Christianity on the Maoris of New Zealand: . . . The impact of Western religion on a non-Western people." M.A. thesis, Yale University, 1934.
Pp. 230-32, the Ratana movement – "a rather naive account."

2106 Dansey, Harry [Delamere Barter]. "As times change . . . will the Ratana Church?" *Auckland Star*, 18 May 1963, p. 7.
By a Maori journalist.

2107 Dansey, Harry [Delamere Barter]. "A Maori town of faith, finance . . . and future." *Auckland Star*, 17 May 1966, [4 pp.], illus.
A well-illustrated current report on the Ratana movement.

2108 Dansey, Harry [Delamere Barter]. "Services of the Ratana Church: Band music plays important part." *Auckland Star*, 20 April 1963.

2109 "Fiftieth anniversary of the Ratana Church." *Te Ao Hou* (Wellington), no. 65 (December 1968-February 1969), pp. 35-36, illus.

2110 Fink, C. "Ein Unabhängigkeitsbewegung der Maoris." *Koloniale Rundschau* 17 (1925): 177-79.
On the Ratana movement.

2111 Gnanasunderam, A. *The birthday celebrations at the Ratana Pa, 1972.* Christchurch: National Council of Churches, 1972, 5 pp.

Ratana

> Report of the official visit by the Secretary of the Church and
> Society Commission of the Council.

2112 Hames, Eric W. "Coming of age: The united church 1913-1972."
      Proceedings of the Wesley Historical Society of New Zealand 28, nos. 1-2
      (1974): 164.
      P. 59, the Ratana movement – a half-page outline of its causes
      and of A. J. Seamer's attitude.

2113 Henderson, J[ames] McLeod. "The Ratana movement." In *The Maori
      and New Zealand politics*, edited by J. G. A. Pocock. Auckland:
      Blackwood & Janet Paul, 1965, pp. 61-71.
      Includes the succession of prophets.

2114 Henderson, James McLeod. *Ratana: The origins and story of the
      movement*. Polynesian Society Memoir 36. Wellington, N.Z.:
      Polynesian Society, 1963, 128 pp., map, illus. 2d enl. and rev. ed.
      Ratana: The man, the church, the political movement. Wellington: A. H.
      & A. W. Reed; Polynesian Society, 1972, 128 pp., illus., map.
      The main historical account.

2115 Jackson, Patrick M[ontague], ed. *Maori and education*. ...
      Monographs of the New Zealand Teachers' Summer School, 1.
      Wellington: Ferguson & Osborn, 1931, xxxi + 481 pp., illus., map.
      Pp. 119-23, Hauhaus, Maoris, and Christianity (by J. C.
      Andersen); pp. 228, 293, criticisms of Ratana (by A. B. Fitt and E. P.
      Ellison) regarding healing, and members selling or mortgaging farms
      to go to live at Ratana village.

2116 King, Michael. "Between two worlds." In *Oxford History of New
      Zealand*, edited by W. H. Oliver. Oxford: Clarendon Press, 1981, pp.
      277-301.
      Pp. 292-95, 300, Ratana, especially on the relation to politics, the
      Labour Party and Maori transtribal identity.

2117 King, Michael. "Labour and Ratana: A marriage on the rocks." *New
      Zealander Listener* (Wellington), no. 2088 [94] (January 1980): 12-15,
      illus.

2118 King, Michael. *Whina: A biography of Whina Cooper*. Auckland:
      Hodder & Stoughton, 1983, 285 pp., illus.

Pp. 90-91, beginnings of Ratana movement, especially among ex-servicemen; its spread to Northland but not among the well-pastored Catholic Church members as at Whakarapa.

2119 Lammas, Fanny. *How I was healed, or a New Zealand miracle: An autobiographical sketch of Miss Fannie Lammas, Nelson ... by Rev. Joseph W. Kemp.* Auckland: Tabernacle Book Room, 1923, 51 pp., illus. 3d ed. 1924.

Especially pp. 28-45, healed through a letter from Ratana; her supporting frames now in the Ratana museum.

2120 Langerwerf, Adrian Cornelius. *Ko te waka o Hato Petera* [The ship of Peter]. Newmarket: M. Smethurst (Printer), [ca. 1940], 30 pp. [text on pp. 5-30].

In Maori: booklet by a Catholic priest written against the spread of Ratana in Tokaanu-Taupo area.

2121 Manchester, Anne. "Old links reaffirmed: Prayer cured his son." *Crosslinks* (Wellington, Presbyterian and Methodist Churches) 3, no. 2 (1989): 12, illus.

Report of Methodist Church president attending annual Ratana celebrations in January 1989; outline of Ratana history and of its relations with the Anglican, Presbyterian, and especially Methodist churches.

2122 "Maori visionary and healer who founded a church." *Auckland Star,* 28 January 1967.

Outline of Ratana movement; report of election of Mrs. Te Reo Hura as new president.

2123 Metge, [Alice] Joan. *A new Maori migration: Rural and urban relations in northern New Zealand.* L.S.E. Monographs on Social Anthropology, 27. London: Athlone Press, 1964, 299 pp., illus.

Pp. 80, 117, 207, Ratana church in Auckland.

2124 Methodist Church of New Zealand. *Minutes of the Annual Conference.* Maori mission reports:

10th Conference 1922, pp. 136, 138, perils and opportunities of Ratana movement; 13th Conference 1925, pp. 115, 116-17, Ratana, and attempt at a new "Maori Church"; 1926, pp. 114-15, extended reference to Ratana, reprinted in *Transplanted Christianity: Documents ... of New Zealand church history,* edited by A. K. Davidson and P. J. Lineham (Auckland: College Communications, 1987), pp. 171-72; 1927,

Ratana

p. 130, "independent church" with some 500 members; 1929, p. 123, affirming previous tolerant attitudes; 1933, p. 131, decrease in opposition to older churches, new cults from America (Theosophy, Spiritism); 1966, p. 172, obituary for Mrs. Puhi-o-Aotea Ratahi, praising her presidency of Ratana and noting a "spiritual resurgence" in Ratana Church.

2125 Methodist Church of New Zealand. [Notes on the Ratana movement.] (a) *Home Mission Reports 1920-1930,* as follows: Home Mission Review, 1920, p. 25, and 1921, p. 31, favorable statements on Ratana Home Mission Report 1925, p. 5, declaration of policy in relation to the new Ratana Church, avoiding opposition; (b) *Minutes of the Home Mission Board 1916-1935,* as follows: 25 August 1921, p. 179, endorsing A. J. Seamer's policy; 15 April 1925, p. 8, endorsing Seamer's plan for appointment by Methodist Board of Agents from among Ratana followers to maintain a full Christian witness in the movement, which should not be opposed on account of its doctrine of angels.

2126 [Methodist Church of New Zealand.] "The Reverend A. J. Seamer and the attitude of the Methodists to the Ratana Movement." N.d., 5 pp. Typescript.
    A detailed account of the Methodist Home and Maori Missions Superintendent's attempts to understand and maintain positive relationships with the movement.

2127 Mirams, Alison. "Murihiku 1970: A survey of the social situation of the Maori population of Otago and Southland." University of Otago (Department of Anthropology) for Presbytery of Dunedin, 1970, 51 pp. Mimeo.
    Pp. 16-17, Ratana members in Invercargill.

2128 Palmer, John Bruce. "Ratana." In *Encyclopaedia of New Zealand.* Vol. 3. Wellington: Government Printer, 1966, pp. 51a-b.

2129 Park, Ruth. "Maori miracle man." *Cavalcade* (Sydney?) March 1946, 12-15.
    A sympathetic, but in parts factually inaccurate account of Ratana's career, especially the healings.

2130 Paternoster, Ira. "Editorial reports and comment." *New Zealand Christian* (Wellington, Churches of Christ), July 1921, p. 6; November 1922, pp. 4-5.

On Ratana's cure of Miss Winter of Nelson; long extracts in J. E. Worsfold (entry 2152), pp. 102-3.

2131 Presbyterian Church of New Zealand. *Proceedings of the General Assembly*. Wellington: The Church, 1921-28.
Reports on Ratana: 1921, pp. 121-22 (Rev. J. E. Ward); 1923, p. 106 (Sister Edith at Whakaki); 1924, p. 133 (Sister Edith); 1925, p. 79 (Sister Jessie at Taupo), p. 92 (Sister Edith); 1926, p. 69 (Sister Jessie), p. 82 (Sister Edith; 1927, pp. 74-75 (Rev. J. G. Laughton), p. 75 (Sister Kearney); 1928, p. 92 (Sister Edith).

2132 Ratana Church. "Constitution of the Ratana Movement; Preamble and Section One: The Spiritual Works: 1 Name. 2 The creed of the Ratana Church." Ratana Pa: Ratana Church, [1970?] 2 pp. Mimeo. [Bound with "Let us learn. . . ." (entry 2135).]
First part of a planned work of lessons in English on Ratana; the Creed is the same as that deposited in 1925 with the Government Registrar General.

2133 Ratana Church. "Creed." Deposited with the New Zealand Registrar General, 21 July 1925. In *Ratana: The man, the church, the political movement*, by J. M. Henderson. Wellington, 1972, pp. 118-19. Reprinted in *Transplanted Christianity: Documents . . . of New Zealand church history*, edited by A. K. Davidson and P. J. Lineham. Auckland: College Communications, 1987, pp. 168-70.

2134 Ratana Church. *Ka Nga Whakahaere Whakamoemiti e te Hahi Ratana*. . . . Printed at Wanganui by A. D. Willis, n.d., 80 pp.
The Order of Worship of the Ratana Church. . . . Eight orders of service for various occasions, together with 71 hymns and 3 canticles. English translation by Canon John Tamahori held at the Centre, Selly Oak Colleges.

2135 Ratana Church. "Let us learn something about our Maramatanga and its founder Tohupotiki Wiremu Ratana. Lesson One, Part Two." Ratana Pa: The Church, n.d., 10 pp. Typescript. [Bound with "Constitution" (entry 2132).]

2136 Ratana Church. *Te Whetu Marama* (Ratana Pa) 1-, 15 March 1924-.
Literally "star-moon" (i.e., "The Shining Light"), the magazine of the Ratana Church and official record, especially for Ratana's work and speeches. Began as a 5-page weekly, became 10 pages, later fortnightly, then monthly; in Maori.

Ratana

2137 "Ratana pilgrimage to Te Rere a Kapuni." *Te Ao Hou* (Wellington), no. 51 (June 1965), pp. 34-35, illus.

2138 "Ratana retires. No benefits for Pakehas." *New Zealand Times* (Wellington), 8 December 1921.

2139 "Ratana, the Maori faith-healer." *Pix*, 26 August 1939, 6 pp., illus.
    Brief text and very good illustrations, especially of personalities, and aerial photo of Ratana Pa as model farming community.

2140 "Ratana–tiny town born of faith." *New Zealand Weekly News* (Auckland), no. 5589 (18 January 1971), pp. 3-5, illus.
    Good illustrations in a feature article.

2141 Raureti, Moana. "The origins of the Ratana movement." In *Tihe Mauri Ora*, edited by M. King. London: Methuen, 1978, pp. 42-59.
    Includes the political influence and "political biographies" of eleven Ratana members of Parliament.

2142 Raureti, Moana. "The Ratana movement." Diploma thesis, Victoria University of Wellington, Social Science School, 1954, 58 pp., illus. Typescript.
    A housing survey for the Department of Maori Affairs. Estimates Ratanas steady membership at about 25,000 throughout its history, more than some census figures show.

2143 Rosevear, Watson. *Waiapu – The story of a diocese*. Hamilton and Auckland: Paul's Book Arcade, 1960, 280 pp.
    Pp. 124, 196, 201, Ratana's relations with the Church of England; extracts reprinted by "Anglo-Catholic" as "The Ratana Church" in *Auckland Star*, 21 May 1963.

2144 Scholefield, Guy H[ardy]. "Ratana, Tahupotiki Wiremu." *A Dictionary of New Zealand Biography*. Vol. 2. Wellington: Department of Internal Affairs, 1940, 571 pp.
    P. 197, brief biography of Ratana.

2145 Sorrenson, M[ichael] P[eter] K[eith]. *Nga to hoa aroha. From your dear friend: The correspondence between Sir Apirana Ngata and Sir Peter Buck, 1925-1950*. 3 vols. Auckland: Hodder & Stoughton, 1987, pp. 269, 284, 296, illus.
    Ngata's hostility to Ratanaism as "bizarre" and antidevelopment, and later allied to the Labour party (see index in vol. 3).

2146 Taylor, David M. "Proposal for study of Maori religions." Christchurch: The author, as Secretary of National Council of Churches in New Zealand, 1972, 2 pp. Mimeo.
On establishing dialogue with the Ratana Church.

2147 Taylor, David M. "The Ratana Established Church." Christchurch: National Council of Churches in New Zealand, 1974, 4 pp. Mimeo.
Report of the General Secretary's visit to the 1974 annual *hui* at Ratana Pa.

2148 Taylor, David M. "Report on visit to Ratana." Christchurch: National Council of Churches in New Zealand. 1970, 2 pp.
The General Secretary's visit to Ratana Pa, 29 January 1970.

2149 [Turner, Harold Walter.] "Ratana"; "Ratana Church." In *Encyclopaedia Britannica*. Micropaedia. Vol. 8, 1974, p. 428b.
Unsigned survey articles.

2150 "T. W. Ratana and the Ratana Church." *Te Ao Hou* (Wellington), no. 42 (March 1963), pp. 32-37, illus. (by Ans Westra).

2151 Williams, Herbert W[illiam]. *The ministry of healing and Ratana and his work.* Gisborne: Gisborne "Herald," 1921, 16 pp.
Pp. 9-16, a very sympathetic sermon in Christchurch (Anglican) Cathedral, 13 November 1921, on Ratana and his healing methods, the treating of whites at a distance, and uneasiness about his non-Christian associates.

2152 Worsfold, J[ames] E. *A history of the charismatic movements in New Zealand.* Bradford: Puritan Press for Julian Literature Trust, 1974, 368 pp.
Pp. 98-103, "Apostle Ratana" and the healing ministry, also pp. 119, 172; includes long extracts from F. Lammas (entry 2119), I. Paternoster (entry 2130), and Anglican Church, Diocese of Waiapu (entry 2097).

Ringatu (New Zealand Maoris)

Ringatu ("the upraised hand") is the oldest continuing and the second-largest Maori religious movement, founded in 1867 by Te Kooti Rikirangi (1830-93) among Maori prisoners in the Chatham Islands. It draws heavily upon the Maori translation of the Bible, especially the Old Testament, and its worship

Ringatu

is focused on the memorized recital of biblical passages, of accounts of Te Kooti's career, and on Ringatu as "suffering Israel." In the 1970s there were some 5,600 census members, largely in the East Coast and Bay of Plenty areas of the North Island. Since the 1920s modernizing tendencies have appeared, with constitution as a "church" in 1938, the printing of the liturgy in the 1960s, and some interest in Bible study and in closer relations with the Presbyterian and other churches. The main essay has been that of W. Greenwood; longer essays from particular viewpoints are by I. Roxburgh (Presbyterian) and L. Tolhurst (Seventh Day Adventist). Some material by the Ringatu Church is also included.

2153 Andersen, J[ohannes] C[arl], and Petersen, G[eorge] C[onrad]. *The Maori family.* Dunedin and Wellington: A. H. & A. W. Reed, 1956, 345 pp., illus., maps.
     Pp. 169-70, Te Kooti's founding of the Ringatu religion and Chatham Islands escape – a hostile account.

2154 "Apologies to men who removed flag." *Hawke's Bay Herald-Tribune* (Napier), 19 December 1970, illus.
     The flag of the Ringatu Te Kotahitanga Church was removed from the Omaha Marae, as belonging to the Te Kotahitanga movement as a whole, and not to the Ringatu Church itself.

2155 Bennett, Enid, and Donovan, Peter, eds. "Ringatu Church." In *Beliefs and practices in New Zealand – a directory.* 2d ed. Massey University, Religious Studies Department, 1980, pp. 131-32.

2156 Binney, Judith [Mary Caroline (Musgrove)]. "The Ringatu traditions of predictive history." *Journal of Pacific History* 23, no. 2 (1988): 167-74.
     Ringatu and Te Kooti's predictions exhibit reinforcement of Maori world-views by biblical traditions of prophetic history; also mentions Rua Kenana and Rongo Teka, a surviving early teacher in Rua's movement.

2157 Binney, Judith [Mary Caroline (Musgrove)], and Chaplin, Gillian. *Nga morehu: The survivors.* Auckland: Oxford University Press, 1986. 2d ed. 1987, 218 pp., illus.
     Life histories of eight Ringatu women, using oral traditions. Pp. 4-18, Te Kooti and Ringatu; pp. 18-24, Rua and the succession to Te Kooti.

2158 Burch, William. "Sectarian survival strategies: The case of the New Zealand Ringatu faith." In *Group Relations in Polynesia.* Papers presented at seminar, Victoria University of Wellington, 23-25 August 1965. Wellington: Department of Adult Education, Victoria University of Wellington, 1966, pp. 36-52.

Theoretical account of sect formation and varieties.

2159 Bush, E[rnest] E. "Address by Mr. E. E. Bush on 'Te Kooti.'" *Journal of the Tauranga Historical Society*, no. 34 (1968), pp. 40-44.

With comment added by reporter, J. P.

2160 Bush, E[rnest] E. "Did this change the course of history?" *Te Ao Hou* (Wellington), no. 64 (1968), pp. 19-21.

On Te Kooti.

2161 Bush, E[rnest] E. Review of *Te Kooti Rikirangi, general and prophet*, by W. Hugh Ross (entry 2191). *Journal of the Tauranga Historical Society*, no. 32 (December 1967), pp. 32-33.

2162 Bush, E[rnest] E. "Te Kooti centenary: Observances at Te Porere." *Te Ao Hou* (Wellington), no. 69 (December 1969-February 1970), pp. 24-25, illus.

2163 "Centenarian Ringatu Woman, Moerangi Ratahi." *Whakatane Historical Review* 20 (1972): 19-27. Abridged from seven articles in *Rotoroa Daily Post*, May-June 1971.

2164 Colenso, W[illiam]. *Fiat Justitia: Being a few thoughts respecting the Maori prisoner Kereopa, now in Napier gaol, awaiting his trial for murder*. Respectfully addressed to the considerate and justice-loving Christian settlers of Hawke's Bay and also to our rulers in a letter to ... the "Hawke's Bay Herald." Napier: Dinwiddie, Morrison and Co. (Printers), 1871, 23 pp.; 2 pp. of "Hauhau" prayers by Te Kooti. Reprinted in *Te Kooti Rikirangi Te Turuki*, edited by F. Davis. Hamilton: Waikato Museum, [early 1970s], [19 pp.], illus. Also in "Religious organization among the Maoris of New Zealand after 1860," by A. J. Gibson. Ph.D. dissertation (anthropology), University of California, Berkeley, 1964, pp. 117-19.

Pp. 1-18, Fiat Justitia; pp. 19-22, another letter, and reprint of Bishop Selwyn's statement in the House of Lords; p. 23, Appendix, Colenso's translation of six short prayers from Te Kooti's notebook.

2165 Cowan, James. "The facts about Te Kooti ... how injustice made a rebel." *New Zealand Railways Magazine* (Wellington) 13, no. 9 (1 December 1938): 17-19, 21.

311

Ringatu

And see quotation by J. Andersen in preface to W. Greenwood (entry 2175).

2166 Cowan, James. *Settlers and pioneers.* New Zealand Centennial Surveys, 4. Wellington: Department of Internal Affairs, 1940, 153 pp.
P. 26, brief reference to Mahuki, King Country prophet; pp. 51-52, Cowan's memories of Te Kooti between 1884 and 1889.

2167 Cowan, James. "Te Kooti, the rebel chief: The facts about his deportation." *Auckland Star*, Enzed Junior, children's supplement, 27 November 1937.

2168 Craig, Elsdon [Walter Grant]. "He preaches peace under banner of Church founded by Te Kooti." *New Zealand Herald* (Auckland), 25 July 1970, Section 2, p. 3, illus.
Paul Delamare, president of Ringatu, gives his life story and interpretation of Te Kooti and Ringatu, in an interview.

2169 Craig, Elsdon [Walter Grant]. "Sown in blood and reaped in harmony." *New Zealand Herald* (Auckland), 24 June 1971, illus.
On Te Kooti and Ringatu.

2170 Craig, Elsdon [Walter Grant]. "Te Kooti, pawn in the power game." *Cavalcade: Stories from New Zealand's Past* (Auckland), no. 1 (1972), pp. 19-23, illus.

2171 Davis, Frank, ed. *Te Kooti Rikirangi Te Turuki.* Hamilton: Waikato Museum, [early 1970s], [19 pp.], illus.
To accompany an exhibition. Includes translation of Te Kooti's vision as in the *Monthly Review* 1, no. 5 (1889); his letter to Governor Grey 1879; W. Colenso's translation of the six prayers found in his pocket notebook (entry 2164).

2172 Fowler, Leo. "A new look at Te Kooti" (Parts 1-2). *Te Ao Hou* (Wellington), no. 20 [5], no. 4 (November 1957): 17-19; no. 21 [6], no. 1 (December 1957): 18-22.

2173 Gibson, Ann Judith. *Religious organization among the Maoris of New Zealand after 1860.* Ph.D. dissertation (anthropology), University of California, Berkeley, 1964, 130 pp. (bib., pp. 120-30).
Reconstruction of the history of Pai Marire (pp. 49-63) and Ringatu (pp. 64-96) and comparison as innovative movements. Appendix 1 (pp. 112-16), Te Kooti's vision text (reprinted from Te

Kooti [entry 2199]). Appendix 2 (pp. 117-19), Te Kooti's personal prayer texts. Useful evaluation of sources including archives.

2174 Greenwood, William. "Iconography of Te Kooti Rikirangi." *Journal of the Polynesian Society* 55 (1946): 1-14.

2175 Greenwood, William. *The Upraised Hand, or the spiritual significance of the rise of the Ringatu faith.* Polynesian Society Memoir 21. Wellington: Polynesian Society, 1942, 88 pp., illus., folding chart on genealogy of Te Kooti. Reprinted from *Journal of the Polynesian Society* 51, no. 1 (1942): 1-80. New ed. with Epilogue (pp. 89-93), covering later Ringatu history, and Appendix: Nga Kawenata (pp. 94-98), being a summary and translation of the covenant section of the Ringatu service book, 1980, 98 pp.

2176 Harrop, A[ngus] J[ohn]. *England and the Maori wars.* London: New Zealand News; Christchurch: Whitcombe & Tombs, 1937, 423 pp., illus., map.
Pp. 341-45, 356-62, 372, 394, 401, 406-7, selections on Te Kooti.

2177 Hawthorne, James. *A dark chapter from New Zealand history: By a Poverty Bay survivor.* Napier: J. Wood, 1869, 41 pp. Reissued 1905, 34 pp. Reprint. Christchurch: Capper Press, 1974, 41 pp.
An educated shepherd's account of the campaign against the Hau Haus and Te Kooti to 1869; note especially pp. 12-13 (in original and 1974 reprint), Te Kooti in the Chatham Islands.

2178 Ihimaera, Witi. *The matriarch.* Auckland: Heinemann, 1986, 456 pp.
Historical fiction closely related to his own family history, with the Ringatu religion as the background. Act 2, chaps. 5-8 (pp. 121-97), "The song of Te Kooti," with description of Ringatu meeting house (pp. 189-95).

2179 Jones, Gordon C[harles]. "Years of the prophets." *Gisborne Herald*, 4 May-22 June 1968, 18 pp.
Series of nine articles on historical background of Ringatu. Religious information: first article, 4 May, Hau Hau and Te Ua; third article, 18 May, Te Ua as a prisoner; seventh article, 8 June, Te Kooti's religious influence emerging; eighth article, 15 June, the escape; ninth article, 22 June, pp. 16-18 on the religion of Te Kooti and Ringatu.

2180 Laughton, J[ohn] G[eorge]. *Ringatuism.* Wellington: Turnbull Library [196?]. Typescript.

Ringatu

First-hand report by a noted Presbyterian missionary. On microfiche, the Centre, Selly Oak Colleges.

2181 Misur, Gilda Z. "From prophet cult to established church: The case of the Ringatu movement. In *Conflict and compromise: Essays on the Maori since colonisation*, edited by I. H. Kawaru. Wellington: A. H. & A. W. Reed, 1975, pp. 97-115.

2182 New Zealand Government. *Appendices to the Journal of the House of Representatives*. Wellington: Government Printer. Items on Te Kooti as follows: 1868, A-15, pp. 1-8, 12-13, A-15B, pp. 3-4, escape and pursuit.

These items show his personality and religious activities; further items little concerned with his religion: 1869, A-3, A-10; 1870, A-8, A-8A, A-8B, A-83; 1870, A-24, A-24A, pardon of; 1871, F-1; 1883, A-8; 1884, G-4A session 1, land for; 1885, G-1, p. 10; 1889, G-8, attempted visit to Gisborne.

2183 Ngata, Apirana Turupu. "The Ringatu religion." Department of Maori Studies. N.p., n.d., 4 pp. Mimeo.

Copy in the Centre, Selly Oak Colleges.

2184 Ngata, Apirana Turupu. *Te kaupapa whakatopu o te hahi Ringatu i whakaotia i te hui whakakotahi i te 25 ki te 28 o Hune, 1938*. Wellington: H. H. Tombs, 1938, 4 pp.

To incorporate the Church and thus register *tohunga* (ministers) to conduct legal marriages, together with discussion of problems affecting Ringatu land.

2185 Presbyterian Church of New Zealand. *Proceedings of the General Assembly*. Wellington: The Church, 1920-41: reports on Ringatu: 1920, pp. 87-88 (Eva Jack, Te Whaiti); 1921, p. 126 (Sister Annie, Ruatahuna); 1922, pp. 124-25 (J. G. Laughton); 1923, p. 100 (J. A. Asher, Missions Committee), pp. 107-8 (Sister Jessie), p. 109 (Sister Tiaki, Waiohau), p. 129 (S. Craig, Maungapohatu); 1926, pp. 75-78 (J. G. Laughton, Maungapohatu), pp. 78-79 (Nurse Doull, Matahi); 1927, pp. 76-77 (E. J. Ward, Taumaranui), p. 80 (Sister Tiaki); 1941, p. 87 (J. G. Laughton as Superintendent).

2186 Renati, Matarena, and Roche, Stanley. "Of love and death: Matarena's story." In *The summer book*, edited by B. Williams and R. Parsons. Wellington: Port Nicholson Press, 1982, pp. 76-84.

A dialogue with a Ringatu woman, Matarena Renati of Te Teko, in 1980.

2187 Ringatu Church. *Rules of "The Ringatu Church Incorporated."* N.p.: The
Church, 20 May 1929, 6 pp.
Copy in the Centre, Selly Oak Colleges, is typed and has some
other author's note appended.

2188 Ringatu Church. *Te pukapuka o nga kawenata e waru a te Atua me nga
karakia katoa a te Haahi Ringatu.* [Gisborne]: The Church (Te Rau
Press, Printer), [1968], 144 pp.
The book of the eight covenants of God and the prayers, hymns,
and chants of the Ringatu Church. See W. Greenwood (entry 2175) for
translation of first part.

2189 "A Ringatu meeting at Ruatoki." *Te Ao Hou* (Wellington), no. 42
(March 1963), pp. 38-41, illus.

2190 Rodgers, Paul. "Lone pakeha attends *hui* of Ringatu sect." *Weekly News*
(Auckland), 2 February 1966.
Bishop Panapa (Anglican, a Maori) and Sir Turi Carroll
attending one of Ringatu's two annual *huis* at home of a senior elder of
this faith.

2191 Ross, W[alter] Hugh. *Te Kooti Rikirangi, general and prophet.* London
and Auckland: Collins; San Francisco: Tri-Ocean Books, 1966, 196 pp.
From viewpoint of a soldier-settler, especially chap. 2, the
Chatham Islands religious development; pp. 30-33, English translation
of Te Kooti's recorded visions. A revised version of articles serialized
in the *Weekly News.*

2192 Roxburgh, Irvine. *The Ringatu movement: A phenomenological essay.*
Pukerua Bay: Privately published, 1985, 104 pp.
Revised edition of 1958 original essay.

2193 Scholefield, Guy H[ardy]. "Te Kooti or Rikirangi also called Te
Teruki." In *Dictionary of New Zealand biography.* Vol. 1. Wellington:
Department of Internal Affairs, 1940, pp. 473-75.

2194 Shadbolt, Maurice. *Season of the Jew.* London: Hodder & Stoughton,
1986, 384 pp.
A novel about Te Kooti, but totally inadequate on his religion.

2195 Simmons, D[avid] R[oy]. "Founded a religion when in prison without
trial." *New Zealand Herald*, 3 August 1968, illus. See also letter from T.
Walsh, 9 August 1968.

Ringatu

On Te Kooti, mainly on military aspects but includes background in Pai Marire and Hau Hau.

2196 Simpson, Frank A. *Chatham exiles: Yesterday and today in the Chatham Islands*. Wellington: A. H. & A. W. Reed, 1950, 182 pp., illus., maps.
Pp. 108-21, "Te Kooti and the Maori Exodus."

2197 Stirling, Amiria Manutahi. *Amiria: The life story of a Maori woman* (as told to Anne Salmond). Wellington: A. H. & A. W. Reed, 1976, 184 pp., illus., map.
Pp. 89-90, experience of having to finish a dance on a Ringatu marae by Friday midnight.

2198 Tarei, Wi. "A church called Ringatu." In *Tihe Mauri Ora*, edited by M. King. London: Methuen, 1978, pp. 60-66.

2199 [Te Kooti Rikirangi Te Turuki]. "Correspondence: Te Kooti." Translated by Arthur S. Atkinson. *Monthly Review* (Wellington) 1, no. 5 (1889), pp. 175-77. Revised from earlier version in *Nelson Examiner*, May 1869.
The visions as in Te Kooti's notebook found at Makeretu December 1868 (present location unknown); reprinted in F. Davis (entry 2171), and also as Appendix 1 in A. J. Gibson (entry 2173), pp. 112-16; Gibson also discusses the contents, history, and authenticity of the manuscript and its copies.

2200 Tolhurst, Leonard Philps. "The religious concepts of the Maoris in pre-European days and a detailed study of Ringatu church today." M.A. thesis, Seventh Day Adventist Theological Seminary, Washington, D.C., 1955, 137 pp., bib.
By son of Elder H. L. Tolhurst, a missionary among the Ringatu for some three years.

2201 [Turner, Harold Walter.] "Ringatu." In *Encyclopaedia Britannica*. Micropaedia. Vol. 8. 1974, p. 591a.

2202 Vine, Ronald. "Te Kooti's church continues its ministry: Biblical beliefs of denomination in Urewera country." *Weekly News* (Auckland), no. 3776 [84] (20 April 1938), p. 42, illus.
An interveiw with the Ringatu Church secretary, a good source for beliefs and practices. Extracts in L. P. Tolhurst (entry 2200), passim.

2203 Wilson, [George Hamish] Ormond. *War in the tussock: Te Kooti and the battle at Te Porere.* New Zealand National Historic Places Trust. Publication no. 2. Wellington: Government Printer, 1961, 72 pp., illus., maps.

Pp. 12-17, 22-25, religion of Te Kooti; Appendix 3 (p. 62), Te Kooti's flag, with illustration.

2204 Winks, Robin W. Documents on the Ringatu Church, now deposited in the New Zealand Collection, Auckland University Library, as follows:

1. A Maori form of Christianity – the Ringatu Church, part 1, 47 pp. [a condensation of the second half of his 300-page manuscript of same title.]

2. Arohatanga a te Wa. Kawenata Ringatu. Hanuere 1919, no. 3, 8 pp.

3. Rules of the Ringatu Church Incorporated. 6 pp.

4. Sundry reports of Church meetings, 1938, and plans to consolidate the Church in 1948, 1949.

5. Various letters and notes from Norman Perry, and book notes, etc., by Winks.

2205 Young, Hugh. "Ringatu and its followers." *Outlook* (Christchurch, the Presbyterian Church), May 1979, p. 4.

A letter defending Ringatu as not un-Christian.

Index of Authors and Sources

Note: References are to entry numbers, not to pages.

319

Index of Main Movements
and Individuals

The entry numbers of the main or more substantial or significant references are included here (i.e., those mentioned in the titles of the items or in the annotations). The list is therefore not exhaustive as to text references, but is fairly complete as to known named movements, apart from those that are designated only by general area or by dates. Founders, leaders, and other significant individuals appear under their most common names, but alternative spellings and names are also given in brackets or cross-referenced.

The materials on the three particular movements placed in three separate sections at the end of the volume refer primarily to the movement concerned. Where these movements are treated along with others they may be found through the various other entry numbers also given.

AAJ2941

4/16/92

BL
80
A1
T8
―――
V.3

0 00 02 0529028 1
MIDDLEBURY COLLEGE